PAULA BYRNE

Mad World

Evelyn Waugh and the Secrets of Brideshead

Harper Press

Harper*Press*
An imprint of HarperCollins*Publishers*
77–85 Fulham Palace Road
Hammersmith
London W6 8JB

Visit our authors' blog at www.fifthestate.co.uk

This edition is produced exclusively for Waterstone's 2011
1

First published in Great Britain by Harper*Press* in 2099

A catalogue record for this book is available from the British Library

ISBN 978-0-00-790371-9

Printed and bound in Great Britain by Clays Ltd, St Ives plc

Mixed Sources
Product group from well-managed
forests and other controlled sources
www.fsc.org Cert no. SW-COC-001806
© 1996 Forest Stewardship Council
FSC

FSC is a non-profit international organisation established to promote the responsible management of the world's forests. Products carrying the FSC label are independently certified to assure consumers that they come from forests that are managed to meet the social, economic and ecological needs of present and future generations.

Find out more about HarperCollins and the environment at
www.harpercollins.co.uk/green

For Timothy and Clare Byrne

CONTENTS

PREFACE AND ACKNOWLEDGMENTS

The story of Evelyn Waugh's life has been told in several admirable 'cradle to grave' narratives. The problem with traditional biographies of this sort is that they tend to lose sight of the wood for the trees. The biographer who seeks to tell the full story has a duty to cover every base, to treat each aspect of the life with equal weight. The essential insights are often buried amidst the incidental facts.

As a literary genre, the heavily footnoted biographical doorstopper had its heyday in the second half of the twentieth century. Twenty-first-century literary biography is already proving to be more varied, more flexible and more selective. Frances Wilson explores the life of Dorothy Wordsworth by working outwards from a single moment and a single document: her journal entry on the day of her brother William's marriage. James Shapiro approaches Shakespeare by way of a single key year, 1599. A pioneer of what I call the 'partial life' was Lyndall Gordon, who, back in 1998 filtered the life and work of Henry James through his relationship with two women, his doomed cousin Minny Temple and the colourful novelist Constance Fenimore Woolson. Experimental approaches such as these have helped to liberate biography from the shackles of comprehensiveness.

I set out to write this book because I believed that Evelyn Waugh had been persistently misrepresented as a snob and a curmudgeonly misanthropist. I did not recognise Waugh in the popular caricature of him. I wanted to get to the real Waugh, so I began asking questions such as 'When and where was he happiest (and unhappiest)?'; 'What were the relationships that mattered to him most?', and 'What was he looking for in life, and how did his quest shape his best novels?' In searching for the answers to these questions, I kept coming back to his relationship with a single family: the Lygons of Madresfield. I came to the conclusion that his feelings about them provided a key that could unlock the door into Waugh's inner world.

Their house, Madresfield Court in the Malvern Hills, which they and he affectionately called 'Mad', has often been described as 'the real Brideshead'. In many ways it was, provided we always retain defensive quotation marks around that 'real'. The genuinely revealing story, though, is not of the house but of the friendship.

In writing this book, I too have made new friendships, above all with Alexander Waugh, Evelyn's grandson. My greatest debt of thanks goes to him. Not only did he put his Waugh archive at my disposal, he taught me how to find passenger lists and old newspaper archives online. He read the manuscript and made many invaluable suggestions and comments. His funniness, his warmth and his kindness (and that of his wife, Eliza) made the writing of this book a great pleasure.

Thanks also to Jean Cannon (Harry Ransom Center of the University of Texas at Austin); Charlotte Heber Percy and Victoria Street for reminiscences of Coote; Wendy and Gordon Hawksley for connecting me to the paintings of William Ranken; Charles Linck for much valuable information about Waugh and Terence Greenidge; Miriam Gross for inviting me to the party where I met Alexander Waugh; Christine Vickers, Michael Meredith and Eric Anderson at Eton College and Anne Drewery and Christopher Whittick at Lancing College; Robin Rhoderick-Jones for sending me some key pages from his unpublished history of the Dukes of Westminster; Nicholas Scheetz (manuscripts librarian at Georgetown University Library) and his assistant Scott Taylor; Jeremy Treglown; Sofka Zinovieff at Faringdon House, Oxfordshire; the staff of the British Library manuscripts room; the many secondhand booksellers reached via www.bookfinder.com for the astonishingly competitive prices and speedy dispatch that enabled me to build my own Waugh library. Also Paul Edmondson for being my guide to Venice and Andrew Wylie for being such a spectacular agent.

Thanks to Karen Chamberlain for reading the entire manuscript and advising on the boring bits, and to Will Hanrahan and Gill Carter for advice on the subtitle. Thanks to Arabella Pike and Annabel Wright and the amazing team at HarperCollins. Thanks too to my copyeditor Katie Johnson. On a more personal note, thanks to my au pairs Martina Jelenova and Lucie Zatecka, Father Matthew Catterick for his friendship, my children Tom, Ellie and Harry for their love and patience and, above all, my heartfelt thanks to my husband Jonathan Bate.

Quotations from the published writings and unpublished letters of Evelyn Waugh are reproduced with kind permission of Teresa D'Arms from the Evelyn Waugh Estate.

So true to life being in love with a whole family
(Nancy Mitford, on first reading *Brideshead Revisited*)

PROLOGUE

Early 1944 and Captain Evelyn Arthur St John Waugh has fallen out of love with the army. He has turned forty and is considering his options. To become a screenwriter? An overture to Alexander Korda comes to nothing. To join MI5, the intelligence service? He is turned down without an interview. Only one possibility remains: to revert to his pre-war occupation.

On 24 January he writes a letter to Colonel Ferguson, Officer Commanding, Household Cavalry Training Regiment. Copies are sent to the Secretary of State for War and to Brendan Bracken, Winston Churchill's Minister of Information and string-puller in chief on behalf of Captain Waugh. 'I have the honour to request,' the letter begins, 'that, for the understated reasons I may be granted leave of absence from duty without pay for three months.' The understated reasons are various. That his previous service in the Royal Marines, the Commandos, the Special Services and the Special Air Service Regiment does not qualify him for his current position in a mechanised unit of the cavalry. That he no longer has the necessary physical agility for active service. That he is no good at admin, so can't do a desk job. And that he doesn't have the foreign languages to make him useful for the purposes of intelligence work.

Assurances are given: the novel to which he will devote his leave 'will have no direct dealing with the war'. But expectations are dampened: 'it is not pretended that it will have any immediate propaganda value'. The necessity of immediate action is stressed: 'It is a peculiarity of the literary profession that, once an idea becomes fully formed in the author's mind, it cannot be left unexploited without deterioration. If, in fact, the book is not written now it will never be written.'

Colonel Ferguson responds by ordering Waugh to go and train the Home Guard at Windsor. A less determined man than Evelyn might have capitulated and the book would never have been written. But he perseveres. By the end of January he has been granted his three months' leave, qualified only by a commitment to a little light part-time work for the Ministry of Information. He leaves his comfortable billet in the Hyde Park Hotel and his military uniform with it.

On the morning of Tuesday 1 February 1944 he is settled in another hotel, deep in the West Country: Easton Court, Chagford, Devon – a thatched fourteenth-century farmhouse with low, dark rooms and small windows. He has been there before, in the late autumn of one of the momentous years of his life, 1931. It is a place that in his memory he cannot separate from a house and a family with which he had fallen in love that year.

In London he had regularly lain in till mid-morning. At Chagford he is up at 8.30 and at work by 10. By dinnertime on that first Tuesday, though his mind is 'stiff' from the tedium of army life, he has written and rewritten 1,300 words. He reports to his wife that he has made a good beginning on what he calls his 'magnum opus'. He has 'bought a very expensive concoction of calcium and halibut liver oil which the chemist thought would restore me to strength but on reading the label more closely I find it to be a cure for chilblains'. This may prove handy, since the lounge he has been given as a private room in which to write has a fire that smokes so badly that he has to choose between streaming eyes and frozen extremities.

By 'close of play' on Wednesday the score is '3,000 words odd'. Through the ensuing weeks he works steadily at the rate of up to 2,000 words a day, occasionally more. He revises arduously as he goes. In the end it takes him closer to five months than three, but the book that he knows in his heart he has to write is completed. The idea that had 'become fully formed' in his mind is 'exploited without deterioration'.

What was that idea? The book's original working title was 'The Household of the Faith'. The story of a household, a family. A journey shaped by religious faith. These are its key themes. But the working title does not find its way into print. When the book is published the following year, its title page reads *Brideshead Revisited: The Sacred and Profane Memories of Captain Charles Ryder: A Novel.*

On the reverse side of that title page there is a notice to the effect that the volume has been 'produced in complete conformity with the authorised economy standards' of wartime publishing. You can tell that this is true when you hold a first edition in your hands and turn the coarse, rough-hewn pages.

Above the routine announcement concerning production standards, there is something more intriguing. A mysterious Author's Note is signed 'E. W.', Evelyn Waugh. It reads: 'I am not I: thou art not he or she: they are not they.'

'I am not I': yet Charles Ryder manifestly *is* Evelyn Waugh. *Brideshead Revisited* contains as large a dose of autobiography as Charles Dickens's *David Copperfield* or Marcel Proust's *À la recherche du temps perdu.* So who, then, was the 'thou' who was and was not 'he or she'? The 'they' who were and were not 'they'? What was 'the household of the faith' that was and was not Brideshead? What were the events that inspired the novel?

This biography sets out to find the hidden key to Waugh's great novel, to unlock for the first time the full extent to which *Brideshead* encodes and subtly transforms the author's own experiences. In so doing, it illuminates the obsessions that shaped his life: the search for an ideal family and the quest for a secure faith. The solution to the mystery can be found in that magical year of 1931. The hidden key will also unlock several of Waugh's other major novels, including his very best one, *A Handful of Dust.* And it will bring us to a secret that dared not speak its name.

But we must begin with two very different childhoods. And then we must go, as Captain Charles Ryder does when he begins his recollections, to Oxford, in the years immediately after the Great War.

CHAPTER 1

A Tale of Two Childhoods

'My name is Evelyn Waugh I go to Heath Mount school I am in the Vth Form, Our Form Master is Mr Stebbing.'

So begins his first extant literary composition, a brief self-portrait called 'My History', written in September 1911, at the age of seven. It is the work of a boy of strong opinions and sharp wit:

> We all hate Mr Cooper, our arith master. It is the 7th day of the Winter Term which is my 4th. Today is Sunday so I am not at school. We allways have sausages for breakfast on Sundays I have been watching Lucy fry them they do look funny befor their kooked. Daddy is a Publisher he goes to Chapman and Hall office it looks a offely dull plase. I am just going to Church. Alec, my big brother has just gorn to Sherborne. The wind is blowing dreadfuly I am afraid that when I go up to Church I shall be blown away. I was not blown away after all.

The child, William Wordsworth once said, is father to the man. Here is Evelyn Waugh the writer in embryo: a good hater of bad masters, a spectator of the world who can make ordinary things (like sausages) look funny. He is just going to church: eventually he will be blown in the direction of Rome. His household is comfortably middle class: prep school, domestic servants (Lucy in the kitchen with sausages), the home dominated by Daddy, with his important-sounding job (Publisher) in his dull London office. And a big brother who has just gone to a big, renowned public school: Sherborne. Some years later, an ill wind will blow dreadfully from there, redirecting Evelyn to another school.

Mother is not mentioned in this first little sketch. But Evelyn was closer to her than he was to his father, chiefly because Arthur Waugh, managing director of the publisher Chapman and Hall, idolised his first-born son Alec to an absurd degree. Albeit with good intentions: Arthur was determined not to be like his own father, a sadistic bully who rejoiced in the nickname 'The Brute'. Arthur, educated at Sherborne School and then New College, Oxford, had married Catherine Raban, a gentle girl from an English colonial family originally hailing from Staffordshire, in 1893. Their first child, Alexander ('Alec') was born in 1898. Arthur called him 'the son of my soul' and, as the boy grew, developed a relationship with him that was intense, exclusive and all consuming.

Evelyn was born on 28 October 1903 at the family home in Hampstead. When Evelyn was four and the family moved to a larger house, closer to Golders Green, Alec left for boarding school. This might have been the moment when the younger son could have come out from under the wing of Mother and Nurse. But he didn't. Evelyn's relationship with his father always remained difficult. There is already a hint of irreverence in that early sketch, with its dismissal of Chapman and Hall's offices as 'a offely dull plase'. Evelyn would grow into a rebellious teenager who carefully cultivated a satirical, worldly, disengaged persona, not least in order to set himself against what he perceived to be his father's nauseating sentimentality and histrionic tendencies.

Arthur Waugh, who was very well respected and connected in the London literary world, had the tastes of his age and class: Shakespeare, the King James Bible, Dickens and cricket (this was the era of the legendary Dr W. G. Grace). The Dickens copyright was the jewel in Chapman and Hall's crown. Arthur Waugh was rotund, diminutive, with twinkling eyes and candyfloss white hair. Ellen Terry, the greatest actress of the age, had the perfect name for him: 'that dear little Mr Pickwick'.

In such a literary household, it was probably inevitable that Evelyn should grow up literary – or at the very least that he should view his own family through the filter of books and plays. Arthur Waugh seemed to spend all his time acting out roles. When he greeted visitors, he was the over-hearty Mr Hardcastle of Oliver Goldsmith's *She Stoops to Conquer*. In deploring the ingratitude of his sons, he was Shakespeare's King Lear. Above all, he was Mr Pooter in George and Weedon Grossmith's *Diary of a Nobody*. 'Why, I am Lupin!' Evelyn cried out delightedly when he first read the book, identifying instantly with Pooter's rebellious, loutish and troublesome son. It remained a favourite book, which he regarded as the funniest in the English language. The hilarious clashes in values and attitude between the respectable lower-middle-class civil servant Pooter and his reckless, extravagant son mirrored to a tee Evelyn's sense of his own disjointedness from his father. It is no coincidence that in *Brideshead Revisited* Lady Marchmain reads *Diary of a Nobody* aloud to lighten the tension generated by her son Sebastian's drunken behaviour at dinner.

Evelyn later displayed his father's gift for adopting theatrical roles, particularly in his middle age when the part that he cast for himself was, as he put it in his autobiographical novel *The Ordeal of Gilbert Pinfold*, 'that of the eccentric don and testy colonel': 'he acted it strenuously, before his children . . . and his cronies in London, until it came to dominate his whole outward personality'.

Arthur Waugh would have been delighted by Ellen Terry's Pickwick comparison. He often read Dickens aloud in his marvellously theatrical voice. Though Evelyn, ever the Lupin, affected to despise his father's theatricality ('his sighs would have carried to the back of the gallery at Drury Lane'), he also later acknowledged Arthur's verbal gifts: 'he read aloud with a precision of tone, authority and variety that I have heard excelled only by John Gielgud'. Had Evelyn lived to witness the celebrated 1981 Granada Television adaptation of *Brideshead*, he would have found it fitting that Gielgud stole the show with his performance in the role of Charles Ryder's father. Arthur kept Evelyn and his friends enthralled with his readings of Dickens and Shakespeare and his favourite poets. In the autobiography *A Little Learning* Evelyn wrote of how his father's love of English prose and verse 'saturated my young mind, so that I never thought of English Literature as a school subject . . . but as a source of natural joy'.

The account of Waugh's happy childhood in *A Little Learning* belies the common view that he was deeply ashamed of his middle-class, suburban upbringing. He paints a delightful picture of the pleasures of life at Underhill, the family home on the edge of Hampstead Heath. He felt lucky to be at a day school and not to be sent away to board: 'it was a world of privacy and love very unlike the bleak dormitories to which most boys of my age and kind were condemned'.

He viewed Hampstead as something like an eighteenth-century pleasure garden. He loved the thrice-yearly fair, with its aromas of 'orange-peel, sweat, beer, coconut, trampled grass, horses' and the rowdy crowd of 'costers' from the East End of London, kitted out in pearl-buttoned caps and suits. Feared by some, they were creatures of fascination to the young boy who saw in them a 'kind of Pentecostal exuberance which communicated nothing but goodwill'. It did not seem to matter that father was forever preoccupied with Alec's triumphant exploits down in Dorset on the playing fields of Sherborne.

At the centre of this small boy's 'paradisal' world were 'two adored deities': his mother and his nurse, Lucy. Mother was associated with 'earthy wash-leather gloves and baskets of globe artichokes and black and red currants'. Lucy was a devout Christian, 'strictly chapel', who loved him unconditionally and was 'never cross or neglectful'.

Equally adored was a trio of maiden aunts who lived at Midsomer Norton in Somerset. When visiting in the summer holidays, Evelyn nosed around their house. It was stuffed with Victoriana: cabinets of curiosities, fans, snuff boxes, nuts, old coins and medals. The smell of gas, fruit, oil and leather. The aunts' life was like something out of the previous century, locked in aspic. A whirl of church bazaars, private theatricals, picnics and games, 'the place captivated my imagination as my true home never did'.

'Save for a few pale shadows' – as, for example, when he almost choked to death on the yolk of a hard-boiled egg – Evelyn's childhood was bathed, he claimed, in 'an even glow of pure happiness'. Like nearly all literary recollections of times past, *A Little Learning* offers up the image of childhood as a paradise lost, an Eden from which the author has been expelled, a secret garden glimpsed through a door in the wall, an alternative world like the one into which the child tumbles in one of Evelyn's favourite books, *Alice in Wonderland.* This theme of exile and exclusion from Arcadia would preoccupy him throughout his life and his work. He always felt as if he did not quite belong. That was what fired his imagination and his comic vision. Whether writing about a deranged provincial boarding school, or the exploits of London's Bright Young Things, or the old Anglo-Catholic aristocracy, he was always the outsider looking in.

His sense of displacement from his own family was there from the start, despite all the genuine memories of a happy and stable early childhood. In later years he was never close to his parents and his brother. With Alec away at boarding school, he was drawn to other families. When Evelyn was six he watched three children, two girls and a boy his own age, playing in a nearby street. He befriended the family. In his autobiography he calls them the Rolands. They were actually called Fleming and they became the first of his substitute families, and remained so for more than a decade.

The children built themselves a fort and formed a gang called The Pistol Troop. They endured tests of courage, walking barefoot through stinging nettles, climbing dangerously high trees and signing their names in blood. Evelyn threw himself into these boisterous games. He was as physically brave as a young boy as he would be when a traveller and a soldier in later years.

The children also devised their own magazine and put on amateur dramatics, writing and acting in their own short plays. The magazine, containing one of Evelyn's first stories, was typed and handsomely bound. So began his lifelong obsession with fine bindings. Whenever he finished writing a novel, he had the manuscript expensively bound, and most of his works were produced in not only a mass-market printing but also a beautiful hand-bound limited edition for presentation to friends.

Mrs Fleming thought that Evelyn was an only child, until she was put right by one of her own children: 'Oh, but he isn't, he has a brother at school whom he hates.' He did not hate Alec. Rather, he accepted with seeming equanimity that the five years that separated him from his brother made 'in childhood, a complete barrier'. Having no sister, he was drawn to female friends and held girls in high regard.

After an appendix operation at the age of nine, he spent time convalescing with a family called Talbot who lived near the Thames Estuary. He was drawn to their stuff – a banjo, old photograph albums, a phonograph, china vases and great coats – but it was the family that really captured his affections: 'the household was extraordinarily Dickensian, an old new world to me. I was very happy there, so happy that I neglected to write home and received a letter of rebuke from my father . . . I returned home and this glimpse of another world was occluded.'

From this time on, he would always be drawn to glimpsed other worlds and large, seemingly happy families. The Talbots were not rich or grand. Far from it: the money they received for Evelyn's board and lodging was used to release furniture from the local pawnshop. The father, an unemployed old sailor, was mildly drunk every night, but he was a jolly drunk. He built the children a makeshift tree house. It was there that Evelyn and the eldest Talbot girl, Muriel, exposed their private parts to each other.

Despite the idealisation of other families, the impression persists of Evelyn as a happy boy in the 'lustrum between pram and prep school', collecting microscopes and air-guns, squirrelling away 'coins, stamps, fossils, butterflies, beetles, seaweed, wild flowers'. Like most boys he went through obsessive phases, one year with his chemistry set, another with magic tricks. He was drawn to dexterity, observing the local chemist melting wax to seal paper packages and the Hampstead shopkeepers working deftly with weights and scales, shovels and canisters, paper and string: 'Always from my earliest memories I delighted in watching things well done.'

Years later, when his Oxford friend Henry Yorke took him to his family's factory in Birmingham, he was able to appreciate the aesthetic beauty of the industrial plant, recording in his diary how impressed he was by the 'manual dexterity of the workers . . . The brass casting peculiarly beautiful: green molten metal from a red cauldron.' This is not to say that he was drawn to the white heat of a technological future. The manual dexterity of those workers was, he said, 'nothing in the least like mass labour or mechanisation'. Rather, it was 'pure arts and crafts'. His delight in watching things well done was bound up with a sense of custom and tradition. As he admits in *A Little Learning*, he was in love with the past. He longed for the loan of a Time Machine. Not to take him to the future ('dreariest of prospects'), in the manner of H. G. Wells, whose *The Time Machine* was published just a few years before he was born, but rather 'to hover gently back through the centuries'. To go back into the past 'would be the most exquisite pleasure of which I can conceive'.

If the adult Evelyn had travelled on his Time Machine back to the childhood of one of the aristocrats who would become his Oxford contemporaries, he would have found – and been pleased to find – that little had altered over the years. Hugh Lygon and his siblings were typical products of a system that had endured for generations. For the boys, prep school, Eton and Oxford; for the girls, very little in the way of formal education – a governess who taught in the schoolroom at home and the use of a well-stocked library were deemed to suffice.

Hugh was the second son of William Lygon, the seventh Earl Beauchamp. His early childhood was as far removed from Evelyn's middle-class background as could be imagined: a heady cocktail of aristocracy, eccentricity and piety. Evelyn was effectively an only child once Alec went away to school; Hugh was one of seven. The Lygon family consisted of William, known from his birth in 1903 as Lord Elmley, Hugh (born 1904), Lettice (1906), Sibell (1907), Mary (1910), Dorothy (1912) and Richard (1916). They divided their time between Madresfield Court, their ancestral home nestling beneath the Malvern Hills in Worcestershire, Halkyn House, their town residence in Belgrave Square (London's smartest address), and Walmer Castle – which genuinely was an enormous castle in Kent, the earl's official residence in his capacity as holder of the ancient office of Warden of the Cinque Ports. The family and their immediate entourage moved between houses in their own private train.

At the time of the 1911 census, shortly before Elmley and Hugh went off to board at prep school, the household at Madresfield included a butler, a valet, three footmen, two hallboys, a housekeeper, five housemaids, a nurse, three nursery maids, a cook and four kitchen maids. A coachman and two grooms lived in the stables, while a skeleton staff of four was retained at Halkyn House.

The family were very devout and when at Madresfield they all attended Anglo-Catholic services twice a day in the chapel. All the staff had to attend too, men on the right and maids on the left, with the family in front. High Church rituals were strictly observed: the candle on the right of the altar would always be lit before the one on the left. Each child had a leather-bound prayer book with their name on it, a flower emblem engraved in gold and a loving inscription from their father.

When they were at their London home, the Lygons would cross the city every Sunday to their favourite church in Primrose Hill. Rather surprisingly, they travelled by bus and the newly opened underground railway; Lord Beauchamp in top hat and morning coat, Lady Beauchamp in satin and fur bedecked with jewels. The earl considered taxies an extravagance and thought that Sundays should be a day of rest for cars as well as horses.

The Lygon children disliked their overbearing, pious mother. Lady Beauchamp always insisted on hiring a nanny who had a neat parting precisely in the middle of her head because this reminded her of the Madonna in Renaissance paintings. She instructed the children personally in religious education. One of her daughters described her mother as 'very odd, a religious zealot'. Within the family, she was nicknamed 'Tomo', because her motto was 'Tidiness, Order, Method and Organisation'. Lady Sibell, the longest-lived of the siblings, recalled that this mantra was 'the secret of the house and she once made me write it out a hundred times'. She also remembered her mother saying: 'I'm right because I'm always right and anyone who says I'm wrong is mad and wicked.'

Madresfield had so many staircases that if the children heard their mother coming up one of them they 'could be sure to go down another'. Each child found him or herself displaced from the countess' special affections when a new baby arrived. 'I had quite a long innings,' said Sibell, 'because she had a miscarriage in 1908.'

The children were encouraged to be hardy and robust, to take regular outdoor exercise. The three boys were taught boxing and lawn tennis. Hunting was encouraged for the girls (side-saddle of course) as well as the boys. Sibell was put on a horse at the age of two and grew up to become a Master of Foxhounds. When riding out, the children were always accompanied by a groom dressed in black, with polished silver buttons and a black silk top hat.

They swam regularly both at Madresfield, where there was an outdoor pool, and at Walmer Castle, which was by the sea. The water in the Madresfield pool was never changed, so must have been somewhat stagnant. Rather than being taught to swim, the children were thrown in at the deep end and told to make movements. When the ladies had departed from a swimming party, Lord Beauchamp would announce that 'Gentlemen may lower their costumes.'

The children loved Madresfield but heartily disliked Walmer Castle, where their mother forced them to swim in the freezing sea. Sibell's birthday was in October. 'Tomo' asked her what she would like to choose as a birthday treat. 'Not to bathe today' was Sibell's answer. The countess replied: 'For that you will go in twice.' When the girl was stung by a jellyfish, 'Mother's cure for that was to fill a bucket with jellyfish and throw them at me.'

Apart from God, the Countess Beauchamp's great passion in life was food. According to her daughters, she would sit alone in the blue sitting room and eat through a mound of bananas, eggs, scones, sponge cake, Gentleman's Relish, a bunch of grapes that had to be peeled and pipped by a lackey, and thick slices of toast cut through and turned inside out. Every afternoon the baker came on his pony to deliver a loaf with a special crust. He was told not to trot because it might disturb Her Ladyship's rest. Sibell remembered her mother as 'frightfully greedy . . . she would eat a whole chicken for dinner'. Lady Beauchamp was conscious of her heavy figure and when a family portrait was commissioned for the twenty-first birthday of her eldest son, the painter, William Ranken, tactfully airbrushed the countess to make her into a much slimmer and more glamorous figure than she really was.

Father, Lord Beauchamp, was a very different kind of parent. Whereas the countess' preferred birthday present for the children was a church candle, the earl tracked down beautiful wooden toys and ordered gifts from Hamley's. For all his love of grandeur and ritual, he was a loving and, as we would now say, very 'hands-on' father. His absorption in the lives of his children was highly unusual for his social class and his time. He may well have been compensating for his wife's reserve and froideur, as well as trying to be different from his own religious and strict father. The Lygon children were devoted to their nanny, as was typical of many upper-class children, but they worshipped their father.

They called him 'Boom', purportedly because of his loud, booming voice, which resembled the sound of the foghorns off Walmer, warning ships to keep away from the treacherous Goodwin Sands. He insisted on formality at home, wearing his blue Knight of the Garter ribbon at dinner and referring to his children by their titles, Lord Elmley for his eldest son, the Lady Lettice, the Lady Dorothy and so on. They had other names for themselves: Lady Dorothy was Coote, Mary was Maimie, Hugh was always Hughie and little Richard was Dickie.

Boom took a keen interest in his children's education and when he was home he read to them and tried to form their literary tastes. At luncheon, the children would have to take it in turns to speak to their father in French, while a footman dressed in livery stood behind each chair. Then when the clock struck two, the sisters would enter the library, greet His Lordship and listen as he read to them from Victorian historical novels, some of which included incidents in which family ancestors had played a part.

Outside his own private rooms, close to the nursery, the earl installed small toilets and basins. As he took his morning bath, the children would chat to him about religion, art and literature, but time was always made for personal troubles such as the death of a family pet or a hunting misadventure. In the evenings, Maimie would bring her father a cocktail while he was taking his bath. Many years later Evelyn Waugh complained that his own daughter's devotion to him did not extend this far.

Politics were rarely discussed during ablutions, but the earl's public career was such that an interest in politics was taken as read. Lord Beauchamp impressed upon his children their long and distinguished ancestry, and the obligations and responsibilities that came with privilege. But, just as he was a Liberal in politics, so he was liberal-minded: Lady Sibell recalled that the abiding lesson that her father taught the family was 'tolerance'. This was a value that would be needed when crisis came.

The family did not weekend at other country houses: that was considered vulgar. Maimie, Coote and Sibell read avidly and played imaginative games. They hunted for birds' nests along the four driveways that led to Madresfield. Lady Sibell remembered being sent out by their mother to collect plovers' eggs in the grounds of the park. It was a trial not to tread on them because they were the colour of the earth. The children played with the chickens in the poultry yard and when the butler's disabled son came to the house in his wheelchair they would take him for a spin around the gardens. They loved animals, especially horses and dogs. Baby Dickie was pushed around the house's extensive grounds in a black pram to which two painted horses on springs were attached. A huge rocking horse was a favourite toy: all seven children could sit on it at once.

The children tended to be dressed shabbily in hand-me-downs from cousins. Their clothes were threadbare and when they were abroad they were mistaken for charity children, which was a source of great amusement. They were encouraged to be stoical in times of illness. Doctor's orders were that champagne was the best cure for all ailments.

Each of the children had their own nursemaid. In their early years they were schooled in the nursery on the ground floor, a spacious room with five-barred sash windows. This was Nanny's domain. Hugh's schoolroom chair was painted blue with forget-me-nots, Maimie's green with snowdrops and Coote's grey with orange blossom. A succession of governesses came and went, with alarming frequency, and included one who taught the children to play Six-Pack Bezique, another called Miss Bryan who always used the word 'deleterious' without really understanding what it meant, and a Swiss woman called Mademoiselle Jenny who was terrified of cows ('so we used to get in a field and drive all the cows at her').

The children spent their time making fun behind the adults' backs, speaking in their nursery patois, and inventing a secret language called 'Iggy Piggy', which involved 'putting an egg behind every vowel'. In later life the girls expressed resentment at their mother's seeming indifference to their needs. Lady Sibell was left-handed but was forced by the governess to write with her right hand. Coote, the youngest girl, was constantly slapped because she had difficulty in reading. In the end, her nanny begged Lady Beauchamp to take the girl to have her eyes tested. Coote was found to be extremely short-sighted and was prescribed thick spectacles. When Maimie contracted measles and she was forbidden contact with her siblings, her diary noted that it was her father who came to her room to read to her whilst she was in quarantine.

Hugh, adored by the sisters on account of his sweet nature, was not an academically gifted child. He preferred to spend time with his beloved horses. Boom despaired of his second son's philistinism, but appreciated his warm, sensitive nature. Hugh, unlike his brother, Lord Elmley, was entirely without pretension and airs. Everyone loved him. Blond and blue-eyed, he was a beautiful young boy with delicate features, though his father's insistence on physical exercise made him strong and robust.

The Lygon children were extremely close to each other, united in their dislike of their mother and adulation of their father. For all the formality of its aristocratic customs and the sanctity of its religious rituals, Madresfield brimmed with vitality and a sense of community. It was a very different place from Evelyn Waugh's Underhill.

Evelyn's day school, Heath Mount, was within walking distance of his home in Golders Green. It was a secure and pleasant environment. A clever and imaginative boy, he was a favourite of the headmaster, Mr

Granville Grenfell ('a name which would seem implausible in fiction'). Being a favourite did not stop him fantasising that the remains of the Head's deceased wife were hidden in a locked chamber.

Evelyn loved his prep school and, looking back, realised how lucky he was: 'When I read the accounts of my contemporaries of the enormities enacted at their preparatory school both by masters and boys, I admit that Heath Mount "had a good tone"' – though it could not be denied that some of the masters 'liked little boys too little and some too much'. There was a tendency to fondle the boys 'in a manner just short of indecency, smacking us and pulling our hair in a manner well short of cruelty'. Evelyn himself was capable of bullying tendencies. He picked on a small and beautiful boy called Cecil Beaton: 'the tears on his long eyelashes used to provoke the sadism of youth'.

Even at a tender age, Evelyn was attracted to seemingly glamorous and sophisticated friends. 'I was early drawn to panache,' he declared, recalling the sangfroid and the louche lifestyle of a little rich boy whose nanny would stand in attendance at football games in order to refresh him with lemon squash from a flask. At the cinema (which Evelyn adored), the rich boy regaled his lowly friend with filthy schoolboy jokes and lurid tales of the private lives of actresses. In return, Evelyn, who was going through a pious phase, tried to interest his friend in Anglo-Catholicism. High Church rituals had captivated him at the age of eleven. His friend, however, had more worldly things on his mind.

Waugh edited a school magazine called *The Cynic*. He collected war relics from the Western Front: bits of shrapnel, shell cases and a German helmet. Academic work was less of a concern. As a day school, Heath Mount did not set its sights at all high. It was not like the boarding schools that existed to feed the great public schools. Heath Mount accordingly provided insufficient preparation 'for the endurances of adolescence'. Waugh later claimed that if he had been sent to a better prep school, he would have been clever enough to win a scholarship to Eton or Winchester. The assumption was that he would go to Sherborne: his father's school and his brother's, a very respectable destination, if not in the top rank beside Eton, Harrow and the rest.

In 1912, nine-year-old Lord Elmley was sent to prep school. His younger brother Hugh followed him there two years later, just after the war began.

The school was a new establishment called West Downs, just outside Winchester. Owned and run by a Wykehamist called Lionel Helbert, who had previously been a House of Commons clerk, it was a small, friendly place in which the boys were treated with great care and affection. Beatings were frowned upon. The boys wore knickerbocker suits on weekdays in winter and grey flannels in summer. Sunday best was Eton suits and top hats. L. H., as Helbert was known, always took a walk after morning chapel, wearing a morning coat, and linking arms with the boys. On Sunday afternoons in summer he read stories of derring-do to the pupils out of doors, while they ate bananas and ginger biscuits.

As an Oxford undergraduate, Helbert had been very keen on drama and music. The hall in the new building at West Downs was called 'Shakespeare' and putting on plays was always a major part of school life – boys would be cross-dressed for *The Taming of the Shrew* and one appeared with a sheet over his head as the ghost in *Hamlet*. Madame Calviou, the French mistress, took charge of plays in French. Here Hugh's acting talents had their first opportunity to shine.

As at all English prep schools, sport was equally important, especially cricket. Sports Day, attended by parents who had to be addressed as 'Mother' and 'Father', was a highlight of the year, as was 'Founder's Day', L. H.'s birthday, when he gave the whole school a break in the countryside. They would load up carts with picnics, and go up onto the downs or further afield.

The war was the constant shadow over Hugh's prep school days. Many West Downs old boys were serving in the Army or Navy and the news of each death was felt by Helbert as a personal blow. The masters, too, were going off to the Western Front, leaving L. H. to shoulder the whole burden of the school himself. He felt that he must prepare the younger generation to go out and serve as soon as they were old enough. He therefore took up Scouting with great enthusiasm. The school was divided into five patrols and the West Downs boys could be seen in pairs going into the town on Scout duties, once even to London with a message for the War Office. Among Hugh's contemporaries were the sons of a general, who wrote vivid letters from the front. These were read aloud to the entire school at Scouting pow-wows. Outside the school chapel, where prayers were said every morning and evening, Helbert put up a notice in large letters under the heading 'Keep on Hopin'':

Keep on lookin' for the bright, bright skies,
Keep on hopin' that the sun will rise,
Keep on singin' when the whole world sighs,
And you'll get there in the mornin' . . .

The boys would sing this at the Wednesday singing class and at their autumn concert.

During the bad weather of late 1915, Hugh's second year at West Downs, troops and horses were flooded out of the local military camp, with the result that the school was requisitioned by the Army in Helbert's absence during the Christmas holidays. He returned to find the Welch Fusiliers sleeping in every room and even in the corridors and kit and equipment piled up on the expensive parquet floor of the new Shakespeare room. L. H. took it all in good humour.

Among Hugh's contemporaries at West Downs was his cousin, a very tall boy called David Plunket Greene. They would go on to Oxford together and meet Evelyn Waugh there.

Evelyn's enormous success as a writer and his assured place as one of the greatest English novelists of the twentieth century has obscured the fact that towards the end of the First World War his older brother became the most notorious young novelist in England. In 1917, Alec Waugh, still in his teens and awaiting active service, published a sensational semi-autobiographical account of school life called *The Loom of Youth*. He wrote it in just seven and a half weeks and it became a bestseller.

The book alluded to the forbidden subject of homosexual love in a boys' boarding school. A storm of fury was unleashed and the novel was condemned by schoolmasters across the nation. Outraged letters were published in the newspapers. Bans were proclaimed in school libraries. Boys found with copies of it were threatened with caning. Anxious parents wrote to headmasters to ask whether such practices really did take place. The ban of course merely whetted the appetite of countless curious schoolboys who devoured the book looking for the offending material. As with D. H. Lawrence's scandalous portrayal of anal sex in *Lady Chatterley's Lover*, equally pored over by schoolchildren, you only had to blink and you missed it. Alec remembered a friend reading the book many years later and asking him 'When do I reach "the scene"?' Alec looked over his friend's shoulder and replied 'You've passed it, ten pages past.' The account seems innocent enough by today's standards:

> Thus did begin a friendship entirely different from any Gordon had ever known before. He did not know what his real sentiments were; he did not even attempt to analyse them. He only knew that when he was with Morecambe he was indescribably happy . . . Morecambe came up to Gordon's study nearly every evening, and usually Foster left them alone together . . . During the long morning hours, when Gordon was supposed to be reading history, more than once there came over him a wish to plunge himself into the feverish waters of pleasure, and forget for a while the doubts and disappointments that overhung his life . . . he realised how easily he could slip into that life and be engulfed. No one would mind; his position would be the same; no one would think worse of him. Unless, of course, he was caught. Then probably everyone would turn round upon him; that was the one unforgivable sin – to be found out.

Nothing more than that.

Alec's book was in part revenge for his expulsion from Sherborne. He had been a model student: prefect, house captain, editor of the school magazine, winner of the English Verse Prize and member of the first XV and first XI. But then he was discovered in a homosexual relationship with a fellow pupil and 'asked to leave'. As *The Loom of Youth* made clear, the 'unforgivable sin' in such all-male establishments was not the act itself, but 'to be found out'.

The trials of Oscar Wilde still lingered in public memory. Alec had been made a victim of what he and others saw as absurd public hypersensitivity and overreaction towards homosexuality. He was not 'the immaculate exception' and he was incensed by the 'conspiracy of silence' and the hypocrisy of those who refused to see such sexual experimentation as entirely common: 'I wonder how many ex-public school boys would deny that at some point in their schooldays they indulged in homosexual practices; practices that had no lasting effect, that they instantly abandoned on finding themselves in an adult, heterosexual world,' he later wrote.

The homosexual controversy, however, was only part of the scandal. An equally serious accusation was that Alec's novel had dared to criticise the public school ethos, the very spirit of which was combating the Hun on the battlefields of France and Belgium. Alec later confessed that his intention had indeed been to expose the myth of the ideal public schoolboy venerated as a pillar of the British Empire. For many, this was his truly unforgivable sin.

English public schools had been undergoing significant transformation since the second half of the nineteenth century. Reforms by Thomas Arnold at Rugby and the bestselling novel *Tom Brown's Schooldays* had popularised a new image of the great boarding schools as nurseries of gentlemanly behaviour and patriotic service. The public school ethos of self-sacrifice on behalf of King and Country, school and friend, reached its apogee in the Great War. On battlefields such as the Somme, the losses were disproportionately high among the public-school-educated officer class. To take Eton as an example. The school had an average of about 1,100 pupils. Imagine the serried ranks of boys in an annual school photograph; 1,157 Old Etonians were wiped out in the war: the equivalent of every child in that photograph. This is what people meant when they talked about the death of a generation.

The much-lauded image of the courageous public schoolboy, educated in a gentlemanly tradition of chivalry, honour, loyalty, sportsmanship and leadership, sacrificing his life for his country, was dealt a body blow by the publication of Alec Waugh's novel. The passage in *The Loom of Youth* that really cut to the quick was not the brief flight of homosexual allusion but a sequence when a young soldier returns to his public school and smashes the ideals of the war: 'All our generation has been sacrificed . . . At the beginning we were deceived by the tinsel of war. Romance dies hard. But we know now. We've done with fairy tales. There is nothing glorious in war; no good can come of it. It's bloody, utterly bloody.'

Days after the novel's publication the soldier novelist, still in his teens, was posted to France. All of this only increased interest in Alec Waugh and his novel. There were already many soldier-poets but he was the first soldier-novelist. He had achieved literary celebrity and sales that ought to have made his publisher father proud. But Arthur was devastated: illusions were shattered and friendships were broken. The son of his soul had betrayed the school that had nurtured them both.

For Evelyn, just thirteen, the immediate effect of his older brother's disgrace was that Sherborne was barred to him just as he was about to go there. Instead he was sent to Lancing, a 'small public school of ecclesiastical temper on the South Downs'. His father had never even seen the place and had no associations with it. Evelyn had an ecclesiastical temper of his own and had expressed hopes of becoming a parson. Perhaps he could do something to absolve the sins of his brother.

CHAPTER 2

Lancing versus Eton

> There was a scent of dust in the air; a thin vestige surviving in the twilight from the golden clouds with which before chapel the House Room fags had filled the evening sunshine. Light was failing. Beyond the trefoils and branched mullions of the windows the towering autumnal leaf was now flat and colourless . . . the first day of term was slowly dying.

So begins Evelyn Waugh's unfinished story, *Charles Ryder's Schooldays*, which was closely based on his experiences at Lancing College in Sussex. A scrim of nostalgia hazes his memory. It was not like this when he left for Lancing on a damp and overcast day in May 1917. Arriving in the summer term meant that it was very difficult for him to make friends. Furthermore, whereas most of the boys had been hardened to absence from home by prep school, for Evelyn it was his first experience of boarding. 'I had lived too softly for my first thirteen years,' he ruefully remarked.

The school itself was built high on the hills of the Sussex Downs, dominating the horizon with its huge chapel. 'Lancing was monastic, indeed, and mediaeval in the full sense of the English Gothic revival; solitary, all of a piece, spread over a series of terraces sliced out of a spur of the downs.' That is how Evelyn described it in his autobiography. Its solitariness was of a piece with his own.

Ascension Day fell four days after he arrived. Having no idea that it was a school holiday, Evelyn had made no arrangements for family visits. No meals were served and it rained all day. The House Room was locked. It was the worst day of his life and he never forgot how wretchedly lonely he felt. He would bring up his own children to 'make a special intention at the Ascension Mass for all desolate little boys'.

Waugh kept a diary during his first two unhappy years at Lancing. He later destroyed it. In part, his unhappiness was a direct result of war deprivations: 'the food in Hall would have provoked mutiny in a mid-Victorian poor-house and it grew steadily worse until the end of the war'. Milkless cocoa, small portions of tasteless margarine, bread and foul stew constituted the very best of the fare. School textbooks were war issue, printed on thin greyish paper and bound in greasy, limp oilcloth, something that offended his taste for fine binding and hand-printed paper.

Many of the best young masters were fighting in the war, and the boys were made conscious of the sacrifices made daily by old boys and schoolmasters: 'On Sunday evenings the names were read of old boys killed in action during the week. There was seldom, if ever, a Sunday without its necrology. The chapel was approached by a passage in which their photographs were hung in ever-extending lines. I had not known them, but we were all conscious of these presences.'

Evelyn's natural fastidiousness and his love of panache also contributed to his unhappiness. He recoiled against the poor table manners of his schoolmates, as they dirtied their napkins and flicked pats of margarine to the high oak rafters. Afternoon bathing was another source of agony, as the boys were forced to share tepid muddy bath water. The latrines were 'disgusting' and lacking in privacy – they had no doors. Rather than waiting his turn, which involved shouting out 'After you' to boys from other Houses, Evelyn preferred to make himself excused during lesson time, for which he paid the punishment of writing twenty-five lines.

He was placed in Head's House, the most prestigious in the school, with the headmaster H. T. Bowlby serving as housemaster, a privilege that cost an extra £10 per year. Evelyn found the school rules bewildering and absurd. For the first two years, boys were dressed in subfusc (black), then they wore coloured socks, then in the sixth form coloured ties. All first years were prohibited from walking with hands in pockets. For the second year they could be inserted, but with the jacket raised, not drawn back. Older boys in year two were permitted to link arms with a 'one-year man', but not the other way round. Only school prefects could walk in the Lower Quad. Treading on grass was generally forbidden. Many vivid details of this sort were captured in *Charles Ryder's Schooldays*, together with schoolboy slang, such as 'dibs' for prayers and 'pitts' for bedrooms. Evelyn was distressed by the dearth of female company.

When the war came to an end, school life changed for the better. Evelyn felt more settled. Food, always of vital importance in the life of a schoolboy, improved greatly. The Grub Shop now offered whipped-cream walnuts, cream slices, ices, chocolate and buns of every kind. One of the privileges for older boys was the 'settle-tea' that each senior member of House Room gave in turn. Hot, buttered crumpets were served in abundance, followed by cake, pastries and, in season, strawberries and cream. Senior boys had their own private studies and tea ceremonies: 'we were as nice in the brewing of tea as a circle of maiden aunts'. They ordered their teas from London and 'tasted them with reverence, discoursing on their qualities as later we were to talk of wine'. They also ordered little pots of caviar and foie gras: 'Fullness was all.'

Respected masters returned from the war. Among them was the legendary figure of J. F. Roxburgh, one of two greatly contrasting figures who dominated Evelyn's adolescence. In his autobiography, he devoted a chapter to his 'Two Mentors'. The other mentor was Francis Crease. Roxburgh and Crease represented the worldly versus the aesthetic life.

Evelyn's interest in graphics – illuminated manuscripts, the design of borders and initials, calligraphy, elaborate scripts – led one of his tutors to approach local scribe, Francis Crease. Evelyn had already noticed Crease at chapel on Sundays. He was not a prepossessing figure. His high nose and pink and white skin made him seem mildly absurd. He was middle aged, effeminate and always dressed in soft tweeds. He had a delicate, mincing gait and spoke in a shrill voice. 'Today,' Waugh wrote in the more open era of the 1960s, 'he would be identified as an obvious homosexual.'

Evelyn went to Crease's home at Lychpole Farm for private lessons. He loved the visits, not only because they offered an escape from school, but also because he was drawn to Crease's aesthetic creed. In the first lesson Crease threw up his hands and exclaimed: 'You come to me wearing socks of the most vulgar colour and you have just written the most beautiful E since the book of Kells.' This he clearly regarded as an inexplicable paradox. Thursdays became a high point of the week, not only for the lessons, but also for their aftermath: 'the best part is when work is put away and we have tea in his beautiful blue and white china. It is such a relief to get into refined surroundings.' Young Evelyn was especially impressed by this sensitive and highly cultured man's devotion to his craft and his belief that 'if one is ever going to do good work one has to give one's life to it'.

Crease was invited to Underhill, the Waugh family home. A defining moment in Evelyn's life came when he asked for Crease's opinion of his father, Arthur Waugh. Crease replied: 'Charming, entirely charming, and acting all the time.' Evelyn asked his mother for her opinion and she 'confirmed the judgement. My eyes were opened and I saw him, whom I had grown up to accept in complete simplicity, as he must have appeared to others.'

The relationship between mentor and pupil was terminated by what seemed to Evelyn a rather trivial incident. In Crease's absence, he had used a quill knife and broken it. Crease had written a furious letter saying that he would never see him again and that Evelyn had broken not just his knife but, more importantly, his trust. A second letter came in the post, apologising for the first. But it was too late for Evelyn: 'the wound did not heal . . . after the incident of the broken blade the old glad, confident morning light never shone on our friendship'.

But the person who really broke Crease's spell was J. F. Roxburgh, upon whom Evelyn looked with unalloyed schoolboy hero-worship. He was as different a man from Crease as it was possible to imagine.

J. F. was a god to nearly all the Lancing boys. At the age of thirty-one he had returned from the war a hero, having been Mentioned in Dispatches and recommended for the Military Cross. He later became the first headmaster of Stowe. It was not difficult to see the attraction. He was handsome, willowy and elegant, and physically strong. Evelyn would always be drawn to this type of physique, so unlike his own. J. F. cut an immensely dashing figure with his colourful hand-woven ties and stylish suits. He liked to make a studied late entrance to chapel dressed in his Sorbonne robes. He was a man of great charisma: witty, charming and learned.

He had a beautiful, sonorous voice and it was a joy, said Evelyn, to hear him declaiming Latin 'like a great Negro stamping out a tribal rhythm'. Over forty years later, in *A Little Learning*, Waugh remembered it as a voice that set up 'reverberations in the adolescent head which a lifetime does not suffice to silence'. J. F. didn't just walk into a room: his entry was always a moment of exhilaration. Evelyn, conversely, had a curiously ungainly walk, a kind of trudge that caused his friends to make jibes about trench foot.

Even whilst invigilating exams, J. F. was unlike the other teachers who sleepily turned over their textbooks. He, by contrast, appeared 'always jaunty and fresh as a leading actor on the boards, in the limelight, commanding complete attention'. Evelyn was also drawn to J. F.'s love of language, his dislike of cliché and slang, his attention to precision in grammar. In the boys' essays 'oo' in the margin stood for 'orribel oxymoron' and 'ccc' for 'cliché, cant or commonplace'. Other comments would include a devastating 'Excellent journalism, my dear fellow.' J. F. used unusual words and phrases, to amuse as well as to educate the boys. Poor reading was a 'concatenation of discordant vocables'. His examination papers were elegantly printed and instead of the perfunctory termly report, he wrote long letters home to parents on hand-woven paper embossed with his name. Evelyn's lifelong disdain for printed as opposed to engraved postcards perhaps came from here.

'Always, in whatever he did, was the panache.' Evelyn was forever drawn to style, even if he felt that he lacked the quality himself. He loved good manners and civilised, cultured people, even though he himself could be rude and abrasive. This contradiction in his personality never changed – later in life, when he was asked why he was so vile despite his religious temperament he replied: 'Imagine how much worse I would be if I wasn't a Roman Catholic.'

J. F. was not overtly religious. He was 'reticent about his scepticism', though would throw in to the school debating society the occasional doubt about life after death that was bewildering to Evelyn. His doubts about God were rooted in the horrific sights he had seen on the Western Front. A stern moralist with a keen work ethic and no time for waste or frivolity, Roxburgh seemed rather like an eighteenth-century Anglican bishop without any of the theological baggage.

'Most good schoolmasters – and, I suppose, schoolmistresses also – are homosexual by inclination,' observed Waugh – 'how else could they endure their work?' His diary records an incident in which J. F. was supposedly caught embracing a boy in his study, but in his memoir he maintained that his teacher was not actively homosexual, though given to intense romantic friendships typical of the time. So called 'Greek love' could have a respectability and innocence, especially for a man such as Roxburgh, whose virility, military demeanour and style by no means conformed to the Wildean homosexual stereotype.

Evelyn was alert to the fallacy of sexual stereotyping: 'Mr Crease . . . was effeminate in appearance and manner; J. F. was markedly virile, but it was he who was the homosexual.' Waugh and his contemporaries believed that J. F. fell in love with individual boys, though without 'physical release with any of his pupils'. One of those he loved was a 'golden-haired Hyacinthus'. J. F. gave the boy a motorcycle. In no time the lad was thrown from it and facially disfigured. J. F. remained close to him until the boy's premature death.

Evelyn was not a particular favourite, although J. F. invited him to tea before he 'had any official position in the school'. In *Charles Ryder's Schooldays*, A. A. Carmichael, the model for J. F., is 'the splendid dandy, and wit . . . whom Charles worshipped from afar'. Evelyn got a bit closer than this: 'I was always in awe of him, so that he was, in a sense, the courtier and I the courted as he sought to draw me into his confidence.' The tea was a great honour: 'I remember as the clock struck five he said "How delightful. We have nothing to do until chapel but eat éclairs and talk about poetry."' Evelyn felt that he had not impressed, but as he went into chapel he was 'giddy with the sense of having been in communion with the Most High'.

The tea with J. F. was another defining moment, a revelation as profound as that when Crease had opened Evelyn's eyes to his father. On this very day, Crease happened to be at chapel in his 'cape and soft cravat'. By comparison with J. F., Crease 'seemed diminished. I did not exactly turn coat, but I knew that Mr Crease and J. F. were opposites and at about that time I transferred my allegiance to the more forceful and flamboyant person.' Following a later afternoon tête-à-tête in which J. F. visited Evelyn and a friend, the friend expressed disappointment that the great man had failed to comment on the specially ordered tea. Evelyn had a more sophisticated reading of the lacuna: 'You see how considerate he is. He never commented because he wanted us to believe that he knew perfectly well that we always drank it.' That, to him, was style.

In later years, the now famous writer heard that J. F. 'deplored my writing and what he heard of my conduct'. Yet he wrote Evelyn a letter, which was kept and treasured, in which he said that 'if you use what the gods have given you, you will do as much as any single person I can think of to shape the course of your own generation'.

At Lancing Evelyn did not find the special friend he had longed for. Like many of his contemporaries, he was drawn to the memory of Rupert Brooke and the ideal of romantic friendship that he represented. Looking through a memoir of Brooke, he noted in his diary: 'I felt very envious reading, particularly the parts about Rugby and friendship. I do honestly think that that is something that went out of the world in 1914, at least for one generation.'

This was a person for whom friendship would become an art, despite a lifelong tendency to infuriate and even to ostracise those who were closest to him. Yet, unlike most of his contemporaries, he made no really intimate friends at school. His intense and enduring friendships were formed at Oxford. Nor, as a schoolboy, was he prone to love affairs with pretty younger boys of the kind known at Lancing as 'tweatles' and at Eton as 'bitches'. He granted that he 'was susceptible to the prettiness of some fifteen-year-olds, but never fell victim to the grand passions which inflamed and tortured most of my friends (to whom I acted as astringent confidant)'.

On the whole, 'indulgences were kept private'. Sexual activity was known as 'filth' and 'was the subject of endless, tedious jokes, but not of boasting'. Evelyn assumed a rather aloof, amused stance to the agonies of his friends who 'played a Restoration comedy of assignations, secret correspondence and complacent chaperones'. In his diary he confided: 'I lead as pure a life as any Christian in the place, always excepting conversation of course.' He advised his friends to show restraint, talking a close friend out of a night's 'whoring' in the holidays.

He was drawn to charming, charismatic boys and was prone to hero-worship. But he despised boys who hero-worshipped him, such as a certain Dudley Carew, who appeared to have an insatiable taste for vulgarity, saying things like 'there's a delightful squalor about Shoreham'.

Crease said of Evelyn: 'You want a friend who is a thorn in the flesh, not an echo.' Evelyn recognised the wisdom of the observation.

The closest he came to real friendship at Lancing was with Tom Driberg – later chairman of the Labour Party, and Hugh Molson – later talked about as a possible leader of the Conservative Party. Molson was nicknamed 'Preters' on account of the fact that when asked if he was interested in politics, he would reply 'preternaturally so'. Flamboyant, highly intelligent and sophisticated, he dazzled with his 'superb pomposity of manner and vocabulary'. Molson had, Evelyn noted in his diary, 'the true aristocrat's capacity of being perfectly at home in anyone's company'. He was perhaps the first of the Sebastian type.

In the upper fifth, Evelyn and his friends formed a debating society called the Dilettanti, divided into three streams. Molson ran the Politics, a boy called Roger Fulford the Literary and Waugh the Arts. The society lasted a year, 'during which time almost every leisure hour was spent in lecturing and heckling one another, in debates, in committee-meetings and in elections'.

As Evelyn's confidence increased, he showed his sadistic side. One boy's life was rendered particularly miserable by his cruel tauntings. Appeals for temperance were met with stony refusal. Evelyn noted in his journal that 'in all these nasty manoeuvres there lay hidden the fear that I myself might at any moment fall from favour and become, as I had been in my first year, the object of contempt'.

Looking back, the mature Evelyn Waugh was appalled by what he read in his own early journals. In a moving letter to his son Auberon, who was unhappy at boarding school, Evelyn wrote that he had read through his own Lancing diaries in order to try to understand his son better. Instead, Evelyn was horrified by the priggish, selfish boy that he encountered amongst the journal's pages. 'Most adolescent diaries are naïve, trite and pretentious: mine lamentably so.' But it was more than this. With his characteristic honesty and self-deprecation, he saw that he 'was conceited, heartless and cautiously malevolent':

> The damning evidence is there, in sentence after sentence on page after page, of consistent caddishness. I feel no identity with the boy who wrote it. I believe I was a warm-hearted child. I know that as a man my affections, though narrow, are strong and constant. The

adolescent who reveals himself in these pages seems not cold but quite lacking in sincerity.

The war had left its mark on Evelyn's generation. Cynical and clever, he was determined to oppose the 'imperialist trash about discipline and the capacity for leading' that was the public school ethos. He was a rebellious boy, though his transgressions seem light by today's standards (giving in homework written in blank verse to catch out his master, for example). Evelyn and his cronies were barred from senior school positions of authority. He gained a reputation as a subversive and was the leader of a group known as the 'Bolshies'. They vented their spleen on those they felt were absurd or inferior. Science masters were treated with contempt and their laboratories were sabotaged by means of minor explosions generated by Bunsen burners.

The Bolshies' contempt was greatest for the school's Officer Training Corps (OTC), to which, like all the boys, they had to belong. Scornful of the school's military ethos, they devised 'rags' – practical jokes – to make the OTC appear absurd. They would march in the platoon with one boot polished and the other muddy, or deliberately drop rifles or turn right instead of left. They were merely expressing what countless other schoolboys around the country felt: a strong reaction against militarism and what they considered to be the huge waste of the casualties of the war.

It was becoming fashionable not to be patriotic. Evelyn noted in his memoir that while the Bolshies made their protests felt through minor delinquencies, other schools expressed their objections to militarism differently: 'At Eton there was a platoon which paraded in horn-rimmed spectacles and numbered off: "ten, Knave, Queen, King." We did nothing as stylish as this, but we outraged local tradition.' The Bolshies' final act of defiance against the OTC was designed to show utter contempt for all that the corps held dear. Evelyn's House (Heads) was well known for its incompetence in drill. His plan was to surprise the school by winning the Platoon Shield but then to have no part in the all-important ceremonial passing over of the shield. The scheme, however, failed as Heads was placed third.

Secretly, he longed for recognition. In *Charles Ryder's Schooldays*, Charles is furious at being passed over for a position of authority in the Settle, just as Evelyn was at Lancing. His House tutor, Mr Woodard, cleverly brought him into conformity. He gave a choice: Evelyn could accept the House captaincy or he could leave. 'I know that you often say and write a lot which you don't really believe,' said Woodard shrewdly. 'Now what do you really think about it?' Needless to say, Waugh chose the captaincy 'and for the next two terms was segregated from my former cronies'. In looking back and assessing his motives, Evelyn concluded that it was not authority that he craved but 'school offices I coveted, such as the editorship of the magazine and presidency of the debating society, which were held by House captains only'.

He knew that he was too much the individualist. But in his diary he showed self-disgust with the way that he had capitulated to authority: 'My position is really impossible – a House-captain as a bribe to make me sober.' It was 'limited Bolshevism' for him from now on. In reality, he felt lonely and dispirited. He was neither an insider nor outsider. Above all, he had not found the golden circle of friends that he craved.

Perhaps his diminutive height and his lack of conventional beauty contributed to his sexual insecurity. His brother Alec had had at least two passionate affairs at Sherborne, and had made his name through his illicit romances, but the most romantic of Evelyn's encounters were late night solitary walks down to the sea with another prefect. The relationship was entirely innocent, but Arthur Waugh found out about it. Fearing a repetition of Alec's disgrace, he wrote a furious letter, which Evelyn found rather bewildering, since he wasn't in full possession of the facts about his brother. Still, at least there was uncharacteristic strength in his father's outburst, with Evelyn commenting: 'I am rather glad that he has taken a strong line against something at last.'

Evelyn's final year at Lancing was more productive than those that had gone before, though not necessarily happier. He enjoyed the privileges of his seniority. He had his own 'pitt' or study, which he decorated in a tasteful blue – blue curtains, blue cushions on the window seat, blue upholstery for his desk. Arthur Waugh's brass candlesticks stood on the desk and Medici prints hung on the walls. Evelyn worked hard for his scholarship to Oxford. 'I must write prose or burst,' he told his diary. He also started writing a novel: 'the study of a man with two characters, by his brother'. He was becoming aware of 'a detached, critical Hyde, who intruded his presence more and more often on the conventional, intolerant, subhuman, wholly respectable Dr Jekyll'. During his final months he edited and contributed to *The Lancing Magazine*, won the poetry prize and the Scarlyn Literature Prize, composed poetry and wrote a very successful three-act play, which was performed to the whole school. He was made president of the debating society, not to mention junior sacristan in chapel.

Outwardly he may have appeared to conform, but his play *Conversion* was aimed to show that he was still a 'Bolshie' at heart. It was a satire on public school values. Its hero, Townsend, clearly a self-portrait, is a rebel blackmailed into conformity. At this time Evelyn wrote in his diary with his usual perceptive candour: 'I am beginning to think that there must be some malignant fate that makes me foul. I never think of the man behind at all. I spend all my attention on trying to get in front of the man in front.'

He half-jokingly toyed with the idea of suicide, drafting farewell notes to friends. Though he admired the beauty of Lancing's enormous chapel (best appreciated, he decided, by lying outside on the grass staring up at the imposing stone and the sky), he felt a loss of faith, sparked by a dynamic divinity teacher called Mr Dawlinson: 'This learned and devout man inadvertently made me an atheist. He explained to his divinity class that none of the books of the Bible were by their supposed authors; he invited us to speculate, in the manner of the fourth century, upon belief in God.'

Evelyn's last term at school, a golden age for most of his friends, was a time of boredom and depression. Or so he remembered them. But there were happy moments. His last Ascension Day, so different from that first terrible day, was spent with Preters, who had borrowed a motor car. The boys drove to Chichester, got very drunk at luncheon and drove round and round the Market Cross shouting out to passers-by that they were looking for the nearest pub. He also enjoyed pleasant late afternoon sessions behind the chapel, smoking 'sweet-smelling gold and silk-tipped Levantine cigarettes'.

The last term meant that he was exempt from all the rules. He was now free to walk on the lawns and wear a bow tie. But instead of revelling in his freedom, he founded the Corpse Club 'for people who are bored stiff'. They wore black ties and black tassels in their buttonholes and wrote on mourning paper. Evelyn was the leader, or 'Chief Undertaker'.

Evelyn's anarchic sense of humour always sustained him, no matter how miserable he felt. His school friend Roger Fulford said that 'without Evelyn's forceful sense of the ridiculous, the spirit of our House would have been unworthy of recall'. Fulford remembers how they stole into a housemaster's room to read his correspondence, only to find a hilarious letter concerning an impudent boy who had the temerity to eat pineapple chunks in class. This incident found its way into Waugh's novel *Decline and Fall.* What Evelyn took particular delight in was the phrasing 'he was pleased to belch rudely in my face'. He relished the choice of the words 'pleased' and 'rudely'. This was the same delight as that he took in Roxburgh's felicitous phrases and put-downs – and indeed in the language of the egregious Dudley Carew. He was honing the ear for dialogue that became so acute in his novels, where pompous people are forever saying serious things that are unintentionally wildly funny.

Even in his final months at Lancing he continued to be plagued by feelings of inadequacy, sensing that he was never first choice in anything, always a sloppy second. Alienated and depressed, generally unpopular, he considered running away: 'I am burdened with failure this term, when I have been most successful really . . . Everything I have had has come to me shop-soiled and second hand.'

Evelyn had an almost pathological fear and loathing of the second-hand and the second-rate. For him, Lancing came into both categories. Even whilst writing about his sabotaging of the OTC, he was thinking wistfully of the stylishness of the Eton rebellion. In a sense, this was not Evelyn's fault. He had already been indoctrinated at home into the view that Sherborne was a much better school than Lancing, and at school, the headmaster, Henry Bowlby, himself a former master at Eton, also impressed upon the boys the superiority of the place where he no longer taught: 'We held him in some awe and he remained aloof from us, never dissembling the opinion, to which we all assented, that Lancing was a less important place than Eton.'

In his biography of Old Etonian theologian Ronald Knox, the adult Evelyn let slip the awe he felt for Eton. He describes Knox's relationship with his school as 'a life-long love'. Like many Old Etonians, Knox found Oxford a very poor second best. Eton, wrote Waugh, 'was the scene of Ronald's brilliant intellectual development and of his ardent and undying friendships'. Waugh went on to write that:

> Most candid Englishmen recognise it as a school sui generis which marks the majority of its sons with a peculiar Englishry, genial, confident, humorous, and reticent; which gives to each as little or as much learning as his abilities and tastes demand; which, while correcting affectation, allows the genuine eccentric to go his own way unmolested; which nourishes its rare favourites . . . in a rich and humane traditional culture which admits no rival.

Lancing had not been like that. John Betjeman in his verse autobiography *Summoned by Bells* has one young man at Oxford saying to him 'Spiritually, John, I was at Eton.' The same might perhaps have been said of Evelyn Waugh. When Fulford came up to Oxford, Waugh recommended him not to talk so much about Lancing: 'If you weren't at Eton or Harrow or Winchester or Rugby, no-one minds much where you were.'

What Lancing schoolboys did have in common with their peers at major public schools such as Eton was the cynicism they felt with regard to the disasters of the Great War. They firmly blamed the 'old men', Arthur Waugh's generation, who had betrayed the golden boys of Rupert Brooke's generation. Evelyn used the phrase 'old men' for the first time in a speech he gave in his final year at Lancing. He would advert to it repeatedly throughout the next decade in his advocacy of the younger generation at odds with the old. This was his manifesto: 'No generation has ever wreaked such disasters as the last. After numerous small indiscretions it had its fling of a war which has left the civilised world pauperised, ravaged, shaken to its foundations.' Evelyn later described his last editorial for *The Magazine*, entitled 'The Youngest Generation', as 'a preposterous manifesto of disillusionment':

> The men of Rupert Brooke's generation are broken. Narcissus-like, they stood for an instant, amazedly aware of their own beauty; the war, which the old men made, has left them tired and embittered. What will the young men of 1922 be? . . . They will be, above all things, clear-sighted . . . very hard and analytical and unsympathetic . . . They will not be revolutionaries and they will not be poets and they will not be mystics . . . they will have . . . a very full sense of humour . . . They will watch themselves with . . . a cynical smile and often with a laugh . . . They will not be a happy generation.

He would become the voice of that unhappy generation.

Evelyn's panegyric to Eton as a school sui generis was written at a time when his male friends were almost exclusively Old Etonians. Eton was then, and perhaps is still, considered to be the best public school in England. It had, and continues to have, an unsurpassed record of future prime ministers. Its aura of elegance and tradition was, and remains, the stuff of legend. Even George Orwell wrote of his old school that it had 'one great virtue . . . a tolerant and civilised atmosphere which gives each boy a fair chance of developing his own individuality'.

When one of Evelyn's friends, the writer Cyril Connolly (whom he nicknamed 'Smarty Boots'), sat his entrance exam at the school, he was utterly entranced. Eton was 'splendid and decadent . . . the huge stately elms, the boys in their many-coloured caps and blazers, the top hats, the strawberries and cream, the smell of wisteria'. When he overheard a boy with a top hat call out in a foppish drawl a remark to a passing sculler, it all seemed 'the incarnation of elegance and maturity'. For Connolly it was a paradise built of 'wine-dark brick'. He was mesmerised by a huge chestnut tree in Weston's Yard. 'I was long dominated by impressions of school,' he wrote in his memoir *Enemies of Promise*; 'The plopping of gas mantles in the classrooms, the refrain of psalm tunes, the smell of plaster on the stairs, the walk through the fields to the bathing places or to chapel across the cobbles of School Yard, evoked a vanished Eden of grace and security.'

Eton College was at the pinnacle of the English social system. It had received its royal charter in 1444. For many it embodied quintessential Englishness. 'The Headmaster of Eton has more to do with the soul of England than the primate of Canterbury,' quipped Winston Churchill's Irish cousin, Shane Leslie. Running in and out of School Yard, dominated by Lupton's Tower and the crumbling cloisters, the boys hurried past the statue of the school's founder, Henry VI: 'the past history was there . . . all this mellowness was continuously sinking into them, a beneficent influence', recalled another old boy, Harold Acton. It was the school where the English aristocracy sent their boys. No school had a higher proportion of titled young men on the roll. It had close links with the royal family. Windsor Castle lies at the far end of the street.

The masters or 'beaks' were in many respects lesser beings than some of the boys. The more servile of them would long to be asked to the boys' great homes, sometimes long even for the mere opportunity to talk to the most important boys.

Yet Cyril Connolly and Anthony Powell (another Old Etonian who would become a novelist and a friend of Waugh's) both stressed that a boy's status depended not on family money or rank, but rather 'on a curious blend of elegance and vitality . . . and the gift of being amusing'. Powell thought that this made Eton different from Oxford, where he too went on to become an undergraduate: 'I recall no sense of inferiority on account of many boys' parents being richer and grander than my own, though of course many were. Indeed the first powerful impact of snobbery and money was brought home to me, not at Eton, but at Oxford.'

Nevertheless, this small and exclusive world existed on a finely graduated but keenly felt code of manners. Editorials appeared in the school magazine on such subjects as 'The Top Hat'. Rules were strict. Boys were prohibited from driving in motor cars on Sundays, for example. One wonders at how many other schools a sufficient number of boys would have had motor cars to make such a rule worth writing.

The education of the Honourable Hugh Lygon and his older brother Lord Elmley at Eton and then Oxford followed a pattern that had endured in the family since the early nineteenth century. They were considered 'important boys' by the masters, since their father, Lord Beauchamp, was a prominent establishment figure. Despite the great wealth and social standing of their father, the boys were lacking in pretension and snobbishness. Anthony Powell thought that it was impossible to conceive a lord less snobbish than young Elmley.

Hugh Lygon went to Eton in 1918. Then as now, there were seventy scholars or 'Collegers', known as 'tugs'. The fee-paying boys were 'Oppidans'. Housemasters were called 'm'tutor'. A 'new-tit' was a new boy. A 'Scug' was a boy who didn't have his colours. A 'dry bob' played cricket, a 'wet bob' chose rowing, a 'slack bob' did neither. Each school term was known as a 'half'. 'Tuck' was known as 'sock', 'messing' was cooking tea together in groups of three (who took turns to eat in each other's rooms). There were no dormitories: each boy was given his own room simply furnished with a 'bury' – a chest of drawers with a desk on top, supporting a small bookcase. A fold-up bed was stowed behind a curtain. Boys were permitted to furnish their rooms to their own taste, typically with ottoman, armchair, boot box, brush box and pictures from Blundell's.

The boys wore tailcoats and top hats, but if a boy was elected to 'Pop' he could wear flamboyant waistcoats, black and white check trousers, and white stick-up collars. Boys in the self-elected and elite group 'Pop' were permitted to beat younger boys. This 'privilege' did not extend to the schoolmasters. Pop was a body of twenty-eight boys, who exercised overall authority as prefects and were generally worshipped by the other boys. The group was based overwhelmingly on athletic prowess but members were sometimes admitted for their good looks, charm and wit. It was regarded as the summit of school distinction. Some boys never got over having been passed over for Pop. Julian Mitchell's play *Another Country* is based on the not outrageous premise that Guy Burgess was so scarred by the experience of not getting into Pop that he turned against his country and became a Russian spy. One desperate boy offered his sister for sex if he were elected. Connolly observed that 'Pop were the rulers of Eton, fawned on by masters and the helpless Sixth Form'. The Sixth Form Select, consisting of twenty or so academically gifted boys, followed Pop in status. The double-file procession of seniors – largely Pop and the Select – into chapel after everyone else was seated was known as the 'Ram'.

Good looks, charm and wit may have been as important as social status, but it was best of all if the whole package came together. When it came to Pop, brains did not count for much. Hugh Lygon was typical of Pop in being admired for his floppy blond hair, his handsome face and his charming demeanour rather than his intellectual capacities, which were distinctly limited.

The dress code and the quasi-feudal system of 'fags' and 'fagmasters' – junior boys performing menial tasks for senior ones – conjure up images of Flashman in *Tom Brown's Schooldays*, but many of the boys of Hugh Lygon's generation had memories of kindly fagmasters. A fag's duties included making boiled eggs and toast and running errands to the shops on Eton High Street. Some fagmasters of course abused their positions and, as Cyril Connolly put it, 'developed into lifelong flagellants'. Connolly claimed that he was damaged for life by his beatings from older boys, often administered for being 'generally uppish'. The small boys would be in their tin baths as they waited in fear for the summons of a 'wanted' man. When his name was called, the victim would be summoned to 'the chair', which would be placed in the middle of the room. The waiting was the worst part. Once the chair was in place, a storm of accusation broke out. It was advisable not to answer back. Then the boy would kneel on the chair, bottom outward and hands stretched over the back. The beating would begin: 'Looking round we could see a monster rushing towards us with a cane in his hand, his face upside down and contorted.' When it was over, one of the older boys would say 'Goodnight'. 'It was wise,' Connolly reported, 'to answer politely.'

A boy's house was very important because Eton was so large, and the housemasters were both autocratic and independent. Each ran his house as he wished. Hugh Lygon boarded at Walpole House, a building of red brick that looked rather like a clinic. Run by Arthur Goodhart, its reputation was as the worst house in the school, with a low sporting record, its only silver trophy being the Lower Boys' Singing Cup. Tolerant scepticism was the keynote. Goodhart was an eccentric, a repressed bisexual who had a fetish for ladies' shoes. This he made no effort to disguise: he would encourage the boys to admire his latest volume of *Feminine Footwear Through the Ages*. In his fifties, with high forehead and walrus moustache, he had a 'look of unreliable benevolence, an awareness of being always prepared for the worst, and usually experiencing it'. Anthony Powell described him as: 'In certain respects a typical schoolmaster; in others, an exceptional example of his profession.' He wore the Eton master's uniform of black suit and white bow tie, and was old-fashioned enough to retain the starched shirt and cuffs of an earlier generation, often remarking that in his own time at Eton a boy who did not put on a clean stiff shirt every day was 'an absolute scug'. Goodhart deplored special sports clothes and considered an 'old tailcoat' to be entirely suitable for the Wall Game (of which he was a star).

Goodhart was a classics teacher whose real love was music. The boys in his house were encouraged to sing a hymn at house prayers every night. Goodhart accompanied them on the harmonium. One night he chose 'Good King Wenceslas'. They reached the verse: 'Heat was in the very sod/ Which the saint had printed'. Goodhart observed a boy laughing. It was Lord Elmley. He kept him behind and gave him a dressing down. Powell takes up the story: '"You were laughing at the word *sod*. Do you know what it means?" He was foaming by now. "It is in vulgar use as short for sodomism – *the most loathsome form of dual vice*".' There was a certain amount of discussion amongst the boys afterwards as to what he regarded as the less loathsome forms of 'dual vice'.

Powell says that 'romantic passions' were much discussed, though 'physical contacts were rare'. He does nevertheless mention 'brutal intimacies' taking place. 'The masters might look on the subject as one of unspeakable horror; the boys behaved much in the manner of public opinion as to homosexuality today; ranging from strong disapproval to unconcealed involvement.'

Goodhart was also responsible for bringing back theatrical performances by the boys, following a ban that had been in place for fifty years. There was no Eton Drama Society, but individual housemasters began to put on plays. In July 1919, Goodhart's House Dramatic Society produced *Doctor Faustus*. Harold Acton remembered it as a 'superlative performance' of Christopher Marlowe's play, with Lord David Cecil playing 'a nervously saturnine Mephistopheles' and Hugh Lygon as a 'cherubic Helen of Troy'. The *Eton College Chronicle* singled out Hugh's performance for praise and the success of this production gave Goodhart the courage to try *The Importance of Being Earnest*. Once again, Hugh played a female role, this time Cecily Cardew. Again, he was singled out for his abilities: 'he proved an excellent *ingénue* and made more of the part than is usually possible in the circumstances'. The best moment of the play, said the *Chronicle*, was when Cecily filled Gwendolyn's tea with sugar. Hugh may not have been a sporting boy, or a clever boy, but he was clearly gifted dramatically. His beauty made him a convincing female. A photograph of him cross-dressed as Cecily shows his delicate features.

At the time, Wilde's masterpiece was considered to be a shocking play, especially when rendered by schoolboys. The author's reputation had contaminated the comedy. The performance contributed to the whiff of deplorable morals that hung over Goodhart's house.

Hugh was a good friend of Anthony Powell. They messed together and became a trio with Denys Buckley, a future High Court judge, until Hugh left to travel abroad before going up to Oxford. Boys were allowed to choose their own messmates, who would not be necessarily of the same year: Powell was a year below Lygon. As at Lancing, tea was the most important meal of the day. After Hugh's departure, Powell messed with a boy called Hubert Duggan, whose glamorous mother (an American heiress) married Lord Curzon, Viceroy of India. The character of the charming, handsome, romantic, dissolute Stringham, who descends into drunken ruin in Powell's *A Dance to the Music of Time* novel sequence, is usually said to be a portrait of Duggan. So he is, but he is also laced with a dash of Hugh Lygon.

Hubert and Hugh were two of a kind: dashing and moving in the highest social circles. They were also prone to melancholy as well as auto-destructive drunkenness. They embodied a type that would come to obsess both Waugh and Powell: the charismatic aristocrat who represents a gilded but decaying world, who lacks direction and is displaced by the grey modernity of a Widmerpool (Powell in *A Dance to the Music of Time*) or a Hooper (Waugh in *Brideshead*). In writing of Eton in his memoir *Enemies of Promise*, Cyril Connolly put forward his theory of 'permanent adolescence'. He proposed that the experience of public school was so intense that it dominated the lives and arrested the development of those who underwent such an education.

Despite his Eton education, Hugh Lygon needed extra private coaching to get him into university. An Oxford don was brought down to Madresfield to tutor him. Another summons came to a successful actor called William Armstrong who served as a kind of dramatic coach-tutor to the family, though his real job was to keep an eye on Hugh's drinking and other failings. Armstrong, who later turned from acting to directing and transformed the Liverpool Rep into the best regional theatre in the country, found it humiliating to have to sit at a separate table for dinner, like an upper servant. But he adored Hugh and always kept in touch. His time at Madresfield, which he remembered with the deer cropping the park and afternoon tea under the cedars on the immaculate lawn, remained one of the high points of his life.

> Remember that the *Eton Candle* is our challenge – our first fruits – the first trumpet call of our movement – it is OURSELVES.
> (Brian Howard to Harold Acton)

Hugh Lygon's Eton generation included boys of extraordinary talent and precocity. The Eton Society of Arts was run by sixth-formers Harold Acton, son of a cosmopolitan artist, and Brian Howard, an American boy born in Surrey who believed that he had Jewish blood. They edited the Society's magazine, called the *Eton Candle*. It had a shocking pink cover. The Society devoted itself to modernism. Acton and Howard were leaders and rebels. Howard was nearly expelled for taking a toy engine into chapel. Acton was beaten for not knowing the football colours of the various houses: 'Smack, smack, smack. I shifted round so that the blows might fall in a different place. "Keep still," he shouted, "it's my religion." I said, "I'm turning the other cheek."'

Brian Howard was considered beautiful as well as brilliant. Connolly remembered his 'distinguished impertinent face, a sensual mouth, and dark eyes with long eyelashes'. Others remarked upon his chalk-white skin and wavy jet-black hair. His eyes seemed to be heavily made-up. He was tall and lean. But it was his speech and mannerisms that made him so unique. Even at the age of thirteen, he seemed like a throwback to another era. He was camp personified, a fop out of a Restoration comedy. Many writers would attempt to capture his character, not only Evelyn Waugh. The Brian Howard voice is unmistakable: 'My dear,' he once said to Harold Acton, 'I've just discovered a person who has something a little bit unusual, under a pimply and rather catastrophic exterior.' Waugh caught the style perfectly in the figure of Anthony Blanche in *Brideshead Revisited*.

His parentage was mysterious. He was grandly named Brian Christian de Clavering Howard, but his friends discovered that his father's real name was Gassaway. The 'Howard' was made up – and rather bad form, since there was no connection with the Howards of Castle Howard. An entirely exotic figure, Brian made no attempt to hide his homosexuality. Yet he was, says Connolly, 'the most fashionable boy at school'.

Harold Acton was tall, with a long thin nose and a high-domed head that was sometimes compared to a peanut. His eyes were like black olives. He had a slightly swaying carriage. He was formal and courteous, with a touch of impishness. The two boys had similar parentage: American mothers, fathers who were art dealers with Italian affiliations. Acton's family home was 'La Pietra', an exquisite Tuscan mansion stuffed with paintings and antiques. The Actons lived like characters out of a Henry James novel. Figures such as Diaghilev the ballet master and Leon Bakst the avant-garde stage designer visited them at La Pietra. Brian and Harold, then, were extremely sophisticated and precocious, the embodiment of cosmopolitan modernity, a culture that could hardly have been more removed from that of the old English aristocracy with their large, cold, shabby homes and annual routines of hunting and shooting.

The two boys cultivated exaggerated mannerisms of speech and gesture. Both had panache and charm. One of their Eton contemporaries described them at the theatre: 'Brian and Harold walked into the stalls, in full evening dress, with long white gloves draped over one arm, and carrying silver-topped canes and top-hats, looking like a couple of Oscar Wildes.' In thrall to Diaghilev and the Ballets Russes, they danced at Dyson's to the pulsating tones of Stravinsky's ballet music. Brian was a wonderful dancer, a worshipper of Nijinsky. They were stylish and elegant – theirs was an altogether far more nuanced rebellion than that of Evelyn Waugh's 'Bolshies' and the 'Corpse Club'.

They loved modernist painting, read Marcel Proust and Jean Cocteau. Edith Sitwell praised their schoolboy writings. They were described as the 'cream of intellectual Eton', full of promise, with their plans for theatre trips and magazines. Their American heritage and modernist radicalism liberated them from the constraints of the English. They despised 'dull frowsy England – awful men in bowler hats and bad tempers trotting up and down wet pavements'. Rebelling against philistinism, as other boys walked up the Eton High Street towards Windsor, they wandered like Parisian *flâneurs*, heading in the opposite direction for Slough in pursuit of the 'bourgeois macabre'. Howard fantasised outrageously about hidden perversions behind respectable facades.

The Eton Society of Arts' sacred meeting place was the Studio, a room in the house of the drawing master. It was a retreat from the school, scruffy and stuffed with pots, jars and drawing implements. The Society comprised an extraordinary group of young men. Henry Yorke, who went on to write novels under the name Henry Green, was secretary; Anthony Powell and Robert Byron, who would become a superb travel writer, were also members, as was Alan Clutton-Brock who went on to be the art critic of *The Times* and then Slade Professor of Fine Arts at Cambridge.

But they were not all artists and intellectuals. The Honourable Hugh Lygon was a member, more on account of his looks than his intellect. He had no artistic pretensions whatsoever. By now he was a slim but muscular youth, always elegantly dressed. It is easy to see why Howard and Acton wanted him in their club. Some said he had a face out of Botticelli, while for Powell he was 'fair-haired, nice mannered, a Giotto angel living in a narcissistic dream'. Unlike nearly everyone else in the Society of Arts, he was sporty and masculine, a boxer and an athlete. As a rule, Harold and his followers set themselves firmly against 'macho hearties'. The code of aestheticism that they lived by was partly a reaction against the hearty public school ethos founded on games worship. But they were happy to make Hugh, with his beauty and his charm, an exception to their rule. There was a suspicion that he was only there because one of the more influential members of the group – Howard, perhaps, or Byron – thought that he was absolutely gorgeous and that he was not averse to their advances. An aura of raffishness, if not outright scandal, surrounded the group as they met on Saturday evenings and discussed such subjects as 'Post-Impressionism', 'The Decoration of Rooms' and 'Oriental Art'.

The shocking pink *Eton Candle* for 1922 was indeed known to its detractors as the Eton Scandal. Extravagantly praised by Edith Sitwell, doyenne of high modernism, it was dedicated to the memory of Eton's most notorious old boy, the arch-aesthete, prolific poet, republican radical and lifelong flagellant, Algernon Charles Swinburne. Beautifully printed on hand-made paper, with yellow endpapers, the *Candle* included a contribution by a young master called Aldous Huxley and an essay by Brian Howard entitled 'The New Poetry', which attacked the staid Georgian poets and praised the innovative verse of Ezra Pound. Like Evelyn Waugh at Lancing, Howard set himself against the 'old men' of the pre-war era who had murdered the golden boys of Rupert Brooke's generation:

> You were a great Young Generation . . .
> And then you went and got murdered – magnificently
> Went out and got murdered . . . because a parcel of damned old men
> Wanted some fun or some power or something.

As Cyril Connolly put it, if you didn't get on with your father in those days, you had all the glorious dead on your side.

Having conquered Eton, it was only a matter of time before the two young Turks took on Oxford. Howard once exclaimed to Acton: 'Do you realise, Harold – please pay attention to this – that you and I are going to have a rather famous career at Oxford?' Both boys seemed destined for great things, dazzling careers in literature or the arts. But it was Eton that made them. University was to be an enemy of promise: it came to seem something of a let down. Ironically, the person who assured their fame and who immortalised their Oxford turned out to be the Lancing boy.

CHAPTER 3

Oxford: '. . . her secret none can utter'

> There is nothing like the aesthetic pleasure of being drunk and if you do it in the right way you can avoid being ill next day. That is the greatest thing Oxford has to teach.
>
> (Evelyn Waugh, *Diaries*)

> He was in love with my brother.
>
> (Lady Sibell Lygon)

January 1922. 'Half past seven and the Principal's dead.' Evelyn Waugh was in bed in his undergraduate rooms in Hertford College, Oxford. He was woken by this call from his servant or 'scout', Bateson, a melancholy man, whose job it was to change the chamber pots twice daily and bring jugs of shaving water every morning. Evelyn was eighteen years of age, and he had come up to Oxford at a different time of year from most undergraduates. He had won a scholarship to read History at Hertford. His original plan had been to spend time in France before Oxford, but his father was anxious for him to start university life without delay. Evelyn felt that it put him at a disadvantage. He was resentful. His rooms, up a poky staircase above the Junior Common Room Buttery, overlooking New College Lane, were modest. All the best ones had been taken in

Michaelmas (autumn) term. Crockery rattled below and cooking smells drifted up to his rooms, though sometimes that meant a pleasant aroma of anchovy toast and honey buns.

It was not merely the inferior student rooms that Evelyn minded, but the fact that it was difficult to form friendships so late in the year. Looking back, as he wrote his memoirs, he remembered his younger self as a somewhat romantic 'lone explorer', a rover on the fringes of various groups ('sets') of like-minded students. His letters at the time show a much less self-confident figure, desperately lonely, shy and ill at ease.

His contemporaries fell into two groups: those who were clever and dull, and those who were foolish and charming. Hertford College he found second-rate, respectable but dreary. It had none of the glamour of the more famous colleges such as Christ Church and Merton, though this had its advantages. It lacked the schoolboyish hooliganism of the larger colleges: 'No one was ever debagged or had his rooms wrecked or his oak screwed up' (undergraduate rooms had an inner door of baize and an outer of oak – if you did not wish to be disturbed, you closed the outer one, or 'sported your oak'). A contemporary described Hertford as 'rather earnest and lower-middle-class'. One of the main reasons Evelyn chose it was to save his father money.

This was not quite the romantic beginning that he had envisioned when as a schoolboy he had daydreamed about Oxford and prepared himself by reading novels such as Compton Mackenzie's *Sinister Street* and Max Beerbohm's *Zuleika Dobson.* For a sensitive boy with a strong aesthetic sensibility, Oxford had an irresistible aura of enchantment. He went up to the 'varsity' with his imagination aglow with literary associations. The sophisticated boys whom he came to know later treated Oxford with studied indifference and cool detachment. Their hearts had been left at Eton. For Evelyn, by contrast, product of a minor public school, there was magic in the beauty of Oxford, its ancient buildings of greys and golds, its tranquil, lush gardens and dreaming spires. 'All I can say,' he gushed to a friend shortly after his arrival, 'is that it is immensely beautiful and immensely different from anything I have seen written about it except perhaps "Know you her secret none can utter?"'

The quotation is the opening line of a poem called 'Alma Mater' by Arthur Quiller-Couch. Known as 'Q', he was the archetypal Oxford man of letters – who by Waugh's time had, with great disloyalty, seated himself in the King Edward VII Chair of English Literature at Cambridge. A typical stanza from 'Alma Mater' reads:

> Once, my dear – but the world was young then –
> Magdalen elms and Trinity limes –
> Lissom the blades and the backs that swung then,
> Eight good men in the good old times –
> Careless we, and the chorus flung then
> Under St Mary's chimes!

Though Evelyn was not the lissom type that might take to the river in a rowing eight, he shared Q's rosy-tinted vision. Oxford was 'mayonnaise and punts and cider cup all day long'. Charles Ryder's voice is his own: 'Oxford, in those days, was still a city of aquatint . . . her autumnal mists, her grey springtime, and the rare glory of her summer days . . . when the chestnut was in flower and the bells rang out high and clear over her gables and cupolas, exhaled the soft vapours of a thousand years of learning.' Late in life, revising *Brideshead* for the last time, Waugh changed that last phrase to 'exhaled the soft airs of centuries of youth'. Oxford ultimately stood for youth more than learning.

What would he have looked like to his fellow undergraduates? He was an attractive young man, short and slim with reddish, wavy hair, a sensuous mouth and a penetrating gaze. He had large hands, which he called craftsman hands. A wonderful hearty laugh, nearly an octave lower than his speaking voice. Those who knew him at this time testified to his peculiar charm, something that had not been nearly so apparent at Lancing. For some he was 'faun-like' – more an allusion to his light-footed energy than his diminutive stature. Despite the fierceness of his blue eyes and his slight swagger, there was an engaging air of vulnerability about him. Nevertheless, he could be impatient and cruel, especially to those less clever. He was not a kind young man, but he was generous and quick to see kindness in others.

For his first two terms he led a quiet and uneventful life. He claimed that he was content: 'I have enough friends to keep me from being lonely and not enough to bother me,' he wrote in a letter, adding that he did little work and dreamed a lot. But in other letters he lamented the lack of congenial friends. He complained of the ones he had met so far, 'a gloomy scholar from some Grammar school who talked nothing, some aristocratic men who talked winter sports and motor cars'. The highlight of his first term was to buy finely bound editions of Rupert Brooke and A. E. Housman's haunting homoerotic poetry collection *A Shropshire Lad*, volumes that he could ill afford. He reported the purchases with relish in letters to his school friend, Tom Driberg.

In his memoir of his early years, self-deprecatingly entitled *A Little Learning*, Waugh described the first part of his Oxford education as typical of a scholarship freshman from a minor public school. Subdued but happy, he purchased a cigarette box carved with the college arms, learned to smoke a pipe, got drunk for the first time, made a speech at the Union and did just enough work to scrape through his first year exams. 'But all the time it seemed to me,' he wrote, 'that there was a quintessential Oxford which I knew and loved from afar and intended to find.'

He knew that he was in search of something, but he was not quite sure what it was.

In *A Little Learning* he quoted Q's line about Oxford's '*secret none can utter*' once again. 'It is not given to all her sons either to seek or find this secret,' he commented, 'but it was very near the surface in 1922.' The clear implication is that he was on the brink of being let into the secret of the quintessential Oxford. At this point in his memoir he named one of his contemporaries: 'Pembroke [College] harboured Hugh Lygon and certain other aristocratic refugees from the examination system.' Pembroke was a college that had a reputation for welcoming the 'cream' of Oxford (rich and thick). Hugh was not the most intellectual of men, but after a period of study in Germany he had duly come up to Oxford. He would hardly have been turned away, given his pedigree.

Evelyn did not care in the least that the place was no meritocracy. Having won his scholarship to Hertford, he was determined to get through his three years with the minimum of work. Like many of his contemporaries, he subscribed to the notion that Oxford was a place 'simply to grow up in' rather than somewhere to gain an education or a step into a career path. More than anything, Oxford was the place where you met the friends that would be with you for life. Initially, it must have seemed to Evelyn that he was doomed to stay with the dull, middle-class friends of his first two terms. Glamorous aristocratic boys such as Hugh Lygon and

Lord Elmley were as remote as Mars. They belonged to sets that seemed impossible to infiltrate, a world that was exclusive, elegant and composed almost entirely of Old Etonians.

In Oxford lore, 1922 and 1923 would come to be regarded as no ordinary years. When Evelyn came to write his own love poem to Oxford in *Brideshead Revisited* he was careful to be explicit that Charles Ryder was of this vintage. A revolution was afoot and two men were its instigators: Harold Acton and Brian Howard. Eton had already made them into legendary figures, thanks to the *Candle*. To begin with, Oxford regarded them as an odd couple: Harold with his tall stooping figure, peculiar gait and abnormally small head, Brian with his swarthy demeanour, slicked back hair, huge dark eyes, and pouting mouth. Flagrantly homosexual, eccentric, worldly and cosmopolitan: Oxford had seen nothing like them since the days of Oscar Wilde. Paradoxically, Acton and Howard themselves considered Wilde effete and second-rate: 'Old Oscar screwed the last nail in the aesthete's coffin' was their view of the matter. They stood for a more robust aestheticism mingled with modernism. They read not Wilde and Swinburne, but Edith Sitwell, James Joyce and T. S. Eliot.

Acton's mantra was plainly set out: 'Now that the war was over, those who loved beauty had a mission, many missions. We should combat ugliness; we should create clarity where there was confusion; we should overcome mass indifference; and we should exterminate false prophets.' In his memoirs, Acton described his group as 'aesthetic hearties': 'There were no lilies and languors about us; on the whole we were pugnacious.' They despised the very things of which they were so often accused: pretentiousness and affectation. As at Eton, Harold was the undisputed leader, on a mission to re-educate Oxford. But Brian was just as influential and it was sometimes hard to separate them. The two men were regarded as rivals, friends, enemies and 'almost twins'.

Harold, to the amusement of his friends, stood on his balcony window with a megaphone, through which he recited poems (usually Eliot or Sitwell) to groups passing below in Christ Church Meadow. He painted his rooms in lemon and filled them with Victorian furniture, artificial flowers and wax fruit under bell jars. This love of Victoriana was a kind of retro kitsch, which almost began as a joke, a rebellion against classicism. These boys wanted modernism with an ironic twist.

News of the extraordinary pair spread like wildfire around drab post-war Oxford. Their highly distinctive turns of phrase were repeated at parties. 'Your etchings are the messes of a miserable masturbator,' Acton told one young man. Brian Howard remarked to a lovesick boy at a party: 'My dear . . . I feel that your fly buttons will burst open any minute and a large pink dirigible emerge, dripping ballast at intervals.'

Most undergraduates wore three-piece broadcloth suits. Brian and Harold were noted for sartorial elegance that set them apart from the crowd. Their clothes were beautifully made, described by one fellow Old Etonian as 'an intoxication'. They wore suits by Lesley & Roberts, cut in early Victorian style with high shoulders and big lapels. Their white double-breasted waistcoats were from Hawes & Curtis of Jermyn Street. They had monogrammed silk shirts, silver, mauve and pink trousers. Their casual wear included cashmere turtle-necked sweaters in bright colours, suede shoes, raspberry crepe-de-Chine shirts, green velvet trousers, and yellow hunting waistcoats. Harold wore a grey bowler, a trailing black coat and his infamous 'Oxford bags' (twenty-six inches wide at the knee and twenty-four at the ankle, covering the shoes).

Acton's nomenclature for their set was deliberately provocative, since Oxford was traditionally divided between Aesthetes and Hearties. Henry Yorke offers a choice description of the braying hearties: 'a rush of them through the cloisters, that awful screaming they affected when in motion imitating the cry when the fox is viewed, the sense curiously of remorse which comes over one who thinks he is to be hunted, the regret, despair and feeling sick the coward has.' A scrum of drunken hearties from the rowing club ducked Harold Acton in his pyjamas in the Mercury Fountain in Christ Church's Tom Quad. This is the origin of the incident in *Brideshead* where members of the notorious Bullingdon Club attempt to duck Anthony Blanche. On another occasion, thirty men – the equivalent of the first and the second rugby fifteens combined – assaulted Acton's room. He recalled the incident: 'I, tucked up in bed and contemplating the reflection of Luna on my walls, was immersed under showers of myriad particles of split glass, my hair powdered with glass dust and my possessions vitrified.' Brian Howard received news of the attack from his mother, who heard it (at Edith Sitwell's recitation of her poem *Façade*) from the mother of one of Harold's assailants: 'If I'd been there I'd have unloosed her corsets on the spot' was his riposte.

* * *

Evelyn, feeling that something essential in Oxford was eluding him, did the minimum of academic work. He blamed his disillusion with academia on his bad relationship with his tutor, C. R. M. F. Cruttwell, who was also Dean of Hertford College. The bad feeling was mutual. Cruttwell disliked Evelyn, convinced that he was wasting his scholarship. He described his student as a 'silly suburban sod with an inferiority complex and no palate'. Evelyn in return despised Cruttwell, describing him as 'a wreck of the war' who had 'never cleaned himself of the muck of the trenches'.

In Evelyn's third term he changed to a more spacious set of rooms on the ground floor of the front quad. This left him vulnerable to people dropping in to dump their bags or to cadge a drink and a cigarette. He decorated the rooms with Lovat Fraser prints and kept a human skull in a bowl, which he decorated with flowers. One night a group of 'young bloods' came into the quad drunk and looking for trouble. One of them leaned into Evelyn's window and was violently sick.

Having failed to be invited to join any of the university's famous drinking or dining clubs, Evelyn formed his own. He called it the 'Hertford Underworld'. His friends would come to his rooms to drink sherry and eat bread and cheese. It all felt rather unglamorous.

His Oxford experience was transformed when he was befriended by the charming, though slightly mad, Terence Greenidge. It was Greenidge who was responsible for introducing him to a new circle of friends. Meeting him was the beginning of a sentimental education.

Greenidge's habits included an obsession with tidiness. His pockets were often crammed with litter from the streets. In his person, by contrast, he was very untidy. He was a kleptomaniac, who filched any trifle that took his fancy: hairbrushes, keys, nail scissors, inkpots. He secreted his ill-gotten gains in orderly heaps behind books in the library. Evelyn was drawn to his zany humour and his child-like aura. Always in trouble with the college authorities, Greenidge loved practical jokes and declaimed Greek choruses loudly at night in the quad. He also invented nicknames that delighted Evelyn. Alec Waugh was 'Baldhead who writes for the papers', the night porter was 'Midnight Badger', another contemporary was 'Philbrick the Flagellant' (who on one occasion beat up Evelyn). Hugh Molson (Evelyn's Lancing friend) was 'Hotlunch', since he often complained about the cold lunches.

Evelyn and Greenidge put about a rumour that Cruttwell was sexually attracted to dogs. They barked under his windows at night and bought a stuffed dog, which was put in the dean's path as he walked home drunk after a college dinner. Greenidge developed a reputation as a dangerous influence. When Lord Beauchamp ('no prude', says Evelyn with typically mischievous understatement) found Greenidge in his elder son's rooms, he took his boy down from the university for two terms, fearing that Elmley had got into a bad set.

Greenidge described Evelyn in his undergraduate days as having 'the attractive appearance of a mischievous cherub'. He recalled him as a well-dressed figure, usually to be seen in a pale blue plus-four suit and carrying 'a short stout stick which was almost like a cudgel'. He remembered that Evelyn's 'conversation, though emotional, always appeared reasonable, his assurance was remarkable, and his wit was remarkable'. The plus fours would become a trademark. Waistcoats were also favoured. Fellow Oxford undergraduate Peter Quennell remembered that the first time he met Evelyn, 'he was small and neat, and dandified, wearing a bright yellow waistcoat'. There was a touch of Mr Toad about him.

Evelyn continued to be attracted to eccentric, anarchic characters. They brought out his own streak of zaniness. Greenidge later suffered from mental illness but nevertheless managed to hold down a job as a minor actor at the Shakespeare Memorial Theatre in Stratford-upon-Avon. He remembered Evelyn as slightly mad, but extremely kind and loyal. In later years, he lent Greenidge large sums of money, always sending it by return of post whenever he was asked for help. Evelyn was uninterested in money. Greenidge had 'a feeling that he was aware unconsciously that his talent was – well – formidable. It is rather pleasant that to him who did not worry about it great wealth came.'

At a lecture given by G. K. Chesterton to a Catholic group, the Newman Society, Greenidge introduced Evelyn to Harold Acton. Evelyn and Acton became immediate and enduring friends. Acton began attending the Hertford Underworld in Evelyn's rooms. Evelyn was convinced that the main reason for his appearance in such a humble setting was that he was infatuated with one of the Hertford men in the group. Refusing to drink beer and eat the plain fare, Acton would sip water and stare at the young Adonis. But in return he invited Evelyn to lunch and introduced him to his Eton friends, including Hugh Lygon.

Acton was now editing a new modernist literary magazine, a successor to the *Eton Candle* called the *Oxford Broom*. Waugh drew the cover for the second edition in spring 1923. Then he wrote a story for the third number, which was published in June 1923. Entitled 'Antony, who sought things that were lost', it concerns a beautiful young aristocrat, 'born of a proud family', who 'seemed always to be seeking in the future for what had gone before'. He was perhaps the first fictional draft for the Sebastian type, created exactly at the time when Evelyn was beginning to be drawn to Hugh Lygon and his kind.

His Oxford life had truly begun.

Evelyn hero-worshipped Acton. He would eventually dedicate his first novel to him 'in homage and affection'. They were an unlikely pair. Even Evelyn was puzzled as to what they had in common. Acton was worldly, sophisticated, cosmopolitan. Evelyn was self-confessedly 'insular': 'At the age of nineteen I had never crossed the sea and knew no modern language.' What drew them together, he said, was what he called *gusto*, a 'zest for the variety and absurdity of life, a veneration of artists, a loathing of the bogus'. Acton was the leader and Evelyn the follower. Evelyn loved the slightly older man's funniness, his cleverness, his eccentricity. 'He loved to shock and then to conciliate with exaggerated politeness . . . he was himself shocked and censorious at any breach of his elaborate and idiosyncratic code of propriety.'

Harold Acton was equally enchanted. He described Evelyn as 'an inseparable boon companion . . . I still see him as a prancing faun . . . wide apart eyes, always ready to be startled under raised eyebrows, the curved sensual lips, the hyacinthine locks of hair'. He detected something behind the shyness: 'So demure and yet so wild.' He loved the mischievous sparkle in his friend's eyes, the capacity for joy, the jokes. Evelyn's wit, charm and gift for irony compensated for the mood swings that Acton also observed: 'Spontaneous, ebullient, vivacious, then silent, sullen, staring at the world with critical distaste . . . his apparent frivolity was the beginning of true wisdom.' For Evelyn 'a sense of the ludicrous' was the essence of sanity.

Though intoxicated by Acton and the new set into which he was drawn, Evelyn was wary of Brian Howard, describing him as Lord Byron was famously described a century before: mad, bad and dangerous to know. Howard's 'ferocity of elegance' seemed to belong to the age of Byron, not the present. Evelyn couldn't quite cope with it. Or perhaps it was the sheer exhibitionism of Howard's homosexuality that both fascinated and repelled him.

Harold Acton gave Evelyn an entry into the Hypocrites' Club. There he discovered hard drinking and firm friendship: 'it was the stamping ground of half my Oxford life and the source of friendships still warm today'. It was at the Hypocrites that he was introduced to Hugh Lygon and his elder brother Elmley.

The Hypocrites was one of many drinking clubs at the university – such clubs were necessary because undergraduates were banned from going into the city's pubs, for fear of town versus gown fisticuffs or liaisons with unsuitable women. The most exclusive of the clubs was the famous Bullingdon, immortalised by Evelyn in his novel *Decline and Fall*, where it becomes the Bollinger Club, characterised by 'the sound of the English county families baying for broken glass'. The Bullingdon was a top-secret (all male, of course) dining club, not strictly a drinking society. Then, as now, it drew its membership from the super rich. It was known then for champagne drinking, ritualised violence and a uniform that consisted of exquisite Oxford blue tailcoats offset with ivory silk lapel revers, brass monogrammed buttons, mustard waistcoat and sky blue bow tie. All members had to endure a humiliating initiation rite that included having their rooms trashed as champagne was binged upon and regurgitated. Freddy Smith, second Earl of Birkenhead (president of Pop at Eton, Christ Church man and future military colleague of Evelyn in Yugoslavia), captured the Bullingdon men with aplomb: 'eldest sons from aristocratic families who drank champagne at breakfast and were often to be found flourishing hunting-whips and breaking windows in Peckwater Quad'.

Harold Acton was not the type (or the class) to have become a member of the Bullingdon. Brian Howard, on the other hand, being a huntsman as well as an aesthete, was once invited to one of their dinners, after which 256 panes of college glass were smashed. He followed up this adventure by spending, as he put it, 'a tumultuous night between the sheets' with a club member.

The Hypocrites' Club did not have quite the same exclusivity, though it too was characterised by a love of fine dining and, most importantly, hard drinking. If the motto of the Bullingdon was an unequivocal 'I love the sound of broken glass', that of the Hypocrites was laced with neat irony: 'water is best'. The watchwords were style and panache. Conversation turned on art and literature rather than deer-stalking and riding to hounds. The club was at this time in a state of transition. Its original members had been heavy drinking but somewhat sombre Rugbeians and Wykehamists (former pupils of Rugby and Winchester, the latter being generally regarded as the most academic of the great public schools). But as Evelyn arrived in Oxford it was in the process of 'invasion and occupation by a group of wanton Etonians who brought it to speedy dissolution'. The Hypocrites' Club was beginning to be associated with flamboyant dress and a manner that had the distinct smack of homosexuality. The name of the club came from the ancient Greek word for an actor: it was a place where you could pose and play roles. The president was Lord Elmley. As the sons of an earl, Elmley and Hugh were natural Bullingdon men. Their presence among the Hypocrites was intriguing and provocative.

'At Oxford I was reborn into full youth,' wrote Waugh apropos of his life once he had been initiated among the Hypocrites. He later denied that he had any ambitions to ingratiate himself with the wealthy or to 'make influential friends who would prosper any future career'. He said that his interests were 'as narrow as the ancient walls'. For Evelyn it was quite simple: he wanted to be loved and he wanted to live fully and freely – 'I wanted to taste everything Oxford could offer and consume as much as I could hold.'

Gone were the days of bread, cheese and beer in the Hertford Underworld. Now it was abundant food and fine wines, claret followed by port. He quickly ran into debt and had to auction all his books.

In his capacity as club president, Elmley promulgated a rule that 'Gentlemen may prance but not dance.' Along with aestheticism and irony, a welcoming of overtly homosexual behaviour was one of the things that set the Hypocrites apart from the Bullingdon, let alone the rowing and rugger clubs.

The Hypocrites initiated Evelyn into the habit of hard drinking. Because of fear that American-style prohibition might be on the way to Britain, there was 'an element of a Resistance group about the drunkards of the period'. The club premises – rooms above a bicycle shop – were described by one of Evelyn's friends as a 'noisy alcohol-soaked rat-warren by the river'. Evelyn remembered a Tudor half-timbered building with a steep and narrow staircase, smelling of onions and stewed meat. He said that the local police constable was usually to be found there, taking a break from his beat, standing in the kitchen, mug of beer in one hand and helmet in the other. The two large rooms beyond the kitchen were decorated with murals by Oliver Messel and Robert Byron. There was a large piano where members played jazz riffs or accompanied the singing of Victorian drawing-room ballads.

Though Evelyn portrayed the place as a den of iniquity, it was actually very civilised. Harold Acton said that there was always someone to talk to 'with a congenial hobby or mania', as if suggesting a tweedy discussion of stamp-collecting rather than a Bullingdon-style debauch. What Evelyn loved about the place was its *conversation*. He relished hearing Acton affect an Italian accent and say: 'My dears, I want to go into the fields and *slap* raw meat with lilies.'

In his memoirs Evelyn gave a roll call of the names of famous people who were members of the club. The best and worst that the university had to offer were either members or guests. The club was beginning to get a reputation. *Isis*, the university newspaper, reported that its members were distinctly alarming on account of their dazzling intellectual catchphrases and cultivated rudeness.

Evelyn's new friends brought him into a circle that was altogether much grander than any he had hitherto known. He found himself among an extraordinary set of young men who would continue to make waves after they left Oxford. There were other pairs of brothers besides the aristocratic Lygons. First the Duggan boys, Alfred and Hubert. Alfred had the aura of a 'full-blooded rake of the Restoration' and his younger brother Hubert – Anthony Powell's Eton messmate – was 'a delicate dandy of the Regency'. Then there were the Plunket Greenes, David and Richard. Both were musical. David was a gentle giant who loved jazz. Many of these young men ended up as alcoholics or suicides (or both). But to young Evelyn they were glamour itself. He and most of his friends were *often* drunk, whereas Alfred Duggan was *always* drunk. The Duggans, stepsons of Lord Curzon, Chancellor of the University, had vast riches at their disposal.

Many members of the Hypocrites, including Evelyn, became members of another fraternity, The Railway Club – motto: 'There is no smoke without fire.' Its founder was John Sutro, a Trinity College undergraduate from a wealthy Jewish family. His home was where Evelyn first tasted plovers' eggs. He became a true friend. Evelyn remembered his loyalty and hospitality, describing him as 'above all humorous; a mimic of genius . . . he has never wearied of a friend or quarrelled with one'.

The Railway was so called because Sutro was an aficionado of night-time journeys on steam trains. Club members would travel around the country, dining on the outward leg and sharing post-prandial drinks in the train bar on the return to Oxford. Dinner jackets were always worn. Hugh Lygon was a member. Even after Oxford, the club continued to hold dinners. Over time, the menus grew more and more elaborate, while, in order to accommodate them, the journeys became longer and more adventurous.

Hugh Lygon's Oxford career was not devoted to academic study. An evening in Magdalen, recorded in detail by Terence Greenidge in his book *Degenerate Oxford?*, may serve as the epitome of the Lygon brothers' life among the dreaming spires.

Elmley was something of a fish out of water. He had matriculated at Magdalen, a college renowned for aristocratic breeding and sporting endeavour. But he disliked rowing intensely and thought that hunting was cruel – a belief translated by Waugh into a trait of Sebastian Flyte's older brother 'Bridey', who refuses to ride to hounds. It was this unorthodox streak in Elmley's character that took him among the Hypocrites, where Hugh was happy to join him. Elmley was clearly recognisable as Hugh's brother, with similar but not such classical features. Even as an undergraduate he had a tendency towards the portly. Evelyn described him as 'a solid, tolerant, highly respectable' Magdalen man. But there is a dig in his observation that Elmley was 'voluntarily rusticating with the yeomanry'.

One evening, in a spirit of mischief, Elmley invited a group of his bohemian Hypocrite friends to a Magdalen 'wine' – a college entertainment evening dominated by the Athletes. Harold Acton turned up in a high-necked scarlet jumper, David Plunket Greene in flowing trousers and a broad-brimmed hat, Terence Greenidge in a black sports coat with Russian-style fur-embroidered edges. Robert Byron – who shared Evelyn's love for all things Victorian – dressed as Prince Albert, and Hugh was as Hugh always was, a representative, in Greenidge's words, of 'the slightly effeminate, elegant type of *jeunesse dorée*'. No sooner had they arrived than a Magdalen undergrad pointed at Terence's fur collar and said 'Jesus Christ, what's that?'

In hall, they drank fine port and joined in with some enthusiastic singing. But Harold insisted on leaning over the chair in front of him and loudly addressing Hugh as 'darling'. To which an Athlete countered: 'None of your tricks here!'

There was then a break, during which they all went down into the Oxford night for 'a breather'. Six members of the rowing crew spotted Elmley and Plunket Greene in the quad. 'Here are two of those bloody Aesthetes,' they said; 'Let's chuck them in the river.' But Elmley was a burly six-footer and Plunket Greene even taller. The rowers had second thoughts and retreated, saying: 'Let's have another drink first, and chuck them in the river afterwards.' At the end of the evening, Elmley had to hurry his friends out of the college in order to save them from a large group of now very drunk Athletes. Hugh just drifted away. He was, according to Greenidge, more secure than the others 'because the *jeunesse dorée* type is not considered pre-eminently Aesthetic and Athletes are apt to respect a man with an Honourable in front of his name'.

Hugh's life at Oxford developed into one of idleness alleviated by pranks. On one occasion he and a group of friends staged a mock duel, complete with pistols and seconds, having previously leaked the news of it to the editor of the *Oxford Times* in an effort to provide a lively story to increase the paper's flagging circulation. Stephen McKenna, a gentleman of leisure who wrote popular fiction about aristocratic life, used the incident as the basis for a novel, published in 1925, called *An Affair of Honour*. He dedicated it 'To Hugh Lygon, to whom I am indebted for the seed of truth from which this tree of fantasy has grown'.

'The record of my life there,' wrote Waugh of his Oxford years, 'is essentially a catalogue of friendships.' In his view, what undergraduates learned they learned from one another, not from the dons: 'the lessons were in no curriculum of scholarship or morals'. He also admitted that 'Drinking had a large part in it.'

Evelyn was a noisy drunk. Once when asked why he was so aggressively loud, he responded: 'I have to make a noise because I am so poor.' This reply delighted his new friends: it had the right sort of panache. Shared drunkenness became a bond. Beer was cheap at the Hypocrites (8 pence a pint), enabling Evelyn to indulge himself to excess. The sight of a drunken Evelyn became familiar: 'very pink in the cheeks, small, witty and fierce, quite alarming, but fascinating'. He lit up the gloomy room like 'a bright spark from the fire', though once he got into trouble for smashing up the furniture with that cudgel-like stick of his.

He was appointed Hypocrites club secretary at his very first meeting. He performed no duties in the role. Alfred Duggan, who was frequently rendered speechless with drink, began to invite Evelyn to luncheon parties. At last the boy from suburban Golders Green and minor public school Lancing was moving among the wealthy, the aristocratic and the debauched. Duggan instructed his scout always to lay an extra place at the luncheon table just in case he had invited someone when he was drunk. The place was always occupied. There were often thirty or forty guests and the parties went on for most of the day. In winter, they drank mulled claret followed by port until long after dusk. Waugh learnt how to finger long-stemmed glasses, sniff the wine and hold it up to the light that slanted in through the narrow Gothic windows. Often Duggan had to be put to bed by his friends.

The Hypocrites' Club found a friend in John Fothergill, proprietor of an old inn called the Spreadeagle at Thame, a town about fifteen miles from Oxford. This was a location where club members could indulge in gaudy nights far from the patrols of the 'bulldogs' (the university's bowler-hatted private police force). Fothergill was an eccentric former art dealer and historian who was very sympathetic to Harold Acton and his set, though less kind to more run-of-the-mill guests. He once charged a party extra money for being ugly. He seemed especially partial to the antics of the Hypocrites; their aristocratic connections no doubt added to their allure.

Fothergill wanted to make the Spreadeagle 'an Eton or Stowe of public houses'. He had a reputation for being an incorrigible snob who bullied his working-class clientele while being 'all over' the aristocrats. But in fact it was appearance, intelligence and style that mattered more to him. His motto was 'not only to have proper and properly cooked food but to have only either intelligent, beautiful or well-bred people to eat it'. The inn was furnished like a home rather than a hotel, filled with Georgian and early Victorian furniture and fine china. As a gentleman innkeeper, he was exactly the sort of man Evelyn admired: rude to those he despised, determined to maintain the standards of a better age. On the publication of his first novel, *Decline and Fall*, Waugh sent a copy personally inscribed to 'John Fothergill, Oxford's only civilising influence'. Fothergill chained it up in the loo and said that it was 'the best comedy in the English language'.

In 1924, Elmley held a twenty-first birthday party at the Spreadeagle for sixty young men, including all members of the Hypocrites' Club. It doubled as a wake for the demise of the club, which had been closed down by the proctors after complaints by the neighbours about riotous behaviour and noise. They went down from Oxford in a fleet of hearses. Elmley, dressed in a purple velvet suit, provided the champagne. Harold Acton made a speech about the beauties of the male body; Evelyn got silently drunk; Robert Byron (wearing lace) passed out and the evening ended in dancing, persimmons thrown against the wall, and couples (all male) having sex in the hearse. In his memoirs, Fothergill noted the impressive amount of champagne that was consumed. Among his abiding memories were Terence Greenidge looking 'quite mad' and after-dinner dancing that reminded him of 'wild goats and animals leaping in the air'.

Evelyn enjoyed heavy drinking because it made him uninhibited. He later acknowledged to his first biographer, Christopher Sykes, that he experienced an acute homosexual phase at Oxford. For the short time it lasted, his homosexual activity 'was unrestrained, emotionally and physically'. This was not at all unusual for male students at Oxford. There were few women at the university (undergraduettes were kept in purdah with the exception of eight weeks) and other heterosexual relationships were frowned upon because they usually meant consorting with the undesirables of the town. Some of Evelyn's friends went up to London for sexual experiences, coming back on the last train, which was known as the 'fornicator'. But in the main, homosexual encounters were more common.

Homosexuality was considered by many to be a passing phase, which young men would grow out of once they had left Oxford and begun to meet young women. In those days it was chic to be 'queer' in the same way that it was chic to have a taste for atonal music and Cubist painting. Even old Arthur Waugh acknowledged as much: 'Alec called on me the other day with a new friend of his, a sodomite, but Alec tells me it is the coming thing.'

'Everyone in Oxford was homosexual at that time,' said John Betjeman, who was there. Though homosexuality was illegal, many senior members of the university, most notably the flamboyant don Maurice Bowra, actively encouraged it, sometimes acting as go-between in setting up assignations for their pupils. Tom Driberg enjoyed *soixante-neuf* with a young don in the rooms where more cerebral tutorials were supposed to take place. The Hypocrites' Club was the epicentre of what would now be called the university's gay scene. According to Sykes, who knew Waugh extremely well, Evelyn was never shocked by homosexuality and remained very interested in the subject. He was, after all, 'interested in all things which shed light on human character'. But later in life he would worry about his son discovering his past indiscretions.

In the spring of 1924, Evelyn informed his old school friend, Dudley Carew, that his life had become 'quite incredibly depraved morally'. Drunkenness at the Hypocrites was part of the story, but hardly sufficient to qualify as incredible depravity. Something else was being hinted at. Tom Driberg, dancing with a fellow member, saw a drunken Evelyn rolling on the sofa with another boy, 'with (as one of them later said) their tongues licking each others' tonsils'. Anthony Powell's first encounter with Evelyn was a sighting of him at the Hypocrites sitting on the knee of another member, Christopher Hollis. A club guest, Isaiah Berlin, also saw him on a settee kissing a friend. Evelyn later teased Christopher Sykes for not having had a homosexual phase, saying that he had missed out on something special.

But it was not just sexual experimentation. There were genuine love affairs. When the staunchly heterosexual Henry Yorke read *Brideshead Revisited*, he told Evelyn that it made him regret not falling in love at Oxford himself: 'I see now what I have missed.' What he missed was what Waugh experienced: real passion. Evelyn's sexual abstinence at school seemed to make his Oxford love affairs even more intense.

Though Evelyn relished the companionship of eccentric and slightly crazed friends like Terence Greenidge and Harold Acton, romantically he was drawn to fragile, beautiful boys. Before being seduced by the Hypocrites, he had become intimate with a shy and scholarly left-wing Wykehamist from Balliol called Richard Pares. Evelyn described him as 'abnormally clever'. In a later letter to Nancy Mitford, he also described Pares as 'my first homosexual love'.

Pares was pale skinned, with a mop of fair hair and large blue eyes that somehow seemed blank. Their affair began in the summer of 1922. Evelyn later recalled: 'I loved him dearly, but an excess of wine nauseated him and this made an insurmountable barrier between us. When I felt most intimate, he felt queasy.' In other words, Waugh needed to be very drunk to release his strongest emotions, whereas Pares could not hold his drink. Nevertheless the young men spent two intense terms together. They only drifted apart when Waugh developed his 'indiscriminate bonhomie' among the Hypocrites. Being drunk was becoming his greatest 'aesthetic pleasure', whereas Pares was more interested in his research on the West Indian sugar trade. He was duly rescued from Bohemia by a homosexual don called Urquhart (known as 'Sligger'), Dean of Balliol, who encouraged him to become an academic. He took a first and was elected to a fellowship of All Souls. Evelyn always remembered him with great affection and late in life Pares, happily married and respectable, remembered the affair as one of the most passionate and intense of his life.

Christopher Hollis, on whose knee Anthony Powell had first spotted Evelyn at the Hypocrites, wrote a memoir of *Oxford in the Twenties*, in which he said that Waugh had two homosexual lovers, first Richard Pares and then Alastair Graham. In *A Little Learning*, Waugh records that Richard Pares' successor as what he called 'the friend of my heart' was a boy that 'I will call Hamish Lennox'. 'Hamish' is described as 'no scholar': he 'soon went down to take a course in architecture in London; but he continued to haunt Oxford and for two or three years we were inseparable or, if separated, in almost daily communication, until like so many of my generation, he heard the call of the Levant and went to live abroad'. 'Hamish,' says Waugh, 'had no repugnance to the bottle and we drank deep together. At times he was as gay as any Hypocrite, but there were always hints of the spirit that in later years has made him a recluse.' This account precisely fits Alastair Graham and Waugh's relationship with him.

The two boys drank deep together of both alcohol and love. In one of his letters Alastair enclosed a naked photo of himself, leaning against a rock face, with arms outstretched, buttocks in full view, along with a description of the best way to drink fine wine: 'You must take a peach and peel it, and put it in a finger bowl, and pour the Burgundy over it. The flavour is exquisite.' The letter ended: 'With love from Alastair, and his poor dead heart.'

Alastair came from the Scottish borders. His father was dead, his mother 'high-tempered, possessive, jolly and erratic'. A southern belle from Savannah, she was the model for the character of Lady Circumference in *Decline and Fall*. She had settled in Warwickshire for the sake of the hunting. She devoted herself to frenzied gardening, disingenuously claiming that she was keeping the place on solely for the sake of Alastair (who in reality was no huntsman).

Alastair invited Evelyn home. His mother's residence in the village of Barford, between Stratford-upon-Avon and Warwick, gave Evelyn his first taste of country-house living. Though on nothing like the scale of Madresfield, Barford House is much the grandest building in the village. It still stands behind a high wall. Albeit more shabby genteel than aristocratic grand, it was still a world away from Underhill. There was a ballroom that had been built especially for Alastair's coming-of-age party.

Alastair, like Hugh Lygon, was a dreamer. He loved lying in the garden looking at flowers, or searching the fields for edible fungi. He drove his mother mad. She befriended Evelyn in the hope that he would persuade her son to cut down on his drinking and start living a less indolent life. He did not oblige.

Though Alastair frequently visited Evelyn in Oxford, he was resident in London. So did Evelyn have another undergraduate lover? Most biographers follow Hollis in identifying only Pares and Graham, but according to the Oxford don A. L. Rowse, Evelyn had three lovers at Oxford. The third man was Hugh Lygon. Rowse was convinced that Evelyn was bisexual and that as a novelist he 'made use of every little scrap of his experience – he wasted nothing'. He remembered a conversation with Lady Sibell, eldest of the three Lygon sisters, who knew Evelyn well. 'He was in love with my brother,' she recalled.

Evelyn's three lovers were of a very similar type: pale and beautiful, with the aura of Rupert Brooke. Richard and Hugh were both blond. After Oxford he fell in love with women of the same ethereal beauty: Diana Mitford, Teresa Jungman, Diana Cooper, Laura Herbert.

Evelyn was drawn to Alastair and Hugh not only because of their delicate beauty and gentility, but also because they were hard-drinking and self-destructive. He liked their child-like qualities and their lack of intellectual fervour (he never fell in love with Harold Acton or Brian Howard, much as he admired their abilities). He definitely had a type: the objects of his desire were invariably richer and better-looking, though never funnier, than he was. They had a dreaminess about them and a fragility that he found irresistible. They brought out his protective instincts. Waugh was speaking equally of himself when he wrote in his biography of the theologian Ronald Knox that he was susceptible to good looks and drawn to those with an air of sadness, of 'tristesse'. Hugh Lygon had exactly this quality. He drifted round Oxford like a lost boy, a Peter Pan who refused to grow up. Terence Greenidge remembered him carrying a teddy bear.

Greenidge, a fervent socialist, admired Hugh's classical good looks and thought he had 'charm and elegance', but said that he was 'rather empty'. But Evelyn found him full of humour. The same things made them laugh. He loved Hugh's eccentricities and was impressed by his lack of snobbery.

Hugh, along with Robert Byron, Patrick Balfour and Brian Howard, was regarded as one of the most sexually active of the Hypocrites. Harold Acton wrote to Evelyn after the publication of *A Little Learning* to reprove him for singling out his homosexuality, whilst failing to mention 'Robert's, Patrick's, Brian's and Hugh's promiscuities'. Evelyn himself called Hugh the 'lascivious Mr Lygon'.

Tamara Abelson (later Talbot Rice) was an exotic White Russian exile, who knew Evelyn at Oxford where she was one of the rare undergraduettes. As far as she was concerned, 'everyone knew that Evelyn and Hugh Lygon had an affair'. She reported that John Fothergill let Evelyn have rooms in the Spreadeagle at Thame at a special midweek rate so that he and Hugh could meet in private.

Not everyone approved of Evelyn's translation to a new set. His brother Alec came to remonstrate about his dissipated lifestyle. But Evelyn was not going to give it up and go back to the loneliness that he had felt as a child. He had found a surrogate family and he had found glamour, wit and intelligence: the 'congenial people' for whom he had longed. No amount of lecturing from an older brother to whom he had never been particularly close was going to change anything. Among the Hypocrites he had found the love that he had been longing for all his life. He was happy.

But there was an element of bravado about his entry into the world of cigars, champagne and Charvet silk ties. In his heart he knew that he did not really belong there. Rather like one of his heroes, Toad of Toad Hall, he had a child-like quality that manifested itself in acute mood swings between hilarious gaiety and sullen gloom. He often felt that he was being treated as a specimen, even a freak. His friendships flared brightly and intensely, but sometimes burned themselves out. He was still the outsider looking in, glimpsing rather than actually passing through the low door in the wall that opened on an enclosed and enchanted garden.

Intimate as they were at Oxford, Hugh did not invite Evelyn to visit his ancestral home while they were still undergraduates. Nor was he invited to Lord Elmley's lavish twenty-first birthday celebrations at Madresfield in August 1924.That was a high-society occasion, very different from the celebration of the same event at the Spreadeagle. Evelyn was never very close to Elmley, who had a more pronounced sense of his status than Hugh.

Evelyn took his final examinations in the summer of 1924, but since he had come up a term late, he was supposed to return to Oxford for a further term in the autumn, so as to fulfil the residence requirement necessary for him to receive his degree. He planned to share lodgings with Hugh Lygon in Merton Street. They were going to take an expensive little house next to the tennis courts. With no exams to worry about, it would be a term of 'pure pleasure' and 'comparative seclusion'.

The plan was aborted with the news that Evelyn had obtained a third-class result. His scholarship was not renewed for the further term and his father did not think that a third was worth the cost of the extra term. Evelyn therefore left Oxford without completing his degree.

Of Evelyn's three Oxford lovers, Hugh Lygon is the one about whom he was most reticent in *A Little Learning*. The name Lygon only appears fleetingly in the book. An aura of concealment hangs over that first naming of Hugh in the passage where Quiller-Couch's line '*Know you her secret none can utter?*' is quoted, together with the mysterious remark that it is not given to all Oxford's sons 'either to seek or find this secret, but it was very near the surface in 1922'. What was the secret none could utter? In the context of an aspiring writer and a beautiful young aristocrat, could it have been something reminiscent of Oscar Wilde and Lord Alfred Douglas? 'I am the Love that dare not speak its name.'

Hugh Lygon's name appears last in Evelyn's list of his fellow Hypocrites: 'Hugh Lygon, Elmley's younger brother, always just missing the happiness he sought, without ambition, unhappy in love, a man of the greatest sweetness; and many others . . .' The wistfulness and the drift into ellipses suggest that something is being left unsaid. Why was it, when Evelyn could be comparatively open about Richard Pares and Alastair Graham, that his love for Hugh dared not speak its name? We may find an answer when Hugh's family story is known.

CHAPTER 4

The Scarlet Woman

After Evelyn's humiliating departure from Oxford, he returned home to Underhill. For a few happy weeks, he hung out with Alastair. They wandered around greater London like Parisian *flâneurs*. But then Alastair departed for Kenya, leaving Evelyn with nothing to look forward to save 'heart-breaking dreariness'. He anticipated 'bills, over-fastidious tastes and a completely hopeless future'.

Evelyn was bored. He resented his father, missed his friends and most of all missed Oxford. He made an abortive attempt to kick-start a career in art, enrolling in a course at Heatherley's Art School in Chelsea. His first assignment was to draw a thin man sitting cross-legged 'with no clothes but a bag about his genitalia'. The place was full of girls in gaudy overalls, who, Evelyn thought, drew badly and distracted the young men who were hoping to make commercial careers for themselves in advertising or 'by illustrating *Punch*'. The model for a 'quick sketch' class was 'a young girl with a very graceful body and a face rather like Hugh Lygon's when very drunk'.

He also began, but soon abandoned, a novel called 'The Temple at Thatch'. It was about an undergraduate who inherited a property of which nothing was left except an eighteenth-century classical folly where he set up house and practised black magic. Later, he destroyed the manuscript, so we will never know whether the (presumably aristocratic) protagonist was in any way inspired by Hugh Lygon or whether a line can be traced from the classical temple at Thatch to the Catholic chapel at Brideshead.

Every morning he walked to Hampstead tube station, hiding pennies along the way, which he then collected on the way home to alleviate boredom. This new life was a shock after the intensity of Oxford. He complained to friends about the dull routine of dinner and early nights after desultory conversation with 'Chapman and Hall' (his nickname for his father). His social life only improved when his brother Alec took him in hand, inviting him to parties and nightclubs. He became a parasite upon his more successful sibling. In his fragmentary second volume of autobiography, he acknowledged his debt to Alec 'as a host who introduced me to the best restaurants of London, on whom I sponged, bringing my friends to his flat and, when short of money, sleeping on his floor until the tubes opened when I would at dawn sway home to Hampstead in crumpled evening dress among the navvies setting out for their day's work'. In fact, home was not Hampstead but Golders Green – Evelyn would walk to a pillar box in Hampstead so that the postmark would not be Golders Green. Alec once remarked that 'there is no stronger deterrent to one's enjoyment of an evening than the knowledge that one has to at the end of it to get to Golders Green'.

The most popular of the nightclubs that they frequented was the Cave of Harmony in Charlotte Street, run by Harold Scott and his partner, Elsa Lanchester. She was a fragile, red-haired beauty who was trying to become an actress. Later, she would become famous for playing the title role in *The Bride of Frankenstein*. The Cave of Harmony was patronised by journalists and actors, who drank late and tried out their short plays and cabaret acts. Alec went there every Saturday night, taking his brother with him. They befriended Elsa, and Evelyn persuaded her to take part in an amateur film that he was making with his Oxford friend Terence Greenidge.

Greenidge had bought a 16-millimetre camera and become a keen amateur cinematographer, casting his fellow Hypocrites in outrageous roles. The first we hear from Evelyn himself of his involvement with this activity is in a diary entry of 5 July 1924, when he and Christopher Hollis go to see one of Terence's films at a dive in Great Ormond Street. Lured by the expectation of seeing Hugh Lygon there, Evelyn was disappointed to find instead 'a sorry congregation of shits'.

Greenidge's short films had been shot under the aegis of the Hypocrites and the Oxford Labour Club in the summer term of 1924. They had such enticing titles as *666*, *The Mummers*, *Bar Sinister* and *The City of the Plain*. The latter was subtitled *A Story of the Oxford Underworld.* A 'burlesque of the American moralising melodrama', it was a celebration of the immorality of the Hypocrites.

Evelyn had acted in at least two of these films, alongside such friends as Hugh Lygon and Chris Hollis. Greenidge was especially impressed with Hugh's performances, especially the lead role he played in *The City of the Plain.* All the reels are, alas, lost: they were last glimpsed in the hands of the Official Receiver in the late 1960s, when Greenidge was a bankrupted dying actor. Little is known of their content, but the biblical titles are suggestive: 666 is the number of the Beast, while 'the City of the Plain' is evidently an allusion to Sodom in the Old Testament. Sin, and sexual 'beastliness' in particular, must have been the (suitably Hypocritical) subject matter. There may also have been some dabbling in black magic, another Hypocrite preoccupation. In one of the films Waugh played the part of a lecherous black clergyman, wearing what Greenidge remembered as 'horrible scarlet make-up, which came out black in those early days'.

Homosexuality certainly seems to have been on Waugh's mind at this time. A few days after the evening in Great Ormond Street when they watched one of Greenidge's films, he recorded an anecdote of Hollis's in his diary:

> Chris turned up in the morning and told me a good story. Mr Justice Phillimore was trying a sodomy case and brooded greatly whether his judgment had been right. He went to consult [Lord] Birkenhead. 'Excuse me, my Lord, but could you tell me – What do you think one ought to give a man who allows himself to be buggered?' 'Oh, 30 s[hillings] or £2 – anything you happen to have on you.'

The Hypocrites' flirtation with early cinema continued over the summer of 1924. Evelyn, whose most significant early short story ('The Balance') was written in the style of a film script, wrote the screenplay for a new Terence Greenidge production. Entitled *The Scarlet Woman: An Ecclesiastical Melodrama*, it was rediscovered in the 1960s and can now be seen on DVD. The outlandish plot turned on an attempt by 'Sligger' Urquhart,

Dean of Balliol (the man who had returned Richard Pares to the academic straight and narrow), to convert England to Roman Catholicism by exercising his dastardly Papist influence on the Prince of Wales. The title plays on the fact that 'scarlet woman' was a colloquial expression for both a prostitute and the Church of Rome. A favourable review in the Oxford student newspaper, *Isis*, had particular praise for Waugh's method of introducing the audience to the leading characters:

> Each figure in this drama of intrigue is disclosed indulging in his favourite sport. So we have a scene in the Papal gardens with the Papal whisky and its owner, the private chamber of the King and the royal gin, the Count of Montefiasco with the Romish cognac, and the eminent Catholic layman [Sligger] with his academic vodka. This convivial introduction had the effect of making us feel that we had known the characters for years.

Filming took place in July, shooting locations being Oxford, Hampstead Heath and Arthur Waugh's back garden. Elsa Lanchester played the heroine, an evangelical cabaret singer called Beatrice who saves the day by drawing the Prince from Urquhart's clutches. Evelyn, kitted out in a blond wig, played Sligger, alluding freely to the dean's homosexuality by fondling the Prince of Wales (played by Greenidge's brother John, known as 'the Bastard'). John Sutro was Cardinal Montefiasco and Alec Waugh the cardinal's mother. Elmley played the Lord Chamberlain, whose real life counterpart would without doubt have banned the script had there been an attempt to release it commercially. Old Arthur Waugh enjoyed the shenanigans immensely.

Evelyn also doubled in the role of a penniless peer called Lord Borrowington who appears to be a cocaine addict. He was unapologetic about advertising the setting of some scenes in the distinctly unglamorous location of North End Road, Golders Green. Elmley was less eager to advertise himself: he acted under the assumed name Michael Murgatroyd for fear of offending his father, who was close to becoming leader of the Liberals in the House of Lords. An officer in the Guards, who played the part of the king, also hid behind an assumed name. Elsa (who later married Charles Laughton) took no fee, only free lunches. The main purpose of the film was to poke fun at Sligger Urquhart for being 'Roman

Catholic and a snob'. We do not know if he ever saw *The Scarlet Woman* but it was shown at the Oxford University Dramatic Society (OUDS) in 1925. Greenidge came to believe that the film had caught the subversive spirit of Oxford in the twenties, and represented 'an Evelyn who had seen through Roman Catholicism and the British aristocracy' – something that could not exactly be said of *Brideshead Revisited*. The script undoubtedly reveals Evelyn's interest in religion, his gift for farce and his early attraction to the more glamorous aspects of modernity embodied in the world of movie-making. The film also features a very fine motor car, which probably belonged to Elmley.

The Scarlet Woman was acted in a style that would now be called high camp. Greenidge was an active homosexual, and the entire film-making project was clearly deeply bound up with the Hypocrites' willingness to push at the boundaries of taste, decency and the law.

Terence Greenidge later remembered Evelyn's mother telling him that her son had changed profoundly by this time, that as a child he was loving, fun and trusting, but that something had happened to put him on his guard. Yet he was always, according to Greenidge, 'joyously, healthily rude, as was the great Dr Johnson'. The combination of guarded watchfulness and unabashed smuttiness may suggest that Evelyn was simultaneously attracted to and repelled by the world in which he found himself.

The bohemian gatherings he attended with Alec were often 'bottle parties' in 'unfashionable areas'. He hankered instead for the statelier world of engraved visiting cards and black velvets. The bohemian set didn't really suit him. The parties were full of actors, painters, and men just down from the university who had no idea of what to do with their lives. Men, in other words, who were all too like himself.

In his diary he recalled one particularly memorable party at Mrs Cecil Chesterton's flat in Fleet Street, at which 'pansies, prostitutes and journalists and struggling actors' all got 'quite quite drunk and in patches lusty'. Among the guests he singled out a certain 'Peter Pusey with whom Hugh Lygon sodomises'. Hugh's taste for the crime that took its name from the City of the Plain was no secret. Alec, meanwhile, turned up late and a little drunk, then proceeded to carry off 'the ugliest woman in the room'.

At another party Evelyn was so drunk that he ended up playing football with the butler's top hat. Parties in private houses were followed by hard drinking at nightclubs, but there was a seedy and unglamorous feel to it all. All the promise of his Oxford days seemed to have evaporated. *The Scarlet Woman* had been a reprieve, but Evelyn had no prospects. It seemed that all his richer friends had places to go after graduating, whereas he sensed himself becoming a hanger-on on the fringes of the artistic world, or, even worse, a sponger (the kind of character he would represent so mercilessly in the character of John Beaver in *A Handful of Dust*).

He was yearning for his lost paradise. Spiritually he was still at Oxford. Its lure, the knowledge that the city of dreams was 'still full of friends', made him quit art school. Invited to an Oxford party by John Sutro, he accepted gratefully, eager to be reminded of what he was missing. His unexpected attendance was greeted warmly. All the old Hypocrites were there: Harold Acton, Hugh Lygon, Robert Byron, even his first lover Richard Pares. It was a luncheon party that seemed to stretch on for ever, as in the old days. They ate hot lobster, partridges and plum pudding, drank sherry, mulled claret and 'a strange rum-like liqueur'. Hugh, as usual, was drinking too much. Evelyn left in time for a tea party and then a beer at the New Reform Club with Lord Elmley and Terence Greenidge. A message then came from Hugh, by this time installed in the bar of the Dramatic Society, proposing a trip to Banbury. But instead they reconvened in the old Hypocrites' rooms, where they drank whisky and watched *The Scarlet Woman*. Evelyn's recollection of the rest of the evening was hazy: all he could remember was that he got hold of a sword and escaped from Balliol via a window after the college had been locked for the night.

The next morning he started drinking again with Hugh, and then they had lunch together. An umbilical cord connected him still to his alma mater. He found himself dressing as an undergraduate again, sporting the latest fashion of turtleneck sweater and broad trousers. He was delighted with the roll-neck top – it was 'convenient for lechery because it dispenses with all unromantic gadgets like studs and ties'. The garment also served to hide the boils on the necks of dermatologically challenged young gentlemen.

The Jazz Age had come to Oxford. Cars full of flappers came up from London every weekend. There was a new smart set. They danced to the Harlem Blues and the strains of Gershwin. Evelyn threw himself into the rowdy, partying atmosphere. He returned every weekend. But he knew that he was becoming self-destructive. He was often in the company of Hugh. Once he was drunk for three days – a condition that for Hugh was perfectly normal. After lunching together they would continue drinking until they were too drunk to stand.

The only way out from this alcoholic spiral was to get a proper job. And the only job that seemed suitable for an Oxford man who had failed to achieve Honours and who had no inclination for either physical labour or further study was schoolmastering. With great reluctance, he began to look for a position.

Before descending into the teaching profession, Evelyn fell in love again. This time, though, it was not with a fellow undergraduate but with an entire family. They were the Plunket Greenes. For Evelyn, they would prove to be the forerunners of the Lygons.

He of course knew David and Richard Plunket Greene from Oxford. They were members of the Hypocrites and very hard to miss: David was six foot seven inches tall and Richard a powerfully built young man. David, a 'languid dandy devoted to all that was fashionable', would die a heroin addict at a tragically early age. Coote (Lady Dorothy) Lygon remembered that he took drugs at a time when that was a very fast thing to do. When Hugh brought him home to Madresfield she used to swoon at the very sight of him. She developed a huge crush.

Evelyn became close friends with Richard, eventually serving as best man at his wedding. The boys' father, Harry, was a singer and their mother a gifted amateur violinist. Harry Plunket Greene was friendly with England's leading composer, Edward Elgar. He sang the baritone part in the first performance of Elgar's *Dream of Gerontius* and was the first to sing settings of A. E. Housman's poems, *A Shropshire Lad.* He frequently appeared in events at Elgar's Malvern Concert Club. This brought him into contact with the Lygons, who were Malvern's most famous family and leading patrons of the festival. Elgar was supposed to have composed the most enigmatic of his famous *Enigma Variations* as a musical portrait of Hugh's aunt, Mary. When Plunket Greene married Gwen Ponsonby, he came into a family relationship with the Lygons, who were cousins to the Ponsonbys.

David was soon to marry and in short order divorce Babe McGustie, the gold-digging stepdaughter of a prominent bookie. Richard fascinated Evelyn with his eccentricities and his tinge of melancholy. He was piratical in appearance, sporting earrings and a cravat, while smoking strong, dark tobacco. Evelyn described him as 'good with boats' and passionate in the way he threw himself into everything: 'he brought to the purchase of a pipe or a necktie the concentration of a collector'. One moment he would be a connoisseur of wine, the next a racing motorist, then a jazz lover, and before long an aspiring writer of detective fiction. But he was never a bore with his passions. He brought to each new hobby 'the infectious absorption of an adolescent'. Not a bore and always amusing: for Evelyn, this was the highest praise.

Evelyn's admiration of the handsome Plunket Greene brothers in his Oxford years transferred itself into infatuation with their sister, Olivia. He lacked the experience and 'force of purpose' to conduct a proper courtship, so the relationship became instead an 'intimate friendship' of a kind that established a pattern for a succession of future liaisons with upper-class, sexually unavailable women. The pattern was always the same: 'doting but unaspiring on my part, astringent on hers'. One cannot help but think of the adventures in unrequited love of Bertie Wooster's friend Bingo Little.

Harold Acton said that Olivia had 'minute pursed lips and great goo-goo eyes'. Evelyn considered this description unfair. She was not a conventional beauty (which her mother was), but she was fashionable and graceful, dressing in black and heavily made up with cosmetics that enhanced her enormous eyes in a pixie-like face. Evelyn loved her personality. He thought that she combined 'the elegance of David with the concentration of Richard'. What drew him to her was the very quality that had drawn him to her brothers: her capacity for passionate but short-lived enthusiasms. She lived every moment to the full.

Some saw a mad streak in her, though for Evelyn this was always tempered by her essential delicacy and fundamental shyness. She did not seek others out: people were drawn to her. Evelyn accepted that she could be a nag and a bully, that she suffered from 'morbid self-consciousness' and was 'incapable of the ordinary arts of pleasing'. Perhaps he loved her because these deficiencies were also his own. 'A little crazy; truth loving and in the end holy', she was his first true heterosexual love. But she made him miserable.

Fiercely loyal to those he loved, Evelyn withheld from his autobiography the information that Olivia went on to have a very unhappy life. She became an alcoholic and died a recluse, unmarried. It was no coincidence or mere ill fortune that so many of Evelyn's friends fell victim to alcoholism: the art of heavy drinking was virtually a prerequisite for his friendship. In sharp contrast to his first male love, Richard Pares, Olivia could hold as much liquor as Evelyn. Like him, she lost her inhibitions when under the influence. Her aura of melancholy made her more like Hugh and Alastair: it added lustre to her beauty, but its corollary was alcoholic dependency and despair.

They met at pubs for lunch and spent days at Underhill. Once he turned up to see her, already drunk, carrying three bottles of champagne under his arm, which they proceeded to consume out of teacups and various pots and other china receptacles that they found around the place. He liked her extremes, her melancholy and wild excesses. They got drunk together, they quarrelled, they read Browning, Plato and Dostoyevsky. She teased him, she loved his intelligence, but she did not want to go to bed with him (even though she was highly sexed, rating her lovers on their performance and counting Paul Robeson among her conquests). 'A ghost with a glass of gin in her hand', she was also in love with religion – to a degree that later became maniacal. She once wrote Evelyn a 'raving sixteen page letter describing a recent visit to heaven'.

Evelyn acknowledged in his autobiography that his feelings for Olivia were a projection of his love for all the Plunket Greenes, who were so different from the Waughs: 'I had in fact fallen in love with a whole family, and, rather as Mr E. M. Forster describes in *Howards End*, had focused the sentiment upon the only appropriate member, an eighteen-year-old daughter.'

Harry Greene, whom Evelyn described as a 'very handsome Irishman', was only occasionally on the scene, having left to live with his mistress. The person who truly cast a spell over him was the matriarch of this magnetic though flawed family, Gwen Plunket Greene. Evelyn encountered her on New Year's Day in 1925. He wrote in his diary: 'I met Mrs Greene for the first time and loved her.' She was a first draft for the magnificent but monstrous Lady Marchmain. Gwen exerted a magic spell over him with her beauty, poise and humour. He later realised that her serenity was a consequence of a 'hidden life of prayer'. She would later convert to Roman Catholicism and was already heading in that direction.

Evelyn's diary records countless invitations to tea, dinner parties and family holidays with the Plunket Greenes. They were unsettled and moved house five times in ten years – 'during which', noted Evelyn, 'I was practically a member of the family'. That the family was on the point of converting to Catholicism may have been an additional attraction.

Richard Plunket Greene was in the same position as Evelyn: 'workless and penurious'. In his case, the position was aggravated by his desire to get married. His decision to apply for a position as a schoolmaster had prompted Evelyn to follow suit. It was the obvious option. As Evelyn once wrote to his school friend, Dudley Carew, 'no one in our class need ever starve because he can always go as a prep school master, not a pleasant job but all roads lead to Sodom'.

The usual route was to sign up with the scholastic agency Gabbitas and Thring (W. H. Auden nicknamed them 'Rabbitarse and String'). Evelyn Waugh, John Betjeman, Graham Greene and the fictional Paul Pennyfeather of *Decline and Fall* all passed through its door. Greene said that to do so was to 'pawn yourself instead of your watch'.

In early January 1925, Evelyn was interviewed by the headmaster of the prep school Arnold House. The name may have been evocative of the great Thomas Arnold of Rugby, but the location was less promising: it was in Denbighshire in North Wales, which could hardly have been further from Oxford.

Mr Banks, the head, 'a tall old man with stupid eyes', offered the post forthwith. He was desperate and, if Evelyn is to be believed (he is probably not to be), only one question was asked: 'Did he possess a dinner jacket?' This was necessary to entertain the wealthier parents. With only a couple of weeks to go before the start of term, Evelyn threw himself into a farewell whirl of socialising with the Plunket Greenes.

There was a disastrous evening at the Café Royal, where champagne cocktails were drunk, followed by oysters and chablis. Olivia disgraced herself. A few days later Evelyn noted in his diary that he had attended a dinner party of his brother Alec's that was 'almost wholly spoiled by the abominable manners of the Greene family, who arrived fifty minutes late'. After dinner they went to the theatre and then on to a nightclub where, drunk again, Olivia began kissing a handsome fellow called Tony Bushell. Evelyn tried unsuccessfully to get equally drunk himself. He was very rude to Olivia, but she was in no condition to take offence. The next day, 'with a glowing resentment against the Greene family', he sent word that he was leaving 'for the country'. But that evening he spoiled his gesture by getting drunk and calling at the Plunket Greenes' in the early hours of the morning, accompanied by two friends. He said that he would not leave until Olivia knelt down and apologised to him. She declined and he broke a gramophone record. A version of the episode was later incorporated into his novel *A Handful of Dust*.

Amends were made before he went north. Olivia came to see him at Underhill where she told him that he was a great artist and should not become a schoolmaster. He was upset at the thought that she was finally beginning to show interest just at the moment when he was leaving for North Wales: 'I went to bed feeling more desolate than I had felt since the embarkation of Alastair.' Whilst he knew that marriage was out of the question, he felt that he was getting close to a romantic and sexual relationship. Women, he was beginning to discover, were far more complex and tricky than men.

He left for Arnold House on 23 January 1925. When he arrived there he found a telegram awaiting him from Hugh Lygon and John Sutro. It read '*On, Evelyn, On*'.

CHAPTER 5

In the Balance

Despite his misgivings, Evelyn enjoyed his brief experience as a schoolmaster. When John Betjeman was forced to turn to teaching, Evelyn assured him that 'You will remember these schooldays as the happiest time of your life . . . not entirely facetiously.' More importantly, the time at Arnold House, in all its glorious awfulness, gave Waugh the inspiration for his first novel.

A letter to his mother on his arrival described the haphazard management of the establishment: 'it is the most curiously run school that ever I heard of. No timetables nor syllabuses nor nothing. Banks [headmaster] just wanders into the common room and says "There are some boys in that classroom. I think they are the first or perhaps the fourth. Will someone go and teach them Maths or Latin or something" and someone goes and I go on making a wood engraving.' The wood engraving was for Olivia, whose hold still consumed him. He felt cut off. The school was in Llanddulas, a tiny town sandwiched between Rhyl and Colwyn Bay.

His wit made him popular with the boys and he in turn found them amusing, usually unintentionally so. 'Yesterday in a history paper,' reads a diary entry written on a cold February night, 'the boy Howarth wrote: "In this year James II gave birth to a son but many people refused to believe it and said it had been brought to him in a hot water bottle".'

One of the new masters was itching to start a mutiny against the amiable and ineffectual headmaster. 'I hope there will be trouble,' responded Evelyn. He found some of the boys ghastly, but warmed to others among them. He let the clever ones read racy French novels whilst he did his own work. When they asked what he was writing, he would reply: 'A history of the Eskimos.' He continued to dress somewhat in the manner of Mr Toad – in plus fours, a tweed jacket and a roll-neck sweater with a check collar peeping out. He took to wearing spectacles and smoking a pipe. He also grew a moustache. Like his fictional alter ego Paul Pennyfeather, Evelyn gave organ lessons despite being not in the least musical.

Though he made the best of the place, he was low in spirits, missing the Plunket Greenes and thinking of his past life. He was desperate for news from the city of his dreams, writing to Harold Acton and pleading for updates on the Hypocrites.

When he returned to London in the holidays he saw a lot of Olivia. As usual, her company was synonymous with heavy drinking and committed party-going. One party in particular ended up with Evelyn under arrest (an incident that turns up in *Brideshead*). Evelyn and Olivia gave a party, to which her cousin Matthew Ponsonby was invited. He came in his car and was sent out to buy more drink with Evelyn, who was, by this time, already drunk. The men stopped off for drinks along the way and were arrested for driving the wrong way around a traffic island. Matthew and Evelyn, 'Drunk and Incapable', were put into police cells. The next day, Evelyn was bound over at the cost of £2. It was far more serious for Matthew, who was the driver of the car. Though his father (the Under Secretary of State for Foreign Affairs) bailed him out, Matthew came extremely close to a prison sentence. In the end he was banned from driving for a year and given a large fine, half of which Evelyn offered to pay: 'After all I was rather more than half to blame and I got off so lightly myself.'

The Ponsonbys blamed Evelyn for the whole business. They described him as a 'disreputable friend of the Greenes'. Their son had been led astray out of his 'good nature'. Evelyn, they contended, was an irresponsible drunk who had appeared at Mrs Plunket Greene's house already inebriated. He had proceeded to decant a bottle of champagne into Gwen's white china ducks, persuading his friends to drink from them. But Ponsonby was far from blameless; he was an incorrigible drink-driver. Before long, there was another, much worse incident, also hushed up, in which he knocked over and 'killed or at least seriously injured' a young boy.

Though he felt guilty about his responsibility for the Plunket Greenes being dragged into the 'Drunk and Incapable' affair, he still spent Easter with them at the disused lighthouse they were renting on Lundy Island. Lady Plunket, as Evelyn called Gwen, met him and Olivia off the boat. In the evening she read aloud to them, while David drew caricatures. Richard and his fiancée Elizabeth were also there, as was Terence Greenidge (revisiting one of his filming locations from the previous year). Evelyn was still unable to cure himself of his love for Olivia: 'While I was in Denbighshire I had hoped that I only loved her as a personification of all the jolly things I had left behind, but here I am with Terence mouthing Kant into a pint glass and David making endless jokes about Lesbos and lavatories, and Richard rowing unseaworthy boats in fearnought trousers, and Lady Plunket serene over it all, but I am still sad and uneasy and awkward whenever I am with Olivia.'

He felt inhibited, not to say mildly disgusted, by the sexual freedoms of the party. One night, after some earnest conversation with Richard's fiancée, he joined the others only to find a girl called Anne, almost naked, 'being slapped on the buttocks and enjoying herself ecstatically'. Another house guest, Julia Strachey (niece of the biographer Lytton Strachey), was looking on. Julia, rather like Evelyn, was a misfit and a writer who drifted through life attempting, as she put it in an unfinished memoir, to 'find some family love after all'. Olivia allowed Evelyn no sexual liberties, but Lady Plunket's madcap world on Lundy was a welcome change from both home and school.

Back at Arnold House after the Easter holidays, things began to look up. Evelyn had applied for a new job as secretary to C. K. Scott Moncrieff, the translator of Marcel Proust. He was assured that he would be successful. It apparently did not matter that he could not type and did not know the languages out of which Moncrieff translated. The position would mean relocation to Pisa: Moncrieff was a homosexual and a Roman Catholic convert who felt more comfortable in Italy than England.

The thought that he would only have to endure one more term as a schoolmaster spurred Evelyn on. He was also pleased with the progress he was making with his novel 'The Temple at Thatch'. 'I am making the first chapter a cinema film,' he reported, 'and have been writing furiously ever since. I honestly think that it is going to be rather good.' Furthermore, the arrival of a new schoolmaster, Dick Young, brightened the picture considerably.

Dick loved to drink and in the local pub would tell the other masters of his transgressions. He had been expelled from Wellington, sent down from Oxford, forced to resign his commission in the Army, 'has left four schools precipitately, three in the middle of the term through his being taken in sodomy and one through his being drunk six nights in succession. And yet he goes on getting better and better jobs.' The reason was that whenever he left a school in disgrace, he always took with him very good references, since no headmaster dared to confess that he had hired a pederast.

Evelyn recorded a day's outing to Snowdonia, which was a bore for all the masters, except for Young. He claimed that he had enjoyed the day enormously. '*Enjoyed* yourself?' asked Evelyn. 'What did you find to enjoy?'

'Knox minor,' Young replied with what Evelyn called 'radiant simplicity'. 'I felt the games a little too boisterous, so I took Knox minor away behind some rocks. I removed his boot and stocking, opened my trousers, put his dear little foot there and experienced a most satisfying emission.'

In his autobiography, Evelyn tactfully referred to Dick Young under the pseudonym of 'Grimes'. He describes him as 'monotonously pederastic and talks only of the beauty of sleeping boys'. He himself had grown fond of the boys and was pleased that they had done well in their history examination.

For a short time during that summer term, his happiness increased. He handed in his notice in the 'benign contemplation of a year abroad drinking chianti under olive trees'. But then news reached him that the job was not his after all. More bad news came with Harold Acton's reaction to his novel, 'The Temple at Thatch'. The verdict was negative: 'Too English for my exotic taste. Too much nid-nodding over port.' Evelyn promptly burnt the manuscript in the school boiler room and went down to the seaside. He took off his clothes and left them in a pile on the beach, accompanied by a suicide note consisting of a quotation from Euripides (in the original Greek, which he had taken the trouble to verify in a school textbook). Then he began swimming out to sea, intending to end it all. But he encountered a shoal of jellyfish, was stung on the shoulder and turned back.

The school year came to an end and Evelyn left Arnold House for London, with no job prospects and no money. He was at his lowest in these months. All his friends seemed to be developing their careers while his was going nowhere. There appeared to be no alternative but to seek another teaching post. Richard Plunket Greene told him about a vacancy at the school where he was teaching. Located at Aston Clinton near Aylesbury in Buckinghamshire, it was within striking distance of both London and Oxford. And Richard would be a colleague. He got the job.

Evelyn was determined to enjoy his summer before starting there in the autumn. Alastair Graham was back from Africa. They renewed their bond. At the end of August, Evelyn stayed with Alastair in Barford for a week. He heard Mass in a hideous church in Leamington Spa. He took a bus over to Stratford-upon-Avon, where Alastair was learning the art of hand-press book printing. They had cocktails at one hotel and luncheon at another, after which Evelyn went to the theatre and found the 'audience most bardolatrous, laughing religiously at the most pathetic puns'. Afterwards, he met up with Alastair again. They had tea together, then returned to Barford 'where we dined in high-necked jumpers and did much that could not have been done if Mrs Graham had been here'. She had left home in a rage on discovering that her son was guaranteeing Evelyn's overdraft.

Several letters from Alastair survive from this time. 'My dear Evelyn,' one of them begins,

> Thank you for your letter. Evelyn, it was very serious for a poor, careless, happy person like me. Of course I want you to treat me like your nature wishes to. I don't understand how one could treat anyone otherwise without being insincere. Travail [?] is a charming spiced memory that I am most pleased to think of in my quiet moments. It is those memories that I live on.

Another one reads:

> My dearest Evelyn, I feel very lonely now. But you have made me so happy. Please come back soon . . . My love to you, Evelyn; I want you back again so much.

Though 'The Temple at Thatch' had been consigned to the boiler of Arnold House, its opening chapter in the style of a film seems to have been recycled in a short story called 'The Balance', which Evelyn finished by the end of that summer of 1925. He thought sufficiently well of it to send it to Leonard Woolf at the Hogarth Press and Geoffrey Whitworth at Chatto & Windus.

The cinematic beginning has four unattributed voices. This kind of dialogue – like the telephone conversation – became one of Waugh's literary trademarks. Each voice reveals the character of the speaker with precision and economy. In creating such voices, Evelyn was finding his own literary voice for the first time.

The main narrative is presented as a silent film whose captions are commented upon by a cinema audience that includes two housemaids and a Cambridge undergraduate. Evelyn drew upon much of his own experience for the hero, Adam Doure (the surname should presumably be pronounced to rhyme with 'Waugh'). Physically, though, the character is created more in the image of Alastair than Evelyn.

Adam, like his creator, is a student at a London art school. He is still spiritually attached to Oxford, from where he has graduated and where his friends still reside. And he tries to commit suicide, leaving a self-dramatising note (albeit in Latin as opposed to Greek). His suicide attempt is thwarted when he vomits up the poison he has administered himself. Adam decides, on balance, that pursuit of his art is better than suicide.

There are other autobiographical details woven into the narrative: Evelyn's sense of not belonging, his sadness, his unrequited love for Olivia (who becomes the excellently named Imogen Quest). Even his sale of his Oxford books is included. Adam's library is 'remarkable for a man of his age and means', consisting of admirably bound volumes, some of them rare editions. Like Evelyn, Adam returns to Oxford in search of his friends and the happiness of his undergraduate existence. The Oxford scene is headed with the line from Quiller-Couch that Evelyn quoted so often: 'KNOW YOU HER SECRET NONE CAN UTTER?' The camera is imagined following Adam from the station through the city of dreaming spires to King Edward Street. Adam is visiting a special friend:

> LORD BASINGSTOKE'S ROOMS. KING EDWARD STREET.
>
> Interior of Lord Basingstoke's rooms. On the chimney-piece are photographs of Lord Basingstoke's mother and two of Lord Basingstoke's friends, wearing that peculiarly inane and serene smile only found during the last year at Eton and then only in photographs. Some massive glass paperweights and cards of invitation.
>
> On the walls are large coloured caricatures of Basil Hay drawn by himself at Eton, an early nineteenth-century engraving of Lord Basingstoke's home; two unfinished drawings by Ernest Vaughan of the Rape of the Sabines and a wool picture of two dogs and a cat.
>
> Lord Basingstoke, contrary to all expectation, is neither drinking, gaming, nor struggling with his riding boots; he is engaged on writing a Collections Paper for his tutor.
>
> Lord Basingstoke's paper in a pleasant, childish handwriting.
>
> 'BRADLAUGH v. GOSSETT. THIS FAMOUS TEST CASE FINALLY ESTABLISHED THE DECISION THAT MARSHAL LAW IS UNKNOWN IN ENGLAND.'
>
> He crosses out 'marshal' and puts 'martial'; then sits biting his pen sadly.
>
> 'Adam, how lovely; I had no idea you were in Oxford.'
>
> They talk for a little while.
>
> 'RICHARD, CAN YOU DINE WITH ME TO-NIGHT. YOU MUST. I'M HAVING A FAREWELL BLIND.' Richard looks sadly at his Collections Paper and shakes his head.
>
> 'My dear, I simply can't. I've got to get this finished by tonight. I'm probably going to be sent down as it is.'
>
> Adam returns to his taxi.

In this poignant little scene, Hugh Lygon enters the fictional world of Evelyn Waugh. His mother is a dominating spirit, as, by way of that nineteenth-century engraving, is Madresfield. Hugh's passions are captured: drinking, gaming, riding. As is his academic weakness: the childish handwriting, the inability to spell 'martial'. But hanging over the pen portrait are the qualities that Evelyn so loved. On the one hand, the capacity for friendship – the photographs of fellow Old Etonians, the invitations revealing that everyone wants his company. And on the other, the sense of sadness and hopelessness. In the flesh, Lord Basingstoke is Hugh Lygon. In the imagination, he is Sebastian Flyte in embryo.

As Waugh developed as a writer, he perfected a technique of combining the characteristics of his friends, enemies and acquaintances in order to create composite characters. His later portraits of Hugh are not of Hugh alone. In that sense, the glimpse of Lord Basingstoke in his Oxford rooms, so clearly evocative of Hugh and no one else, is the closest we ever come to the most elusive of Evelyn's lovers.

Another aspect of Waugh's creative sophistication was his way of splitting his own identity into more than one character. The full extent of this practice has not always been noticed by his critics and biographers. They have seen that Adam Doure is a self-portrait, but a second double has escaped observation. Adam goes around Oxford trying to find an old friend to dine with. Everyone is engaged. But then as a last resort he calls on a certain Ernest Vaughan. This E. V. has ugly rooms in a second-rate college. They are situated (symbolically) between 'the lavatories and the chapel'. Caricatures and messy drawings line his walls. Among them is an 'able drawing of the benign Basingstoke'. Ernest is carefully described, sitting in his wicker chair as he mends darts 'with unexpected dexterity'. He is 'a short, sturdy man, with fierce little eyes and a well-formed forehead'. His well-made tweeds are stained with drink and paint. The two men proceed to get drunk over dinner. Ernest sketches Adam. Later, after more drinking in another Oxford pub, Ernest 'beset by two panders, is loudly maintaining the abnormality of his tastes'. Then with 'swollen neck and staring eye', Ernest almost gets into a fight with Imogen Quest's brother. He is violently sick at the last minute, foreshadowing Adam's reprieve when he vomits up the poison.

The story ends with a conversation between the Quests and some aristocratic Oxford friends who pass judgement on the hapless Vaughan: 'Just the most *awful* person in the world . . . Isn't he short and dirty with masses of hair.'

Imogen, bored and repelled by Adam, is intrigued by a glimpse she has had of the awful Ernest: 'I think he looked very charming. I want to meet him properly.'

'Imogen, you can't, *really*. He is too *awful*.'

The story ends with Imogen determined to persuade Adam to orchestrate a meeting with his funny little friend. Ernest Vaughan is on his way to becoming an unlikely romantic hero.

Adam Doure is Evelyn Waugh, but so is Ernest Vaughan. On returning to Oxford, Adam meets his own other self, a doppelganger who is also drawn to Basingstoke/Hugh, and who becomes a device for Waugh to fantasise about succeeding in his doomed quest for the love of Imogen/Olivia. Many things are in the balance in this most accomplished of Waugh's early stories: not only the choice between life and death, but also the question of sexual orientation and the writer's need to hold together his personal experience and his gift for fantastical invention.*

September 1925 and the new term at Aston Clinton beckoned. It was time once again for Evelyn to say goodbye to Alastair. He felt more ready on this occasion. Alastair and his friend Christopher Hollis were beginning to bore him with their endlessly rehashed conversations about just two subjects, 'Catholicism' and 'the Colonies'.

Aston Clinton did not meet expectation. Its common room (always the key to a teacher's happiness) was 'frightful'. The boys were 'mad' and 'diseased' (i.e. spotty). It was no more than a crammer for the rich and thick. There was a pub close by, which was something. 'Taught the poor mad boys and played football with them' is a typical diary entry. Or 'Taught lunatics. Played rugby football. Drank at Bell.' Evelyn was trapped here for the next seventeen months. The one compensation was that he was closer to his friends.

Most weekends were spent at Oxford or London. In October, Evelyn and Richard Plunket Greene returned to Oxford, where they dined with Hugh Lygon and John Sutro: 'they gave us champagne and we gave them brandy'.

He was disappointed when he hosted an early birthday dinner and not one of his Oxford friends turned up. The day before his birthday, he

* There seem to be two private jokes for Hugh Lygon's benefit in the story's names. 'Ernest' inevitably evokes Oscar Wilde's play: Evelyn would have known of Hugh's triumph at Eton in the role of Cecily, who is in love with 'Ernest'. And in Gilbert and Sullivan's well-known comic opera *Ruddigore*, 'Basingstoke' is famously used as a code word by Sir Despard Murgatroyd to soothe his new wife, Mad Margaret, when she seems in danger of relapsing into madness – the name of Lord Basingstoke is thus linked to the Lygons by way of the code name 'Murgatroyd' used by Elmley when they filmed *The Scarlet Woman*.

began a drawing intended as a present for Hugh on his twenty-first, which was to be a week later. Richard, meanwhile, had got a new job at Evelyn's old school, Lancing. The prospect of Aston Clinton without a real friend in the common room was grim.

He was not invited to Hugh's twenty-first birthday party at Madresfield. But around the same time, Evelyn and Richard had a party of their own. Three carloads of Oxford friends came down to play a rugby match against the schoolboys. It was a great success. The grown-ups won, though not by such a large margin as Evelyn had feared that they would. He even scored a few tries himself, which would have been an unusual sight. In the course of the drunken evening that followed, Arthur Tandy, a Magdalen man of a thespian bent who hung around on the fringes of their Oxford set, 'made love' to Evelyn – that is to say, professed his love for him. He spoke in no uncertain terms: 'Everything that I said about him cut him to the very soul; throughout the giddy whirligig of his life – and he had been up against things, in his time, face to face with the scalding realities of existence – the one constant thing that had remained inviolate in spite of all else had been his love of me.' This all took time to say and, according to Evelyn, it bored him inexpressibly. Tandy eventually became British ambassador to the European Economic Community.

Two days later, at the beginning of half term, Evelyn headed for Oxford. He had promised to act in Terence Greenidge's latest film. They were filming in the Woodstock Road but Evelyn was cross about the other actors, who were people he couldn't stand: 'After an hour I could bear it no more and when we came to a scene in which a taxi was to be used I got in it and drove away, rather to everyone's annoyance.' That evening he went with friends to the George Bar. A scandal ensued from the night's activities, though Evelyn managed to escape all the trouble.

A party was in full swing. But not solely with the usual Oxford set. A gang of wealthy homosexual stockbrokers and businessmen had come to Oxford to see Hugh Lygon. There was a rumour that one of them owned 107 newspapers and wore platinum braces. When they arrived, they discovered that Hugh was not there. He was still at Madresfield, celebrating his coming of age. His failure to turn up for the party to which he had invited the stockbrokers was characteristic: Hugh was notorious for bad time-keeping, always arriving late, or sometimes not appearing at all, despite assurances given when arrangements were made. So great was his laxness in this regard that a considerable number of his friends and family had the same idea for a twenty-first birthday present: he was overwhelmed with numerous gifts of clocks and watches of all sizes and designs.

Robert Byron, one of the most active homosexuals among the Hypocrites, opportunistically took Hugh's place and enjoyed a wild night with the Londoners. Writing to Patrick Balfour with a graphic account of their activities, he cautioned him not to leave the letter lying about. There was, according to Anthony Powell, a fear that the police might become involved. Though homosexuality was tolerated when indulged in privately by undergraduates, group encounters between gentlemen and stockbrokers were a step too far in an era that had not forgotten the trials of Oscar Wilde.

Evelyn was in at the start of the evening, but not its climax. The 'syndicate of homosexual businessmen' stood him champagne cocktails at the George, but he then went off to another bar, the Clarendon, with some friends of his cousin, Claud Cockburn. He was then pursued by Richard Plunket Greene and his fiancée, Elizabeth. Feeling perverse, he didn't want their company. In order to escape them, he climbed out of a window and broke his ankle on his descent.

CHAPTER 6

The Lygon Heritage

'A party of queer men from London arrived to see Hugh yesterday,' wrote Robert Byron to his mother from Oxford. 'As he is at Madresfield celebrating his majority with becoming pomp, I looked after them.'

A night in their company provided some compensation for his not being at Hugh's party himself. The previous year, by contrast, Byron had attended the coming-of-age party of Hugh's older brother, Elmley. He had been overwhelmed by the sheer scale of the event, and deeply impressed by the organisation of Lord Beauchamp, who had conducted the celebrations as if they were a military campaign. Hugh's coming-of-age party was also held at Madresfield Court. Once again, no expense was spared – even though Hugh was the 'spare' and not the 'heir'.

Until Evelyn Waugh appeared at Madresfield in 1931, Robert Byron was the most favoured Oxford friend of the aristocratic Lygons. He had known them since Eton. During the summer months he stayed with them at Walmer Castle in Kent, where Lord Beauchamp put in an annual stint in his capacity as Warden of the Cinque Ports. It was there that the earl acquired his family nickname (only to be used behind his back) 'Boom'. At Walmer, Byron met the striking Lygon sisters. Lettice, the oldest of them, was particularly lovely. He judged her 'the most beautiful human being I have ever seen – oversize feet and yet the most lovely figure'. Byron in turn made a lasting impression on eleven-year-old Coote: she never forgot his 'café au lait suit' and his pince-nez spectacles.

In 1923, Lord Beauchamp invited Byron to accompany him and his sons on a tour of Italy during the Easter vacation. Byron later credited Hugh's father as the man who opened his eyes to the world and the wonders of foreign travel. He himself became a renowned travel writer. Many critics consider his book *The Road to Oxiana* (1937) to be the foundation stone of the modern genre of literary travel-writing.

Byron kept a diary, and his remarks about the earl shed light on how someone of Evelyn's generation (with their well-documented anger at their fathers) saw this rather unusual patriarch. Venice was Lord and Lady Beauchamp's favourite Italian city, so the travel party went there first before moving on to the historic towns of northern Italy, after which they headed south to Naples and the island of Capri.

Byron remembered that Hugh's father was an indefatigable sightseer 'who maps out every moment of every day, weeks beforehand'. Whilst they were in Venice their travel bible was Ruskin. In Florence and Rome, it was Augustus Hare. Byron's diary details the churches and galleries they visited, as well as the obscure little restaurants that Lord Beauchamp insisted upon frequenting – he had a passion for local Italian dishes. Byron was suspicious that the *secondi piatti* sometimes consisted of horse meat.

It was this visit that first inspired Byron's love for Byzantine art, and he had the most knowledgeable of teachers in Lord Beauchamp. Byron's greatness as a travel writer came from his way of finding the essence of a culture in a magical alchemy of its architectural history and the customs of its people. It was Beauchamp who sharpened the young man's eye, wherever he went, for both the buildings and the locals. For his part, the earl was delighted to have a boy in the party who shared his interests and enthusiasms. Hugh was emphatically uninterested in culture – his boredom was an endless source of exasperated amusement to the other men. Lord Elmley took a little more interest, but Robert was the passionate sightseer. He was the kind of son for whom Beauchamp had longed. In Florence the party dined with Harold Acton at his exquisite family home, La Pietra. Acton took them to the famous tea-rooms, Doney's, and to the nightclub, Raiola's. This was the first time that Hugh became animated.

Byron recalled his wonder as the party climbed to the top of Giotto's bell tower in Florence. Hugh showed little interest in the magnificent view. He stood reading the *Daily Sketch* whilst Robert was overcome by the view of the Duomo and the other historic buildings. Hugh was more interested in the racing news and the gossip column report on the London party scene.

In Assisi, Lord Beauchamp and Robert Byron inspected in minute detail Cimabue's frescoes in the vault of the upper basilica of the church of St Francis. Hugh complained about missing breakfast and then moaned about the luncheon menu. Doting father that he was, Beauchamp could not help calling his adored second son 'something of a little philistine'. But Hugh, tall, languid and charming, could get away with anything.

They had arrived in Florence by train. Having exhausted the sights of the city, Beauchamp hired an enormous motor car for the drive south to Assisi and Rome. By this time they were all beginning to be fatigued by their exertions with Ruskin and Baedeker in hand. After ten days' recuperation on the island of Capri, they left for England.

Byron thought Lord Beauchamp a man of exquisite and unusual taste, despite his being a stickler for punctuality with a mania for timetables. Beauchamp, for his part, wrote to Robert to thank him for being a delightful travelling companion, and for setting such a good example to Hugh: 'It is . . . so much more delightful . . . to take an interest in everything – religious functions and daily customs. Everything that is different from England. Too many people bury their noses in a detective novel as they go thro' beautiful scenery and prefer internationalism in cookery to the native delicacies.' No doubt he was thinking of his son with his nose in the *Daily Sketch* and his unadventurous attitude to foreign food. Byron told his mother (whom he always addressed as 'Mibble') that he had been transformed by Beauchamp from an idiot into a person.

Lord Beauchamp took a great interest in his sons' friends, dropping into Oxford to see them and taking them out to dine. It was on one such occasion that he met the scruffy Terence Greenidge and, horrified by the young man, temporarily removed Elmley from the university. Lady Beauchamp did not visit, but she never forgot to send presents for the young men. Once she sent Byron a delicate box covered in shells.

Byron was so besotted by the family in these early days that he began writing a love story based on an incident with Elmley, when a young lady turned her head and said '*Are* you a Viscount?' He was more than a little starstruck, impressed that Lord Beauchamp appeared in newsreels around the country. He reported his sightings to his doting Mibble: 'Hugh and I spend our days visiting cinemas in search of Lord Beauchamp meeting foreign royalties on Dover pier.' Years later, Dover pier would have very different associations for 'Boom'.

In May 1924, Lord Beauchamp visited Oxford, full of plans for Elmley's coming-of-age party. Byron noted that the handsome earl had 'grown fatter' and spent a couple of hours with the boys. Byron was invited to take luncheon with them in the Magdalen College guest room. Pride of place was given to 'a bottle of Tokay, that the steward had brought from the cellars of the late Emperor Karl of Austria'. Byron, still impressed with Lygon largesse, was mesmerised: 'It has the most wonderful taste – so extraordinary as to be like seeing a new primary colour.'

His birthday present for Elmley was a gigantic scrapbook 'bound in white suede with gold ciphers, which I spent *hours* designing'. Byron excitedly told Mibble all about the plans for the party at Madresfield. The celebrations were to begin on 5 August with the annual agricultural show in the grounds. There would be a house party of thirty. Boom had timetabled the weekend in such a way that it would be necessary for Elmley to make seven speeches.

No one loved throwing a party more than Lord Beauchamp, whether it was a ball for the servants or a spectacular birthday celebration for the children. Madresfield parties were famous for their extravagance and style. Back in the Edwardian years a visiting lord had described a weekend party for forty guests: 'Everything was done in great style: minstrels in the gallery at dinner, numbers of footmen in powder and breeches and a groom of the chambers worthy of Disraeli's novels.'

For Elmley's twenty-first, some guests had to be accommodated in tents in the grounds. The guest list survives. It assigns the bedrooms and gives details of meal times, post times, and, needless to say, daily prayers in the family chapel.

William Ranken, the society artist who had been commissioned to immortalise the occasion with a magnificent family portrait, was given Bachelor Room Number One (he was indeed a confirmed bachelor). There were four other Bachelor Rooms and a host of other berths for visiting worthies – the Blue Bedroom, the Japanese Bedroom, the Ebony Bedroom, the Stanhope Bedroom, the Pyndar Bedroom and so on. On the principle that what was good enough for the least among their guests was good enough for the hosts, Boom, Elmley and Hugh gave up their own rooms and decamped to the tents in the grounds. Young and undistinguished guests such as Byron were under canvas, but they had the benefit of a mess tent.

For Byron, the celebration was the embodiment of 'a phase of civilisation either forgotten or derided'. Lord Beauchamp was always in control, only losing his cool at one point: 'he reached such a pitch of exasperation that he took to ordering the girls about as if they were servants'. Byron thought that the organisation was marvellous. No detail was spared, down to the typewritten slips indicating who was to take whom in to dinner.

For the servants' ball, Lord Beauchamp wore the insignia of the Order of the Garter and 'the frequenters of such functions who were there say there never has been a party on such a scale before'. A delegation consisting of the Mayor and the entire Corporation of the City of Worcester arrived in full civic regalia in order to present an address to Elmley. The family, looking rather glum, was photographed in their company in the great hall. Reporters and photographers from the *Daily Sketch* and the *Tatler* attended, though Byron had fun running away from them. He asked his mother to keep copies of the news articles. To his astonishment, 'Elmley remained quite oblivious of everything.'

There was also a part of Byron which recoiled against the extravagance and tedium of country-house living: 'Really Madresfield was tiring. What a horrible existence it must be flitting from one house party to another, making meaningless conversation to vapid girls, who for all you know expect to be made love to, wandering aimlessly about, worried to death lest you have not got an invitation to the next.' The homosexual Robert felt uncomfortable around the young female guests.

He refused his next invitation to a Madresfield party in January: 'if it's going to be anything like the last I don't think I shall face it. I cannot stand the smart guards officer with his loud voice and *savoir-faire*.' Once one has turned down an invitation to a place such as Madresfield, one is not asked back. Robert did not attend Hugh's coming-of-age party, even though he continued to idolise Beauchamp and to be good friends with the brothers. Lord Elmley helped him with his journalism by sending his credentials to Barbara Cartland, who passed his name on to Lord Beaverbrook. Barbara Cartland was in love with Elmley and desperate to marry him. Elmley did not reciprocate the affection, though he did take Miss Cartland's virginity.

It was clear to all the Eton and Oxford friends of the Lygon boys that their father's devotion to his children was extraordinary. And they repaid him amply with warmth and loyalty.

It is not hard to understand why Lord Beauchamp cast such a spell over Hugh's friends, first Robert Byron and then Evelyn Waugh. William Lygon was the perfect aristocrat, not only tall, dark and handsome, but also intelligent, cultured and very artistic. He was an energetic and highly successful public servant, driven by a sense of noblesse oblige.

His father, Frederick, the sixth earl, was pious and severe. Frederick was a second son who inherited the title after the death of his brother, Henry. The latter was a delicate and sensitive child who grew up to become a soldier and a passionate horseman. A family history records, in a tactful phrase, that Henry 'never seems to have formed any long-term attachment'. He spent long periods abroad with a 'friend', Gerard Noël, and their two valets. Algiers and Egypt were favoured destinations, partly in the pursuit of better health but perhaps also because of the opportunities they offered for short-term attachments. He died a bachelor, brought low by consumption in his mid-thirties.

Frederick, by contrast, was a scholar, bibliophile and music lover who was deeply interested in religion. He became closely involved with the Oxford Movement and there was real concern that he would cross over to Rome. He made a vow of celibacy in the hope that within his lifetime there might evolve a united church in which Canterbury would be in communion with Rome and that he might then become a priest. He converted two rooms at Madresfield into a private family chapel, as if in readiness for the day. But once he became earl, with the need to beget an heir, he extricated himself from his vow and married the beautiful and talented Lady Mary Stanhope.

On becoming the Earl Beauchamp in 1866, Frederick threw himself into the life of the house and the county of Worcestershire (his Catholic sympathies meant that he was viewed with suspicion in royal and political circles, so he confined himself to the shires). He rebuilt large parts of Madresfield in the Gothic style. He beautified the gardens. And he began the tradition of an agricultural show for his tenants (in *Brideshead*

Revisited Charles and Sebastian watch just such a show whilst sunbathing on the roof of the house).

Frederick and Mary's first child was a daughter, named after her mother. She was the one who became a very close friend of Edward Elgar. In 1872, when little Mary was three, a brother, William, was born to great jubilation. Madresfield had an heir. Church bells were rung in celebration all across the three counties of Worcestershire, Gloucestershire and Herefordshire. When William was only five his father took him to the House of Lords and sat him on the steps of the throne, as was a peer's privilege with his heir.

Despite all his wealth and privilege, William never got over the loss of his mother. She died in childbirth when he was three years old. Queen Victoria, still mourning her beloved Albert, wrote to Frederick to commiserate, telling him that 'having gone through the same terrible trial, she is able to understand his present suffering and feel deeply for him'. Little William was devoted to his father, but, like many pious people, Frederick lacked warmth. He was described by his peers as bigoted, pompous and disagreeable. William would grow up to marry a woman with some of the same characteristics as his father.

From Eton he went on to Christ Church, Oxford, as was the custom for the family. He was styled Viscount Elmley until he succeeded to his father's earldom in 1891. At Oxford he was popular, a clever and articulate man, cultured and studious. He was President of the Union. He was following in his father's footsteps as an ardent Anglo-Catholic, but he also had a strong Evangelistic streak and became president of the Oxford Mission, which was dedicated to bringing poorer men to Oxford. It was rumoured that he was seen preaching for the Salvation Army in the open air in the East End of London.

His glittering academic career was halted after he attended a twenty-first birthday party at Blenheim Palace, a few miles from Oxford, without having a proper *exeat* for absence from college. Refusing to apologise, William was sent down. The dean had been waiting for an opportunity to get rid of him. The young earl had already attracted the unwelcome attention of the college authorities when he had put up notices criticising the expulsion from the university of certain members of the Bullingdon Club after one of their riotous evenings of debauchery and window-smashing.

Beauchamp's rancorous relationship with the Dean of Christ Church, curiously akin to Evelyn's feud with Dean Cruttwell, stemmed from a deception that had been practised on him over the news of his father's death. In late February 1891, William had travelled home to Madresfield from Oxford in order to celebrate his nineteenth birthday with the family. On his return to college, he was met by the dean who told him that his father was ill and that he must return home at once. On arrival at Worcester station he saw a newspaper billboard announcing in the headlines 'Death of Lord Beauchamp'. He bought a paper and later cut the article out and pasted it into his scrapbook. Next to it was a handwritten note that said 'this was the first intimation I had of my father's death'. He never forgave the dean for what he considered to be a gross act of cowardice in keeping news of the death from him.

None of this is enough to amount to sufficient cause for the expulsion of an earl from the university. One senses that there may have been some grosser misdemeanour that was never publicly acknowledged. After Beauchamp was sent down, he was said to have suffered a mental breakdown. He was sent on a cruise to recuperate, spending many months in the Mediterranean, with a stay at Madeira. When he returned, he began to take his place in public life.

In 1895 he was elected Mayor of Worcester, the first peer in England ever to be chosen for a civic office of this kind. His commitment to the betterment of the working classes also led him to become a member of the London Board of Education. He gave a garden party for the National Union of Teachers in the gardens at Madresfield. The *Christian Review* described him as 'tinged with Christian Socialism'.

He was beginning to look like a dangerously progressive radical. This may have been one of the reasons why at the remarkably youthful age of twenty-seven he was appointed Governor and Commander in Chief of New South Wales. Some saw it as Secretary of State Joseph Chamberlain's ruse to remove a potentially awkward young man from the Upper House, whilst the *Daily Mail* considered the posting to be 'experimental, interesting and original'. Further afield, where the newspapers were less deferential, the story went that he was shipped out to the colonies because he had formed an indiscreet attachment to his mother's maid; thus claimed the *Boston Globe* and various other American papers. There may well be a grain of truth in the story – save that the servant in question was almost certainly not a maid.

Letters and telegrams poured in to congratulate him on his new position. He took his sister Lady Mary with him as his hostess. She was a much-loved lady-in-waiting to Queen Victoria. Not amused to lose her, the aged Queen commented drily: 'Well, I suppose he must take his nanny with him.'

Beauchamp was a keen sportsman (as his son Hugh would be), being especially fond of swimming and boxing. A photograph of him at the time shows him resplendent with tricorn hat and plumes, sword and sash. He cuts an equally striking figure wearing morning dress in a caricature by 'Spy' published in *Vanity Fair*. He had something of the dandy about him. To Robert Byron and Evelyn Waugh, he was the quintessential Englishman: dashing and at ease with himself.

His radical opinions and tactless comments made him both friends and enemies. In Australia he earned the nickname 'Big Chump', a pun on the name Beauchamp, for his occasional gaffes, such as when he made a reference to the country's criminal past. He was frequently outspoken. At Cobar in 1899 he enraged French colonists when he condemned the controversial Dreyfus trial, in which the framing of a Jewish army officer revealed the anti-Semitism of the French establishment. Beauchamp publicly thanked God that he was an Englishman and not a Frenchman.

He travelled around the country, going deep into the outback in order to meet the real people of Australia. He insisted on stopping at every small settlement. In one of his speeches, he said that the lessons of true Christianity could be learned from the natives. Imperialism, he protested, could lead to 'a policy of force and repression and war'. He advocated 'not only the gospel of trade, but the Gospel of love and Christianity'. These were not the orthodox views of a Victorian imperial proconsul.

Though he travelled throughout Australia, he loved Sydney. It would become a second home to him in his lonely later years. He felt free there, responding to the city's energy and excitement, its lack of class distinctions, the absence of that rigidity of views which was so much part of his life in England. The wood-blocked roadways were crammed with steam trams, omnibuses, hansoms and carriages. The brightly lit streets remained thronged until midnight and there were hundreds of bars and clubs full of young people. He frequented a thriving scene of arty bohemian private clubs, such as 'The Dawn and Dusk Club'. Artists and writers, rather than politicians and petty officials, were his friends.

Sydney was synonymous with youth and vitality. The weather was bright and sunny and the beaches a huge draw. Later, Beauchamp would write 'the men are splendid athletes, like Greek statues. Their skins are tanned by sun and wind, and I doubt whether anywhere in the world are finer specimens of manhood than in Sydney. The lifesavers at the bathing beaches are wonderful.'

In October 1900, after just a year and a half in his new post, he returned to England on half-pay. He held the governorship for another year, but did not return to Australia. It is not clear whether injudicious words or deeds were the reason for his being called home so soon.

When he returned to Malvern in 1901, there was a cheering crowd three miles long to greet him. He was thirty and beginning to feel the pressure to produce a son and heir. A year later he married Lady Lettice Grosvenor, sister of the Duke of Westminster. It was the society wedding of the year. She had the right credentials and character to become a great society hostess.

Lord Beauchamp was known for his love of formality, but he was interested in people of all classes. This was a trait that his children inherited. An American tourist visiting the Madresfield Agricultural Society was amazed to see the earl bareheaded in a grey summer suit, speaking warmly to the agricultural workers, shaking them by the hand and stopping to chat.

He was soon immersed in politics as a member of the Liberal Party in the House of Lords, setting himself against his father's Conservatism, particularly over the question of free trade. His Belgravia home became a meeting place for party grandees. When the Liberals came into government under Henry Campbell-Bannerman in 1905, Beauchamp had great expectations. 'We shall 'ave Hindia or Hireland, but we don't know which,' his valet was said to have declared with eager anticipation. But there must have been some black mark against his name, because rather than becoming a viceroy he only accumulated an assortment of minor appointments: Member of the Privy Council, Captain of the Corps of Gentlemen-at-Arms, Lord Steward to the Royal Household, eventually Lord President of the Council. Honours were showered upon him: he was created KCMG in 1899 and a Knight of the Garter in 1914. At King George V's coronation in 1911, it was Beauchamp who carried the sword of state. That same year he was appointed Lord Lieutenant of Gloucestershire and in 1913 Lord Warden of the Cinque Ports. In August 1914, he represented the government at Buckingham Palace when the King signed the declaration of war.

Like many children who lose a parent at a very young age, Beauchamp idolised his late mother and the memory of her devotion to the underprivileged. She had undertaken welfare work in the Newcastle slums and had opened a school for orphaned girls. He followed in her footsteps, undertaking charity work in the East End and becoming Chairman of the Church of England Liberal and Progressive Movement. He spoke in the Lords on a wide range of subjects from free trade and tariff reform, to juvenile smoking, vivisection, and the employment of women. He was active in pushing through a bill that set up juvenile courts and abolished prison sentences for children. He was described as having 'an impish spirit of mischief which has caused him to be described as the Lloyd George of the House of Lords'.

He also supported home rule in Ireland. The Irish took to him, but they were aware of his foibles. A miner told an English newspaper that 'he's a decent man and he'll shake hands with anybody'. To which another remarked: 'Though he always looks first to see if your hand's been properly washed.'

In May 1918, he introduced a Sexual Offences Bill which included a provision that the transgressions of both sexes should be dealt with on a basis of equality. In June he moved all the stages of a bill enabling women to become Justices of the Peace. In 1924, just two weeks after Elmley's coming-of-age party, an opportunity arose for Beauchamp to gain a position of genuine political eminence. Earl Grey resigned for personal reasons from his position as Leader of the Liberal Party in the House of Lords. Beauchamp positioned himself for the succession and was duly elected by his peers in the autumn. 'No better choice could be found than in Lord Beauchamp,' remarked one commentator; he 'is known to possess those qualities of tact and personal charm, which, equally with his stock of personal acumen and his alertness in debate, are essential to every successful leader'. His first task was to position his party on the opposition front bench in the chamber: he was bitterly disappointed when Lord Curzon, Tory Leader of the House, ruled that the new Labour Party should take precedence. The Liberals were a fading cause.

Another of his positions was as Chancellor of London University. In his installation speech, he contrasted London with the ancient universities (Oxford and Cambridge) that were not accessible to 'all comers'. London was the first university to 'open its doors to women' and also made it easier for those from poorer backgrounds to benefit from a university education. He honoured those students who worked in employment all day and then spent their evenings preparing for examinations: 'At a time when universities were becoming more and more the playground of the rich, London University came into existence as an intellectual treasure house for the poor.' Beauchamp must have felt frustrated by his sons and their contemporaries, who viewed Oxford as their playground. It is easy to see why Lord Elmley used a pseudonym when he appeared in Terence Greenidge's frivolous amateur films.

Lord Beauchamp was also an artist and craftsman. He had his own studio at Madresfield Court, mainly devoted to sculpture. It was there that he produced his finest piece, *The Golfer*, which was displayed in the Paris Exhibition of 1920. It depicts a naked golfer, raising his club as he concentrates on his shot. It is still in the smoking room, though the club is missing. The piece was widely acclaimed for the perfection of detail 'in the portrayal of an exceptionally difficult pose'. In the library at Madresfield there is another fine sculpture of a naked youth. Beauchamp was also keenly interested in embroidery. There seemed to be no end to his talents.

CHAPTER 7

Untoward Incidents

> The nearer you get to the hub of the wheel . . . the easier it is to stay on.
>
> (Evelyn Waugh, *Decline and Fall*)

The broken ankle sustained while escaping from an Oxford bar was something of a turning point in Evelyn's life. He was forced to return to the family home, sit still and read quietly. Enforced absence from the party scene made him think seriously about becoming a writer.

Boredom was alleviated by visits from the Plunket Greenes. They brought him a silver flask as a get-well present. Richard and his fiancée Elizabeth were delighted that her parents had finally agreed to their marriage. The wedding was fixed for 21 December, with Evelyn hobbling along as best man. Though pleased for them, he felt they were 'remote from me behind an impenetrable wall of happiness'.

He turned his attention to a study of the Pre-Raphaelite Brotherhood. They formed a subject that brought together his love of Victoriana, his fascination with beauty, his interest in both painting and writing, and his yearning for a 'brotherhood' of like-minded young men. He worked on it back at Aston Clinton, where he also finishing the drawing of Hugh that was to be his twenty-first birthday present. He was growing ever fonder of the boys, some of whom he thought charming. The best part of the day was when he went to talk to them in the evening.

At Elizabeth and Richard's wedding, he was depressed. A few days later he went with Olivia to a debauched party full of Russian émigrés. He despised Olivia for dancing 'the disgusting dance of hers' – the Charleston, about which she was crazy. She was drinking as much as ever. Whilst she kept him at arm's length she flagrantly threw herself at other men in his presence. He planned a Christmas trip to Paris and seemed relieved, for once, to escape the Plunket Greenes.

This was Evelyn's first trip abroad. He went with Bill Silk, a 'toping actor-manager', who, like many of his kind, was homosexual. Silk was in love with actor Tony Bushell, another of Evelyn's friends. It rained constantly and most of the art galleries were closed for the Christmas season. The second evening they visited a male brothel. Evelyn and Silk asked how could they amuse themselves and were told '*Montez, messieurs, des petits enfants*' ('Come upstairs, gentlemen, we have little boys').

After drinking expensive champagne, they were presented with the *petits enfants* who 'howled and squealed and danced and pointed to their buttocks and genitalia'. A boy dressed as Cleopatra sat on Evelyn's knee and started to kiss him. He claimed that he was nineteen and said that he had been in the brothel for four years. Evelyn found him attractive, but he had better uses for the 300 francs that the patron demanded for enjoyment of him. So he decided instead to arrange 'a tableau by which my boy should be enjoyed by a large Negro'. They went upstairs to a squalid room, and the boy lay there waiting for the black man's advances, but at the last minute a further argument over the price of witnessing the scene led Evelyn to take a taxi back to his hotel 'and to bed in chastity'. His diary entry ends with an equivocal: 'I think I do not regret it.'

Evelyn's school-mastering life at Aston Clinton was rendered much more bearable by a present given to him by Richard Plunket Greene: a motorbike. 'It is called Douglas and cost £25.' He dined with Julia Strachey in London, noting in his diary that she had cut off all her hair, making her look like Hugh Lygon. This was the era when girls were beginning to bob their hair and cultivate the look of lovely androgyny. The fashion pleased Evelyn at a time when his own sexual preferences were veering ambiguously.

He went on his motorbike to Oxford where he had luncheon with

Brian Howard and Harold Acton. It was quite like the old Hypocrite days: eating fried oysters, 'trying on the hats of strange men, riding strange bicycles and reciting Edith Sitwell to the chimneys of Oriel Street'. But his accounts of these visits seem tired and sad. Once again, he was trying to recapture his undergraduate years whilst knowing in his heart that it was time to move on.

Evelyn's popularity as a schoolmaster was greatly enhanced by the motorbike. From the moment he first rode up the driveway astride it, he became 'the idol of the school'. He would bribe the boys into behaving better by letting them tinker with its engine. His two favourite pupils, Charles and Edmund, were extremely fond of him, and he of them. His diary mentions them often. On one occasion they took him to see a pond that they had been digging in great secrecy, and he helped them catch fish to put in it. He was upset when he caught Edmund out of bounds and had to beat him. He gave him a Sulka tie as recompense. He also invited the boys to tea. Every evening he would go to their dormitory to say goodnight to them (but nothing more). He took over the school's literary society and designed the cover for the school magazine. He was trying to recapture his own schooldays – or to reinvent himself as a version of J. F. Roxburgh.

Evelyn loved his home comforts and was pleased that the headmaster had given him a room over the stables, which he converted into a sitting room. He went running with the boys and in return they helped him to fit out his rooms.

The summer term of 1926 began with just a handful of boys in residence, owing to transport problems caused by the General Strike. Evelyn took little interest in the strike other than the opportunity it gave him to relieve boredom under the colour of duty by motoring up to London on his bike and signing up as a volunteer police dispatch rider. On his second day the strike was called off and he returned to school.

He enjoyed the fine weather, reading aloud his favourite *Wind in the Willows* to the boys in his sitting room, while eating strawberries. And he completed his extended essay on the Pre-Raphaelites, dashing it off in between marking exam papers, and delighting his father with the result.

The long school holidays were spent almost entirely in Alastair's company. First they went to see Mrs Graham in Scotland. Evelyn loved Edinburgh. As a mark of their intimacy, Alastair took him to see his old nanny, to whom he was devoted. But the 'Queen Mother', as they called Alastair's redoubtable mama, was not in the best of tempers. She resented Evelyn's presence and accused him of being consistently rude to her.

In late August, Alastair and Evelyn went to Paris. Evelyn was delighted to hear that Elmley and Hugh Lygon were there. They dined together in a fashionable restaurant, visited the Luna Park, and drank a great many champagne cocktails. Being in the company of the Lygons was exhilarating and turned Evelyn off Alastair: 'I did not see much of Alastair, nor did I want to. He is so ignorant about Paris and French. I think I have seen too much of Alastair lately.' Evelyn was fascinated by the Luna Park and especially the big wheel. In *Decline and Fall* Otto Silenus illustrates his philosophy of life by reference to this particular fairground attraction.

These were the years during which the wheel was turning for Evelyn and Hugh. With the Pre-Raphaelites book Evelyn had found his vocation as a writer and over the next few years his career would rise spectacularly. Hugh, by contrast, was descending rapidly from the giddy heights of Eton, Oxford and his coming-of-age party at Madresfield. He was now working at a bank in the Boulevard St Germain. He was drinking heavily. One night, Robert Byron, who was also in Paris, had a call from a hungover Hugh, who had slept in and failed to arrive at the bank. He was in a bad way and asked Robert to go around and help him. The younger sons of the upper classes who dabbled in merchant banking in the capital did not have to put in a great deal of work or show a high degree of financial acumen, but Hugh could not live up even to the limited expectations that were placed upon him. An understanding with the bank was reached and he soon returned to England.

Evelyn went to Oxford and paid off his creditors with a pocket-book full of £5 notes lent by his mother. He dined and partied with Hugh Lygon and the 'smart set' at Christ Church. But he was depressed by the parties, describing one of them as 'all gramophones, cocktails and restlessness'. He resolved upon a life of 'sobriety, chastity and obedience'.

He published his very short book *The Pre-Raphaelite Brotherhood* in November – printed, with copious typographical errors, by Alastair Graham on his private press in Stratford-upon-Avon. He began writing a new book called *Noah: or the Future of Intoxication.* He also finally got his short story 'The Balance' into print in an anthology called *Georgian*

Stories and was pleased to be paid £2. 5s. 6d. The book was edited by Alec Waugh and published by Arthur Waugh's firm, Chapman and Hall.

A Christmas holiday with Alastair in Athens was disastrous. Alastair had finally escaped his mother, and taken up a post as honorary attaché to the British legation. Evelyn was repulsed by what he saw as the sordid life of the homosexual expatriate. The talk was all of male prostitutes and Alastair's flat was 'usually full of dreadful Dago youths called by heroic names such as Miltiades and Agamemnon with blue chins and greasy clothes who sleep with the English colony for 25 drachmas a night'. This is the kind of expat life that Waugh would recreate so brilliantly in his depiction of Sebastian's downward spiral in *Brideshead Revisited*. Evelyn chose instead to spend his time visiting churches and a deserted monastery.

He set off for Italy, hoping that Alastair might rejoin him there. In Rome, he played the tourist, 'gaped like any peasant at the size of St Peter's', took a cab to the Forum 'and enjoyed myself shamelessly marching about with a guide book identifying the various ruins'. He took a conducted Cook's tour to the Vatican and was disappointed with the Sistine Chapel. He enjoyed the Colosseum and then one of the sights that made the most impression on him: the Church of St Sebastian Outside the Walls, 'where I saw the footprints of Our Lord and arrows of St Sebastian'. This was an ancient basilica housing a beautiful and highly eroticised horizontal statue of Sebastian, by the baroque sculptor Antonio Giorgetti, together with alleged relics such as one of the arrows that pierced him and part of the column that he was tied to when he was martyred.

Alastair never turned up, so Evelyn headed home. The new term began and 'an admirable' new matron arrived at Aston Clinton. She had previously been a dame in Hugh Lygon's house at Eton. She gave Evelyn a ham very soon after becoming acquainted with him, but she was to be his nemesis. On 20 February 1927 he wrote in his diary: 'Next Thursday I am to visit a Father Underhill about being a parson. Last night I was very drunk. How odd those sentences seem together.' Five minutes later, the headmaster came in and fired him. The matron had told the head that Evelyn had tried to seduce her. This would have made a very amusing story to tell Hugh Lygon: that he was sacked for trying to seduce his friend's old school matron. Evelyn 'slipped away feeling rather like a housemaid who has been caught stealing gloves'.

It all seemed like an awful and distorted replay of the Alec Waugh expulsion. He told his mother that he had been sacked for drunkenness rather than indecent behaviour. He was sad that he had been unable to say goodbye to Charles and Edmund, his favourite pupils, though he had written to them. Edmund sent a charming letter in reply: 'Dear Evelyn, I cannot tell you how sorry I am that you have left. I do not know what Pig and I will do now without your room to go up and tidy or wash.'

'It seems to me the time has arrived to set about being a man of letters,' Evelyn wrote in his diary. This was another turning point. After a lunch with Gwen and Olivia Plunket Greene, he realised that his love affair with the family was over. Olivia was boring him with her constant harping on jazz, drink and, above all, 'Negroes'. All she seemed to want was a big black man. He began to see why many of his closest friends had disapproved of his obsession with her. Harold Acton thought that he was well rid of the entire family, whom he condemned as 'esurient narcotics'.

He decided to write a biography of Dante Gabriel Rossetti. The publisher Duckworth showed initial interest in the project. As Evelyn pondered his future, he made a further note in his diary: 'I have met such a nice girl called Evelyn Gardner.'

Dudley Carew, Evelyn's old Lancing friend, claimed that he introduced the two Evelyns, adding that she was impossible to dislike, 'or, rather, I could imagine only one person who might dislike her, and that was Evelyn Waugh'. It may, however, be that they were introduced by Alec Waugh, who had recently interviewed Evelyn Gardner for an article he was writing about the 'Modern Girl' – otherwise known as the 'flapper'. The slang term was purportedly a description of the physical awkwardness of the fledgling woman as she hovered between girlhood and womanhood.

Evelyn Gardner epitomised the 'Modern Girl'. She smoked, drank and danced. She cut her hair short, wore lipstick and went to parties, 'jazzing her way over a floor parqueted with broken hearts'. She was very pretty, with a snub nose and round eyes, and very androgynous. Some of her contemporaries said that she looked like a painted doll. She wore her hair not just bobbed, but in a pixieish Eton crop. She often cross-dressed for parties. In order to create the 'garçonne' (female little boy) look popularised by Coco Chanel, girls tied tight strips of linen around their chest to flatten their breasts. F. Scott Fitzgerald, America's bright young novelist who immortalised the flapper, described the ideal girl as 'lovely, expensive and about nineteen'. As with Fitzgerald, who wrote *This Side of Paradise* with the express purpose of winning over the family of Zelda Sayre, Evelyn Waugh's relationship with an upper-class young flapper was the catalyst for his writing career: brother Alec suggested in his memoirs that Evelyn wrote his first novel in order to raise money for his marriage to Evelyn.

Duckworth's interest in the Rossetti biography was now translated into a formal commission. By July Evelyn had written 12,000 words without much difficulty. 'Think it will be fairly amusing,' he noted in his diary. By the end of August, he had reached 40,000, more than half the acceptable length for a decent book. The noise of the traffic outside Underhill was a distraction, but he was becoming the complete man of letters, consumed by his work, reviewing for *The Bookman* and mentioning in his diary for the first time that 'I have begun on a comic novel.'

Rossetti, dedicated to Evelyn Gardner, was a colourful, opinionated biography mixing a grandiose manner with an informal, chatty tone (the brother of the model Lizzy Siddal is described as 'slightly dotty'). Evelyn had great sympathy with Rossetti. They both hated music, loved craftsmanship, suffered from insomnia and felt that they had been born out of their time. To a greater or lesser extent, all biographers project themselves into their chosen subjects. Evelyn was no exception: even Rossetti's mother seems to be an exact description of Catherine Waugh. There is more than a little of himself in the description of Rossetti as 'sensual, indolent, and richly versatile . . . a mystic without a creed; a Catholic without the discipline or consolation of the Church'. He ultimately describes his subject – as he thinks of himself – as second rate, lacking the 'moral stability of a great artist'.

He rounded off his endeavours with the words: 'The End. Thank God'. With his school-teaching experiences fresh in his mind, he was keen to turn his full attention to the comic novel. He was happy to share his work with his friends. He read the first fifty pages of the story aloud to Anthony Powell and then Dudley Carew, who would never forget 'the happiness, the hilarity, that sustained him that night . . . he roared with laughter at his own comic invention and both of us at times were in hysterics'. Waugh's first biographer Christopher Sykes remembered Tom Driberg reading passages to him but being unable to continue because they were both laughing so much. John Betjeman said that when he read it, it seemed so 'rockingly funny that nothing else would seem funny again'.

Its working title was 'Untoward Incidents', which seemed to set the 'right tone of mildly censorious detachment'. Like all of his novels, Evelyn's first had a strong element of autobiography. The novel initiated the 'spot the portraiture' game that his friends revelled in, though he sometimes went too far in this regard and risked trouble. Grimes was clearly based on Dick Young from Arnold House, Lady Circumference on Mrs Graham, 'little Davy Lennox' was Cecil Beaton, 'Jack Spire' of the *London Hercules* was J. C. Squire of the *Mercury*. Philbrick, the Balliol flagellant who beat up Evelyn as an undergraduate, gives his name to the mysterious school butler, and the egregious Cruttwell becomes a burglar. Two homosexual characters called 'Kevin Saunderson' and 'Martin Gaythorn-Brodie', clearly based on his acquaintances Gavin Henderson and Eddie Gaythorne-Hardy, were too close to the bone. Evelyn was forced to change the names to 'Miles Malpractice' and 'Lord Parakeet'.

Another working title for the book was 'Picaresque: or the Making of an Englishman'. As in the great satirical novels of the eighteenth century, Paul Pennyfeather is a picaresque hero. He is unjustly sent down from Oxford for indecent behaviour and stumbles from one disaster to the other. His adventures revolve around three worlds, Oxford, a grotesque private school in North Wales, and Mayfair in London. He ends up exactly where he began, though now studying to become a clergyman. Paul Pennyfeather is clearly a version of Evelyn himself.

The novel skewers every aspect of English society from the establishment's education system to the Church to high society to the legal and penal code. With unerring skill, Waugh satirises cowardly unscrupulous dons and aristocratic philistines ('the sound of the English county families baying for broken glass'). Its most brilliant comic creations are Captain Grimes the pederastic schoolmaster and the redoubtable Lady Circumference, based on Alastair's mother, who is forever complaining of her son, 'The boy's a dunderhead. If he wasn't he wouldn't be here. He wants beatin' and hittin' and knockin' about generally.' In many ways it is the perfect comic novel. Every sentence is delicately weighted, every joke impeccably timed.

It also introduces those macabre fantasy elements that make Waugh's world so different from the gentler comic universe of P. G. Wodehouse. A schoolmaster called Prendergast has his head sawn off in Egdon Mire Prison with one of the tools issued to the Arts and Crafts School. One of the little boys, Lord Tangent, is accidentally shot in the ankle at sports day – a comic incident, save that he dies. Grimes, who stages his own apparent suicide, is the only true victor among the characters. An unrepentant pederast and bigamist, he is the ultimate survivor, 'one of the immortals': 'He was a life force . . . he would rise again.'

Nevertheless, despite its anarchic elements, morality is at the very heart of the novel. One of the questions it poses is how a person can be ethical in an unethical world. Paul Pennyfeather is the only one, despite his passivity and weakness, who is moral and who does the right thing. He doesn't lie or cheat, and he protects Margot, the upper-class girl he adores, even though he knows that she is unworthy of the sacrifice. He is an innocent in a world of unscrupulous monsters. Waugh also introduces one of the concerns that would become a refrain throughout his novels: the destruction of the country house. The wanton demolition of the ancestral home King's Thursday, the 'finest piece of domestic Tudor in England', and its replacement with a modernist nightmare is indicative of Margot's inner corruption.

At the end of the novel, the tone changes dramatically. Back in Oxford there is a poignant scene between Paul Pennyfeather and handsome aristocratic Peter Pastmaster. Peter is an alcoholic, and has become a member of the very Bollinger Club that had been responsible for Paul's debagging and his unmerited expulsion from Oxford:

> Peter Pastmaster came into the room. He was dressed in the bottle-green and white evening coat of the Bollinger Club. His face was flushed and his dark hair slightly disordered.
>
> 'May I come in?'
>
> 'Yes, do.'
>
> 'Have you got a drink?'
>
> 'You seem to have had a good many already? . . . You drink too much, Peter.'
>
> 'Oh, damn, what else is there to do?'

This scene anticipates a crucial encounter between Charles Ryder and Sebastian Flyte in *Brideshead*. Though Peter Petermaster, son of Lady Metroland, has strong elements of that other Oxford acquaintance Hubert Duggan, son of Lady Curzon, his aristocratic demeanour and his despairing sense that there is nothing else to do in life other than get drunk is clearly suggestive of Hugh Lygon. The name Peter Pastmaster is dangerously close to that of 'Peter Pusey with whom Hugh Lygon sodomises'.

Evelyn knew that his book was special and he also knew that publishers would be worried about its indelicacy. The book contained a homosexual relationship between Grimes and a schoolboy, not to mention references to incest and to the Welsh mating with sheep. It also features a brothel and a stationmaster who offers his sister for sex. Publishers in the twenties were very cautious about potential lawsuits and Duckworth wanted too many changes, so Evelyn took his manuscript down the road to his father's firm. Chapman and Hall persuaded him to make some minor changes. It was not until 1962 that Waugh restored the edits.

Most of Evelyn's friends were amused by his love affair with Evelyn Gardner. They became known as 'He-Evelyn' and 'She-Evelyn'. But not everyone was complimentary. Diana Guinness thought she 'had a head full of sawdust'. The Fleming girls, his long-standing friends, were lukewarm. One of them, Jean, described Evelyn Gardner as 'very pretty' but the other, Philippa, considered her 'a tight-lipped snobby little thing'. One of her more annoying traits was her slang: 'angel-face', 'sweety-pie', 'Prousty Wousty' for Marcel Proust, a 'complete Pinkle-Wonk' for Arthur Waugh. But the fact is, Evelyn was not romantically drawn to intelligent men or women. It didn't worry him in the least that She-Evelyn was child-like. On the contrary, it brought out his protective instincts.

She was wholly unlike Olivia and this was one reason why she appealed to him. She helped to break the spell. Shortly before meeting She-Evelyn, he saw Olivia at a fancy-dress party dressed as the celebrated beauty and drug addict Brenda Dean-Paul: 'she seemed so unhappy'. She had invited a black man from Manchester for the day and, in a sorry state, had then phoned Evelyn to help her out. He was no longer interested.

Initially, the Evelyns were good friends rather than lovers. She was relieved that, unlike other men, he didn't put her under pressure. He-Evelyn had learnt from the disaster with Olivia not to seem over-keen. This kept She-Evelyn's interest. On the one occasion that he let his guard down by getting drunk, and insisting that he take her home, she refused. She got back in the early hours of the morning and received a telephone call. A polite voice asked: 'Is that Miss Gardner?'

'Yes.'

'What I want to say is, Hell to you!' Clang went the receiver. She laughed uproariously. Evelyn apologised the next day. 'He is so sweet,' she noted. When he proposed, apparently on a whim, at a dinner at the Ritz, she said that she would think about it. The next day she accepted.

Evelyn Gardner was the daughter of Lord and Lady Burghclere. His Lordship had been a Liberal Party politician who was devoted to his four daughters, but had died when they were young. She-Evelyn's mother was a strong character, the author of historical biographies. She was vehemently opposed to the match with He-Evelyn. She thought him middle class and entirely unsuitable. He said: 'It never occurred to me that I wasn't a gentleman until Lady Burghclere pointed it out.'

He-Evelyn seemed to be plagued by bossy older women of the kind he had caricatured in *Decline and Fall*. Evelyn had learnt from experience that the best response to such redoubtable women was to stand his ground. Secretly, he rather admired the *grandes dames*, who were like nothing so much as Bertie Wooster's aunts in the stories of P. G. Wodehouse.

Lady Burghclere was determined to find out more about her daughter's suitor. She was appalled at her discoveries. With admirable doggedness she travelled to Oxford to conduct her enquiries. Unfortunately for He-Evelyn, she spoke to his old *bête noire* Cruttwell. She-Evelyn remembered her mother sitting her down and furnishing the information that her suitor ill-treated his father and used to 'live off vodka and absinthe and went about with disreputable people'. There followed a string of French remarks about certain English vices. Lady Burghclere informed her daughter in no uncertain terms that Evelyn Waugh would drag his wife 'down into the abysmal depths of Sodom and Gomorrah'. It looked as if Cruttwell would have his revenge.

Lady Burghclere insisted that the couple wait for two years. He-Evelyn merely replied that he would marry She-Evelyn in a week. He had the tenacity to hammer out a compromise. He gained Her Ladyship's reluctant consent to a match the following September. 'Victory for the Evelyns!' her daughter declared to a friend who had been following the saga.

In time-honoured fashion, the opposition to the match only drew the couple closer together. In equally time-honoured fashion, the mother was proved right: the marriage was a disaster. The only compensation was that She-Evelyn kick-started He-Evelyn's writing career.

Evelyn Gardner, in common with many girls of her generation – Diana Mitford prominent among them – made a hasty marriage in order to escape from home and a domineering parent. For his part, it is not difficult to understand the attraction of marriage to a pretty, vivacious high-society girl, who gave him acceptance and confidence as she propelled him into a new set of glamorous people. They were only twenty-four.

The marriage was held in secret, in a rather tawdry low church. Harold Acton was best man, while Robert Byron gave She-Evelyn away. The date was 27 June 1928. They had not even waited until September as agreed.

After a short honeymoon at a hotel in Beckley, Oxfordshire, they set up home in a flat in Islington, which Evelyn took great pains to renovate. He covered an ugly coal scuttle with stamps and then varnished it. He-Evelyn and She-Evelyn even looked like each other, she with her Eton crop and doll-like features. Nancy Mitford, a friend of She-Evelyn's who soon became one of the very closest friends of He-Evelyn, thought that they resembled a pair of fresh-faced schoolboys.

Decline and Fall was published in September 1928. By December it was in its third impression, bolstered by some very positive reviews. An inevitable consequence was resentment from jealous friends. At Oxford, Harold Acton had been the leader of the Aesthetes, but since Oxford his fame had dimmed. He published a book called *Humdrum* at the same time as *Decline and Fall*. It suffered the inevitable comparison: it was indeed humdrum, where Waugh's was sparkling. Evelyn complained that when he invited Harold to the Ritz he would invariably reply, 'Of course you're a famous author, but you can't expect a nonentity like me to join you there.' And if he suggested that they should go to a pub, Acton would reply, 'My de-ar, what *affectation* – a popular novelist going to a pub.' The balance had tipped, and the friendship was different. Evelyn was no longer the protégé.

The marriage got off to a bad start with She-Evelyn suffering poor health. She caught flu, which turned into German measles. In February the couple went on a Mediterranean cruise, the voyage to be paid for by Evelyn publicising the ship. He also planned a number of travel articles, which he eventually published as a book, *Labels*. The cruise also served as a more extended honeymoon and a chance for She-Evelyn to convalesce. However, her health worsened and she was diagnosed with double pneumonia and pleurisy. At one point, she was coughing up blood and He-Evelyn was worried that she might die. As she recuperated in hospital He-Evelyn nursed her devotedly, reading P. G. Wodehouse to her aloud.

Whilst on the cruise, the couple visited Alastair Graham in Cyprus. He was there with his boyfriend, Mark Ogilvie-Grant. Evelyn noted how relaxed Mark was with the relief of not having to keep up appearances, 'and having terrific affairs in an atmosphere of garlic and Charlie Chaplin moustaches'. Abroad, as Sebastian discovers in *Brideshead*, is the place where you do not have to keep up the pretence of being straight.

CHAPTER 8

Bright Young Things

The Evelyns returned in May to the greatest London season since the war. 1929 was the summer of parties. There was a new Labour government under Ramsay MacDonald, promising that the rule of the rich was over. Women under the age of thirty had been given the vote for the first time (the so-called 'flapper vote'), but in the society pages it was the antics of the aristocrats that filled the pages of the gossip columns. The young couple threw themselves into the London scene.

Nancy Mitford said: 'We hardly saw the light of day, except at dawn; there was a costume ball every night: the White Party, the Circus Party, the Boat party.' As she recalled, most parties had themes. There was a 'Mozart Party' where everyone dressed in eighteenth-century costume and listened to a symphony orchestra playing the 'Jupiter'. Another was a 'Second Childhood' party at which guests wore baby clothes and arrived in prams. A Cowboy party was given by the Acton brothers. Especially memorable was the Swimming Party, hosted by Brian Howard, Eddie Gaythorne-Hardy, Babe Plunket Greene (sister-in-law of Olivia) and Elizabeth Ponsonby, held at the St George's Baths, Buckingham Palace Road. The invitation said 'please wear a bathing costume and bring a towel and a bottle'. This was the first recorded 'bring a bottle' party.

Another huge party, also hosted by Howard, on the occasion of his twenty-fourth birthday, was 'The Great Urban Dionysia'. It had a Greek mythology theme and was announced via an outsize invitation that had to be brought along in order to secure admission. Often there were fights, and the White Party became infamous when it ended in tragedy as a young man drunkenly crashed his car and killed himself. There was a literary party, where people dressed as the titles of famous books. John Heygate's 'Never-ending party' did what it said on the invitation: it went on all day and all night. 'Oh Nina, *what a lot of parties*,' says the hero of Evelyn's new novel. There is simply no better description of the partying of the aristocratic young in 1929 than that in the book which Evelyn was beginning, *Vile Bodies*:

> Masked parties, Savage parties, Victorian parties, Greek parties, Wild West parties, Russian parties, Circus parties, parties where one had to dress as somebody else, almost naked parties in St John's Wood, parties in flats and studios and houses and ships and hotels and night clubs, in windmills and swimming-baths, tea parties at school where one ate muffins and meringues and tinned crab, parties at Oxford where one drank brown sherry and smoked Turkish cigarettes, dull dances in London and comic dances in Scotland and disgusting dances in Paris – all that succession and repetition of massed humanity . . . Those vile bodies.

The definition of the true twenties party, according to Anthony Powell, was that it was given by a hostess of no great distinction who did not know half of her guests. The gramophone would belt out jazz. Cocktails were the drink of choice. Indeed, it was supposedly Alec Waugh who invented the cocktail party. Certain parties had black jazz bands of the kind that are memorably described by Anthony Blanche in *Brideshead*: 'No, they are not animals at a zoo, Mulcaster, to be goggled at, they are artists, my dear, very great artists to be revered.'

Evelyn saw the hit revue 'Blackbirds' many times, once with Alastair before moving on to a lesbian party, where Sir Francis Laking 'dressed first as a girl and then stark naked danced the Charleston' while a Russian played a saw like a violin. On another occasion he saw the show and met its star, the beautiful black American cabaret dancer, Florence Mills, in her dressing room afterwards. Oliver Messel threw a party to which 'all the Oxford Brian Howard set' and the Blackbirds troupe were invited. One man was so drunk that, as Evelyn noted with his usual weary eye, he 'vomited and pissed intermittently'. Robert Byron appeared dressed as Queen Victoria.

Most of the parties went on into the early hours of the morning. Policemen who were called in were entreated to join in and disrobe. It was at this time that the press dubbed the upper-class partygoers the 'Bright Young People' or 'Bright Young Things'. Evelyn loved to use the term ironically to describe his particularly serious friends, such as 'Bright Young Henry Yorke'.

Nancy Mitford remembered the sea of fancy-dress costumes that littered the floor of her tiny room in the Waughs' flat in Canonbury Square, where she was renting the guest room. That summer she accompanied Lady Sibell Lygon to the Circus party, given by the couturier Norman Hartnell. Performing bears and Siberian wolf cubs entertained the guests, along with a circus orchestra and a jazz band.

Newly-weds Bryan and Diana Guinness were the acknowledged leaders of the Bright Young People – though they vehemently denied the tag. Diana was another of the famous Mitford girls, the most beautiful of them all, with a face like a Grecian goddess: huge blue eyes and blonde hair. She was intelligent and well read, more elegant and individual than the average flapper. She had married an heir to the Guinness fortune when she was only eighteen and they had both embraced high-society life, hosting dinners and parties at their country residence in Sussex and their town house in Buckingham Street. In *Vile Bodies,* dedicated to Bryan and Diana, Evelyn would write: 'The real aristocracy [were] the younger members of those two or three great brewing families which rule London.'

Diana was typical of the young well-born women who, once they were out in society, had very little else to do but party. They didn't work, and if they did have a baby, it was handed over to nanny. Her eldest sister Nancy's rebellion led the way for her and her sisters. Tiny blows were struck for flapper freedom: 'Nancy using lipstick, Nancy playing the newly fashionable ukulele, Nancy wearing trousers, Nancy smoking a cigarette . . . she had broken ground for all of us.' The flappers even had their own jargon: 'Darling, too, too divine, too utterly sick-making, how shame-making . . .', which He-Evelyn delighted in and incorporated into *Vile Bodies.*

The 1920s was a good time to be a posh girl. The popular press was buoyant, with numerous daily newspapers and weekly magazines seeking to fill their column inches with society news and the doings of the upper classes. It was a celebrity culture: people wanted to read about the antics of the Bright Young Things and their latest crazes, which might be sunbathing or conducting treasure hunts through London's department stores. Lady Lettice Lygon, Hugh's eldest sister, made the headlines for her appearance in a circus party where she performed a comic cycling act, while her hostess danced the Charleston in a top hat and red shoes.

Not everyone was quite as idle as they sometimes made out. Because of income tax and death duties, some young aristocrats needed to earn a living, training as journalists, selling cars or working in fashion stores. Nancy Mitford was a typical cash-poor aristocrat who spent most of her time weekending with richer friends while making abortive attempts to work during the week, before finding her niche as a novelist. There was a feeling that the new regime had finally overthrown fusty Edwardian society. Socialists had forced their way into Parliament and the wealthy had taken to trade. Patrick Balfour (later Lord Kinross) became a journalist with the *Daily Sketch*. He depended on his friends to give good copy for his society columns; some years later he wrote a book called *Society Racket* that remains the definitive factual account of the Bright Young Things – as Waugh's *Vile Bodies* is the definitive fictional account.

Though she didn't need the money, Lady Sibell Lygon worked variously as a journalist and in a hairdressing salon in Bond Street. The *Illustrated London News* carried a photograph of her having a manicure, while in another photoshoot her sister Maimie posed in a fur coat as part of an advertising campaign for the department store Marshall & Snelgrove. Hugh, meanwhile, was a fixture on the party scene. A caricature in *Punch* called 'Our Cartoonist in a Savage Mood – at a Bright Young Party', shows him draped over the banisters, looking distinctly the worse for wear.

Nightclub owners and professional hostesses such as Rosa Lewis of the Cavendish Hotel provided venues for the young people to drink to late hours. The parties got wilder and drug abuse – particularly cocaine and hashish – was rife. Fast cars, faster women and sexual experimentation: Evelyn Waugh scrupulously chronicled every excessive detail for the satirical novel that was germinating in his mind.

One account of the mad antics of the aristocracy caught his eye and provided one of the great comic set pieces for *Vile Bodies*. This was a story to top them all, involving the unlikely collision of Bright Young People and politics. It was probably passed on to Evelyn via Hugh Lygon.

Lady Sibell and Lady Mary Lygon had been to a party and stayed out late. Dressed in their white Norman Hartnell party dresses, they enjoyed a night's dancing and drinking. But when they returned to their London home off Belgrave Square, they found the door locked and the night footman fast asleep. The girls had only five shillings between them, so instead of going to a hotel they decided to beg a bed from a friend. There was another family they knew well who had a night porter: the Baldwins, near neighbours from Worcestershire. So they traipsed from Belgravia to Whitehall. The Baldwins' current address was 10 Downing Street.

The night porter woke the Prime Minister and his wife. They came downstairs in their nightclothes. Mr Stanley Baldwin was wearing striped pyjamas. Mr and Mrs Baldwin greeted the Lygon girls and arranged for them to sleep in one of the spare rooms. In the morning, Mr Baldwin rang Lord Beauchamp to ask if he would send a maid round with day clothes for the girls. 'Balderdash and Poppycock!' he retorted – and made them walk home in broad daylight in full evening dress.

In Evelyn's hands, this episode was transmuted into the sublime comic episode where the wild flapper girl Agatha Runcible unwittingly gate-crashes 10 Downing Street and then appears for breakfast in her party clothes, to the incredulity of the Prime Minister and his wife.

Once he had an agent and a critically acclaimed novel to his name, Evelyn was keen to present himself as the voice of the young generation. He wanted to be seen as the Modern Young Man. He began to take a keen interest in the marketing of his own image. In an article on 'The Way to Fame' he advised writing a shocking novel, and taking little notice of the reviews, 'as long as people talk about it'. For several years, he had been trying out a range of voices in his diaries – the dissolute drunkard, the coolly detached outsider, the outright cynic. Now he saw that in a world dominated by the popular press, he needed a public image that would get people talking.

This is something that he never forgot. The key mistake of his critics and biographers would be to assume that his later pose – as the old buffer, the crusty colonel – revealed his true self rather than originating as a comic impersonation of the type. But the mistake is easily made, not least because – as Waugh would ruefully recognise – he ended up becoming his own caricature.

He became very good at self-promotion. He so desperately needed the money, writing to his agent: 'Please fix up anything that will earn me anything – even cricket or mothers' welfare notes.' When the *Evening Standard* misread a proposal of his for a piece on 'The Manners of the Younger Generation' as 'The Mothers of the Younger Generations', he was not deterred. The misunderstanding 'is unfortunate, but not disastrous'. He duly dashed off an article about the Mothers.

Evelyn decided that he would return to the scene of his honeymoon to write his new novel. He would spend the weeks in isolation, working hard at the Abingdon Arms in Beckley, and then return to his wife at the weekends. The Evelyns invited Nancy Mitford to sublet a room in their Islington flat. She-Evelyn was delighted to have Nancy as a flatmate, and Evelyn asked his male friends to keep an eye on them and chaperone them at parties.

On 25 June 1929, Bryan and Diana held a magnificent 1860s party at their house in Buckingham Gate. Nancy was photographed for the papers wearing a huge crinoline skirt whilst She-Evelyn went dressed as a street-urchin in cami-knickers, carrying a bowling hoop. Harold Acton wrote to Evelyn to say that he had danced with his wife at the party.

Evelyn was engrossed in his novel at Beckley. He described it as 'rather like a P. G. Wodehouse all about bright young people . . . I hope it will be finished by the end of the month'. Despite his appetite for hard drinking and good company, he was never really a party animal. He preferred the intimacy of small gatherings with people that he knew and loved. At large parties, he reverted to the stance of the outsider. This made him an effective fly on the wall. He wrote to Harold Acton and Henry Yorke, asking them if they were going to Bryan and Diana's party. 'I might go up for it,' he said, 'if I thought there would be anyone who wouldn't be too much like the characters in my new book.' The pub at Beckley suited him. He could drink beer in companionable silence, without the pressure of being witty and interesting, of singing for his supper. And he enjoyed the company of the working classes. 'I like so much the way they don't mind not talking.'

He didn't go to the party. His next letter was written to his parents: 'Dear Mother and Father, I asked Alec to tell you the sad and to me radically shocking news that Evelyn has gone to live with a man called Heygate. I am accordingly filing a petition for divorce.' They had been married for little more than a year.

'So far as I knew,' he told his parents, 'we were both serenely happy.' The shock was devastating. Adding to his distress was the fact that she had betrayed him with a friend, a handsome man called John Heygate, who worked for the BBC. He was also an Old Etonian. He-Evelyn had entrusted She-Evelyn to his care.

One of the most popular venues for partying was an old sailing ship moored at Charing Cross Pier. It was called *The Friend Ship*. Nancy and She-Evelyn attended a party there, chaperoned by Heygate. Shortly afterwards, She-Evelyn became his lover. He was descended from the famous seventeenth-century diarist John Evelyn. His parents had debated long and hard as to whether they should give their son the first or the second name of their famous ancestor. They finally chose the former. Had they gone for the latter, Evelyn would have left Evelyn for Evelyn.

He-Evelyn returned immediately to London. The Etonian had rewarded the Lancing boy by sleeping with his wife on his first wedding anniversary. He-Evelyn promised to forgive She-Evelyn if she never saw Heygate again. At first she agreed and they tried to make a go of the marriage. They attended a tropical-themed party on board *The Friend Ship*. A photograph of them in fancy-dress costume, taken at this time, reveals their deep unhappiness. The press commented that the famous author looked rather scared.

The salvage attempt did not work out. On 1 August, He-Evelyn returned home to a cold and empty flat. The cleaner told him that his wife had moved out. She had gone to Heygate, whom she later married.

It was a massive blow to Evelyn's confidence and self-esteem. His marriage had brought him acceptance and love, but now he felt a fool. The marriage was over almost before it had begun and the manner of its ending had been most degrading. For the rest of his life he found it hard to talk about his 'mock marriage' and he expunged most of the references to Evelyn Gardner from his diary. He removed the dedication to her from all later editions of his biography of Rossetti. Many years later John Heygate, by then a converted Catholic, asked for Evelyn's forgiveness. He responded with a postcard bearing the briefest of messages: 'O.K. E.W.'

His friends were little comfort, except the ones who unequivocally took his side and refused to have anything to do with She-Evelyn. Nancy Mitford was horrified by her friend's behaviour and severed the relationship, perhaps feeling a little guilty at her part in facilitating the affair, however unwittingly. Best man Harold Acton was hopeless. Evelyn wrote to him: 'Evelyn has been pleased to make a cuckold out of me . . . I did not know that it was possible to be so miserable and live.' Harold's response was tactless: 'Are you so very male in your sense of possession?' Evelyn noted: 'it is extraordinary how homosexual people however kind and intelligent simply don't understand at all what one feels in this kind of case'. His Oxford life seemed to be very remote from him.

There has been speculation that the main reason for the failure of the marriage was sexual incompatibility. She-Evelyn suspected that her husband preferred men to women, and that his technique, learnt from men, ensured that he was 'bad in bed' with women. Whilst it is true that Evelyn lacked experience with women, he had several affairs with women after his divorce, which indicate that he was at least capable of inspiring sexual passion. Evelyn Gardner, on the other hand, found it difficult to stay faithful. She married three times. John Heygate killed himself in 1976.

Like the cuckolded Tony Last in *A Handful of Dust*, Evelyn could hear nothing but 'the all-encompassing chaos that shrieked about his ears'. He explained his position to Harold Acton: 'my reasons for divorce are simply that I cannot live with anyone who is avowedly in love with someone else'. Unlike the fictional Tony, who does the gentlemanly thing and lets his wife Brenda divorce him (leading to a hilarious scene in a seedy hotel in Brighton where he pretends to commit adultery for the benefit of some private detectives), Evelyn initiated the proceedings, citing Heygate as co-respondent.

The divorce, finalised in September, had very important consequences. His male friends noted a change in character: he became more brittle and harsh. Neither Alastair nor Harold could comfort him. His deep humiliation would be reflected in his novels for years to come: the theme of the betrayed husband is reprised throughout his literary career. More practically, and ultimately more significantly, the break-up of his first marriage meant that Evelyn had no settled base for a number of years, from 1930 to 1937. Friendship, always important to him, now became something sacred, as many of his friends old and new opened their homes to him. He became an honoured guest in their world.

Many commentators have presented Evelyn Waugh as a social climber, a parvenu who was hopelessly in love with the aristocracy and deeply ashamed of his middle-class upbringing. This view does not chime with the people who loved him the most. Diana Guinness, Nancy Mitford, Coote and Maimie Lygon, Diana Cooper, all members of the aristocracy by birth, emphasised that it was they who sought out his company rather than the other way round. He judged people not by their class but by their ability to be funny and entertaining.

Diana Guinness gave him hospitality in the months after the divorce. She was the first in a long line of devoted, beautiful, intelligent friends that fell under his spell (as he fell under hers). Physically, she was a female version of the ethereal blond man he had fallen for in his youth, and the forerunner of the three women he idolised throughout most of his life: Maimie Lygon, Diana Cooper and his second wife, Laura Herbert. Like all of those women, Diana Guinness was aristocratic, blonde and fragile-looking, but with a steely inner strength. She was just nineteen and pregnant with her first child. Her capacity for laughter was the single most important aspect of their friendship, which was no less intense for being short-lived, especially since the year after his desertion by She-Evelyn was such an important time in his life.

They were barely apart for the whole autumn and winter. He did not inflict on her any sense of the depression he felt over the collapse of his marriage. In a very English way, she helped him to cope with adversity through laughter. 'When Evelyn was there,' she later recalled, 'it was impossible to be dull for an instant.'

It was in the company of Diana that he finished his novel about the Bright Young Things, now called *Vile Bodies*. He dedicated it to her and her husband. He was also still working on his travelogue, *Labels*, and that too would be dedicated to Diana and Bryan 'without whose encouragement and hospitality this book would not have been finished'. He spent Christmas with them and was touched when they presented him with a handsome gold watch, which he treasured for years. He told them that he had nothing to give in return except his friendship and talent.

Among the guests at their Christmas party was Hugh's beautiful sister,

Mary – 'Maimie' – Lygon. Hugh himself was with Patrick Balfour when a satirical Christmas card arrived from Evelyn – sending these was one of his annual customs. On one side it printed a gallimaufry of newspaper headlines ('Women and Bones Mystery', '18 Atrocities This Year') and advertisements ('Why Have Indigestion?', 'Nearly Everyone Can Write', 'Bunions Go!', 'Be a Successful Artist: There is Joy and Profit in Creative Art'). On the other side were extracts from unfavourable reviews of *Decline and Fall.*

Evelyn noted at this time that 'I was not one of the young men to whom invitation cards came in profusion' and that he thought of himself 'less as a writer than an out-of-work schoolmaster'. This was to change. On 14 January 1930, three days before the granting of his decree nisi, *Vile Bodies* was published. It was an instant success.

> BRIGHT YOUNG PEOPLE AND OTHERS KINDLY NOTE
> THAT ALL CHARACTERS ARE WHOLLY IMAGINARY
> (AND YOU GET FAR TOO MUCH PUBLICITY ALREADY
> WHOEVER YOU ARE).

This light-hearted epigraph to the novel was later removed, but, as would always happen with Evelyn Waugh's novels, his friends and enemies pored over the pages to find portraits of themselves. Evelyn got into the habit of writing to his friends: 'Your turn next.'

In fact, only a few minor characters were the result of direct portraiture: the radio evangelist Aimée Semple MacPherson as Mrs Melrose Ape, the 'Duchess of Duke Street' Rosa Lewis as Lottie Crump and, most importantly, the party-mad politician's daughter Elizabeth Ponsonby as Agatha Runcible. The novel's aristocratic gossip columnists were based on Lord Castlerosse and Lord Donegal, as well as Evelyn's two friends Tom Driberg ('Dragoman' of the *Express*) and Patrick Balfour ('Mr Gossip' of the *Daily Sketch*).

Rosa Lewis was so furious with Evelyn that she banned him from her establishment, the Cavendish Hotel in Jermyn Street (which is easily recognisable in the novel as Shepheard's Hotel in Dover Street). 'There are two bastards I'm not going to have in this house,' she declared: 'One is rotten little Donegal' (she was threatening to sue him for libel) 'and the other is that swine Evelyn Waugh.' She also sent a letter to Chapman and Hall threatening litigation. Evelyn responded by writing a column in the *Daily Mail* entitled 'People Who Want to Sue Me'.

As was becoming his custom, the novel is peppered with private jokes. The egregious Cruttwell becomes a Conservative Member of Parliament, while the life of Miles Malpractice is based on those of Alastair Graham and Mark Ogilvie-Grant in their diplomatic postings abroad, where they lived their homosexual lives – an existence 'punctuated by ambiguous telephone calls and the visits of menacing young men who wanted new suits or tickets to America, or a fiver to go on with'.

One of the novel's themes was the ease with which the public could be duped into slavish conformism. Thus Adam Fenwick-Symes's gossip column invents the kinds of fashions that were lapped up by the Bright Young People, such as the combination of black suede shoes and green bowler hats or a taste for scruffy cafés on the Underground. Bizarrely, real events fictionalised by the novel were turned into real events by admiring readers. So for example, Evelyn's account of the Lygon escapade at 10 Downing Street gave rise to a real bottle party at Number 10, given by Isabel MacDonald in honour of *Vile Bodies*.

With its treasures hunts, nightclubs, parties, sexual experimentation, motor racing, ocean liners and aeroplane travel, *Vile Bodies* is *the* English novel of the Jazz Age, as the very different *Great Gatsby* is the definitive American imagining of the era.

Waugh's ear for idiom enabled him to breathe life into his characters: '"*Well*," they said. "*Well!* how too, too shaming, Agatha, darling," they said. "How devastating, how unpoliceman-like, how goat-like, how sick-making, how too, too awful."' 'Goat-like' is a private joke for the benefit of the Mitford girls – young Jessica Mitford adored sheep and disliked goats, so the adjective 'sheepish' became a term of approbation and goat-like was used for anything bad. In 1962 Evelyn said in an interview that the flapper slang was one of the key ways in which his novel had captured the spirit of its age: 'I popularised a fashionable language, like the beatnik writers today, and the book caught on.'

The shallow Nina owes much to She-Evelyn. Her brittleness, her slang, her beauty and her callous infidelity to both her husband and her lover are brilliantly conveyed through the dialogue, often via the briefest of telephone calls (a device pioneered in 'The Balance'). Nina's moral blackness is rendered brilliantly in the sparse dialogue of the telephone conversation in which she makes it quite clear that she intends to marry a man she doesn't love at all (Ginger, for his money) while expecting to carry on being the lover of Adam.

Evelyn later confessed that a 'sharp disturbance in his private life' changed the tone of the book 'from gaiety to bitterness'. What had started out as a light-hearted satire on the Bright Young People became a brutal castigation. The selfish, drifting Bright Young People unconsciously condemn themselves out of their own mouths. Their language is the mark of their shallowness.

Never afraid to take revenge in print, he includes many a dig at She-Evelyn and Heygate. But a more serious point as well as a personal one is being made when Adam says: 'I do feel that marriage ought to *go on* – for quite a long time. That's the thing about marriage.' Waugh was perfecting the art of simultaneously laying out a moral vision and turning his private quarrels into art.

This was the book that propelled Evelyn into the big time, establishing him as a brilliant young author, the voice of the young generation. It was ironic that he became identified as the leading spokesman of the Bright Young Things at the time when, because of She-Evelyn's betrayal, he felt most alienated from them. But he relished his new status. The Lancing boy had trumped the Etonians: Evelyn suddenly found himself much sought after by the newspapers and magazines. He could up his price for articles and reviews. With mock pomposity he insisted on 'feature articles (not side columns like Heygate) – with photograph of me and general air of importance'. He wrote regularly for the *Daily Mail* and had a slot reviewing books for a glossy society magazine called the *Graphic*.

He had risen from relative obscurity at Christmas 1929 to become the most widely discussed author of his generation by the end of January 1930. His diaries begin to read like the roll call of the rich and famous. He was feted in London's most fashionable circles, while remaining loyal to Diana Guinness, who was now in the last trimester of her pregnancy. He always preferred the company of his good friends to wild parties. Even at the height of his fame, he was happy just to 'chat' – Diana's favourite pastime. In the final weeks of the pregnancy, he would sit in her bedroom eating at a small table and telling funny stories while she ate in bed. In the afternoon, they would visit London Zoo. He felt that he had her undivided attention and it was personal attention of this kind more than public fame that rebuilt the confidence that had been shattered by his wife's infidelity.

For all the success of *Vile Bodies*, he had to work hard to keep his name in the public eye. He quickly finished writing up *Labels*. Diana gave him the necessary privacy by lending him her country house in Sussex. He travelled back to London for weekends.

In March, Diana gave birth to her son Jonathan and asked Evelyn to be a godfather. The other godfather was an Eton and Christ Church man: Randolph Churchill, son of Winston. Evelyn met him for the first time over the font at the christening. The relationship between the two men would be long-standing and tempestuous.

It was at this time that Evelyn sat for his portrait. Diana and Bryan commissioned Henry Lamb, a follower of Augustus John and the 'Camden Town' school. His finely executed oil reveals an attractive young man with auburn hair, pipe to his mouth and the fierce and piercing stare that all his friends remembered so vividly. In tribute to the couple who paid for it, and who did so much for him at this time, he is holding a glass of Guinness in his large craftsman's hands.

Sadly, however, the friendship came to an end. Once Diana's baby was born, she was keen to rejoin the social scene. But Evelyn wanted her all to himself. There were quarrels and then Evelyn severed the friendship. Many years later, she wrote asking what went wrong. He gave a forthright answer:

> Pure Jealousy. You (and Bryan) were immensely kind to me at a time when I greatly needed kindness, after my desertion by my first wife. I was infatuated with you. Not of course that I aspired to your bed but I wanted you to myself as especial friend and confidante. After Jonathan's birth you began to enlarge your circle. I felt lower in your affections than Harold Acton and Robert Byron and I couldn't compete or take a humbler place. That is the sad and sordid truth.

To her credit, Diana remained loyal to his memory, always considering him 'a perfect friend' who to her infinite regret 'bestowed his incomparable companionship on others'.

But there were more complicated undercurrents. Both friends were at crossroads and would take paths that would lead them in very different directions: Evelyn to the Catholic Church and a new circle of friends, Diana to the Bloomsbury set of Lytton Strachey and Dora Carrington and then to an intense passion with Fascist leader Oswald Mosley, which would take her to Adolf Hitler's Germany and then Holloway Prison during the Second World War.

In the end, politics divided Diana from most of her friends, and she and her second husband, Mosley (whom she married in Goebbels' drawing room in the presence of Hitler), became in her own words 'social pariahs'. Diana's most endearing and most destructive quality was her loyalty. Her loyalty to Mosley ruined her life. She remained loyal to Evelyn, upset and angry when he was attacked in the press or in reviews. She was deeply upset by the publication of his diaries, which she felt gave a 'totally false picture' of him: 'I felt angry to think this brilliant and delightful man might be judged by a new generation, who had never known him, by his exaggerated self-caricature.' 'Don't worry,' her son Alexander comforted her, 'we've got the books.'

But she was right to worry: the caricature has stuck. A great many entries in Evelyn's diaries smack on first reading of malice or inveterate snobbery. They need the gloss that Diana added to a letter from Evelyn in which he noted that he had been with a group of people whom she wouldn't like because they were even more humbly born than he was: 'for the literal-minded: this is a JOKE'.

Without the stabilising friendship of Diana, Evelyn became the very thing he had made his name by satirising: a shiftless Bright Young Thing. Through the summer of 1930 he was feted by society hostesses and the Ritz became his second home. His days were filled with luncheon parties, his evenings with cocktails, dinners and dances.

Then he fell in love. The girl's name was Teresa Jungman, known to her friends as 'Baby'. She was a famous flapper, noted for starting the craze for treasure hunts and private theatricals. She and her sister Zita were frequently photographed in the *Tatler*, wearing fancy-dress costumes or lovely flapper dresses. As well as being beautiful and intelligent, Baby was Roman Catholic. And it would be Baby who would provide the link through which he finally found himself in Hugh Lygon's family home.

* * *

The autumn of 1930 was marked for Evelyn Waugh by a momentous event. On 29 September he was received into the Roman Catholic Church. It is often said that the failure of his marriage propelled him into the arms of Rome. This is probably because when he was asked whether he was a Catholic when writing *Vile Bodies* he said: 'Not at all, I was as near to an atheist as one could be.' Then shortly after the novel was published he converted. But this was a path that Evelyn had been travelling for some time. His father called it his 'perversion to Rome'.

After Olivia Plunket Greene's death, Evelyn claimed: 'She bullied me into the Church.' Though Evelyn's friends blamed the Greenes, his confessor Father Martin D'Arcy SJ denied the charge, saying that 'his close friends Gwen Plunket Greene and her daughter helped to make him act, but they did not make up his mind for him'. His diary records his meetings with Father D'Arcy, whom he described brilliantly as having a 'blue chin and fine, slippery mind'. They talked about 'verbal inspiration and Noah's Ark', then, on another morning of instruction, 'infallibility and indulgences'. In *Brideshead Revisted* Waugh is exceptionally funny on the subject of conversion. The scenes of Rex Mottram's instruction are based upon Evelyn's own readiness and willingness to accept the tenets of Catholicism without demur. Rex, like his inventor, is 'matter of fact' about the whole business – and, like Evelyn, he starts going to the Roman Catholic church at Farm Street, Mayfair. D'Arcy wrote: 'I have never myself met a convert who so strongly based his assents on truth . . . he had convinced himself very unsentimentally – with only an intellectual passion, of the truth of the Catholic faith, and that in it he must save his soul.'

In July, he had met and lunched with Noël Coward, himself a Roman Catholic, and told him of his plans for conversion. Coward advised that conversion was such a grave step that it was best preceded by a trip around the world. Evelyn did things the other way around. He converted at the end of September and then went abroad in October. He got himself a journalistic assignment covering the coronation of the Emperor Haile Selassie in Abyssinia.

During the Second World War Evelyn was forced to undergo a psychometric test (he abhorred psychology – 'the whole thing's a fraud'). After being asked a number of questions about his parents and childhood, he countered: 'Why have you not questioned me about the most important thing in a man's life – his religion?' He took his Catholicism very seriously, believing in the supernatural element, the 'Alice-in-Wonderland side of religion' as Lady Marchmain memorably describes it in *Brideshead*. He was convinced that his life was saved by divine intervention. One of the most spiritual moments of his life came at the deathbed conversion of one of his closest friends.

Later, after *Brideshead*, when some critics accused him of glamorising Catholicism and converting out of a 'love of money' and a preference for 'the company of the European upper classes', he denied the charge: 'I can assure you it had no influence on my conversion. In England, Catholicism is predominantly a religion of the poor. There is a handful of Catholic aristocratic families, but I knew none of them in 1930 when I was received into the Church.' Many of his closest friends were Catholics, some of them converts (Harold Acton, Alastair Graham, Christopher Hollis, Frank Pakenham, Douglas Woodruff). Others, such as Tom Driberg and John Betjeman, were devout Anglo-Catholics. Perhaps more significantly, the women with whom he fell in love were all devout Catholics: Olivia Plunket Greene, Teresa Jungman and later his second wife, Laura. The influence of Gwen Plunket Greene was undoubtedly very strong – more so than that of her daughter. Olivia, who had recently converted, had the typical zeal of a convert. For her, it was all an affair of the emotions. For Gwen, by contrast, 'the call came unadorned by any joy or emotion, only a hard and naked will to follow God'. Evelyn understood this response.

It was not something undertaken lightly. He saw that he was making a sacrifice of home, marriage and children. As a divorced man he would be unable to marry again. His reasoning was simple: the world was 'unintelligible and unendurable without God'. He was twenty-six. He later said to Alec: 'The trouble about the world today is that there's not enough religion in it. There's nothing to stop young people doing whatever they feel like doing at the moment.' To Father D'Arcy he wrote: 'As I said when we first met, I realise that the Roman Catholic Church is the only genuine form of Christianity.' It was perhaps that simple. The Catholic Church was the 'True Church' and that was all there was to it.

Evelyn had embraced the Scarlet Woman.

CHAPTER 9

The Busting of Boom

> O child of Uranus, wanderer down all times,
> Darkling, from farthest ages of the Earth the same,
> Strange tender figure, full of grace and pity,
> Yet outcast and misunderstood of men.
> (Edward Carpenter, *Towards Democracy*, 1902)

One afternoon in July 1930, Evelyn Waugh took tea with Victor Cazalet, the MP for Chippenham, on the terrace of the House of Commons. On the way he bumped into his old Oxford friend, Lord Elmley, and Oliver Baldwin, the homosexual son of the former Prime Minister, Stanley Baldwin. That evening Evelyn noted in his diary: 'Oliver Baldwin grown fatter and Elmley a little thinner.'

Elmley was following his father into politics. His life since Oxford had followed a typical trajectory for a man of his class. He had done a stint in the Army (second lieutenant in the 100th Worcester and Oxford Yeomanry Field Brigade, then transferred to the Royal Tank Corps, where he stayed for the next four years). After that, he went on a world tour.

His brother's life was rather different. Since Oxford, Hugh had drifted aimlessly. Having been forced to abandon his banking job in Paris, he was often to be seen hanging around in the Packard limousine showroom in

Piccadilly, driving around in the vast cars whenever the fancy took him. Every now and then his name crops up in the Court Circular or the gossip columns, accompanying one or other of his sisters to a society reception, a wedding or a dance. He sometimes provided dutiful help to his father, entertaining dignitaries to luncheon in Belgrave Square. He was happier at the Madresfield Agricultural Show and the annual Hunt Ball in Worcester.

In 1929 he decided that he wanted to work with horses, so he became an amateur jockey. His chances of success were slim, given that he was six feet two inches tall. In July 1930, he was on the card to ride a horse called Alan Malone in the Amateur's Cup at Salisbury. But he was not among the finishers: he must have either scratched or fallen. His next scheme was to train racehorses.

A couple of weeks after Evelyn bumped into Elmley, the newspapers noted that Lord Beauchamp was departing on a world tour. At the end of July 1930 he left London for Australia. He had taken up the position of Chancellor of the University of London and as ambassador on its behalf he intended to visit various universities in Canada and the United States on the way back. In early September he wrote to tell his daughter Coote that he had just crossed the equator: 'I hope for news of Madresfield and especially of mummy, though I fear it might take her a little time to settle down.' The wording suggests that there had been some trouble before Lord Beauchamp left Madresfield. Was the countess ill, or worried about her husband's safety? It is not clear what he meant by her needing time to 'settle down'. What Lord Beauchamp did not know was that a plot for his downfall was underway.

Beauchamp planned to return to England at the end of January 1931, in time for the opening of Parliament. He travelled home on the *Europa*, stopping off at San Francisco, Washington and New York. In New York he met Evelyn's elder brother, Alec, at a party given by Franklin D. Roosevelt's mother. Alec Waugh told him that he was acquainted with Elmley and that he knew Hugh well. 'A dear, dear boy,' said Beauchamp; 'If only he would write to me more often.' The comment would take on an extra poignancy in the light of the events of the coming year. Alec Waugh recalled that 'the great man was very gracious and urbane, embellishing his role of guest of honour'. 'Had he any knowledge,' Alec wondered, 'of the trouble that awaited him back in England?'

* * *

Lord Beauchamp was said to have 'exquisite taste in footmen'. When interviewing male staff he would pass his hands over their buttocks, making a similar hissing noise to that made by stable lads when rubbing their horses down. If the young man was handsome and pleasant, Beauchamp would remark: 'He'll do well. Very nice indeed!' The fingers of the footmen of Madresfield were said to be glittering with diamonds. One could hear the clunk of the jewellery as they served dinner.

The diplomat and diarist Harold Nicolson recalled a dinner at Madresfield when he was asked by an astonished fellow guest, 'Did I hear Beauchamp whisper to the Butler, "Je t'adore"?' 'Nonsense,' Nicolson replied, 'He said "Shut the door".' But Nicolson, bisexual husband of Vita Sackville-West, knew that the other guest had indeed heard correctly. The Madresfield butler, Bradford, was an exceptionally handsome man. According to Lady Sibell, even her prudish mother thought he was delicious: 'Not birth-control – self-control,' she would say in front of him, to the bemusement of her children.

Not all Lord Beauchamp's servants were homosexual, though many were. One day a heterosexual servant, finding the door to the Belgrave Square drawing room locked, peeped through the keyhole to find the earl and his doctor sexually engaged on the sofa.

At a certain exalted level of society, Lord Beauchamp's homosexuality had been an open secret for years. His 'persistent weakness for footmen' was familiar to many of his friends. Indeed, his proclivities were reasonably well known even to his political opponents. But it was not thought gentlemanly to make them a subject for public attack. Beauchamp felt confident that he could continue his double life without being exposed by his colleagues or the press.

Even his children knew of their father's secret double life, advising their male friends to lock their bedroom doors at night when they came to stay at Madresfield. If a particularly handsome young man was staying, Beauchamp would try the guest-room door. On finding it unavailing, he would complain at breakfast the next morning: 'He's very nice that friend of yours, but he's damned uncivil.'

At Walmer Castle, where he was frequently without his wife, he held parties for Kentish lads, fishermen and prominent London homosexuals. It was there that he indulged in unseemly behaviour with figures such as the flamboyant actor Ernest Thesiger, subsequently co-star with Boris Karloff and Elsa Lanchester in *The Bride of Frankenstein*. When Lady Christabel Aberconway was invited to the Beauchamps' London residence for tea, she was amazed to find herself being introduced to Thesiger, who was naked from the waist up and adorned with ropes of pearls. He had just been cast in a film called *The Vagabond Queen*. At Madresfield, Lady Christabel also met a beautiful young man who described himself as a tennis coach. She could not help noticing that he had no idea how to hold a racquet.

Lord Beauchamp took an intellectual as well as a practical interest in homosexuality. He was an admirer of Edward Carpenter, the poet, homosexual activist, vegetarian and socialist reformer. He read Carpenter's epic poem *Towards Democracy*, which boldly linked homosexuality to political freedom in a style much influenced by the energies of Walt Whitman. He also treasured Carpenter's *Iolaus: An Anthology of Friendship*, a celebration of 'Greek love' published in 1902 that became an underground hit in homosexual circles.

It was Carpenter's long-term partnership with a working-class, uneducated odd-job man called George Merrill that led him to believe that same-sex couples had the power to subvert class boundaries and that homosexuals could be in the vanguard of radical social change. A visit to Edward Carpenter inspired E. M. Forster to write his one openly gay novel, *Maurice*. The template for the affair between middle-class Maurice and Alec the gamekeeper was the relationship between Carpenter and Merrill. Like Carpenter, Beauchamp was drawn towards young men of a lower social class. His lovers were invariably tall, handsome grooms or manservants.

He was comfortable in the company of homosexuals and gave patronage to men who shared his own orientation. He commissioned the Arts and Crafts designer C. R. Ashbee (also a friend and admirer of Carpenter) to redesign Madresfield. The artist William Ranken, who painted portraits of the family for Elmley's coming of age, was also homosexual.

Ashbee was lanky and intense, with eyeglass, moustache and wispy beard. Known to be solitary and foppish, he was extremely close to his mother (his father was infamous for possessing Victorian England's most extensive collection of erotic, and especially flagellant, literature). Like Lord Beauchamp, Ashbee continued to have homosexual affairs after he married. Being a bohemian type as opposed to an eminence in society, he could be quite open about his preferences, insisting to his wife upon his need for 'comrade friends': 'My men and boy friends [have] been the one guiding principle of my life . . . You are the first and only woman to whom I have felt I could offer the same loyal reverence of affection that I have hitherto given to my men friends. Will not the inference be obvious to you? There are many comrade friends, there can only be one comrade wife.' Lord Beauchamp would have wished but never dared to write thus to his pious wife.

He would not, then, have felt alone in his leanings, but his downfall came as a result of his increasingly indiscreet conduct. As the years went on he found it more and more difficult to hide his orientation. This was extremely risky for a senior politician in an age when homosexuality was a criminal offence.

By 1927 the high-society figure Lord Lee of Fareham was 'painfully cognizant of Beauchamp's unsavoury moral reputation'. He protested when the earl presented the prizes at a school speech day. The novelist Hugh Walpole told Virginia Woolf of a visit to 'the Baths at the Elephant and Castle [where he] saw Lord Carisbrooke naked: saw Lord Beauchamp in the act with a boy'. Sooner or later, this sort of thing was going to become public.

The final straw was Beauchamp's behaviour during his 1930 tour in Australia. He was accompanied by a rising figure in the Liberal Party, Robert Bernays, a former President of the Oxford Union, now in his late twenties and with one unsuccessful parliamentary bid behind him. Bernays was employed as Beauchamp's secretary. Travelling with them there was – not unusually – a young valet. George Roberts, a handsome nineteen-year-old plucked from the Madresfield estate, was His Lordship's 'joy-boy'.

Beauchamp was well received on his return to Sydney, so many years after relinquishing the governorship, but eyebrows were raised when it became clear that young George Roberts was living with him as his lover rather than his servant. There was to be a visit to Canberra, in advance of which the hosts requested Bernays to let it be known to the earl that Roberts would not be welcome. Bernays reported this news in a letter back to his own lover in London, Harold Nicolson. Soon the story was doing the rounds in London society. Boom may have thought that being abroad he could get away with behaviour of a kind that would have been impossible at home, but he could not stop the spread of gossip.

If there were to be a scandal, the countess would suffer and the person who took it upon himself to protect her was her brother, Hugh Richard

Arthur Grosvenor, the second Duke of Westminster, one of the richest men in Europe (he supposedly earned a guinea a minute from his rents). Known as Benny or Bendor (after Bend Or, a racehorse of his grandfather's that had won the Derby), he had long been waiting to act against his brother-in-law.

Bendor had many reasons to resent Lord Beauchamp, who had borne the sword of state at the coronation of King George. A duke ranks above an earl. But it was the Earl Beauchamp, not the Duke of Westminster, who had been elevated to the Most Noble Order of the Garter. Bendor was jealous. He sneered at Beauchamp's pomposity. Why, the man was to be seen flaunting his blue Garter ribbon whenever he threw a servants' ball. Bendor also believed that Beauchamp was behind an attack on him in a Church newspaper after his first divorce back at the time of the Great War. He was now on his third marriage. His two divorces had made him persona non grata at the court of King George and Queen Mary, where there was a rigid sense of propriety and deep disapproval of anything so public and vulgar as divorce.

The success of Beauchamp's marriage was a thorn in Bendor's side. Perhaps most significantly, given the importance of inheritance to an aristocrat, he was also profoundly jealous of his having produced three sons. It seemed grotesquely unfair that his brother-in-law should have three sons, a loyal wife, a string of homosexual lovers, a glittering career and great standing in politics, while he himself had got through three wives without producing a surviving male heir. The duke's only son had died at the age of four back in the Edwardian era. There were reports that the duke had contributed to the little boy's demise by forcing him to ride to hounds. The child had complained to his father of severe abdominal pain, but the duke had insisted that he should join the hunt. He was suffering from appendicitis. Following an emergency operation, he died of peritonitis. The boy, Edward George Hugh, first cousin to the Lygon children, had been born in the same year as Hugh. The duke never recovered from the loss. There may be an echo of the story in Evelyn's homage to Madresfield Court, *A Handful of Dust*, when the beloved only son is killed in a hunting accident.

As an ardent right-wing Tory, Bendor saw incidental political advantage in a campaign to destroy Beauchamp. Since the earl was the Liberal Party's leader in the House of Lords, his demise would be a great embarrassment to his colleagues, a further nail in the coffin of the party that had been a shadow of its former self since the split between Asquith and Lloyd George. Indeed, Beauchamp was doing his best and most important political work in these years, attempting to reunite the fractured party. A glimpse of his efforts behind the scenes is seen in a letter that he wrote to the wife of a fellow Liberal, Walter Runciman, after she had scuppered efforts to patch over differences with her husband:

> I came to see you at your request. I was advised not to come by those who know you. In your home to which you had invited me, you entertained me to an hour and a half of studied insolence such as I have never experienced in a varied life. You took advantage of the fact that you were a lady to whom I must speak with respect in her own house. I hope I may never have such an experience again. I am afraid we must disagree as much on the principles of hospitality as we do on our ideas of what Liberalism means.

Lord Beauchamp's capacity to speak his mind in this way meant that he was well prepared for the battle to come, which was to be both personal and political.

Bendor was also homophobic – as were most men of his era and class. But he was in no position to take the moral high ground, given his own habit of seducing underage girls. On one occasion, he had to pay a wronged family £20,000 as hush money. He was a known womaniser, famous for his pursuit of, and love affair with, the fashion designer Coco Chanel. He therefore had to proceed carefully.

Westminster employed private detectives to spy on his brother-in-law. Witness statements were compiled. When he had accrued enough incriminating evidence, he arranged a meeting with King George V. This had to be held at a private location, since as a divorced man the duke was ostracised from court. At the meeting Bendor told the King that he had conferred the highest honour of Knight of the Garter on a licentious homosexual. The rumoured response of the King, often repeated when the story circulated in aristocratic circles, may or may not be apocryphal: 'Why, I thought people like that always shot themselves.' Another version had the King saying that he was under the impression that people only did such things abroad.

The King asked his legal adviser, Lord Buckmaster, sometime Solicitor General and Lord Chancellor, to undertake further investigations into Beauchamp's conduct. Personal statements were taken from servants at Walmer Castle, Madresfield and Halkyn House. The evidence, Bendor reported, was indisputable and overwhelming. It was kept in the Grosvenor family archive in a box marked 'The Beauchamp Papers' until the 1960s, when the contents were destroyed.

The King decided that a scandal of this nature should not taint the court, where Beauchamp had once been Lord Steward of the Household. It should at all costs be kept out of the public eye. According to the Lygon family version of events, this was not what the duke wanted. He demanded a public trial and went so far as to insist that his nieces and nephews testify against their father. They stoutly refused. This, in their eyes, was the most heinous sin: that they could be requested to betray their own father. Instead they blamed their mother. The duke was incensed by their attitude. Only Elmley took the side of his mother. As far as the other Lygon children were concerned, the hounding of their beloved father was entirely Bendor's doing. The Lygon girls always maintained that it was not their father's proclivities but their uncle's malice that ruined everything. They never changed their minds about this and they never forgave their uncle.

Whenever there is a family dispute, the opposing parties have different histories of the events. The Grosvenor account of the affair has one crucial difference from the Lygon. It is not denied that Bendor bore a grudge against Beauchamp. Nor that he was the major player in the story. The fact that the Beauchamp Papers were held in the family offices in Davies Street shows that he was the man who took it upon himself to gather the evidence. And the fact that the fifth Duke of Westminster ordered a senior employee to burn those papers suggests that the family were long embarrassed by the extreme lengths to which Bendor was prepared to go in his determination to bring Beauchamp down.

The point in dispute is whether it was really Bendor who *initiated* the chain of events that led to the collapse of Beauchamp's marriage and career, or someone else. Bendor was fingered not only by the Lygon family, but also by everyone in the limited high-society circle who knew about these events. However, one detail in the story seems odd. Given that Bendor had had no dealings with the royal family in the decade since his first divorce, why did he involve the King and the King's Counsel, Buckmaster? It would have been perfectly possible for him to orchestrate his brother-in-law's downfall through a combination of innuendo, divorce proceedings and the threat of prosecution for illegal homosexual acts without the high-risk strategy of involving the royal family. And for that matter, given Bendor's marginalisation from the royal court, how easy would it have been for him to gain the ear of King George?

These questions evaporate if we believe the Grosvenor account, reconstructed by their authorised family historian, Robin Rhoderick-Jones, from the testimony of the employee who destroyed the papers. According to this version, it was not Bendor who sought a meeting with the King, but the King who got in touch with Bendor. Discreetly, indirectly, of course, using Buckmaster as intermediary.

So why did King George V, that aged embodiment of tradition and moral rectitude, sully himself by becoming involved in such a sordid affair? According to the Westminster family history, it was because two of his sons, Prince Henry and Prince George, were friends of Beauchamp and occasional visitors to Madresfield. If the stories of the earl and his footmen reached the press, in however veiled a form, the consequences could be catastrophic. One imagines the King's advisers having nightmares about newspaper headlines along the lines of: 'Royal Princes in Immoral Country House Parties'.

But the connection between the Lygons and one of the royal princes was much closer than this account supposes. Prince Henry was a stolid military type, who later became Governor-General of Australia. No taint of scandal attached to his name. But his younger brother Georgie was a very different character.

Born in 1902, Prince George was educated at a preparatory school in Broadstairs where, unusually for a member of the royal family, he proved himself a very bright pupil. His father sent him into the Navy, which he loathed, but he escaped by doing well in exams at the Royal Naval College. He then persuaded his father to allow a change of career: he entered the civil service, working as a health and safety officer for the Home Office Factory Inspectorate. Like his eldest brother, David, the future Edward VIII, he took an interest in the plight of the working classes in a time of sharply rising unemployment.

But he also shared with his brother a love of serious party-going and a voracious sexual appetite. They would go to all-night jazz clubs and kick their top hats through the streets in the small hours of the morning. Georgie drove fast cars and loved fast women; he flew, sailed, played the piano and was cultured. Tall, handsome and dark-haired, he could have any woman he wanted. One of his lovers was the American cabaret artist Florence Mills who danced in the show called Blackbirds that was enjoyed by Evelyn Waugh. Another princely paramour from across the pond was a girl called Kiki Whitney Preston, who was a member of the Kenyan expatriate 'Happy Valley' set. Known as 'the girl with the silver syringe', she introduced His Royal Highness to cocaine and morphine.

Prince George, known to his friends as Babe, was bisexual. In 1923 he began a nineteen-year affair with Noël Coward, whose play *The Vortex* offered the most explicit portrayal of homosexuality and drug addiction yet seen on the London stage. The threat of scandal was ever present. On one occasion, the royal household had to pay a substantial sum of blackmail money to a Parisian boy to whom Babe had written compromising letters.

On 22 May 1928, Lady Mary 'Maimie' Lygon, eighteen years old, had her coming-out ball at Halkyn House. Princess Ingrid of Sweden was there: Maimie was being lined up for a position as her lady-in-waiting. The next day the King and Queen held court at Buckingham Palace. Top of the list of those in attendance was Prince George. Top of the list of the debutantes to be presented was Maimie. She wore pearls and a gown of white silk tulle over silver lamé, embroidered with bright silver thread motifs on the bodice and a long floating tulle skirt. Her train was of silver lace and tulle flounces. The design was by Norman Hartnell.

Maimie had grown into the great beauty of the family. She was the deb that everyone wanted at their party. Prince George had recently broken up with another debutante, Poppy Baring, with whom he'd had a full-blown affair. There had been talk of marriage until Poppy let it be known that she 'couldn't bear the royal family'. The relationship was terminated. Now it was Maimie who caught the prince's roving eye.

A year later, her portrait by William Ranken, who had painted all the Lygons, was exhibited at the Royal Academy summer show. The piece was singled out on account of her beauty as much as Ranken's art. Though painted in the studio, it shows her standing by an urn in a landscape intended to evoke the grounds of Madresfield. She is a willowy blonde, wearing her coming-out dress and a shoulder scarf flecked with gold. It may be assumed that Ranken chose it for his contribution to the annual Academy exhibition because Maimie had suddenly become a prominent, talked-about young beauty in high society.

In early June 1930, not long after the opening of the exhibition, there was perfect weather for Ladies' Day at Ascot. Maimie was an honoured guest in the Royal Stand. Prince George strolled around the paddock looking very relaxed among his friends. The affair between them began around this time. Six months later, they were seen dancing together at a charity masked ball. Baby Jungman, with whom Evelyn Waugh had fallen in love, was also there.

On the surface, Maimie was an ideal candidate to become a royal bride. Prince George was nearly thirty, with an alarming array of extra-curricular activities to his name. Marriage would settle him down. She was the beautiful daughter of an earl from an ancient line, a Knight of the Garter with an impeccable record of service to both the royal household and the state. Her mother was the sister to a duke. The family had hopes that an engagement might have been on the way.

Society rumours about Lord Beauchamp's flaunting of his homosexuality in Australia therefore came at the very worst possible moment. If Prince George were to propose, there would suddenly be the prospect of the royal family allying itself to the household of a man who buggered his footmen. The lethal combination of a possible match and the prince's own bisexual tendency was too high a risk to countenance. Something had to be done.

The Duke of Westminster's hatred of his brother-in-law being well known, the obvious course of action was for him to undertake the dirty work on behalf of the King. Buckmaster was therefore dispatched to Bendor and they worked together to gather sufficient evidence to force Beauchamp to do the honourable thing, which would mean allowing his wife to leave him quietly. He would have to resign all posts and slip out of the country. In private exile on the continent – or back in Australia – he could do what he liked with his valets and his 'joy-boys'. And there would be no question of the relationship between Babe and Maimie progressing beyond a fling. Ironically, she would eventually become a princess, but of a very different kind from those of the House of Windsor.

Given how high the stakes were, it is not surprising that everything was kept from the public. The Beauchamp story never got into the newspapers. Lady Sibell, who always placed herself at the centre of things, liked to claim credit for this. She was having an affair with Lord Beaverbrook, who owned the *Daily Express*. The reality is that the most powerful forces in the land had a vested interest in keeping everything private. After all, if it came to a criminal prosecution Lord Beauchamp could have exercised his ancient right to a trial by all his peers in the House of Lords – and Prince George might have been dragged in as a witness. Nor was it only the King who was involved: the leader of the Conservative Party and sometime Prime Minister Stanley Baldwin was a Worcestershire neighbour and close personal friend of Lord Beauchamp's. Since his son, Oliver, also a politician, was also homosexual – this was accepted by his family, but not known to the public – the last thing Baldwin wanted was a public scandal turning on the sexuality of a prominent political figure.

The royal archives are silent on the affair. We may never know whether it was King George V or the Duke of Westminster himself who fired the starting pistol. Whichever of them it was, Bendor set about his task with great relish and ruthless dispatch.

His first task was to get his sister out of the marriage. He prepared a house for her, Saighton Grange, on his estates in Cheshire. He then arranged for Buckmaster and two other very senior barristers to inform the Countess Beauchamp of her husband's double life. The story went that the news was delivered with such brutality that she suffered a nervous collapse. It was said that she had no idea what 'homosexuality' meant: 'Benny tells me it's because he's a bugler,' was her alleged response. The duke had to resort to drawing diagrams in order to make the position completely clear. There is, however, no evidence for these more colourful claims: they are part of the froth of anger and innuendo that was provoked at the time and sustained for decades to follow.

Countess Beauchamp's account is to be found in a letter that she wrote to her children after the event:

> Enquiries were made, tho' not by me, or with my knowledge, and most terrible things were discovered. These were laid before 3 of the greatest and wisest barristers – they considered most anxiously, the

situation, not once or twice, but many times. I myself saw them twice; and they advised the thing was so dreadful, that the best and kindest way, was to give daddy the opportunity to leave England, and sign a document, undertaking to remain abroad, and thus *avoid* any legal step being taken either by me, or the authorities.

In February 1931, she left for Cheshire, having first visited her youngest son Richard at his boarding school near Broadstairs in Kent. He was just fourteen. From this time forward, he would spend his holidays with her, not at Madresfield. The girls, with the exception of the eldest, Lady Lettice – who had recently married a guardsman, Richard Cotterell, the son of a Herefordshire baronet – divided their time between 'Mad' in the country and Halkyn House in London.

A pious but poignant letter survives from the first days of Lady Beauchamp's exile, which clearly reveals her sorrow at being absent from Madresfield on the day of her youngest daughter's birthday:

My darling Dorothy,

It is such a lovely spring morn: – I am just waiting for the Car to take me to Eaton [the Grosvenor seat], for the Celebration in the Chapel there at 9.30 a.m.: so I write this ere I leave, to tell you that my Prayers will be for you – I wish you were with me today, but as it could not be, I know that nothing can really separate those who love one another – and perhaps from a distance, we can help each other more – I found this green-edged paper on which to write to you – and I live over again, past happy birthdays, and you and Mary in snowdrop wreaths, which 'Dewy Bunty' used to make you – they (snowdrops) are lovely in the garden here. I thought of sending you some – but know how Madresfield garden is filled with them, to greet you on your birthday morn: I had a sunset walk in Eaton gardens yesterday eve. So heavenly – the Spring House, *filled* with hyacinths and wisteria – and another one, with different sheds of cyclamen.

Later – it was Beautiful this morn in Eaton chapel – bathed in sunlight. The organist did not turn up – so I played the great organ, which I loved – hymns (A and M) 323 – 322 – and 164 – also 'Nunc Dimmittis' to the Barnby tune. I had a talk after, with

> Mr Okell – Nurse Gray was there – and many others – so I was able to remember your birthday in a heavenly chapel. I found this prayer, which Granny used to say for us, in one of her books, so I send it you for your P.B. [Prayer Book] – to keep always. In a few days, I hope to send you a beautiful book, with coloured illustrations, which belonged to darling Granny. It is for you and Mary – and I have written something for you to read in one of the first pages. God bless you, my darling Dorothy – every loving wish always, from Mummy.
>
> p.s. I have a found a little Seal – which translated means ('Mizpah') 'The Lord watch between thee and me, while parted one from another.' It is a message for you all 3 – with my *blessing* and all my *love*.

Enclosed with the letter was a 'Prayer for My Children': '*My Lord, I pray Thee for the children of my love, keep Thou the little faces pure, and the white raiment undefiled, and the dear feet steadfastly walking in the way that leadeth to Eternal life.*' Tentative plans were made for Coote and Maimie to visit their mother in March. But their thoughts and concerns were much more with their father.

On his return from Australia and America, Lord Beauchamp made a brief visit to Madresfield, where his wife informed him that she was leaving him. He returned to Belgrave Square, where he hosted a coming-of-age dinner-dance for Maimie. Halkyn House was decorated with pink flowers and green candles, but it was difficult to celebrate in such circumstances. Something would have had to be said about the absence of Lady Beauchamp. A few days later, acting in his capacity as Chancellor of London University, Lord Beauchamp hosted a dinner for the president of Columbia University. Despite the escalating rumours in society, he was carrying on as normal. Three weeks later, he gave a large reception, again in his Belgravia home, for the Eighty Club, which had a membership of senior Liberal Party men. Most of the guests were accompanied by their wives. Lady Beauchamp was conspicuous by her absence. Among those attending was Lord Buckmaster, the only one who knew what was really going on.

On the last weekend in March, Lord Beauchamp entertained a house party at Madresfield Court, guests including Mr and Mrs Stanley Baldwin and the exceedingly handsome Sir Michael Duff, a *bon vivant* and society figure, and a favourite of the royal family. He was also a bisexual, as was his second wife. This was to be Boom's last big country house party. He was gathering his supporters around him as the net closed in.

Bendor struck again. Baldwin was close to becoming de facto Prime Minister on account of the Ramsay MacDonald government's failure to put together an adequate response to the Great Depression. On discovering that the Tory leader and his wife had both spent the weekend at Madresfield, Bendor wrote to Baldwin suggesting that in the circumstances this was highly inappropriate. For good measure, he persuaded his other sister, Lady Shaftesbury (known as Cuckoo), to write a similar letter.

Lord Beauchamp carried on with his duties, but the strain was telling. Given Buckmaster's role in the business, it was not easy for Beauchamp to speak just before him in a House of Lords debate in early May on the Agricultural Land Bill, a subject dear to his heart. Then the following week, at the Presentation Day Ball following the University of London degree ceremony, he was accompanied by his daughter, Sibell. His wife's absence could only continue for so long without being remarked upon.

The offer from Bendor, via the senior lawyers, was clear. The alternatives were public disgrace for Lord Beauchamp or a marital separation without formal divorce, resignation from all duties – ill-health could be cited – and departure from the country, with a written undertaking never to return. But Beauchamp would never willingly relinquish his public duties and the appurtenances of office and status. Let alone abandon Madresfield and his children. His opponents now considered that they were left with no choice but to deliver an ultimatum.

Reluctant as she was to make any public statement, the countess placed a notice in the papers saying that she had separated from her husband and was in good health. She regretted even the little amount of publicity that this caused, but maintained that it was necessary because of Boom's refusal to agree to the conditions.

Urged on by her brother, she then took a step from which there was no turning back. On 14 May 1931 she filed a petition for divorce in the High Court. The grounds for the petition were laid out in an affidavit sworn by the countess the previous day in front of a commissioner for oaths at her brother's home, Eaton Court, near Chester, and then dispatched to her London solicitors, Lewis and Lewis of Holborn. The contents of this document were so explosive that when it was filed in the Public Record Office it was stamped to remain closed until the year 2032.*

The Humble Petition of Lettice Mary Elizabeth Lygon, Countess Beauchamp, for dissolution of marriage begins innocuously enough in standard format. The date of marriage to William Lygon, the Earl Beauchamp ('hereinafter referred to as the Respondent') is recorded – 26 July 1902 – and the dates of birth of the seven children are listed. But in paragraph five, on the second page, the grounds are given. It would have been possible to allege cruelty, neglect or a trumped-up fiction of adultery of the kind that occurs in Waugh's novel *A Handful of Dust*. But the duke had insisted on the truth, the whole truth and nothing but the truth. His sister's blushes would not be spared. The grounds were: 'THAT the Respondent is a man of perverted sexual practices, has committed acts of gross indecency with the male servants and other male persons and has been guilty of sodomy.'

The following paragraphs then lay out the litany of evidence that had been gathered by Westminster, Buckmaster and their detectives:

> 6. THAT throughout the married life at 13 Belgrave Square, Madresfield Court, and Walmer Castle, aforesaid, the Respondent habitually committed acts of gross indecency with certain of his male servants, masturbating them with his mouth and hands and compelling them to masturbate him and lying upon them and masturbating between their legs. The said servants with whom the Respondent committed the said acts of gross indecency were John Scown, Samuel John Scown, Redvers George Rolfe, Edward Hyatt, George Roberts, Frank Webb, William Cann and Ernest Edward Tippell.
>
> 7. THAT from the month of May 1909 to the month of April 1912 in the Chauffeurs rooms at 13 Belgrave Mews, West, the Respondent frequently committed sodomy with the said Samuel John Scown.
>
> 8. THAT on an occasion in the month of January 1911 at 13 Belgrave

* The closure has now been cancelled and the document has been released to me for the first time by the National Archives at Kew.

Square, aforesaid, the Respondent attempted to commit sodomy with one Frederick Moore.

9. THAT from the year 1922 to the year 1925 at the Garage, 13 Belgrave Square, West, the Respondent frequently committed sodomy with Redvers George Rolfe.

10. THAT in or about the month of October 1924 in the Library at 13 Belgrave Square, aforesaid, the Respondent committed sodomy with a man named Cook.

11. THAT in or about the month of November 1927, in the Library at 13 Belgrave Square, aforesaid, the Respondent committed sodomy with a man whose name is unknown to Your Petitioner.

One familiar name in this list is that of young George Roberts, whose presence had caused all the trouble in Australia. The specific allegations of sodomy all refer to events in the house in Belgrave Square and the chauffeur's mews behind it. They were incriminating enough, but Bendor undoubtedly had a further selection of statements from staff at Walmer and Madresfield.

A poignant final paragraph claimed that 'by reason of the aforesaid conduct of the Respondent Your Petitioner suffered acute mental agony and misery and her health was undermined'. The countess was accordingly petitioning for the dissolution of the marriage, custody of the two children who were still minors (Lady Dorothy and the Honourable Richard Lygon) and 'such further and other relief as may be just'.

On 19 May a little notice appeared in the 'Invalids' column of *The Times*: 'Earl Beauchamp is resting at Walmer Castle, where it is expected he will soon recover his usual health. Although indisposed, he attended as Lord Warden of the Cinque Ports the ancient meeting of the Courts of Brotherhood and Guestling at New Romney on Saturday, but the exertion overtaxed him, and he had to remain in bed on Sunday.' A week later, though, he insisted on returning to London to open the University Inter-College Athletic Championship. He then headed home to Madresfield. He had hosted his last public engagement. The ground was being laid for a withdrawal from public life: on 30 May, he was absent from an important Liberal Party meeting to launch a new free trade campaign. He let it be known that his doctors had advised him that he must not undertake any public work for some time to come.

With a heavy heart, he tendered his resignation to Lloyd George on health grounds. The wily old Liberal Party leader sent a graceful reply by return of post:

> My dear Beauchamp,
>
> I am very grieved to hear from your Doctor that you are suffering from cardiac fatigue, and that a period of comparative rest is essential to your recovery. Your partial and temporary retirement from the very hard work you have done for us will be a real loss to the Party. We have come to rely so much upon your ready and very effective help in all our difficulties, that we shall miss it more than I can tell you. However, I hope that you will consider your health as first and foremost, so that you may have a full chance of an early restoration to complete vigour.

There was to be no restoration, only another twist of the knife, a final dramatic confrontation.

At the behest of Buckmaster, three of Beauchamp's fellow Knights of the Garter arrived uninvited at Madresfield just after six o'clock on a warm early June evening. The hope was that they were sufficiently respected by him to stand a chance of twisting his arm. Lord Crewe was a Liberal elder statesman, while Lord Chesterfield could speak for Baldwin and the Conservative Party. Most telling of all, Lord Stanmore was given authority to let it be known that they had been sent upon 'the highest authority in the land'. With the knowledge that he had lost the support of the King, combined with his wife's initiation of formal divorce proceedings in such full and explicit terms, Beauchamp knew that the game was up. No written record survives of the meeting, but the Lygon children gained the impression that he had been told that there was actually a warrant out for his arrest, though the police had been given to understand that if he left the country immediately (by midnight, in some versions of the story; within twenty-four hours in others), he would escape prosecution and public infamy.

The children joined him for dinner. He told them that the only honourable thing to do was to kill himself, but that he would arrange matters to make it look like an accident. He would leave the country first, to minimise the impact. They tried to talk him out of it: they would always remain loyal to him; they could visit him abroad. When they said goodbye to him, the girls still feared that he might commit suicide. As for the option of a new life abroad, almost everything would be lost, but at least money wasn't a worry. Recalling the breathtaking speed with which these events unfolded, one of the daughters casually remarked: 'Suppose my father hadn't had any money available? Luckily, he always carried a thousand pounds.'

The undertaking never to return was signed. Bendor ensured that the Home Office warrant for his arrest on the charge of committing acts of gross homosexual indecency was kept on file. This meant that the earl's legal status was that of an involuntary exile who would be liable for arrest if he re-entered the country.

It took a little more than twenty-four hours to make the necessary arrangements. He said goodbye to his daughters and Madresfield, and returned to London. On 8 June, with considerable sangfroid, he put in an appearance at a reception given by the Royal Institute for International Affairs at Chatham House. The next day, he crossed the Channel. On Wednesday 10 June a notice appeared in *The Times*: 'Earl Beauchamp, accompanied by his son, the Honourable Hugh Lygon, left for Nauheim yesterday to take a cure. His daughters will join him later.' The absence of any reference to Lady Beauchamp was pointed.

Remarks appeared in less exalted newspapers concerning his need for 'mud baths'. Further letters of resignation were dispatched. The Baldwins remained loyal. Gossip and sneers circulated in high society: 'Well, you must expect anything from a man that has his private chapel decorated like a barber's pole and an ice-cream barrow.'

For the purposes of public consumption, the family maintained the fiction that their father was taking a rest cure for heart problems. In a sense, it was not a lie – his heart was indeed broken. Broken by being forced out of his beloved home and away from his children. Bendor and the countess had their revenge.

But Beauchamp had something that his wife lacked – the love and devotion of his children. It was they who decided to fix a rota to ensure that he always had one of them for company. Hugh led the way, again talking his father out of suicide once they were in Germany. As favourite child, he spent more time with Boom than any of the others, later travelling to Australia to be with him and keep him from depression and suicidal thoughts. Though he was doomed to become an exile, Beauchamp kept in constant contact through letters to and from his children. Only Elmley refused to write to him, severing all contact, until he married and his new wife brokered a reconciliation.

Sibell, Maimie, Coote and Hugh took Boom's side completely and would not hear a word against him. Their unwavering loyalty, despite the fact that he was seemingly the wrongdoer, was a source of anger and sorrow to their uncle, Bendor, and their mother. This caused a bitter rift that never healed.

Lady Beauchamp was determined to tell her side of the story. In May, as things were gathering to a head, she sat down to compose a letter to her children. But she could not bring herself to post it for nearly two years. She wrote copies – with minor variants – for each of the girls. She was determined to convince her children that she was the wronged party, emphasising that she had no part in the hiring of detectives and the threat to expose the scandal. Her dignified and candid account belies the story that she had no idea what homosexuality was. She told her children that their father had been shown the greatest mercy and consideration, more than any man of similar conduct could expect. She confronted the issue as boldly as she dared: 'I think you should now be told by me first what seems right and necessary about the facts.'

In contradiction to society whispers about her being innocent of her husband's proclivities, she now confessed: 'For many years, I had strongly suspected that (with Daddy) all was not as it should be – and that one side of his life and desires went contrary to everything that is right, normal and natural.' She was at pains to make his homosexuality clear without actually saying the word: 'I think you are old enough to understand what I mean and that you will not wish me to explain further but if any of you do not understand the seriousness, then I must.'

She continued with great poignancy, saying that for the children's sakes when they were young she refrained 'through many years of anguish and anxieties from converting my suspicions into actual knowledge'. Such was her mental anguish that she welcomed physical pain because it helped her to escape from her 'agony of mind'. In justification for her actions, she asked her children to understand what she had undergone for so many years and asked that the 'old love will be restored in its fullness and perhaps even increased, for indeed nothing has been done without the greatest and gravest consideration, compassion, understanding and wisdom'. She added that it was for Dickie's, her youngest's, sake and his future that she left the marriage – to 'keep him clear of all the ills that otherwise would doubtless have befallen him'.

She concluded by saying that the hardest thing of all for her to bear was that she would never again be able to see her husband, telling the children to 'assure him that my forgiveness will never cease and that my prayers for him will be unceasing'. She was clearly finding comfort in her faith: 'All I can do is to accept the inevitable and trust Daddy to God's mercy which never fails us when we turn to him . . . I pray that peace and forgiveness may be granted to him and that his soul may yet find peace and solace – if not in this world, in the world beyond . . . Out of it let us rise in Newness of Life and may it yet be used for good in helping others.'

If Lady Beauchamp expected her children to be softened by her appeal, she was badly mistaken. No sympathy was forthcoming. As for her brother, his last word on the affair took the form of a curt letter to the exiled earl: 'Dear Bugger-in-law, You got what you deserved, Yours, Westminster.'

In June 1931, shortly after her father's departure, Lady Dorothy Lygon, aged nineteen, took up her pen to write to 'Mr Gossip' of the *Daily Sketch*, aka her friend Patrick Balfour (who relied on such missives for his copy). She bewailed the lack of juicy gossip: 'What meagre news there is in our great metropolis this summer.' There was talk of a Castlerosse divorce, she noted, but that had come to nothing. There were reports of dreary virgins' or debutantes' parties, dull charity balls, rumours of love affairs, new restaurants opening ('Douglas Byng is singing at a new restaurant called the Monseigneur, damnably hot and stuffy, crowded too, but his songs are good'). And the other latest trendy eating establishment, the Malmaison: 'not too good, but I'm told it's cheap'.

As for the Lygon news, well, all was quiet too. She and Maimie had just returned from a visit to Hugh in Tilshead, where he had set himself up as a racehorse trainer. They were off to a society dance in the evening. 'Sibell has a new job earning £2.10s at my Aunt Violet Cripp's hair shop in Bond Street and has hair, face and nails done free as well. She only started yesterday, so is quite a novice as yet. Letty and Richard continue to be very happily married. Elmley is The Complete Politician, and there we all are – Hughie is also very well and probably better than usual, since my evening paper tells me that he has trained 2 winners this afternoon.'

Coote joked about how boring her news was: 'This letter is reading like a country Cousin's Guide to London.' The hidden agenda of this newsy letter, with its protestations of happiness amongst her siblings, was to dispel the rumours. She told Mr Gossip that her father was in Germany taking the health cure for his heart, nothing more: 'Halkers [Halkyn House, the Belgrave Square residence] has been shut up since Boom went abroad – poor man, his heart wasn't at all too good, but I am afraid he will be horribly bored at Nauheim, especially as he is on a diet!'

When he received this letter Patrick Balfour happened to be in the south of France, with Evelyn Waugh. They had arrived in Villefranche on 9 June, and met up with Evelyn's brother Alec. Mr Gossip was to become one of Alec's closest friends, but at the time the older Waugh brother was wary of him: 'Gossip Writers had a dubious reputation in the days of the "Bright Young People",' he recollected.

One morning, Alec came down to breakfast to find Evelyn and Balfour discussing over coffee a report in the *Continental Daily Mail*. A divorce suit was being brought against one of the richest and most prominent peers of the realm, a man in his sixties, who had been very active in political and public life. 'So the story has broken,' Evelyn said.

It is clear, then, that Balfour knew all about the scandal and so did Evelyn. His first concern was for his friend Hugh.

Alec Waugh's book about 1931, *A Year to Remember*, gives a detailed account of the scandal and its impact on his brother. He explicitly states that the events of that summer inspired *Brideshead Revisited*. Refusing to name the peer, even in 1975, the year of the memoir's publication, Alec decided to call him Lord Marchmain:

> In real life Lady Marchmain was the sister of a prominent Duke, and the case was being brought because of a quarrel between her husband and her brother, at her brother's instigation. A groom for whom Marchmain had formed an attachment many years before was to be cited. The case was never brought because the King inter-

vened. He could not allow a man who had been his own representative to be exposed to scandal. But the case was only dropped on the condition that Marchmain left the country.

Of Hugh, also not named, he writes: 'His younger son was very good looking, very charming. He was also a very heavy drinker.' Alec remembered that the wealthy and distinguished bisexual expatriate writer Somerset Maugham, who knew the family well, made the connection between Hugh Lygon and Sebastian Flyte in New York in 1945: 'We all know, of course, who Sebastian was. A charming boy. He drank himself to death.' Hugh had stayed with Maugham in the south of France.

Before recounting the story of the Beauchamp affair, Alec Waugh told of another encounter that took place in the summer of 1931. It involved W. Somerset Maugham and a young playwright called Keith Winter, who was a friend of Evelyn's and Balfour's. Winter was taken to the Villa Mauresque, where Maugham resided. Various other guests came and went, but Winter spent the night with Willie Maugham, teaching him a new sexual trick with his fingertips. Maugham was reminded of the boys he had enjoyed in Bangkok. Winter hoped to be taken up as Maugham's new paramour, but Maugham dropped him unceremoniously. And the moral of the story? Winter (also unnamed in Alec's memoir) went on to become a well-known writer, married with three children, a presenter for the BBC, a member of the Savile Club, a lecturer in American universities. Alec Waugh's message is clear: promiscuous homosexuality is not in itself an impediment to success in life. As with Alec's own disgrace at Sherborne, it was the discovery and not the act that did the damage. Boom's big mistake was to get busted.

CHAPTER 10

Madresfield Visited

1931 was a year that marked the end of one epoch and the beginning of another – the watershed of the modern world. It was the banking crisis of that year, more than the Wall Street crash of '29, which ushered in the Great Depression. The frivolous age of the Bright Young Things had come to a sudden end.

Evelyn was also in a period of transition. He was a recent convert to Catholicism; he had divorced his wife; he was feted as one of the most brilliant young novelists of his age. But he had no fixed abode. 1931 was the year when he would meet and befriend the Lygon girls, whose friendship would endure for the rest of his life. He became part of the family, making their ancestral home in Malvern the nearest place to a home at a time when he owned 'no possessions which could not conveniently go on a porter's barrow'. Their story would inspire the book that was in his words his 'magnum opus' or, in Nancy Mitford's, his 'Great English Classic': *Brideshead Revisited.*

He returned from his five months in Africa as a special correspondent for the *Graphic* magazine. Eventually, he would get two books out of his experiences there, a comic novel *Black Mischief* and a work of witty reportage, *Remote People,* which covered the coronation of Emperor Haile Selassie. For much of the year, he continued to drift between the houses of different friends. When he stayed with his brother Alec in the south of France and read the news of the Beauchamp affair, he did not know that his life would become so closely entwined with the Lygons. In 1959, acknowledging a friendship that had endured for three decades, Evelyn wrote to Maimie Lygon: 'I think it is just 38 years no damn it I mean 28 since I first came to stay in the hotel at Malvern and met you and your pretty sisters.'

It was Baby Jungman who brought Evelyn to the Lygon sisters. He took up her recommendation to enrol at Captain Hance's Riding Academy in Great Malvern. It was the autumn of 1931. Baby, an accomplished rider, had been at the academy recently, along with her friend Mary Milnes Gaskell. Both were friends of the Lygon sisters. Whilst at the academy they had stayed at Madresfield. Evelyn wrote to Baby there, sending his love to Hugh and Elmley, his old Oxford chums. He knew the crisis that had befallen the family, but he did not yet know the sisters. Nor had he seen the magnificent family seat.

Evelyn met Maimie at a party given by Baby Jungman's mother. Hearing that Evelyn was about to start riding lessons in Malvern, Maimie offered him a lift down to Worcestershire in the family's chauffeur-driven limousine, an American Packard. In the event, Evelyn took the Great Western Railway to Malvern Link. In future years he would travel to Worcester on a quicker train, where Maimie would pick him up in the car and drive him back to Madresfield: the experience of being a passenger driven up to a stately home by a beautiful flapper girl would be recreated in *Brideshead*.

On this first visit to Malvern he booked himself rooms at the County Hotel, a vast building adjoining the spa. It was a stone's throw from the Riding Academy in Church Street and close to the cinema – filmgoing was still a favourite pastime for Evelyn.

Baby Jungman's friendship with the Lygons helped to ease Evelyn's passage into this new environment. Maimie and her younger sister Coote introduced him to the ferocious Captain Hance. Evelyn wrote to Baby to tell her how grateful he was that the girls had helped to break the ice with Hance, who was devoted to the Lygon family. Evelyn and Captain John Hance got along well, despite Hance's formidable reputation. Hance had spent eleven years as an army riding-instructor. He swore profusely and could reduce hardened cavalrymen to jelly with his barbs. Famously he had shouted at one unfortunate horseman: 'You're not a cadet. You're an old Piccadilly prostitute on a night commode!'

Hance had set up the very first residential riding school in Malvern.

He ran it with his wife 'Mims', his son Reggie and his daughter Jackie, teaching men and women from all over the country, steeplechasers and competition showjumpers, as well as those who wanted to improve their hunting skills. Several of their pupils went on to win at Aintree, the toughest jumping racecourse in the land.

At the time Evelyn attended the school, Hance was at work on a book called *School for Horse and Rider*, in which he argued that the problem with the British civilian attitude to riding was that after a course of ten or a dozen lessons people would be left simply '*to pick up* the rest by haphazard experimentation upon a horse'. His book is a passionate manifesto for a newly rigorous and systematic equestrian education. He explained that the minimum period of enrolment in his school was a week, with lessons from 9.30 to 11.30 and 2.30 to 4 in the afternoon, followed by a lecture at 5.30. Every aspect of horsemanship was covered, with particular emphasis on correct posture and good jumping technique. The book is full of illustrations with such captions as 'A good jump over a blind and hairy place', 'A very common sight – the rider's leg drawn too far back', and 'A correct half-passage side-saddle without the help of the leg on the off-side. Note delicate handling of the reins.' Though he did not say so in the book, he was a hard taskmaster who would throw horse manure at people who could not get their technique correct.

Evelyn joked to his friends that he had taken up riding as a means of social advancement, but this was not strictly true – he had begun to take riding lessons when he was in North Wales, far from high society. Of course it was the case that invitations to big houses in the country carried the expectation, even the obligation, of a ride to hounds, but the real reason for his enrolment at Captain Hance's was that it was Baby Jungman's suggestion. Improving his riding was a way to be close to her.

Despite his determination, he never became proficient. His passion only lasted a couple of years, though he later hunted with the Lygons, despite frequent falls. Coote – like all her siblings, a superb rider – laughingly described Evelyn as one of the worst riders she had ever seen, but she said that he and Captain Hance developed mutual admiration for each other's very different capacities.

The Lygon girls took immediately to Baby's writer friend. They insisted on his coming to dine at Madresfield. Maimie picked him up after Captain

Hance's lecture and he found himself being driven up to the great house.

Evelyn had by this time been a house guest in several stately homes. English country houses were becoming a passion, their demise a theme of his novels. Like many, he saw them as a symbol of England. At the same time, his affection for the stability of the country house was connected to his own rootlessness.

Madresfield was special because it had been home to the same family for eight centuries. Like the mythical Brideshead, the real Madresfield had been remodelled several times. Parts were Jacobean, but there had been a major renovation in the style of Victorian Gothic.

Madresfield is a red-brick, moated manor house with yellow stone facings around the doors and windows. On sunny days one could see the golden carp and the blue flash of a kingfisher in the moat, which is twenty feet wide. (Charles Ryder compares Julia Flyte to a kingfisher.) On autumn days such as those when Evelyn first saw the place, a mist would rise out of the moat. The surrounding parkland was once royal hunting country. The house is set in 4,000 acres and has 136 rooms, many of them immense, some tiny.

Four separate avenues of oaks, cedars, poplars and cypresses lead up to the house. There is an enclosed lawn with a succession of statues of Roman emperors. The grounds boast a rock garden, a yew maze said to be better than that at Hampton Court, a wonderful variety of trees and flowering shrubs. In the topiary garden there is a bronze sundial which has carved on it: 'That day is wasted on which we have not laughed.' Evelyn and the girls made that motto their own.

This was the house that was the nearest place to home for Evelyn during these nomadic years. Despite its vast size, it feels homely and inviting, but it is nevertheless a million miles away from Underhill. For Evelyn, it was like entering an enchanted world. A door leading from the hall opened into the library, one from the library led up to the chapel, another to the long gallery and a side door to the minstrels' gallery above the old Tudor dining room. Room upon room was filled with treasures, old masters, fine porcelain, antiques, objets d'art. In *Brideshead*, with all the careless ease of the aristocrat, Sebastian says to Charles, who is fascinated by the house and its treasures, that there are a 'few pretty things I'd like to show you one day'.

The hybrid of Tudor and Victorian features appealed to Evelyn, who was a great apologist for the Gothic Revival. The house had its major reconstruction in the 1860s, but Evelyn would have been told by the girls that the most remarkable renovations and improvements were entirely new, undertaken by their father. A leading patron of the Arts and Crafts movement, he had imprinted his taste on every detail from the decoration of the chapel and the library to the many artefacts, lamps, tiles, wall-hangings, window panes, William Morris fabrics, doorplates and carvings that had been introduced. His hand and eye were everywhere in the house that he loved and from which he had just been exiled.

When one sees Madresfield today, the Arts and Crafts style merges seamlessly into the hybridity of the house, yet at the time when Evelyn Waugh saw it, it was contemporary, fresh and cutting edge. It shows Lord Beauchamp as a pioneer.

He and his wife had commissioned C. R. Ashbee to decorate the library. Ashbee's decorations were original and unique: among his materials were silver-wire, hammered metal, coloured stones and enamel from his guild workshop. His designs ranged from architecture to furniture to jewellery. In 1902, he moved his workshops to Chipping Campden, hoping to create an Arts and Crafts paradise for skilled labourers in the beautiful Cotswold town. This placed him in close proximity to Worcestershire, the county dominated by the Beauchamps.

Between 1902 and 1905 Ashbee designed carvings for the four doors of the library and two large bookcase ends. The latter show the Tree of Knowledge and the Tree of Life, forming the centre of a series of images depicting the many paths to learning and wisdom – the scholar, the doctor, the musician, the reaping farmer. At the very bottom of one of the stack ends is a little boy filching a volume, a jokey allusion to the proverb carved above, 'Thou shalt not steal'. The design, finished by means of intricate pewter doorplates, played simultaneously to Beauchamp's aestheticism and his wife's piety.

Above the flight of stone stairs to the chapel is a slightly later addition, a stained-glass window executed by the artist Henry Payne to a design by Beauchamp. It is an illustration of the story in St Matthew's Gospel of the Roman centurion who begged Christ to heal his servant. The centurion is kneeling at the feet of Christ, in his hand a huge sword. In the left-hand corner of the window is a woman lying on her deathbed whilst a young boy, in tears, is being comforted by his elder sister. The face of the kneeling centurion is Beauchamp's own, the sword an allusion to the Sword of State which he bore at the coronation of George V in 1911 (it was shortly after this that the window was designed). The scene behind him replays the death of his mother, his own grief at her death and his sister's support. At the top of the window there is a grass enclosure with five lambs, representing his children. The face of the Christ resembles that of the earl's late father.

The figure with the face of the earl himself is sometimes described as that of a sinner seeking forgiveness, but this is to miss the point. In the Gospel story the centurion is not a sinner, he is a master asking for his beloved servant to be healed – the earl always cared for his servants, one way or another. Matthew's purpose is to illustrate that the high-ranking Roman centurion has extraordinary faith despite being a pagan. He says to Jesus: 'Lord, I am not worthy to have you enter under my roof; only say the word, and my servant will be healed.' Jesus's reply is 'in no one in Israel have I found such faith'; he heals the servant. There is an underground theological tradition of reading this story as Jesus's endorsement of a homosexual relationship. Historically, it was certainly the case that many Roman masters had sexual relations with their male servants. Whether or not this thought occurred to Lord Beauchamp, there was clearly a complex set of emotions at work in his design of the window – guilt, sorrow, love and faith, but perhaps also desires recognisable to only a few.

Close to the stained-glass window is a little door that opens into the chapel. It was originally two bedrooms known as the King's Rooms, where Charles II was supposed to have stayed during the Battle of Worcester. The chapel was built as part of the 1865 redesign in the days when there was a resident chaplain taking services for the household every morning and evening. But the extraordinary feature is the Edwardian Arts and Crafts decoration. It was commissioned in 1902 as a wedding present from Lady Beauchamp to her husband. Beauchamp took a deep interest in every aspect of the design. The paintwork, stained glass and metalwork were designed and made by the Birmingham Group, the altar cross an elaborate creation of Arts and Crafts metalwork, decorated with *champlevé* enamel. Everything is of a piece, from candlesticks to sanctuary lamps to gold-embroidered altar frontal.

Most startling of all are the wall frescoes, which feature the Lygon children amongst a profusion of delicate flowers, all of which could be found in the gardens of Madresfield. There are also lifesize portraits of the earl and countess, fully robed and kneeling in prayer on either side of the altar, below angels and the figure of Christ. The countess is in her bridal gown and veil, the earl in his Garter robes. The frescoes took so long to complete that by the time the chapel was finished all seven of Beauchamp's children were included. They are represented as beautiful blond cherubic children picking flowers at the feet of an angel. The angels wear printed cotton smocks – the quintessential Arts and Crafts fabric. The whole effect is of a kaleidoscope of colour.

In *Brideshead* Sebastian insists on showing his family chapel to Charles, mockingly describing it as a 'monument of *art nouveau*'. Waugh's prose takes flight:

> The whole interior had been gutted, elaborately refurnished and redecorated in the Arts-and-Crafts style of the last decade of the nineteenth century. Angels in printed cotton smocks, rambler-roses, flower-spangled meadows, frisking lambs, texts in Celtic script, saints in armour, covered the walls in an intricate pattern of clear, bright colours. There was a triptych of pale oak, carved so as to give it the peculiar property of seeming to have been moulded in plasticine. The sanctuary lamp and all the metal furniture were of bronze, hand-beaten to the patina of a pockmarked skin; the altar steps had a carpet of grass-green, strewn with white and gold daisies.
>
> 'Golly,' I said.
>
> 'It was Papa's wedding present to Mamma. Now, if you've seen enough, we'll go.'

Evelyn changes the gold triptych to pale oak and the sanctuary lamp and metal furniture to bronze, but otherwise there is no mistaking the Madresfield chapel.

'Golly' is an appropriately ambiguous reaction. Charles is distinctly underwhelmed by the art nouveau chapel: 'I think it's a remarkable example of its period. Probably in eighty years it will be greatly admired . . . I don't happen to like it much.' Evelyn's first impression of the real thing was also far from the usual one of unqualified admiration. He wrote to Baby Jungman: 'I thought the Boom chapel at Madresfield the saddest thing I ever saw.' This may be partly because he sensed that its style did not suit Baby's Catholic sensibility, but the reaction was also shaped by the knowledge that the family represented as the picture of perfection had been fractured beyond repair.

The third room that Beauchamp dramatically remodelled was the Staircase Hall: a vast room that had been created out of three smaller rooms and made in part to house the enormous Italian pink marble fireplace that was an ostentatious wedding present from the Duke of Westminster to his sister. On either side stand tall freestanding Venetian lanterns collected by the earl and countess on one of their many trips to Venice, their favourite Italian city. When Evelyn saw the room, it had two enormous art nouveau hanging lamps. Carved into the cornice circling the room is a quotation from Shelley's elegy on the death of Keats, *Adonais*, 'Shadows fly: Life like a dome of many coloured glass stains the white radiance of eternity until death tramples it to fragments. The one remains, the many change and pass: Heaven's light for ever shines.' This was a text that could be read differently according to disposition: the pious countess took comfort in the eternal light of Heaven, while the earl could contemplate the beauty and transience of the youthful male form embodied by the fragile figures of Keats and Shelley.

Ancestral portraits still line the walls of Madresfield. Those of Lord Beauchamp are among the most impressive. A half-length painting of him as a young man on his coming of age is flanked by portraits of Hugh and Elmley. There is a delicate pencil sketch of Maimie by Harold Acton's brother, who drew similar sketches of the six Mitford sisters. Another fine portrait shows Beauchamp in his Garter robes, bedecked with medals, leaning on his sword and holding a plumed helmet like a young god.

The many portraits of his children show him as he was: a devoted father, the proud head of a large and beautiful family. At the top of the staircase is the huge William Ranken family portrait celebrating the occasion of Elmley's twenty-first. The earl and his heir are very formally dressed in dark tailcoats; Hugh is impeccable in a white linen suit, the girls in flowing white dresses. The painting was executed in the newly finished Staircase Hall. The men are standing in front of the pink marble fireplace and in the background one can see the extraordinary crystal staircase, the fine paintings, the bust of the countess that guarded one side of the door. There was a matching bust of the earl opposite it. Before long, the bust of the countess would be thrown into the moat as a mark of what the children regarded as her betrayal of the family. Years later, it would be fished out and restored.

The dining room where Evelyn first ate with the Lygon girls was dominated by a hammer beam roof and a minstrels' gallery (from which the local choir would sing at Christmas). He described it exactly in *A Handful of Dust*.

Madresfield was a community as well as a building. Like any stately home, it depended on an army of servants to make it run smoothly. Bradford, the beautiful butler, was adored by the family. There was a kindly spinster called Miss Jagger, a permanent house guest always happy to run errands. A dull and ineffectual governess taught the girls and the place swarmed with under servants – six housemaids, a cook, a kitchen maid, a scullery maid, twenty-four gardeners. The footmen were smart and formally dressed. They wore morning suits in the morning and at dinner tails and waistcoats in the Beauchamp colours of maroon and cream. Bradford the butler was resplendent in his snowy waistcoat, with a gold watch chain.

A servant called Rose Nash, who started work at Madresfield during the years when Evelyn became a regular visitor, recalled that all the housemaids used a contraption called 'the Donkey' to clean the staircase and front hall. It was a flat piece of iron with a broom handle. They would put old blankets (or a servant's old fleecy-lined knickers) underneath it to polish the floors. The homemade polish was a mix of beeswax and turpentine. Clouds of dust would fly from the Donkey, causing bronchial coughs. There was always work to be done: carrying hot water in cans to the bedrooms, emptying the ashtrays in the Drawing Room. But at least there was never a shortage of food in the Servants' Hall.

Just as Lord Beauchamp was exiled from his ancestral seat, so Evelyn was given the chance to find his spiritual home. He was falling in love with a house, but also – once more – with a family.

CHAPTER 11

The Beauchamp Belles

God, what a family.
(Evelyn Waugh)

'Mad', as they called Madresfield Court, was a topsy-turvy Alice in Wonderland world. Fun and fantasy reigned, though always with an undertow of sorrow. Over the next few months, as Evelyn grew increasingly close to the three girls, he would discover the intimate details of their beloved father's downfall, still raw and painful for the children.

His imagination was fired by this charming family, just as he had been entranced by Diana Guinness's tales of her and her sisters' eccentric childhood in rural Gloucestershire. That household had been dominated by the large and colourful personality of Lord Redesdale, the patriarch of the Mitford family, who tried unsuccessfully to tame his brood of wild, unconventional girls. The household that Evelyn stumbled upon in 1931 was without parental guardian: the mistress had absconded and the master had been forced out.

The Lygon sisters, known in society circles as 'the Beauchamp Belles', had the house to themselves. Sibell was twenty-four, Maimie twenty-one and Coote nineteen. Lettice had left home and married shortly before Lord Beauchamp left on his world tour. Elmley, the man who once dressed in a purple velvet suit and acted as president of the wild Hypocrites' Club, was now a dull and rather pompous MP, living mainly in London and in his Norfolk constituency. Hugh drifted in and out intermittently. Dickie, the youngest, was at school or with his mother in Cheshire.

Evelyn had not forgotten Hugh Lygon, who had done so much to shape his taste for aristocratic manner and almost pathological insistence on being charming and amusing. Hugh and Evelyn's lives had diverged, but their friendship was still strong. Hugh was increasingly dependent on alcohol, his career was going nowhere and his life was spiralling out of control. He was suffering from what his sisters called 'second son syndrome'.

Evelyn now saw at first hand the legendary girls whose antics had inspired one of his most celebrated scenes in *Vile Bodies*, the gate-crashing debacle of 10 Downing Street. The girls invited their friends to stay for house parties and weekends, as in the old days, but without the forbidding presence of their pious mother they were free to invite undesirables such as Evelyn. A middle-class Roman Catholic would not have been allowed to darken Her Ladyship's door.

Evelyn was pressed to dine every night and the girls, especially Maimie and Coote, liked him from the start. They shared his outrageous sense of humour. Sibell, the difficult sister – known by a close friend as a 'sacred monster whose mind works like magic' – was more tricky. Coote described her as 'a stormy petrel – and a great wielder of the wooden spoon: if mischief was going to be made, she made it'. One of her cousins confessed to two great hatreds in her life: Sibell and custard.

Sibell was very tall, over six foot. She towered over the diminutive Evelyn. She wrote a gossip column called 'Hectic Days' for *Harper's Bazaar* and was embroiled in her on-off affair with the equally diminutive but extremely powerful Lord Beaverbrook. She was often in London, leaving the two younger sisters alone at Mad with Miss Jagger and the servants to keep an eye on them.

Evelyn was captivated by the Beauchamp Belles. Seven years older than Maimie and nine years older than Coote, he became like an older brother. The girls had been forced to grow up fast in the wake of their mother's departure and their father's disgrace. On the surface they seemed to have everything: beauty, grace, elegance and the ease of the aristocrat. They had their own private incomes and long gone were the days when they were dressed in threadbare clothes. They ordered their dresses from Norman Hartnell, designer to Queen Mary, rode around in the chauffeured Packard (or, in Maimie's case, drove it herself), dined lavishly and moved freely between their London home and their ancestral pile. Like their brother Hugh, they gave themselves no airs, and delighted in clever, stimulating conversation. Sibell remembered that they all liked Evelyn instantly because 'he had our sense of humour'.

Evelyn's favourite was blonde Maimie – he was always drawn to blondes. She was a female version of beautiful Hugh, with a face of classical proportions. Her beauty was such that, allegedly, when she walked into a ballroom the band would stop playing to gaze at her. Tall, with blue eyes, she had her hair fashionably bobbed and her lips painted red. Photographs show her dressed in furs and cloche hat, carrying her ferocious one-eyed Pekingese, Grainger.* She was the epitome of glamour. She had a sensuous mouth, flawless skin and was always laughing.

Just as they refused to condemn their father for his unorthodox behaviour, so they had no qualms about brother Hugh's homosexuality. They themselves were often drawn to bisexual men. Though their outlook was unusually liberal-minded in this regard, in other respects they were typical of their class: subservient to their brothers (whom they adored) and waiting for marriage to transform their lives. 'To be married, soon and splendidly, was the aim of all her friends,' writes Waugh of his heroine Julia Flyte. But, like Julia, the Lygon girls were tainted and there were no respectable offers of marriage coming their way. Big sister Lettice was lucky to have got married before the scandal broke.

To outsiders, however, they lived a charmed life. When Elmley's wife first met the sisters she was amazed by the sense of privilege and largesse. She noticed, somewhat bitterly, that they were 'financed by their father in a big way'. Each had her own bank account and an open travel account at American Express. They could spend more or less what money they liked. Many people were surprised that Mad was kept open for them, their friends and their parties. The expected state of affairs in the circumstances would have been for white sheets to be thrown over the furniture and the big house closed up until the parental difficulties had been resolved.

Maimie and her sisters were shunned in certain areas of society, though

* Named after Mr Grainger, the Warden of Walmer Castle during Maimie's childhood.

they still made regular appearances in the Court Circular, attending balls, weddings and charity events. Sebastian Flyte describes his family as 'social lepers'. If that was what the Lygons were, then as far as Evelyn was concerned Mad was the world's loveliest leper colony. He adored Maimie and was the most faithful of her friends. She was another of the beautiful, aristocratic and cultivated female friends that were so important to him but whom he did not – would never have dared to – pursue sexually. In his biography of the Catholic theologian Ronald Knox, Evelyn reveals much about his own character. He thought that among the keys to Knox's character were the deep friendships he made at Oxford and his special capacity for friendship with women. The Lygons provided Evelyn with these two kinds of friendship in a single family. When he writes of Knox, 'he found among women most of the happiest friendships of his middle and later life', he might as well have been writing of himself. Ever since his boyhood days basking in the love of his mother and nanny, he had always felt safe and happy with women. But of the very wide circle of female friends who adored him, he valued above all the friendship of the Lygons. Because of his strong protective instincts, and his attraction to beauty and vulnerability, he counted them first among equals.

Maimie's wild side appealed to Evelyn. She was unrestrained, known as the sister who danced on the tables in the local pub. Like Hugh, she loved to drink – an important qualification for any friendship with Evelyn. Coote always maintained that Evelyn was closest 'first to Maimie, then myself'. Maimie's vitality drew him like a magnetic force and Coote was happy to be pulled along behind. Coote was the only plain-looking child in the family. She had round, full cheeks and thick glasses. She was tall and ungainly with large feet. It must have been extremely difficult to be the ugly duckling in a family of swans. But she had a caring and sweet nature. She was also intelligent and a great reader.

Once Evelyn had found his way to Mad, he renewed his Oxford friendship with Hugh. Elmley was a different kettle of fish. He wasn't often there, and when he was he seemed, in Coote's words, a forbidding character, difficult to get on with: 'Shy, serious'.

Life at Mad was an odd mixture of the formal and the unrestrained. With only Miss Jagger and the hapless governess Miss Bryan as chaperones, the girls led a wild life. From abroad, Lord Beauchamp issued orders concerning the upkeep of his home. Madresfield had long been known for its lavish hospitality (Hugh's parents once entertained 2,366 visitors in the course of a single month). But now the socialising was on the children's terms. Hunting, of course, was essential. The young people threw dinners, drank copious amounts of champagne and frequented the local pubs, the Forester's Arms at Barnards Green and the Hornyold Arms Hotel in Malvern Wells.

The Forester's Arms was owned and run by a great friend of the Lygons, a man called Wally Weston. He had lost a leg while serving in the First World War. For two days and nights he lay unnoticed in the mud of the Dardanelles, shot through the thigh and the knee. He was only nineteen at the time. Taken to Liverpool, he had his leg amputated and a prosthetic, cork one fitted. He worked on the railways before becoming a landlord.

Wally was something of a local hero. He trained boxers and wore a Stetson. One of his most famous pupils was Jack Hood, the British middleweight champion of the day. A local girl remembers seeing Wally 'running like a stag' as she walked to school: 'With his walking stick, he would hop and run, hop and run, with the boxers, all the way down Guarlford Road.' Wally also trained Hugh Lygon, who was an excellent boxer. He became one of Hugh's great friends. Wally kept a gymnasium at the back of the pub, where he would train and give massages to Hugh and his friends. Mad itself also had a training gym.

Another local girl, Mary Wells, recalled that Wally often entertained the Lygons in the special back room of his pub. When she was twelve years old Wally encouraged her to go into the back room and meet the family from the big house. There the young ladies would be sipping drinks. They would let little Mary sit on their laps. Robert Bartleet, the vicar's son from Malvern Priory, a hearty beer-drinker, was another great favourite of the Lygons, whom Evelyn would come to know well. When Evelyn was away from Mad, he would crave news of Bartleet and Wally Weston. He found another source of amusement in the dashing Master of the Hounds, Tommy MacDougal, whom Evelyn affected to believe was illiterate.

Also at Malvern at this time was the Tory leader's son, Arthur 'Bloggs' Baldwin. The Baldwins were neighbours of the Lygons and had been one of the very few families of high standing who had supported Lord Beauchamp. Most people in society had taken the Duke of Westminster's side, and the duke made it very clear that one was expected to take sides.

Lord Beauchamp lost all but a very few of his most loyal friends. The Prime Minister, Stanley Baldwin, was one of them.

One of the reasons for the Baldwins' support was their own family experience. Their eldest son, Oliver, lived happily with his male lover for over thirty years, and was completely accepted by his family. Lady Baldwin once wrote to his partner Johnny Boyle, to whom she was devoted: 'Thank you for loving my Oliver.' Her view contrasted sharply with that of her husband's cousin, Rudyard Kipling, who found homosexuality repulsive.

Arthur Baldwin, a second son like Hugh, was also in love with Baby Jungman, though with his round face and ginger whiskers she did not find him very attractive. Coote Lygon remembered that a great friendship arose out of the hopeless rivalry between Arthur and Evelyn. Being in the company of Baldwin and the Lygons allowed Evelyn to indulge his feelings for Baby and to discuss her endlessly.

If Evelyn's friendly rivalry with Arthur Baldwin was one source of constant amusement, another was the banter that centred upon the riding academy. According to Coote, Evelyn transposed Captain Hance and his family to an 'Olympian level': 'he invented lives for them which, like the gods in ancient Greece, were still linked with the mortals below; their least pronouncement was debated and scrutinised for omens and auguries. The Captain's name was always succeeded by the initials GBH – which stood for God Bless Him, and his health was frequently drunk.' When Maimie and Coote left Mad to go to Norfolk to campaign on behalf of their brother in the October 1931 general election campaign, Evelyn wrote to say that Malvern was not the same without them. 'I miss you both very much at school and in play time.'

The Madresfield set invented nicknames for one another. Maimie was 'Blondy', Coote was 'Poll' or 'Pollen', Baldwin was 'Frisky', Evelyn was 'Boaz' or 'Bo' – a Masonic soubriquet* purportedly intended to annoy Elmley who had joined the Freemasons, something of which Evelyn, as a Catholic, disapproved. Baby Jungman was 'The Dutch girl', on account of her family origins.

* 'Boaz' was the name for the secret handshake of an Entered Apprentice in the Freemasons. By adopting it, Evelyn and the girls were implicitly forming their own secret bond of friendship. It is probably also relevant that the original biblical Boaz was a man who befriended the good-hearted women Naomi and Ruth at a time of family trouble (in the Old Testament Book of Ruth).

Because Baby was so impossible to woo, the word 'dutch' was used to indicate something awkward or difficult. Thus in the manner of a secret society, they invented their own language. A 'jagger' meant someone or something kindly and helpful, in honour of spinsterly Miss Jagger. An Anglican priest was a 'lascivious beast'. To 'laycock' was to chuck at the last minute (this was in honour of Robert Laycock, a family friend who had been best man at Lettice's wedding). To bagpipe someone was to have sex with them, and so on. In his biography of Ronald Knox, Evelyn suggested that 'the accumulation of common experiences, private jokes and private language . . . lies at the foundation of English friendship'. Such things were certainly the foundation of his world at Mad.

My brother drank, you know.
(Lady Sibell Lygon)

Evelyn was being drawn into the life and world of the glamorous Lygon sisters. But what about his old Oxford love? What had happened to the 'lascivious Mr Lygon', the beautiful young man with whom he had been besotted, imploring Tom Driberg 'if you come across Hugh . . . or anyone else I love give them a kiss from me'?

Hugh had become an assistant trainer in the stable of Edgar Wallace on Salisbury Plain in Wiltshire. For a time, he had a little house in the local village of Tilshead, a pretty hamlet of flint houses. He seemed happy and settled. He had his first success when a horse called Evaporate that he had trained became a winner in 1931. But all Hugh's brief successes had a way of evaporating. That was the summer when the family tragedy erupted, and it was sensitive Hugh who took it worst. He was the one who talked his father out of suicide and accompanied him to Germany.

If habitual lateness was one of Hugh's faults (he was even late for his own funeral), another was his reluctance to put pen to paper. The lack of letters makes it very hard to recover his voice, in contrast to those of his sisters, which come across so vividly in their correspondence with Evelyn Waugh.

Letters were to take on increasing significance following Lord Beauchamp's expulsion; they were his lifeline, and he rarely lost the opportunity to impress upon his children their importance. He was forced to write to the others to ask for specific news of Hugh, who did not remain in Germany for long. Shortly after Hugh returned to England in June 1931 Boom wrote to Coote from Berlin desperate for news of him: 'How is Hugh? He will be the centre of fashion again when the manoeuvres begin. I want to see a photo of the new bowler hats.' Poignantly, Boom also refers in this letter to his youngest son, who was only fourteen and away at boarding school: 'Do you think there would be an awful row if I sent Dickie a snapshot of me? I don't suppose he has a photo. Does he ever write to you? Poor darling! How he would love to come to the Show!' He was referring to the Madresfield Agricultural Show that always took place in August and that was one of the high points of the Lygon year. It is recreated in a charming scene in *Brideshead* when Cordelia first meets Charles Ryder.

He later wrote from Berlin that he was enjoying the museums, especially the Botticellis and the Greek sculpture. Ever the cultivated tourist, he wrote ruefully that he was lost without a Baedeker (there wasn't one for Berlin). And still the concerned politician, he also noticed the poverty and how 'the lower classes' had to put up with a very poor standard of living.

By the end of August, Beauchamp was in Paris, having set himself up in an apartment near the Place de l'Étoile: 'after an agitated time with much voluble conversation, here I am settled in to the flat – with a very nice spare room'. He was thinking about the children and the possibility of their visiting him. He described smoking his first cigar and taking dancing lessons. 'Altogether, you won't know me!' The strikes in England depressed him: 'On the whole Japan and Java may be better places to live than in England during the next few months.' Coote made plans to visit him in Paris, but by October he had set sail for the Far East and Australia. She always remained a superb correspondent. Her father relied on her to pass on messages to Hugh, always imploring him to write, which he never did.

Hugh's poor letter-writing habits were to have disastrous consequences, especially when he failed to keep his father informed about his pressing financial difficulties. Towards the end of October 1931, Hugh was at Madresfield. He too planned to leave for Paris. Lady Sibell was with him, but the younger sisters had left Malvern to canvass for Elmley in Norfolk. The general election would see a huge victory for the 'National Government', with the result that Stanley Baldwin would once again become the most powerful man in the land.

Evelyn and Frisky Baldwin promised to write to the sisters and keep them informed about all the Malvern news. Frisky dutifully wrote to Coote, gossiping about staff squabbles. The governess Peglar, who had taken over from the hapless Miss Bryan, had been causing trouble and 'stirred up a false mutiny among Bradford the Butler and his peers'. 'I find myself saturated with a nauseating pity for the lonely old bleeder,' he wrote, 'sitting in her little cold old room, and feeling that she's gone too far and she can't turn back and that they're all against her.' Speaking of governesses, Frisky joked, if Coote failed to go carefully with money, she might be reduced to earning her own living: 'she didn't want to end up as a governess, peglaring for a living'. It must have seemed unthinkable that one of the daughters of Lord Beauchamp would end up as a governess.

Other bits of gossip from Mad were not so amusing. Frisky reported that there had been trouble between other family members. The night before Hugh was due to leave for Paris had been full of tension and unease. Frisky had argued with headstrong Sibell, who had been repeating confidences, then Hugh had been drowning his sorrows in the time-honoured fashion: 'Hugh was tipsy and drank more and more and more, God it was sad.'

Evelyn had been spending time on his own at the Malvern hotel since Maimie and Coote had departed. He was busy correcting the proofs of *Remote People*, his non-fiction book about his months in Africa. Sometimes, though, Frisky was ordered by Lady Sibell to swing by the County Hotel and pick up Mr Waugh to bring him to Mad for dinner. Sibell later took against Evelyn, but in those early days she was very fond of him and craved his company as much as her other sisters did.

Evelyn's letters to the sisters, sent from the County Hotel that late autumn of 1931, were the beginning of a correspondence that was to last over thirty years until his death. Captain Hance was finishing his book and his daughter Jackie was modelling on horseback for the photographs. Evelyn found the whole business very funny and reported with glee of how a pupil had asked to be photographed being whipped by Captain Hance: 'it is called Masochism and if you ask Elmley and he thinks you are old enough he will explain what that means'.

He joked about his success with Hance, who is 'dead nuts on me'. They would smoke cigars together and talk about politics and art. 'I am well in with that family,' he wrote, adding: 'Give Elmley a rousing cheer from his old Varsity chum.' Elmley would duly be re-elected with a greatly increased majority.

The family he really wanted to be in with was the Lygons. He didn't have to try very hard. He won them over by a combination of self-deprecation and mock insults. They loved a man who was willing to say the unsayable. His jokes often alluded to his inferiority: he had been promised straps to wear on his riding clothes – 'so I am very classy now' – and had been promoted to a better horse. He was also aware that people mocked his decision to learn to ride. He responded by saying that he was doing it for medicinal reasons. As a cure for what? 'Drink.'

In his next letter he joked that his stock had fallen because his horse Tom Tit threw him off and the captain had wrongly assumed that he was an Eton man, and when he found out he wasn't Hance had walked out of the bar where they had been having a drink. His jokes about his social inferiority were just that – jokes, but they were also a way to let the Lygons know that he wouldn't presume too much. In *Black Mischief* there is a character called Viscount Boaz. This is a self-mocking joke, though it may also have been a dig at Elmley and his disapproval of the nickname.

Evelyn continued to write funny letters, joking about back injuries and how Jackie Hance had false teeth because her real ones had been 'rolled out' by a horse when she was fourteen. But, as with Frisky's letters, there was a serious undertone concerning Hugh's increasing dependence on alcohol. Hugh had telephoned Evelyn at the County Hotel and invited him to Madresfield for the evening. Evelyn continued the tale: 'Well I hate to say it but the truth is that Hugh had been at the bottle and he was walking about the house with a red candle saying he thought the lights might go out.' This was alarming behaviour. Evelyn told them that he had stayed to have some brandy with him, but that Hugh became more and more despondent. He was worried about money and had bought many racehorses that he couldn't afford. Eventually they went upstairs and found Sibell, ill and also despondent because she couldn't think of what to say in her gossip column. He ended the letter lightly: 'I think Jackie is in love with me only I often think this about girls and it is hardly ever true so I daresay she isn't.'*

* Waugh's letters to the Lygon sisters are often lacking in punctuation and sometimes idiosyncratic in spelling (all the more so when he was writing while drunk). I have not corrected them in quotations.

One of the most dispiriting aspects of alcoholism is the way in which it reduces adults to irresponsible children who need to be guarded and protected from themselves. The fact that both Frisky and Evelyn reported on Hugh's drunken behaviour to his sisters suggests a degree of complicity. At some level they were in the unenviable position of spying on Hugh. Evelyn would later depict with compelling truthfulness the fictional Lady Marchmain's attempt to have Sebastian spied upon, whilst alcohol is hidden from him.

Hugh's financial worries were certainly contributing to his depression and heavy drinking. It must have been difficult for the sisters to see their sweet-natured brother on such a course of self-destruction, so soon after the collapse of their parents' marriage and their father's humiliation. In later years, they still found it painful to talk about Hugh's alcoholism. The sisters put his troubles down to his being a second son, and the pressures of their father's scandal. But they never uttered any blame, always showing great compassion and tolerance. Hugh's homosexuality was not mentioned in their retrospective accounts, but it undoubtedly contributed to his despair, given what had happened to his father when he was outed.

He did go to France that autumn and meet up with his father. But he did not tell of his own woes either then or later. There were other distractions in Paris, not least that Lady Beauchamp and her brother the Duke of Westminster were continuing to employ private detectives. Beauchamp still cherished hopes of returning to England, but the Grosvenors' opposition was implacable, and it seemed that he would be forced to continue a wanderer for the foreseeable future. He wrote to Coote to tell her that he was also being spied upon: 'The detectives in Paris annoyed me a great deal – when will she relax her hatred of us all? . . . There seems to be no use in coming back if your mother is still implacable.' Lady Beauchamp was clearly angry that the children continued to take her husband's side, even though she was the injured party.

Evelyn went from Malvern to Mary Milnes-Gaskell for the weekend, where he reported that he met Nancy Mitford who 'played cards all night in a dashing way'. This other Mary, Baby Jungman's friend, lived with her brother at nearby Great Tewkesbury and had been in the Riding Academy with Evelyn. Their father had died in September that year, and the house was now owned by her younger brother Charles. It was another fatherless home where Evelyn could play the surrogate brother. By the time he returned to the academy after the weekend, the Lygons had left Madresfield. It was time for him to move on.

In his next letter to the sisters he told them that he would be visiting the family of his Oxford friend Henry Yorke at Forthampton Court, near Tewkesbury. Still in love with Baby, he wrote to Frisky Baldwin: 'I am sorry I made bad blood with Teresa [Baby] but you must know, old boy, that alls fair in love. Anyway I can tell you this that whenever I plot and make bad blood – as I do pretty often I may say – it is always I who lose in the end.'

In early November, *Remote People* ('Remoters' in Lygon parlance) was published to mixed reviews. Evelyn returned to London to be best man at a wedding and then wrote to the Lygons to inform them where he was going next. He pleaded with them to write to him at the Easton Court Hotel, Chagford in Devonshire. The hotel was an extraordinary place discovered by 'Mr Gossip' of the *Daily Sketch*, Patrick Balfour. He had told Alec Waugh about its peculiar charms, and Alec in turn had passed the tip on to Evelyn. Chagford was a writer's paradise, with comfortable rooms, delicious food, lovely gardens, and many miles distance from the temptations and distractions of London. One could even hunt if one wished. It would remain a haven for Evelyn in his wandering years.

Easton Court was run by an American woman, Mrs Cobb, and her partner, Norman Webb (affectionately known as the Cobwebs). They adored Evelyn. This would be the place to which he would retreat during the war to write *Brideshead Revisited*. Evelyn begged the Lygons to write to him in his exile, as he intended to spend all day writing and needed to keep up his spirits. 'At Chagford,' he wrote, 'I pretend to my London chums that I am going to hunt stags but to you who are my intimates and confidantes I don't mind saying that I shall sit all day in my bedroom writing books, articles, short stories, reviews, plays, cinema scenarios etc etc until I have got a lot more money.'

In the usual fantastic style of conversation that characterised his relationship with the Lygons, Evelyn described the Chagford hotel as a 'distributing centre for white slaves or cocaine or something like that. They never give one bills.' Mrs Cobb 'mixes menthol with her cigarettes' and 'we drink rye whisky in her bedroom'. He wrote to the girls that he had been riding and would be out with the hounds in the morning. He was becoming one of them.

But he was worried about Christmas. He had little desire to be at Underhill with his parents, and another festival season with the Guinnesses was out of the question after his estrangement from Diana. So he was delighted when Coote wrote to him at Chagford to invite him to Mad for the festivities.

The Lygon girls were turning their minds to the winter holiday season. Christmas Day had always been a huge event at Madresfield, not least because it was both Lady Beauchamp's birthday and that of her youngest son Dickie. She was very proud that they shared a birthday not only with each other, but also with their Lord in Heaven. For the servants it was a season of extra work, what with house parties and long hours of darkness necessitating the household's huge consumption of candles (the wax that dropped from the chandeliers had to be scraped laboriously from the polished floors). But for the girls, Christmas 1931 was going to be very difficult. With their mother in Cheshire and their father abroad, none of the old family traditions could be maintained. They decided to invite their new friend and confidant to join them. Evelyn was thrilled: 'Dearest Lady Dorothy, It would be just too lovely for any words to join in your Christmas cheer. Deevy' – this was Nancy Mitford's word for 'divine' – 'in fact hot stuff. Oh but you can't mean really mean it. Oh you are an awful tease.'

His first task, he said, would be to replenish his wardrobe for the occasion: 'the prospect of coming to Madresfield relieves all my gloom and HOW!' Over the coming weeks, his anticipation filled his delighted letters to 'those sweet orphan girls': 'I Hope Lord E will dress up as Father Xmas and go round putting oranges in stockings. May I bring fireworks?'

He was writing furiously and asked Lady Sibell to plug his new book in her *Harper's Bazaar* column: 'Tell Lady Sibell to say that all the smart set are reading *Remote People* the brilliant book by that well known hunting gent, E. W.' The thought of Christmas kept him going through the November gloom ('Very depressed. Rain all day. No money. Can't write. Fire smokes . . . Looking forward to Yuletide'). The next day he wrote again to say that his bicycle was lame, so he didn't make it to the meet, which was at a pub run by a 'mad major with a falsetto voice who thinks he is descended from Thomas a Becket': 'it was all a trifle eccentric'. He ends by saying yet again that it will be heavenly to come to Madresfield for Christmas. He would indeed remember the experience for the rest of his life.

CHAPTER 12

Christmas at Mad

Maimie picked Evelyn up from Worcester station and drove him to Madresfield. Balls of mistletoe were secured high in the oak and lime trees. In the hall a huge tree was lit up for an hour after tea, with footmen standing on either side with sponges in case any of the candles set it alight. Open fires crackled in the grates of the various rooms, brought to life for the festive season. The young people loved to congregate in the comfortable smoking room, just off the library.

Despite the absence of their parents, the Lygons were determined to put on a good show. Maimie took the place of her mother and distributed Christmas presents to the staff, who lined up according to rank. Guests were also given presents. Christmas dinner was traditional, with paper hats and crackers. Guests were served burning brandy in silver ladles. There were indoor fireworks and games of charades. In the evening, the local choir sang Christmas carols in the minstrels' gallery above the Dining Room. After singing they were given hot punch and biscuits. All of these details were lovingly recreated in Waugh's description of Christmas at Hetton Hall in *A Handful of Dust*.

The girls invited a range of house guests that year. As well as Frisky and Bo, there was Patrick Balfour (Mr Gossip, who did not gossip about Boom), a young aristocrat called Edward Jessel and 'an elegant and amiable young social butterfly' (Harold Acton's description) – Hamish St Clair Erskine. More guests arrived after Christmas – Baby Jungman, Diana

Coventry, Lord Berners, Phyllis de Janzé. One of the guests was an acquaintance of Evelyn's from his Oxford days, Hubert Duggan.

Hubert – witty, handsome and wild, described by Evelyn as a rakish dandy – was having an affair with Maimie. He was a stylish rider, a lapsed Catholic and an ardent womaniser. He had left Oxford prematurely because of the lack of female company. He seems to have been one of the few in Evelyn's set who did not have a 'homosexual phase' at Oxford. Hubert was a close friend of Hugh's and had been captain of Goodhart's, his house at Eton.

Evelyn and Hubert became close friends. Some years later, Evelyn, having witnessed Hugh Lygon's desperate slide into alcoholism, tried to save Hubert's brother, Alfred, from a similar fate. But it was Hubert Duggan who was responsible for the most spiritually compelling moment of Evelyn's life, a momentous event which would kickstart the writing of *Brideshead*.

For now, the young people were only concerned with having a good time. The company was incomparable, champagne flowed in abundance (decanted into jugs in accordance with Boom's custom) and jokes were as plentiful. The family felt liberated from their mother's presence and found amusement in everything. Edward Jessel bore a present of foie gras and then amused the others by tucking into it himself. Even the foie gras makes a guest appearance among the private jokes in *A Handful of Dust*.

After lunch, they took a walk to the 'noble line' of the Malvern Hills and when they reached the top one of the party pushed Hubert Duggan, who could not stop running until he finally ended in an exhausted heap at the gates of the girls' school at the foot of the hills. Charity visits were also undertaken. Evelyn and Hamish Erskine went with Coote to Lord Beauchamp's Home for Impoverished Clergymen.

Trips were taken to the local pubs. That year of 1931, Robert Bartleet, the son of the vicar, designed a Christmas card for the Hornyold Arms. Inside was a verse:

> There are sometimes famous writers, for instance Evelyn Waugh,
> And Lady Sibell Lygon, though seldom Bernard Shaugh.
> For its rest and recreation after writing books and plays
> To meet Remoter People during these Hectic Days.

In just the few months since his first arrival at Captain Hance's Riding Academy, Evelyn had turned himself into a local celebrity.

Maimie later recalled that, 'Our great thing was to be with people who made you laugh . . . Bores, *whoever* they were, simply never set foot anywhere.' Lady Dorothy remembered the time as positively Arcadian: 'we were young and foolish, and just enjoyed ourselves very much. Hubert Duggan used to come and stay at the time. He was very attractive . . . very amusing and great company. He and Evelyn got on very well. They were great friends.' Coote was more than a little in love with Hubert despite (or maybe because of) the fact that he was having an affair with her older sister.

Hubert and Evelyn shared the painful bond of divorce, in strikingly parallel circumstances. Each of them had married in 1928 and divorced not much more than a year later; each union was brought to an end by the wife's adultery while the husband was working away from home – Evelyn writing in Bognor, Hubert serving in Parliament. (In each case, the lover went on to marry the wife, then eventually committed suicide.)

The Lygon girls were of course aware of both divorces, but did not talk about them. 'Nor did we feel,' said Coote, 'that Evelyn ever wanted to, his spirits were resilient and he seemed to live entirely in the present.' This wasn't entirely true: Evelyn was still hurt by the failure of his marriage, but he was forever grateful to the Lygons for the 'decencies of hospitality' at a time when he needed to feel loved and cared for. He would always look back on this Christmas at Madresfield as a golden time. In 1944, enduring a rotten, solitary Christmas as an intelligence officer in Yugoslavia, he told Coote that 'Christmas makes me think a lot about Malvern.' His letter to her listed all that he had held in his memory for so long: the staff standing in line to be given their handsome presents, the walk to the hills, Jessel's foie gras. 'Well well never again,' he wrote sadly. The war had split them all apart.

Later still, in 1957, when Maimie had fallen on hard times and was desperately poor, Evelyn sent her a cheque, as he often did: 'Darling Blondy, I want to send you a Christmas present and I don't know what you would like. Will you get yourself something comforting? Do you remember how all the five-to-twos [Jews] went to Holy Communion at Madresfield on Christmas day? And how Jessell's boy tucked into the pate he brought? And what a lot of fine gifts we showered on Capt H GBH.'

The Lygons put on a good show that first year without their father and mother. Two days after Christmas, Lady Beauchamp sent a letter to Coote, with a heartfelt postscript (her and little Dickie's Christmas-cum-birthdays had been distinctly subdued): 'I can say, what once you said to me – "only God knows how much I love you".'

Evelyn left Mad on 28 December to spend New Year with 'the bright young Henry Yorkes'. He called them this because they were so serious and the antithesis of the Bright Young Things. Whilst at Forthampton Court, the country home of Henry's family, Evelyn was sent a message from his agent telling him that Basil Dean was prepared to commission a film scenario. Dean was the founder and chairman of the Ealing Studios. Evelyn readily agreed to write the treatment, as he needed the money. The salary was good: £50 per week. He then returned to Mad to celebrate with the girls for a couple of days. He spent hours drinking with Frisky Baldwin and talking of Baby Jungman, who was still keeping him at arm's length but not wishing to lose his friendship.

Evelyn returned to his parents' home after the festive season was over. His father's diary recalls that he came to Underhill carrying beautiful white lilacs to celebrate the news that Basil Dean had engaged him. Evelyn may well have been feeling guilty that he had been away from his family at Christmas.

On 14 January, he wrote to Frisky to boast that he was living in paid lodgings in the Albany near the Ritz. This was one of his favourite haunts: 'Well. I am living like a swell, in Albany, as it might be Lord Byron, Lord Macaulay, Lord Lytton, or any real slap up writer!' He also recalled the 'deep man-to-man intimacies which we reserve for the Madresfield Crème de Menthe', adding: 'Jolly sporting of you not to put Boaz in the moat, old boy.' He was missing Mad: 'I have been trying to recreate Worcestershire in London.' He had been drinking and socialising with the Lygon set in London, going to see Noël Coward's new play *Cavalcade* with Lady Sibell (it reduced her to tears) and indulging in a staring match with Maimie's one-eyed Pekingese – 'the malignant Cyclopean-eye of Grainger winking across the Ritz lounge'. But it wasn't the same 'away from the Captain, (God bless him!)'.

Evelyn's brief tenure as a screenwriter provided him with a life of ease that he revelled in. He was looked after by a studio representative called

Paddy Carstairs, who 'found him delightful, urbane and of course with that dry, witty sense of humour which abounded in his novels of that time . . . I found him warm and approachable. It was the time when he was much in the news and he was clear[ly] enjoying his success.' Paddy paints a picture of Evelyn's working day: arise mid-morning, cocktails at the Ritz, then a leisured lunch and a long chat that would be about anything other than the script. The moment Paddy tactfully guided the conversation towards the writing assignment, Evelyn would jump up exclaiming: 'Good heavens, is it nearly six? I must go to a cocktail party, so shall we start tomorrow?' And so it would be the next day and the next. Paddy was charmed: 'I remember when he was off to the Ritz he was sartorially elegant and he would inevitably say: "See you about three, then, Paddy?" and as he moved off he always winked at me as if to say "It's great to be lionised, but don't for a moment think that I am taking it seriously".'

Paddy was intrigued by his schoolboy humour and his love of fantasy. There was a fire in the hotel and Evelyn re-enacted a preposterous scene of a character groping for his false teeth in panic: 'It was odd to find, despite his very sophisticated comic books, he seemed to adore slapstick, the cornier the better. I found this very bizarre. Our completed treatment was never filmed and I don't think either of us was very surprised.'

He frequently took Maimie to lunch at the Ritz. Their friendship was going from strength to strength. Often when she was in London, Maimie would meet Evelyn for cocktails *à deux* before supper with a larger party. They discussed their love lives. He dwelt incessantly on Baby Jungman, always making a joke of his haplessly unrequited passion. Far from being ashamed of his parents, as is sometimes suggested, Evelyn invited the girls to meet them. Coote remembered visiting Mrs Waugh in Highgate. She was given a warm welcome and a glass of sherry.

When he was out of town writing in Chagford, or they were down at Mad, they exchanged letters. These are as filled with private jokes as their conversation was. Evelyn reported that his friend, Eleanor Watts, was in love with a one-eyed actor, 'as it might be Grainger'. The one-eyed Pekingese was a constant point of reference. Evelyn sent him invitations to cocktail parties, addressing the envelope to Mr Grainger. Many of his letters were written when he was drunk. In that condition, he could be lewd, but the girls never regarded this as an insult or a breach of decorum: 'I hope you have fun with SOCIETY this week. Look after that dear dutch girl [Baby] and don't let her roger anyone with clap . . . I hope your clitoris is very well. Good idea for Hughie to marry Sykes, then he will be catholic like me.' He would chide Maimie for not writing to him as often as he did to her: 'sad that all your letters to me have been stolen in the post'. But she offered him the use of the Belgravia home, 'Halkers', and of Mad, whenever he wanted to write in peace. Some of his letters are written from Belgrave Square, with thanks for letting him sponge.

In April 1932 the Vaudeville Theatre staged a dramatisation of *Vile Bodies*. It was not a roaring success. Arthur Waugh noted in his diary, 'a good show but an indifferent audience'. There would have been even more empty seats had it not been for the presence of a large body of Waugh friends and relations. Evelyn was determined to make the most of his venture into theatreland, and planned a lavish party to celebrate the opening. He wrote to the Lygons, boasting that it was the hottest ticket in town: Lady Cunard ('the old trout') had just phoned to complain that she had been given seats in the eighteenth row – how could she take her guest Prince George and sit him in the eighteenth row? Lady Castlerosse, meanwhile, refused to pay for her tickets: 'oh dear these great ladies . . . still it makes me feel like a social figure which is good for my low spirits because no one knows how despised I am in the theatre'. Evelyn had given his parents front row seats. He took his mother dressed in her best to dine at the Ritz. The Lygons, whom he now considered to be part of his family, were at the top of his guest list.

Sadly, there was a poor showing from them. They all had ailments of one sort or another. Little Poll, as he called Coote, had broken her collarbone in a riding accident, Sibell was in a nursing home 'having her wisdom teeth removed' (which seems to be a euphemism for a more embarrassing operation), and Maimie had hurt her 'arse'. Baby Jungman was in Ireland: 'Did little Miss Jungman send me a line of good wishes from Ireland? Not on your life,' he complained to Frisky. He also wrote to Coote to commiserate on her injuries, joking that he had put up a monument to her bravery and popularity: 'nothing like suffering to sweeten the soul'. Then to Frisky: 'The slow extermination of our Lygon chums saddens me. First little Blondy's arse. Now Pollen's breastbone. Blondy came to see my play but went away in great pain before supper.'

Still, at least Blondy had made it to the show. His party also included Hubert Duggan and an assortment of minor aristocrats. Among them was Hazel Lavery, wife of the famous painter Sir John Lavery. An Anglo-Irish beauty, now in her early fifties, and an artist herself, she sat for her husband over four hundred times (his image of her as the personification of Ireland appeared on the banknotes of the Irish Free State). She was intimate with figures as various as George Bernard Shaw, Winston Churchill and the Irish Republican, Michael Collins. She was having a casual, on-off affair with Evelyn. He joked to Frisky about his social success, though drawing attention to the renowned hostess Lady Cunard rather than his part-time lover Lady Lavery: 'So Boaz is momentarily a social lion and Lady Cunard . . . calls him Evelyn and makes him sit on her right hand at luncheon and dinner . . . but is his head turned by these favours? NO: he remains the same simple lad who bounced around Malvern Academy on the broad back of Mater.'

He was deep into *Black Mischief*, known to the Lygons as 'his feelthy novel'. He wrote to Coote from the Savile Club:

> Darling Pollen,
>
> God how sad about tiny breastbone. What an unfortunate family you are to be sure. There was little Blondy with her arse too and Hugh with his baldness. Well I am ill too and despondent and I have no money and I get so despised at the theatre where they are acting my play that it has given me that distressing and well nigh universal complaint the inferiority complex.
>
> I have had a lot of SOCIETY of a pretty high and dashing kind so on Sat I am going to a monastery for three weeks to write my feelthy book. How I long to see you all again and will too when I have written the smut.
>
> My word I am miserable about everything
>
> xxxxxx

Evelyn needed to write in peace. He spent time at the Catholic School, Stonyhurst, where his Oxford friend Christopher Hollis was a teacher.

And he also went back to Chagford. Coote wrote to him there with the latest family update. As always with the Lygons, it was black news borne with grim good humour and delivered with a light touch. But Evelyn was able to find just the right tone for his response: 'Sweet Poll, Golly what a family. Hugh in a mad house and now Sibell at my ex-aunt Almina's abortionist parlour. How my heart bleeds for you all.' The nursing home where Sibell was 'having her wisdom teeth removed' was run by a relation of She-Evelyn's. Hugh was in even more serious trouble, despite the jokes about his premature baldness and being in a madhouse.

His drinking had worsened. His good looks were being ravaged by hard living and his reluctance to write to his father meant that there was no one left to bail him out financially. On 18 March 1932, shortly before Evelyn's play opened, a notice appeared in the *London Gazette* to the effect that the Honourable Hugh Lygon of 'The Elms', Tilshead, Wiltshire, had petitioned for bankruptcy in the court at Bath. This disaster seems to have precipitated some sort of mental collapse.

Evelyn had seen Hugh and Sibell at Halkers. He had taken brandy with them and had long talks with Hugh saying, as he put it in his letter to Poll, 'a great many things that I can't say now'. Lady Beauchamp was informed of the disaster. She wrote to Coote: 'I am so grieved for all you are suffering . . . let us be united in facing the sadness of this tragedy which has befallen us.' On the same day that she wrote from Saighton Grange, Lord Beauchamp sent a letter to his daughter from Australia, telling her that he had received a cable telling him the shocking news of Hugh's bankruptcy: 'Never would it have happened if I had known.'

In later years, Coote blamed Lady Sibell and her brother Elmley for refusing to save Hugh from bankruptcy. For Coote, this was the beginning of the end for her beloved brother. She (like Cordelia Flyte with Sebastian) had always been the sister who had loved him best. Following this disaster his drinking increased. Over the years he would have abortive attempts to go on the wagon, but all were unsuccessful.

Hugh made plans to go to Italy with Evelyn in the summer, where they would meet Lord Beauchamp. Meanwhile, Maimie and Coote begged Evelyn to come to Madresfield to write his novel. He tried to put them off, knowing that he needed isolation and no distractions from his work. A lovely letter thanks them and explains his dilemma:

> Now I am going to write the important part of my letter. Oh how I should love to live in your Liberty Hall but the trouble about poor Bo is that he's a lazy bugger and if he was in a house with you lovely girls he would just sit about and chatter and get d. d. [disgustingly drunk] and ride a horse and have a heavenly time but would he write his book? No, and must he? By God he must. So you see, but listen.
>
> How would it be for me to stay in some inn or farm in your neighbour[hood] and then every time I have written 5,000 words I could have a reward and walk to your lovely house and have heavenly tea party with you? . . . Not too far away so that when you have week-end orgies [Madspeak for 'parties'] I could come tripping in to see them and get ideas that way for my famous book.

Despite their entreaties he remained in Chagford. 'How I wish I were in your stately home with all you popular girls. But it cannot be . . . I can't leave this hotel until some money comes for me. But that ought to happen in a day or two if that Interesting Play [*Vile Bodies*] is still going on and then Heigh Ho for the Lygons' arms. Will you be there *next* weekend? Say Yes?'

He kept them up to date with his novel, especially Coote, the sister who took most interest in his work. He even copied into her letter passages from it, such as the menu for a character's dinner party.

For all his good intentions, he could not stay away. Liberty Hall was too much of a draw. He was back at Mad in May, sending a telegram to announce his arrival. It was a return to Arcadia and an entrance into the full embrace of a substitute family. This was the summer when he really got to know Mad intimately, living and working there as a member of the family. In the course of 1932 he stayed at Madresfield in January, February, May, June, August, October and several times in November and December.

His friend from his Oxford days, Peter Quennell, used a striking phrase in reflecting on Evelyn and the Lygons: 'I'd heard from Coote Lygon that when Evelyn first joined the Lygon family, they told him he ought to become a hunting man.' 'Joined the Lygon family': the girls treated him as if he were their own brother. He had always wanted a sister, and now he had a whole gaggle of them. Quennell added that from the moment Evelyn went to Madresfield 'he felt that was his world'. Mad World and Waugh World were as one.

He arrived on 7 May, determined to finish *Black Mischief* as quickly as possible. Like Charles Ryder at Brideshead, he had found his 'enchanted palace'. Being treated as family meant that, again like Charles, he could 'wander from room to room' and undergo a new aesthetic education. His feelings were the same as those he projected onto Ronald Knox years later: the theologian was also drawn into 'an enchantress's palace', a big country house with 'expanses of carpet and parquet, abundant well-conducted servants, roaring fires, glittering leather bindings, laughter and music . . . deliciously exciting to those reared in narrower circumstances'.

He leafed through rare books in the library and walked in the extensive grounds. The gardens were at their best in May: the Moat Garden, the Rock Garden, the Yew Garden, the Lime Arbour, the Herbaceous Garden, the Greek Temple and Caesar's Lawn, with its busts of twelve Roman emperors. A dapper-looking Evelyn posed next to the Emperor Vitellius for the benefit of a *Tatler* photographer. The picture appeared with a caption that provided good publicity:

> Mr Evelyn Waugh, the young novelist whose book, *Vile Bodies*, has been transformed into a successful play, was snapshotted recently as above when staying at Madresfield Court, the seat of Lord Beauchamp. He is posed beside a bust of the gluttonous Roman Emperor Vitellius – certainly a classical 'vile body'! Mr Waugh's new novel, which contains an account of a cannibalistic banquet, will soon be published.

With no parents to spoil the fun, they could all be Mad Hatters at a tea party. Innumerable details of daily life amused Evelyn and were embellished in surreal fashion. The mundane and its capacity to be transformed into something fantastic was the key to his comic vision.

The Lygons and Evelyn shared an irreverent sense of humour. Coote kept a juvenile diary that was 'remarkable only for its dullness'. Evelyn found the diary entries 'confined to weather, dogs and horses', and enlivened them with references to incest and an assortment of other immoralities. He pretended that Coote was engaged in orgies and sexual misconduct. This was all the more funny because, in sharp contrast to her older sisters, she was the epitome of innocence. A watercolour of a carthorse that she had carefully painted in the diary was defaced by Evelyn and given a large penis – just as carefully painted. A present of handkerchiefs from Maimie elicited the response: 'I have tied them to my cock, they look very becoming.'

'It was,' recalled Coote, 'like having Puck as a member of the household.' The description is apt: there was definitely something of the malicious sprite about him, and he was (at this time) slim and small and extremely attractive, with his intense stare and piercing wit. What the girls loved most was his 'consistent, spontaneous, irreverent wit and his capacity for turning the most unlikely situations into irresistibly funny jokes which continued to be woven into our conversations and letters with an increasing richness of texture over the years'. He was always cheerful and rarely showed them his darker side during these halcyon days.

Plays and books were incorporated into their daily chat. Sibell remembered him selecting books from the library and reading aloud to the girls in the evenings, eliciting shrieks of laughter. Favourites included *Letters of a Diplomat's Wife* by Mary King Waddington, which 'missed the point of everything', and also the memoirs of an Arctic explorer entitled *Forty Years in the Frozen North*, in which a character called Pitt underwent terrible hardships and privations. When his nose became frostbitten he rubbed it with snow: 'The best thing in the world, the only remedy.' This became another catchphrase that they applied to a good many unsuitable things. The sisters also remembered there was a novel set in India, which included the line: 'The East has got me, Granger, but thank God I'm still a pukka sahib.' 'Evelyn loved that' – especially because of Grainger's presence. Evelyn proposed that Maimie's dog should be made a member of the Lord's Day Observance Society under the name of P. H. Grainger, the initials standing for Pretty Hound.

Jane Austen was high on their list. A 'Collins' was their term for a thank-you or 'bread and butter letter', named after the unctuous Mr Collins in *Pride and Prejudice*. In one of Coote's letters to Evelyn she complained that her brother, Elmley, and his wife were 'becoming more and more like Mrs John Dashwood every day'. This is a revealing allusion to what was at the time one of Austen's lesser-known novels,

Sense and Sensibility. Mr and Mrs John Dashwood are two of her most unpleasant minor characters. They disinherit the three Dashwood sisters. The parallels with the Lygons are obvious.

Literary jokes, some light-hearted, others more hard-edged, abound in the letters that passed between Evelyn and the girls over the years. They quoted lines from Noël Coward's *Private Lives*: 'What fools we were to ruin it all, utter utter fools . . . very flat, Norfolk – That's no reflection on her, unless *she* made it flatter . . . I swear I'll never mention it again.' When Evelyn and Maimie met Coward in the Ritz one day, they both collapsed into giggles and ran away. One of Evelyn's favourite games was marrying off Coote, who was not exactly overwhelmed with beaux. This became a running joke, with Evelyn asking her every time a new man appeared: 'Would he do?'

Evelyn fell ill with the flu and was very pleased to be given the prescription that the family doctor at Madresfield, Doctor Mackie, always swore by: 'get the girls to give you a dozen oysters and a pint of champagne'. This they did and the cure was instantaneous. He wrote later to say that he had no business being there when he was ill: 'Please forgive me for being such a boring and inconvenient guest and thank you all for being so kind.'

It was impossible for Evelyn to be boring. The laughter that he brought sustained the girls at this most difficult time of their lives. Waugh's first biographer, Christopher Sykes, who knew them intimately, recalled that 'the Lygons were (and are) among people who, even when confronted by catastrophe, never face life without a sense of humour. It is a rare spirit that shallower people regard as shallow.' This is astute: to an outsider the banter and play that characterised Mad World appear frivolous and jejune, but in reality the comedy was a means of survival and a manifestation of love. One day they were walking in the garden and came upon the sundial inscribed with the words: 'That day is wasted on which we have not laughed.' Evelyn remarked to the sisters: 'We haven't wasted many days, have we?'

It was hard to concentrate on work. Evelyn groaned loudly as he shut himself away for a few hours a day in the old day nursery in order to finish *Black Mischief.* They hindered more than they helped, having no qualms about disturbing him and dragging him away to join them in whatever was going on. Sometimes the girls simply joined him in the nursery and chatted. As he wrote, they stitched away at an enormous patchwork quilt that was never finished.

Evelyn still saw himself as an artist as well as a writer. He had illustrated *Decline and Fall* and designed his own cover for *Vile Bodies*. He decided to illustrate *Black Mischief* with some sketches, for which the girls and other house guests sat as models. Lady Sibell recalled how 'he drew me sitting on the edge of the bath with a bathrobe on, getting cramp'.

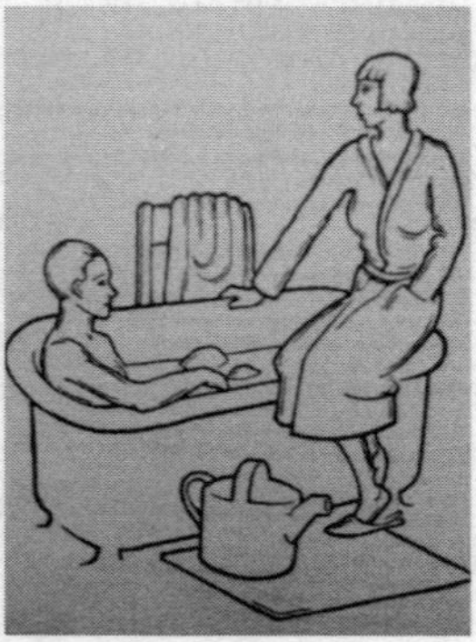

Despite the distractions, the book was finished at Mad. *Black Mischief*, with nine drawings by the author, would be published in October 1932. He dedicated it: '*With love to* MARY AND DOROTHY LYGON'.

CHAPTER 13

An Encounter in Rome

The truth is that self-respecting writers do not 'collect material' for their books, or, rather, they do it all the time in living their lives.

(Evelyn Waugh, *Ninety-Two Days*)

I think people's sex lives are their own concern.

(Lady Mary 'Maimie' Lygon)

He is the last, historic, authentic case of someone being hounded out of society.

(*Brideshead Revisited*)

After completing *Black Mischief* in May 1932 and receiving the cheque for the balance of his advance, Evelyn decided to reward himself with a holiday in Venice. This was the Venice before package tours, when only a handful of wealthy Europeans and Americans went there. For Evelyn there was also a serious mission, a spiritual pilgrimage: he had arranged to be confirmed in Rome by Cardinal Lépicier.* There was always a conflict

* Few people know about this important event in his life. The trip to Rome has escaped his biographers partly because the published edition of his letters only partially prints his 'Open Letter to the Archbishop of Westminster' (written in May 1933), omitting the key sentence: 'I was confirmed privately in Rome last summer by Cardinal Lépicier.'

within Evelyn between the religious side and the hard-drinking hedonism. This was a trip in which he hoped to reconcile the two.

His friendship with the Lygon sisters was deepening. After spending time with his parents in London, he was back at Madresfield for long stretches in June, July and a long weekend at the beginning of August. Sometime that summer he wrote a 'Collins' (thank-you letter) to his Dearest Blondy: 'How can I thank you for my long and delightful visit to Mudersfield. It was all heavenly – the pansies and the play and the batting, the idleness and recuperation of spirit. I look forward impatiently to the autumn when we will be reunited.' He was proud of his friendship with the family, and in July he sent his parents a 'shame-making' article by Lady Sibell Lygon called 'Dinner Party Wits', numbering him among 'the people she liked to talk with'.

He also made an appearance in the pages of her magazine, *Harper's Bazaar*, with a hilarious short story called 'This Quota Stuff: Proof Positive that the British Can Make Good Films'. A wildly exaggerated riff on his brief experience in the world of movie-making, it tells of a newly successful but still impoverished young novelist, Simon Lent, quite clearly based on himself, who is hired by a studio to produce 'An Entirely New Angle' (the title under which the story appeared in American *Harper's*) on *Hamlet*. His task is to write the dialogue. 'But, surely, there's quite a lot of dialogue there already?' Lent points out. Studio head Sir James Macrae explains:

> 'Ah, you don't see my angle. There have been plenty of productions of Shakespeare in modern dress. We are going to produce him in modern speech. How can you expect the public to enjoy Shakespeare when they can't make head or tail of the dialogue? D'you know I began reading a copy the other day and blessed if *I* could understand it. At once I said, "What the public wants is Shakespeare with all his beauty of thought and character translated into the language of everyday life."
>
> 'Now Mr Lent here was the man whose name naturally suggested itself. Many of the most high-class critics have commended Mr Lent's dialogue.'

Shortly after the story was published in the August *Harper's*, Evelyn went into town to lunch with Lady Sibell. They talked about their magazine work and plans for Italy. He then went back to Underhill to pack.

Evelyn had earlier written to Coote to tell her how glad he was that Hugh was going to be in Italy, because 'between you and me and the w.c., Raymond de T. is something of a handful v. nice but so BAD and he fights and fucks and gambles and gets D.D. [disgustingly drunk] all the time. But Hugh and I will be quiet and chaste and economical and sober.' Evelyn had previously met wild 'desperado' Raymond de Trafford in Kenya. He was famous for being shot by his girlfriend after a lovers' quarrel. She then turned her gun on herself. They both survived but were badly hurt. Maimie was convinced that this incident had been recreated in F. Scott Fitzgerald's soon to be published novel *Tender is the Night*.

Since no Evelyn Waugh diary survives from this period, his trip has to be reconstructed from letters and reminiscences that are not specific about dates and travel details, but it seems that he visited Rome for a week, with a fortnight in Venice thereafter.

After his trouble with the detectives in Paris the previous summer, Lord Beauchamp had returned to the privacy of more distant shores. In November 1931 he was writing home from the Europe Hotel in Singapore, explaining that he was going to Sydney but that he did not know what he would do after that. By Easter Sunday the following year, he was at the Grand Hotel in the resort of Rotorua on New Zealand's Bay of Plenty, saying that he would return to Europe the following month, though was rather dreading the journey: 'The thought of the heat rather dismays me for my return – the Gulf of Serpentine, the coast of Java – Singapore Ceylon and the Red Sea in June!!!' He duly made it back to Dieppe, and thence to Paris and Rome, where he spent the summer.

He rented a lovely little apartment from the eccentric composer and writer Lord Berners. The address was 3 Foro Romano, overlooking the ruins of the ancient Forum. Berners had bought the property in 1928, and it was lavishly styled in the flamboyant manner that was his hallmark. The bedroom walls were painted in a dirty parchment colour, with the furnishings in deep crimson damask. The bed had an elaborately carved gilt head. There was only the one bedroom, but this suited Berners's homosexual appetite. Above all, the apartment had a beautiful and spacious drawing room with a balcony commanding a magnificent view of the Forum. Berners said that 'on a moonlit night it is pure magic'. One looked directly out on the Temple of Saturn and the ruins of the Basilica Julia, which had been commissioned by Julius Caesar in 54 BC. Round the corner was the Piazza della Consolazione. For many exiles and outsiders Rome was indeed a place of saturnine consolation.

Berners added a garage for his Rolls-Royce, which he had customised with a butterfly motif and in which he was purported to carry a piano – actually a tiny clavichord, adorned with butterflies and flowers. More beloved than the vehicle was its chauffeur, a handsome man called William Crack, described by Siegfried Sassoon as 'the blue-eyed charioteer' – his eyes were violet and his presence at Berners's beck and call was much envied by various homosexual friends. Harold Nicolson described him as 'William, the Adonis chauffeur'.

In Rome, Berners found a man called Tito Mannini to look after the apartment. He also happened to be a brilliant cook. Tito came to regard the place as his own. Some of Berners's guests found him difficult, one or two leaving instantly because of his rudeness. Others loved him. Diana Mitford adored his sour cream chocolate cake. Tito bred canaries. Once, one of his enemies released them and they flew all over the Forum. Tito was distraught and would not return home until he had persuaded his birds to return to their cages. He was just the sort of character that Evelyn loved. Tito later prospered as king of the post-war black market. Lady Dorothy once met him in Rome wearing one of Berners's suits. He was devoted to Lord Beauchamp and accompanied him to the Palazzo Morosini in Venice in the summer of 1936.

It was customary at 3 Foro Romano to take breakfast prepared by Tito (hot rolls and butter with coffee, followed by peaches and figs) out on the loggia overlooking the Forum. For the guests, the Forum was the garden, where they sat in the sun and wandered about. Rome was quiet in those days, 'not yet the wild noisy hub of crazy traffic, tearing bicycles, scooters and cars'.

This was where it had been arranged that Evelyn would stay with his new friends. The Lygon children were going to see their exiled father again and Evelyn was finally meeting the man he had heard so much about, whose presence lingered in every room at Madresfield, whose handsome image he had seen in the numerous paintings, and whose undoing he had heard about in intimate detail. He knew that Boom was an extremely cultivated man; he knew of his love for formality, his love for his children, his eccentric habits such as decanting champagne into jugs. His hatred of his wife. His shame at his pariah status.

Evelyn saw Lord Beauchamp as a Byronic figure. He did indeed have a strong physical resemblance to Lord Byron: his black curly hair, though now greying, the cleft in the chin, the deep blue eyes and full sensuous lips, the slight overweightness, the air of voluptuousness. But there was also the parallel situation of the two lords, exiled to Italy for sexual indiscretions involving charges of homosexuality, leaving their families behind in England. Like Byron, Beauchamp kept fit by boxing and swimming. Evelyn noticed too, despite the inherent grace and nobility, that Boom cut a tragic figure.

The visit was a great success. Lord Beauchamp, his daughters later recalled, was 'extremely fond' of Evelyn and they got on 'tremendously well'. They visited the sights together, particularly the churches. Boom, always an assiduous planner of social and cultural events, took them all over Rome. They climbed the dome of St Peter's, a terrifying ascent up a steep and narrow stone staircase set at an angle. They ate ices in the Piazza Navona. A favourite destination was the ancient basilica of San Sebastiano fuori le Mura (St Sebastian outside the walls, otherwise known as St Sebastian at the Catacombs). This was the basilica with the gorgeous statue of Sebastian and his arrows that Evelyn had visited when he was first in Rome in 1927, with his heart and head full of Alastair Graham.

They visited the Vatican. Years later, Evelyn wrote to Maimie to say that he had been back to Rome and had seen the Pope and a great deal of porphyry: 'They have taken away the urinal outside the Vatican where Boom peed in his Garter robes.'

No record survives of the exact circumstances of Evelyn's confirmation by Cardinal Alexis Lépicier, Prefect of the Sacred Congregation of the Affairs of Religious, though he may have benefited from a change in ecclesiastical regulations enacted in June 1932, whereby for the first time it was permissible for confirmation to take place after first communion, instead of before it. He described his confirmation as 'private', so he was probably alone for the actual ceremony, but it is possible that the Lygons accompanied him to the Vatican. Could it have been in honour of Evelyn's meeting with the Cardinal that Lord Beauchamp donned his Garter robes?

As with Robert Byron all those years ago, Evelyn was a charming and interested companion, who pleased Boom because he was far more interested in churches and art than the Lygon children. Lady Sibell recalled that although her father liked Evelyn very much, he could be irritated by his lack of grace: 'Father once told me "I wish Mr Waugh would not genuflect because he does it so clumsily".' Evelyn, in Rome for his confirmation as well as the chance to meet Beauchamp, was as yet a novice – and perhaps a little over-enthusiastic – when it came to the external signs of his faith. Lady Dorothy, too, remembered that Evelyn and her father got on well and that for Evelyn it was tremendously exciting to be in Rome to have his new faith confirmed.

Evelyn would always remember this time with great affection. He wrote to Maimie on more than one occasion to recall the happy days that they had shared: 'Wasn't it extraordinary that we were all there in one room?' Another letter from 1950 says that he was in Rome and went back to visit Berners's home, 'now in the hands of a soldier'. 'I had quite forgotten there was only one bed-room. What fun you and I and B[oom] – and Byron must have had. Youth youth . . . there is a wonderful porphyry font in Verona. Did B[oom] know? Love BO.' Boom was an admirer of porphyry, to the point of being a bore in his enthusiasm. This became a running joke between Evelyn and the Lygon children.

The reference to 'Byron' in this letter is intriguing. It is not an allusion to the Byronic quality of Lord Beauchamp. Nor does it refer to Robert Byron, the Hypocrite and travel writer, who accompanied Beauchamp on that earlier trip to Italy, but does not seem to have met him again. It would seem, therefore, to be a reference to a third Byron. Ocean liner passenger lists reveal that the Earl Beauchamp was accompanied on his wanderings by one Robert Harcourt Byron, an Australian in his mid-twenties. Born in Sydney, six feet tall with fair hair and blue eyes, he is sometimes described as Beauchamp's 'valet' and sometimes as his 'secretary'.

When Evelyn returned to Rome four years later for the final stages of the annulment of his marriage, he wrote to Coote Lygon: 'So I am in the eternal city god it is cold and I have to wait to be cross-examined by beasts re my wife.' He was clearly thinking of Lord Beauchamp and Maimie: 'Then I will come to London to my boom at Highgate . . . I miss porphyry arse very much also Blondy.'

'My boom at Highgate' is a projection of the Lygons' fond nickname for their father onto Arthur Waugh. Blondy is of course his name for Maimie. 'Porphyry arse' would appear to be Boom himself. This is the playful Evelyn, fuelled by alcohol, indulging in what he calls 'filth'. Other letters, though, reveal a different side. In February 1960, he again reminisced to Maimie about Rome, this time in a serious and reflective mood that shows his deep and abiding love for her: 'I was in Rome and thought much of our days in the Forum. I was in Venice and thought of Brandolin. I think of you always.'

'Brandolin' was the Palazzo Brandolini on the Grand Canal in Venice, where Richard Wagner had once stayed. It was there that Evelyn and Maimie went after saying goodbye to Boom. That summer of 1932, Venice was full of society people, among whom the most glamorous was Diana Cooper. Another Nordic blonde like Diana Mitford, she was witty, elegant, charming and unconventional. Brought up as the daughter of the Duke of Rutland (though almost certainly the result of the duchess's liaison with a dashing writer called Harry Cust), she was regarded by many as the most beautiful woman in England. An actress as well as a society fixture, she married the diplomat Duff Cooper and entranced every man who met her. Evelyn too fell under her spell. His cup filled to overflowing as he found himself in the company of Diana as well as Maimie.

English society in Venice was orchestrated by an ambitious American called Laura Corrigan, a professional hostess who offered high-class accommodation and entertainment for wealthy visitors. The Guinnesses, Cecil Beaton, Lady Cunard, Randolph Churchill and many others from the 'smart set' were all to be seen at candlelit dinner parties in crumbling palazzi, the tables adorned with heavily scented tuberoses. By day the guests were ferried to the Lido on Mrs Corrigan's outsize motor-launch. Liveried footmen arranged backgammon boards on the beach, poured drinks and served elaborate luncheons. It was a time of late nights and sleeping in till noon. At cocktail hour, people would gather at Harry's Bar to drink Bellinis and plan the rest of the evening.

Evelyn wrote up his experience of this trip in a 'letter' entitled 'Venetian Adventures' for *Harper's Bazaar*. The argument of the piece was that Venice was a superior destination to the French Riviera. He defended the delicious scampi that was unfairly given a bad name by the English: 'It is pure legend that they are caught in the canals. I spent a night last week trawling in the Adriatic with one of the boats of the Chioggia fishing fleet, and watched netfuls of scampi being drawn in from the deep water for the Venice markets. We cooked them on a charcoal brazier and ate them in their shells at dawn.' But he then characteristically deflates his own lyricism, adding 'with cups of hideous coffee compounded, it seemed, of chicory, garlic and earth'.

Evelyn, Maimie and a group of others visited the monastery island, San Lazzaro, once a leper colony but now home to Armenian monks. The island was made famous by Lord Byron, who would row out there to learn the language and help the monks to compose an English-Armenian dictionary. Evelyn enjoyed talking to the brothers in Latin. One of them complained about '*Mulieres stridentes et vestitae immodestissime*' ('noisy and immodestly dressed wives'). Evelyn gave a donation and tried to explain that there were six English Members of Parliament in the party ('*Hic sunt sex senatores Britannici*').

He painted a rosy picture of Venice, which he was to draw upon many years later when he wrote *Brideshead*. He loved the evenings, when the city 'really becomes itself' and 'we can drift quite silently, except for the gondoliers' cry at corners, on black water among the smells'. He stayed drinking until late in the Caffe Florian, where he admired the locals' sense of the need for formality of demeanour. If foreigners wish to sit at Florian's in the evening, he informed the readers of *Harper's Bazaar*, 'they must dress as the Venetians think suitable'. He despised tourists wearing informal sun wear: 'Young Englishmen who attempt to appear like gross schoolboys in shorts and vests present a very vulgar spectacle indeed under Venetian eyes.'

He liked the compactness of the city, the fact that it could be walked in an hour. In contrast to the sprawl of the Riviera, with all its hotels, villas, beaches and casinos: 'Here there are at the most about forty English or Americans, who know exactly what everyone is doing every minute of the day. They all meet every evening on the Piazza and discuss how they dined, and on the morning after a party I love to see the convergence of patinas, canoes and bathers, sometimes into a Sargasso Sea of gossip, sometimes into rival camps with rare swimmers travelling between and fanning the dissension.'

Even the Lido, with its noisy backgammon players and general grubbiness, did not deter him. But the heat did not agree with him. A 'confirmed heliophobe', he left it to the others to sunbathe while he escaped 'in the cool depths of the churches and palaces'. In *Brideshead* Lord Marchmain advises sticking to the cool of the churches rather than the beaches where endless games of backgammon were played.

Evelyn welcomed the cool of the evening when he could watch the locals: 'I like the evening carnival, when all the poorer Venetians decorate their boats with lanterns and flow in procession down the Grand Canal, not to collect money or attract tourists, but simply because it is their idea of an agreeable evening.' Italy, the home of Catholicism, released his long-repressed romanticism. He loved the Venetian architecture and painting. He liked the food and the wine. He could see no ills – even the traditional complaints about the smells of the sewage and the mosquitoes were not to spoil the mood. The mosquitoes, he noted, disappeared at dawn, 'and as none goes to bed much before that they are very little nuisance'. Even the smell of sewage in 'garlic-eating countries' he found preferable to those of the north.

For *Brideshead*, the only one of his novels in which he fully unleashed his emotional and romantic side, he drew on his memories of 1932 in an evocative passage:

> The fortnight at Venice passed quickly and sweetly – perhaps too sweetly; I was drowning in honey, stingless. On some days life kept pace with the gondola, as we nosed through the side-canals and the boatman uttered his plaintive musical bird-cry of warning; on other days, with the speed-boat bouncing over the lagoon in a stream of sun-lit foam; it left a confused memory of fierce sunlight on the sands and cool, marble interiors; of water everywhere, lapping on smooth stone, reflected in a dapple of light on painted ceilings; of a night at the Corombona palace such as Byron might have known, and another Byronic night fishing for scampi in the shallows of Chioggia, the phosphorescent wake of the little ship, the lantern swinging in the prow, and the net coming up full of weed and sand and floundering fishes; of melon and *prosciutto* on the balcony in the cool of the morning; of hot cheese sandwiches and champagne cocktails at the English bar.

When Charles Ryder first arrives in Venice he experiences a heady, intoxicating response to the city's beauty: 'conifers changing to vine and olive . . . the sun mounted high, the air full of the smell of garlic'. The liveried gondoliers, the butler dressed in 'rather raffish summer livery of striped linen', the *piano nobile* in full sunshine, 'ablaze with frescoes of the school of Tintoretto': every detail is a loving recreation of the visit in the company of the Lygons.

Not even the bouts of diarrhoea – the habitual inconvenience of the English abroad – spoiled Venice for Evelyn. He was among friends, where they accepted him as a celebrated young novelist and an amusing companion. His wit was legendary, as long as he could control his equally famous sharp tongue. He was at his happiest in the company of beautiful women and there were plenty to be found on the Lido that summer. He listed them in his article for *Harper's*: 'Diana Cooper, Diana Abdy, Bridget Parsons, Mary Lygon, Mrs Bryan Guinness, Doris Castlerosse, Anne Armstrong-Jones and Tilly Losch'.

Passions ran high in the summer humidity. Michael Parsons (Earl of Rosse) 'boxed the ears' of Anne Armstrong-Jones in a jealous rage provoked by her stepping out on a balcony with another man. She sent back the tuberoses he sent in apology but married him three years later. Evelyn noted wryly that there were always apologetic tuberoses lining the tables of the Palazzo Brandolini.

Another legendary quarrel broke out on the island of Murano. It took place during 'a placid, English birthday party when glassblowers and gondoliers joined in and danced with the guests'. This was a party to celebrate Diana Cooper's fortieth birthday on 29 August, but it all ended in disaster – 'placid' is a joke. The trouble began when the 'Lucky Strike' cigarette heiress Doris Duke accused Sir Richard Sykes of making a pass at her in her car before the party. She was incensed and asked her chauffeur to throw him out of the car. Then, at the party, Sir Richard deliberately burnt the back of Miss Duke's hand with a cigarette. Randolph Churchill sprang to her defence. Diana Cooper's account was this:

> Everyone had been drinking like fishes for an hour before. Now all the wives were clinging to their men to stop them joining in . . . Oliver Messel and Cecil Beaton were fighting like bears and, as I thought, doing *splendidly*! . . . The next day I was covered with tuberoses, which were sent when you'd behaved outrageously.

Evelyn wrote: 'I shall never smell tuberoses again without envisaging queues of repentant young men apologising after parties.'

It became known in Evelyn's circle as the 'Murano incident' and the word 'Syksed' was added to the pool of in-jokes and private language shared with his friends: it was applied to anyone who had been roughed up or to anything broken. Writing to Diana after returning to England, he mourned the end of 'all the fun in Venice. How I loved it'. He also reported that in the version of the Murano incident that was circulating around London society the Earl of Rosse was purportedly thrown into the canal by twenty gondoliers. He added that Lord Donegall thought that 'we were all hired by Miss Duke to bash Sykes' – this suggests that Evelyn must have been at least a fringe participant in the famous brawl.

At the end of the summer Lord Beauchamp left Rome. He travelled through Provence, stopping off in Avignon, before joining Hugh in Marseille, where they boarded a ship for Australia.

It is not clear whether the unreliable Hugh made the Italian trip after all. This most elusive of the Lygons does, however, speak in his own voice in a letter to his little sister Coote written from on board ship during the voyage out with his father. 'Darling Coote,' he begins, 'Thank you so much for coming to see me off. It was sweet of you and I did love it.' He writes of the lovely swimming pool on the ship, which is mostly reserved for 'all the horrible children on board'. He rather poignantly tells her that he is 'on the wagon' and therefore does not have to spend money and that he works out at the gym every morning, on the rowing machine and that he boxes, and swims before trying to 'sink into a coma for the rest of the day. Proust is very helpful.' He also mentions that High Choral Mass has started next door in the bar. He seems not to be fond of women: 'There are lots of little women on board but the Captain is nice and is going to show me the engines.' He also notes that: 'There are 120 Malay stewards which is quite quaint.' He says that he is going to Cairo for the day the next morning and that 'Boom is hopping about everywhere with his embroidery.' He says that the women on board also have their embroidery, 'so soon we shall have a cosy little circle'. He asks 'how are the poor animals?' He adored his shooting dogs and missed them desperately when he was away.

On arrival down under, Boom was in good spirits despite a leg injury. He was delighted to have his favourite son with him for company. They settled in Darling Point, 'with a small but efficient staff' and magnificent views.

Darling Point was a prestigious suburb of Sydney with supposedly the best outlook on the harbour. Boom and Hugh lived in Carthona, a magnificent harbourside sandstone mansion located at the end of Carthona Avenue. Built in 1841 for the Surveyor-General Sir Thomas Mitchell, it was one of Sydney's finest properties. Designed in Gothic style with arched and leaded windows, Carthona resembled a miniature Madresfield on the other side of the world. Boom wrote to Coote with a vivid description of his new home, describing furniture that was comfortable but horribly stained, a big room with gold walls and green furniture, the dining room in black and deep blue and 'my little room with blue gold chairs and nondescript paper'. A fastidious man of great taste, he noticed every little detail. Though the interior was gloomy, the view more than compensated: 'I write looking over towards one of the bays with a promontory beyond covered with house half-buried in trees of which many are in purple flowers just now'. He had a daily massage, which took up 'a heap of time'. He also told Coote that Hugh was hoping to see the Test Match.

There was much talk of cricket in his letters: this was the season of the infamous 'Bodyline' series, when the controversial tactics of England captain Douglas Jardine and his fast bowlers led not only to the regaining of the Ashes but also to a major diplomatic incident when the Australian government protested that it was unsportsmanlike to aim at the batsman's body rather than the stumps. If Hugh did manage to get a ticket for the packed Sydney Test Match in the first week of September, he would have seen the fast bowlers Larwood and Voce decimating the Australians (who were for once without the mighty Don Bradman), while the English batsmen Herbert Sutcliffe, Wally Hammond and the Nawab of Pataudi all scored centuries. It was a famous victory.

Raymond de Trafford came to stay. Boom reported that he had taken a tiny flat and is 'launched upon a sea of gaiety'. They had taken him to a play and a wrestling match. Boom recovered some of his dignity by becoming President of the Australian Sporting Club. He became involved in the boxing scene, especially enjoying the heavyweight bouts. The physiques of the lifeguards on Bondi Beach remained a source of much admiration. All in all, Boom wrote to his youngest daughter, 'Sydney is as delightful as ever and I see just those I like.'

Evelyn returned to England confirmed in his faith and exhilarated by his Italian trip. Meeting Lord Beauchamp had had a profound effect upon him. The theme of the aristocrat in exile, far from his beloved ancestral home was to haunt him. Like Lord Beauchamp, he too was a wanderer, and he now went to Pakenham Hall in County Meath (home of his Catholic friend Frank Pakenham, who later became Lord Longford).

Still he was in love with Teresa 'Baby' Jungman. Her letters dating from this time give a good indication of the state of affairs. Baby keeping Evelyn at arm's distance, Evelyn wanting more and becoming increasingly frustrated: 'Darling Evelyn, Don't be cross with me and keep ringing off all the time . . . what do you expect me to do when you say that you might fall in love with me and that your intentions are evil . . . I mean to try as hard as I possibly can not to behave badly.'

It has been suggested that their relationship was at stalemate because Baby simply did not find Evelyn physically attractive. But it was more complicated than this. Baby, despite her flapper reputation, was very serious about her religion. That is part of the reason Evelyn so loved her, as he did Olivia and as he would later love the woman who became his second wife. Evelyn wanted to have a sexual relationship, but for Baby this was not possible, especially since in the eyes of the Roman Catholic Church he was still married. Yet she was also being frustratingly ambivalent: 'If you weren't married you see it would be different because I might or I might not want to marry you but I wouldn't be sure.'

Maimie and Coote, who had witnessed Evelyn's despair, were furious with her. Sibell recalled that Maimie had a 'frightful row' with Baby on Evelyn's behalf and said: 'If you're going on like this with Evelyn, why don't you go and sleep with him?' Baby replied: 'Because I'm saving him from committing a mortal sin.'

In October *Black Mischief* was published. With this book, Evelyn began the practice of lavishly binding a first-edition copy for each of his closest friends. The dedicatees, Maimie and Coote Lygon, would have been top of the list to receive theirs. Evelyn told Diana Cooper that he thought that the book was good 'in just the same sense that Capt Hance's horsemanship is good'. By which he meant professionally most accomplished. But also, 'I don't credit it with any real value.'

The reviews of 'Blackers' were mixed. Some saw it as a transitional work of increasing seriousness, others as a humorous *jeu d'esprit* in the manner of Ronald Firbank. The novel, drawing on Evelyn's 1930 visit to Abyssinia for the coronation of Haile Selassie, tells the story of the efforts of the English-educated 'Emperor Seth', assisted by a fellow Oxford graduate Basil Seal, to modernise his Empire, the fictional African state of Azania. As Evelyn himself explained, the real 'savages' in the novel are the Bright Young Things and European middle-class emigrants. In its juxtaposition of sophisticated and 'primitive' cultures, it was an experimental dry run for *A Handful of Dust*, the great novel that grew from his love of Madresfield and his sensitivity to the effect of Lord Beauchamp's exile on his children.

CHAPTER 14

Up the Amazon

Evelyn spent time with his parents that autumn, 'pretty gloomy on account of being v. old and poor'. He often escaped to the Ritz for lunches and dinners. On one occasion he saw Sibell sitting at the next table. Evelyn was cross with her for a bitchy reference to Diana Cooper's 'raucous laugh' in one of her articles. He invited her for cocktails only to tear a strip off her for her betrayal. He only forgave her when she cried and then admitted that her lover Lord Beaverbrook had written the article.

In order to escape from home, he now planned a trip to British Guiana and Brazil, wanting to go 'among the wildest possible forest people'. South America had caught his fancy in part because of an article that he read in *The Times* on 29 October. Peter Fleming, brother of future Bond-creator, Ian, had written about an expedition in search of an explorer called Colonel Fawcett, who had ventured into the Brazilian jungle in 1925 in search of the fabled lost city of El Dorado. Fawcett was never seen again, but there were rumours of his being held captive by natives, or being worshipped as a god. Fleming's completed account was published the following year under the title *Brazilian Adventure.* Evelyn met Fleming in London and got his advice about an adventure of his own.

The trip would also be an escape from matters of the heart, the dispiriting relationship with Baby and his casual affair with Lady Lavery.

But the main thing was to get new material. With the publication of *Remote People* and *Black Mischief*, he had exhausted the stock of his African trip. South America would provide him with plenty of fresh copy. He booked a passage to Georgetown, the capital of British Guiana. His plan was to travel on horseback through the jungle to Boa Vista, making full use of the riding skills learned from Captain Hance. Then Manaos, and back to Europe.

Before departing for South America he made a valedictory visit to Madresfield, first to the Lygons and then to Captain Hance. His 'Collins' to Maimie (dated November 1932) shows him in good spirits:

> Darling Blondy,
>
> Well goodbye-ee don't cryee wipe the tear baby dear from your eye-ee tho it's hard to part I know I'll be tickled to death to go na pooh tootle oo good bye eee.
>
> So it was lovely at Mad and I cant thank you enough for all the innocent pleasure I had there.
>
> Best wishes to you all for the New Year. I hope that before I return you will all be married to royal dukes, mothers of many children and the idols of the populace.
>
> All love and xxxxxxx

A diary entry for 4 December 1932 describes his visit to Mad in the week before his departure. 'Arrived at Madresfield to find everyone still in bed. Three girls and Hubert in the house. Bloggs and Thom Lea to luncheon, later Lord Dudley, very jaunty. Saw Mr Harrison and Captain Hance and left early next morning with Hubert in his car.' A letter to Maimie written from the Savile Club, when he was more than a little drunk, suggests how deeply he had fallen in love with Mad:

> Well you will say how Bo must have hated staying with me this week-end. However, no, not at all, quite the reverse. I love it and will look back on the noble lines of the Malvern hills that I love so dearly . . . I was going on to enumerate all the glories of Malvern then I would say how wistfully and with heartache I would look back on them from the jungle.

Already the seed of his next novel was germinating: a man deep in the jungle looking back with wistful heartache on an English country house created in the exact mould of Madresfield.

He met Hazel Lavery in the vestibule of the Savile, and she drove him to North End Road to pick up clean clothes and then took him to have his passport photograph taken for his Venezuelan visa. He tried to see as much of Baby as he could. There were many church visits together, and he was delighted when she presented him with a gold St Christopher to wear around his neck. He later attributed the saving of his life to this medallion. Baby saw him off as he embarked for Georgetown: 'Deadly lonely, cold, and slightly sick at parting . . . Down the river in heavy rain and twilight. Heart of lead.'

Christmas was especially difficult. In *Ninety-Two Days*, the travel book he wrote about this trip, he commented that: 'Everyone has something to be melancholy about at Christmas, not on account of there being anything intrinsically depressing about the feast but because it is an anniversary too easily memorable; one can cast back one's mind and remember where one was and in what company, every year from the present to one's childhood.' Inevitably, spending Christmas of 1932 so far from England, he cast his mind back to Madresfield and the Christmas of 1931. He was invited to Government House in Georgetown for Christmas dinner, and his thoughts returned to the Malverns. He wrote to Maimie: 'So yesterday it was Christmas and we had very far flung stuff – turkey and mince pies and paper hats . . . and we drank to "Absent Friends" and everyone cried like Mr Hanson and I thought of you and little Poll and Lady Sibell and Hughie and Lord Elmley . . . and the Capt. G.B.H. and Min and Jackie and Reggie and Bartleet . . . God how S[ad].'

He was writing regularly to Maimie and, as usual, kept up an amusing account of his travels and the eccentrics he had met along the way, including an elderly man who talked in his sleep ('Buy something, fuck you! Why don't you buy something'). He would soon meet a more sinister eccentric, who would provide him with the starting-point – which became the end-point – for his next novel.

Christmas was also a low-key event for Hugh and his father in Australia, a world away from the lavish traditional celebrations at Mad. Beauchamp took pleasure in small things such as a gift of a beautiful orange and white dressing gown from his son. He and Hugh were planning a trip to the Blue Mountains, the spectacular range famous for its wildlife and flora and the blue mist in the air, an effect of the oil of the Eucalyptus trees.

Hugh was making the most of the opportunities afforded by Australia in the summer season. He went sailing and speed-boating. Boom wrote to Coote to tell her that he had finally convinced his son of the value of letters, especially to those in exile. 'Hugh appreciates the fact now! A sinner converted indeed!'

Beauchamp went on to give a poignant depiction of his life. While Hugh was out in the harbour on a speed boat, he sketched his own routine: reading a book in Hugh's room, a daily morning massage, cocktails at the club, home for luncheon, surfing at Bondi, lawn tennis at home, dinner at 6.45, sleep by ten, embroidery every day. He was still feeling the lack of yellow silk, about which he had complained in an earlier letter. A skilled embroiderer, he sent home as a Christmas gift for Mad the seat covers that he made for the dining chairs. Embroidered in bargello (Florentine flame stitch), they remain there today.

The children would not go to see their mother and Lady Beauchamp wrote that she was missing out on great happiness. There was an element of revenge in their refusal to visit her: they were ensuring that she felt as much of a pariah in Cheshire as their dear father did in Australia. He may have been missing Dickie, but at least he had Hugh. Boom wrote constantly, with Madresfield always on his mind. He had always loved his home, but now that he was in enforced exile his longing for it increased achingly.

Evelyn too, in his shack in the jungle, was thinking of Madresfield, as he was often to do. He wrote to Coote on the first day of the new year of 1933:

> Dear Poll,
>
> It is only five weeks since I left Madresfield. Now I am four thousand miles away and oh what a changed world. Instead of the smiling meadows of Worcestershire and the noble lines of the Malvern hills that I love so dearly, I look out upon a limitless

> swamp broken only by primaeval forest, desert and mountain. This club, if club it can be called so different is it from the gracious calm of Bucks and Punches, is a low shack on the edge of the jungle. A single oil lamp sways from the rotting beam and so thick are the mosquitoes round it that it sheds only a pale glow. The table has long ago been devoured by ants and I write on my knees crouching on an empty cask . . . Outside in the night air I can hear the tom-toms of hostile Indians encamped around us and the rhythmic rise and fall of the lash with which a drink crazed planter is flogging his half caste mistress.

He paints a vivid and unromantic picture of a world in which corrupt officials gamble away their bribes and missionaries, drunk with rum, 'have long forsaken their vows and live openly with native women infecting them with hideous diseases'. The contrast between the jungle and Madresfield could not be greater. There was a novel in that thought.

Evelyn was unimpressed with Georgetown. With his guide Haynes (in *Ninety-Two Days* he is called Bain), he left for Boa Vista, travelling by train, then boat, then horse. On the boat, a rancher joined them: 'Conversation was all between Mr Bain and the rancher, and mostly about horses. Quite different standards of quality seemed to be observed here from those I used to learn from Captain Hance.' Haynes was a farcical figure, prone to tales of exaggeration or pure fantasy. He had mood swings and wheezed with asthma. Evelyn grew increasingly worried, whilst also aware of his comic potential. Haynes told Evelyn to 'Listen out for the six o'clock beetle.' Why?

'Because he always makes that noise at six o'clock.'

'But it's now quarter past four.'

'Yes, that is what is so interesting.'

He was finally able to leave Haynes and head off for a Jesuit mission on the Brazilian frontier. The journey was fraught, with fierce heat and winds by day, freezing cold at night. On the way there was an incident that he related to the Lygon girls: his stallion reared and rolled on top of him, 'but luckily he was so small that it did not kill me outright'.

His face was burned from the intense savannah heat, despite his broad-brimmed hat. 'All through the blazing afternoon,' he reported to Maimie and Coote, 'I found that I thought of nothing except drinking. I told myself very simple stories which consisted of my walking to the bar of my club and ordering one after another frosted glasses of orange juice; I imagined myself at a plage, sipping ice-cold lemon squashes under a striped umbrella, beside translucent blue water.' He was plagued by insects, the worst being 'jiggers', the eggs of which had to be dug out of his feet with pins.

The only respite was to be found at travellers' ranches, though these were hardly luxurious. At one of them he encountered a man called Mr Christie, reclining in a hammock and sipping cold water from the spout of a white enamelled teapot. Christie was a religious maniac. Evelyn was enthralled:

> He had a long white moustache and a white woolly head . . . I greeted him and asked where I could water my horse. He smiled in a dreamy, absent-minded manner and said, 'I was expecting you. I was warned in a vision of your approach . . . I always know the character of my visitors by the visions I have of them. Sometimes I see a pig or a jackal; often a ravening tiger.'

Evelyn could not resist asking: 'And how did you see me?'

'As a sweetly toned harmonium,' replied Mr Christie politely.

Christie plied Evelyn with rum: 'The sweet and splendid spirit, the exhaustion of the day, its heat, thirst, hunger and the effects of the fall, the fantastic conversations of Mr Christie, translated that evening and raised it a finger's breadth above reality.' The latter phrase recurs in *Brideshead* when Charles falls under the spell of Sebastian: 'We . . . lay on our backs, Sebastian's eyes on the leaves above him, mine on his profile, while the blue-green shadows of foliage, and the sweet scent of the tobacco merged with the sweet summer scents around us and the fumes of the sweet, golden wine seemed to lift us a finger's breadth above the turf and hold us suspended.'

Another ranch belonged to a Mr Hart. Evelyn examined his well-stocked library, 'much ravaged by ants'. His next destination was the St Ignatius mission outside Bon Success, where he met and befriended a Jesuit called Father Mather. He stayed nine days, attending Mass in the mornings and reading during the day, as well as observing Father Mather's missionary work as priest and doctor. Despite the isolation and loneliness of the outpost, Evelyn found him 'one of the happiest men I met in the country'. Father Mather gave him a haircut and made him presents of a walking stick and a camera case.

On leaving Father Mather, he tried to reach Manaos via Boa Vista on horseback. This journey was extremely arduous, with little water or food. The thought of Boa Vista, 'a town of dazzling attractions', assumed even greater importance in his mind, so he was vastly disappointed when he arrived to find that it was no more than a 'squalid camp of ramshackle cut-throats'. He was bored and lonely. He wrote to Maimie and Coote:

> Well I have gone too far as usual and now I am in Brazil. Do come out and visit me. It is easy to find on account of it being the most vast of the republics of South America with an area of over eight million square kilometres and a federal constitution based on that of the United States. You go up the Amazon, easily recognisable on account of its being the largest river in the world, then right at Rio Negro (easily recognisable on account of being black) right again at Rio Bianco (easily recognisable on account of being white) and you cannot miss this village on account of its being the only one. The streets are entirely paved with gold which gives a very pretty effect especially towards sunset. But otherwise it is rather dull.

He was, of course, homesick:

> I am rather lonely and have to wait here for some weeks until it rains and there is enough water in the river to go to Manaos. When I get there it is quite near Malvern and I will come over if you will have me and take a glass of beer with you and Bartleet at the Hornyold.

His letters are peppered with references to their Malvern friends, especially the beer-drinking vicar's son ('Tell Bartleet the local beer is called Superale Amazona and is rather nasty on account of it being so warm').

To relieve the boredom he turned to writing: 'Wrote a bad article yesterday but thought of a good plot for a short story.' That story, based on his encounter with the deranged Mr Christie, would be a stepping-stone towards his masterpiece, *A Handful of Dust*.

He never made it to Manaos. He planned to return to Georgetown in what became an absurd misadventure that involved leaving Boa Vista, returning, leaving again, lost horses, lame horses and a potentially catastrophic attempt to return to Bon Success and Father Mather, in which he set off alone without his guide, Marco, and found himself hopelessly lost, without food or drink, exhausted and dehydrated. He was in danger of collapse and felt that he was close to death. In his desperation Evelyn turned to his faith: 'I had been given a medal of St Christopher [patron saint of travel] before I left London. I felt that now, if ever, was the moment to invoke supernatural assistance. And it came.' The odds he knew were against him – he later calculated them at 1:54.75 million. But he stumbled upon an old English-speaking Indian about to leave for Bon Success, who saved his life. He was equally grateful to Baby's medal. He thanked God that he was a Catholic, and took the short ride to Father Mather at St Ignatius, who was amazed to see him arriving on his weary horse.

Whilst he waited to complete the last stage of his journey, Evelyn read books from Father Mather's library, where he found copies of Charles Dickens. He had always associated Dickens with his father – sentimental Victorian tosh – but rediscovering the novels so far from home he felt reconnected to England and quintessential Englishness. He read *Nicholas Nickleby* with 'avid relish' and when he left he took with him a copy of *Martin Chuzzlewit*.

On the last leg of the return journey he reached a riverside camp belonging to a man he had met before, who ran a primitive trading-post that sold, amongst other things, mechanical mice. Like so many other details of his adventure, they would find their way into his novel. At the camp, he rested in a hammock, reading Dickens and recuperating, waiting for his feet to heal from the wounds gouged by the pins that extracted the jiggers.

By the first week in April he was back in Georgetown and able to dispatch a letter to Mad: 'Darling Blondy and Poll, Well I am back in Georgetown and all the world is Highclere' (Highclere was their phrase for all that was luxurious: Sibell had stayed at Highclere Castle and declared it the epitome of splendour). Relieved to be alive and safe, he was full of jokes and high spirits, sending messages to Grainger the Pekingese: 'Tell Grainger I had luncheon in a Chinese restaurant yesterday and ate a bird's nest.' Full, too, of plans for their reunion – 'Will you lunch with me at 1.30 on May 7th' – and telling them that he was so thin his trousers fell down and asking them if they'd like a present of a stuffed alligator. He longed for news of Madresfield, such as the meeting between Cecil Beaton and Captain Hance. He relished the thought of the effeminate 'Sexy Beaton' with the blustering Capt. G.B.H, but feared that the gossip would have left him behind: 'I suppose that I shall not be able to understand any Madresfield jokes by the time I get home.'

CHAPTER 15

A Gothic Man

> The scheme was a Gothic man in the hands of savages – first Mrs Beaver etc. then the real ones.
>
> (Evelyn Waugh to Henry Yorke, September 1934)

> I believe that man is, by nature, an exile and will never be self-sufficient or complete on this earth.
>
> (Evelyn Waugh, *Robbery under Law: The Mexican Object-Lesson*, 1939)

> I wanted to discover how the prisoner got there, and eventually the thing grew into a study of other sorts of savage at home and the civilised man's helpless plight among them.
>
> (Evelyn Waugh, 'Fan-fare', *Life* magazine, April 1946)

When Evelyn arrived back from South America on 1 May 1933 he went to his parents' home, 'cheery, red-cheeked, with a car load of luggage, and five stuffed crocodiles in a crate'. This was his last visit to Underhill, as his parents were moving to a small flat in Highgate. Evelyn visited the new flat the following day and offered to pay for the redecoration of the rooms.

He was shocked to read an announcement regarding *Black Mischief* that had been published in the Catholic newspaper *The Tablet*, while he had been in South America. Refusing even to name the title or the publisher, it said that a book of such 'coarseness and foulness' could not have been written by a true Catholic, which Mr Waugh purported to be, following the public announcement of his conversion a year or two before. Evelyn composed a long open letter in defence of his novel, addressing it to His Eminence the Cardinal Archbishop of Westminster. His father described the letter as 'masterly but libellous'. Evelyn and many of his friends were horrified by the viciousness of the attack on him. In the end, the open letter was not published, although Evelyn had copies privately printed and distributed to friends.

He went to the Yorkes for a visit and then it was to the Grand Pump Room Hotel in Bath, where he planned to read, sort and reply to his huge backlog of correspondence. Among the gossip to catch up on was the shocking news of the break-up of the Guinness marriage. Diana had been having an affair with the Fascist leader, Oswald Mosley. She had left Bryan to be Mosley's mistress. 'Don't tell Hazel I am back,' he also warned Yorke, for fear that Lady Lavery was still in pursuit of him. He was bored with the demands of this older society woman.

He also wrote to Maimie: 'Well I have come back and I have bought you an Indian rubber boat with rubber Indians in it . . . I have a stick of Brazilian tobacco for Capt GBH and it will make him sick.' He told her that he had seen her pictures in the press and that he would soon be back in London where they could get drunk together: 'Bath is awfully decent and I drink some very old and expensive port . . . come and see me. No alright then lunch at the Ritz Wed May 17th.' He promised to send Bath Buns to little Poll, whose healthy appetite was another standing joke. He would soon spend a few days at Mad, and wrote again to Maimie in advance: 'Longing to see the dignity prosperity and peace of Mad again. Will come Tues and let you know with telegrams.'

The Lygon girls had still not seen their mother, though in the spring they had sent her violets from Madresfield and a letter. Lady Beauchamp was thrilled. She wrote back: 'They slept near me, as did your dear letter.' Violets, she pointed out, denoted 'balm and healing'. If she thought, however, that forgiveness was on the way, she was very much mistaken.

Evelyn was deeply in debt and owed travel articles, which he was having difficulty writing. For the first time in his life he was writing badly. His agent, A. D. Peters, apologised to his editors: 'Evelyn has not been doing his best lately . . . he agrees it is time he pulled up his socks.' But Evelyn, always honest about himself, knew that he was in trouble: 'You can't tell me a thing I don't know about the quality of my journalism.' *Vogue* was refusing his articles because he was charging so much, although *Harper's* remained faithful, perhaps because of Sibell and her relationship with Beaverbrook.

In July, he wrote a short story called 'Out of Depth', which would be published in the *Harper's* Christmas number. He also wrote up 'The Man Who Liked Dickens', which was published in America in September and then in England in November. Both are on the theme of exile and the loss of paradise.

'Out of Depth' tells the tale of a forty-three-year-old man who has lost his faith. He time travels to the future, London (Lunnon) in the twenty-fifth century. All civilisation has disappeared and the city is merely fifty or so huts on stilts raised above the mudflats of the Thames. The people are no more than savages. His sanity is saved by his faith and his discovery of a church in the wilderness: 'Rip knew that out of strangeness, there had come into being something familiar; a shape in chaos.' He finds a congregation in prayer, two candles burning. He then awakes from his 'dream' to find a priest at his bed, where he makes a confession: 'I have experimented in black art.' It is the first fictional work in which his faith plays a significant part, a first tentative step towards the Catholic apologetics of *Brideshead*.

The image of the 'savages' and their huts by the muddy river obviously came from his experience up the Amazon, but the notion of placing a man of deep faith who has lost his way in the ruins of a once great civilisation suggests that he was also thinking about Lord Beauchamp sitting on Lord Berners's balcony looking out on the ruins of the Forum. The sometime proconsul is exiled among the remains of the great empire that he has served.

'The Man Who Liked Dickens' is based more directly on the Amazonian adventure. It combines Evelyn's meeting with the sinister Mr Christie and the Dickens library of Father Mather. The Christie figure, Mr McMaster, detains the traveller in the jungle, reading Dickens to him. There will be no escape: 'We will not have any Dickens today . . . but to-morrow, and the day after that, and the day after that. Let us read *Little Dorrit* again. There are passages in that book I can never hear without the temptation to weep.' The hapless traveller, ironically named Henty (after G. A. Henty, the author of popular imperial adventure stories for boys), is a young man of means who has closed up his country house and gone abroad while his wife remains in London, 'near her young man'. *A Handful of Dust* would be developed as a back story to the set piece of reading Dickens in the Amazon. The short story, slightly reworked, and with Christie renamed Mr Todd, suggestive of the German word for death, would form the climax of the novel.

That summer found him back at Madresfield for extended visits throughout May, June and the first half of August. Hugh had returned from Australia and there was yet another upsetting incident involving his alcoholism.

Evelyn wrote to Baby Jungman from Madresfield on 2 August, telling her that no one was there except for Maimie, Coote and Hughie. Hugh was in serious disgrace as he had been drunk all weekend and had 'Sykesed' the servants and tried to 'murder' Charlie Brocklehurst (a landowner from Sussex who was in love with Baby and many years later left her money). Wally Weston, the boxing maestro, had given Hugh what-for and Hugh was deeply remorseful. Evelyn described him sloping about not raising his eyes from his plate all weekend. He had been put into 'Lady Sibell's old room', which, he wrote, was full of bad taste objects and Eastern squalor. And he had once again been given the old day nursery as his study. Instead of having children themselves, the Lygon girls were serving as midwives to Evelyn's books.

Hugh's disintegration was devastating for his family and friends. His looks were fading and his violent outburst towards the staff and a family friend showed that he was no longer the gentle and sensitive young man of Oxford days. His guilt over his homosexuality was also part of the story. Evelyn tried to assist his old friend, but Hugh was beyond help. His battle against alcoholism continued, and in the meantime, Evelyn, unable to do anything, tried to save another Oxford friend who was also alcoholic, Alfred Duggan. From Madresfield he wrote to Nancy Mitford to tell her his latest plan: 'You will think me insane when I tell you that I am just off for Hellenic Society Cruise.'

The cruise was an attempt to return Alfred Duggan to the faith and help him abandon his heavy drinking – as well as being a more relaxing jaunt than the journey up the Amazon. Evelyn wrote from shipboard to the Lygon girls in the highest of spirits:

> Darling Blondy and Poll,
>
> So I am in the sea of Marmora and it is very calm and warm and there are lots of new and old chums on board and I have seen numbers of new and old places and am enjoying myself top-hole . . . Alfred (brother of bald dago) has behaved very well so far except for once farting at Lady Lovat . . . The ship is full of people of high rank including two princesses of ROYAL BLOOD. There is not much rogering so far as I have seen and the food is appalling . . . Perhaps that handsome Dutch girl is staying with you. She was expelled from Capri by Mussolini for Lesbianism you know.* Give her my love and a kiss on the arse and take one each for yourselves too.
>
> Bo
>
> And kiss Lady Sibells arse too if she is with you
> And Mims
> And Jackies
> I don't think Mr Hood would like it but give him one if he would.

(Mims was Captain Hance's wife, Jackie's mother; Mr Hood was the Birmingham boxer trained by Wally Weston.)

This new gang in which Evelyn had started to move became known as the 'Catholic Underworld'. After dinner they would form a group and listen to Father D'Arcy expound on doctrine. Prominent among them was Katharine Asquith, a friend of Diana Cooper, who was a Catholic convert and had inherited a large house in the West Country called Mells Manor. She noted in her diary that there was the 'usual rather unusual conversation' with Father D'Arcy explaining religious principles to Evelyn and Alfie, 'Mr Duggan rather drunk, but very attentive.' Evelyn added Katharine to his list of beauties. He noted that she 'spreads scandal and

* This sentence was suppressed from the published text in *The Letters of Evelyn Waugh* (1995).

nicknames them all . . . is exceedingly amusing and a great collector of ship's gossip'.

At the end of the cruise Evelyn and Alfie Duggan found themselves at a loose end. They accepted the invitation of one of the other passengers, Gabriel Herbert, to stay at her family's house in Portofino. It was there that he met for the first time Laura, Gabriel's younger sister, whom he described as a 'white mouse'. She was blonde, very pretty and fragile looking. The Herberts, all Catholic converts, were related by marriage to Evelyn Gardner. The visit was marred by Duggan's attempts to find strong liquor and Evelyn's attempts to stop him – all distressingly reminiscent of Hugh, but good originating material for the portrayal of alcoholism in the figure of Sebastian.

Evelyn was still desperately in love with Baby Jungman, though he felt that his prospects were bleak because of their Catholicism. The only hope was an annulment of his first marriage. On his return to England in October he began the first stage of what was to become a protracted and painful process. His case was submitted to the Ecclesiastical Court in five sittings during October and November and a report was sent to Rome. The whole business, he hoped, would be settled in six months. The case rested on whether there was a 'lack of real consent': according to canon law, if a couple married with the explicit understanding that the union might not endure for life, this was defective consent and therefore possible grounds for an annulment.

Evelyn gave his ex-wife lunch, where they discussed the tribunal. She-Evelyn had agreed to testify. He wrote to Coote telling her: 'I shall be in London on Wed to take my poor wife to be racked by the Inquisition.' The judgment at Westminster looked favourable, but the petition that was sent to Rome got lost and forgotten about for almost two years through a clerical error. Evelyn expected to hear from Rome by the following Easter, but in the end the annulment was not granted until 4 July 1936.

Following the Adriatic adventure, Evelyn increased his involvement with the Mells Catholic set. Like Madresfield, the lovely manor house in the Mendip Hills of Somerset became a haven for him. But it wasn't quite the same: he had to behave himself at Mells, something he always found difficult.

This was not a happy time. He needed money and his journalism was drying up. Diana Cooper had a house near Bognor in West Sussex, which was a present from her mother. It was a large cottage with Gothic windows separated from the shingle beach by a walled garden. In October 1933 she lent it to Evelyn who needed a period of isolation to write up his South American travel book *Ninety-Two Days*, which he dedicated to Diana. He wrote to Maimie, making light of his depression: 'had my hair cut in a bad taste way and came back to solitude, sorrow and my tear drenched pillow . . . yesterday I couldn't stand the disillusion, death, bitterness any more . . . I will see you on Wednesday when the sun has passed its zenith. In the evening, unless shes dutch I shall be with Miss J. Can't help loving that girl.' He also jokily alluded to thoughts of suicide: 'wish I was dead like Reggie Beaton' (Cecil's elder brother had just thrown himself under a tube train).

Maimie and Diana held very special places in his heart not only because they were beautiful but also because they were vulnerable and prone to unhappiness. His letters to them released his sentimental side. In Bognor, he wrote to Diana, opening with a parody of Noël Coward's *Private Lives* (a joke that he shared with the Lygon girls). He mentioned a 'tearful dinner with little Blondy when she talked about Duggan, very drunk, with such shining generosity that I could only say don't say any more you are making me cry so terribly' (the latter phrase is also a quotation from *Private Lives*). He also said in this letter that Blondy was expecting a proposal from Captain Malcolm Bullock, whose wife had died in a hunting accident in 1927. If he did propose to Maimie, she must have refused him. Evelyn was further depressed by a 'severe beating from my agent for idleness'. He signed the letter off with the words: 'Hate everyone except you and Maimie.'

Out of courtesy he told Diana that he liked the house, but he revealed the truth to Poll: 'It is a very sad life I lead, very lonely, very uncomfortable, in a filthy cottage in the ugliest place in England with only mice for company like a prisoner in the tower.' He found it hard to work and was still thinking of Baby, telling Diana Cooper: 'Trouble is I think of dutch girl all day and not sweet voluptuous dreams, no sir, just fretful and it sykeses the work.' To Maimie he revealed more: 'The Pope GBH won't let me use her (nor will she). God how S[ad].'

On 28 October he wrote to Maimie again: 'I was thirty on Saturday and feel sixty. I celebrated the day by walking into Bognor and going to the Cinema in the best 1/6 seats. I saw a love film about two people who were in love; they were very loving and made me cry . . . I bought myself Sitwell's new book and find it as heavy as my heart . . . It is very hard to be 30 I can tell you . . . oh dear oh dear I wish I was dead.'

Two letters to Coote also date from this time: 'Darling Poll,' he begins before launching into some typically affectionate abusive banter: 'Filthy Bitch – so much for your promise to write to me and cheer me up.' He complains of being lonely and miserable, writing his boring book, 'while you meanwhile are having lesbian fun with six toes and Capt GBH . . . so yesterday I went to London to get more divorced and I lunched at Ritz with little Blondy and saw a lot of repulsive people . . . it was awful going by train and not having you to see me off . . . But the important thing I have to say is that GRAINGER KISSED ME spontaneously and with evident relish.'

In the other letter to Coote, sent from Bognor, he noted it was 'the 2nd anniversary of my first visit to Mad'. And, 'So you were not really a filthy bitch because you were writing to me just when I had despaired of a letter.' He told her that he had grown his hair and a beard and looked 'very effeminate and bohemian'. 'I am very lonely and very well and sober . . . I am looking forward to the next war. I shall get a medal and lose a leg and that is irresistible for sex appeal.'

Hugh was also travelling that year. After his long stay in Australia with his father over Christmas 1932 and into the New Year, he returned via the Pacific route, with a month's stop-over in New York in April 1933. The passenger list describes his occupation as 'horse trainer'. He is listed as six feet one inch tall with fair hair, fair complexion and blue eyes. 'In good mental and physical health', says the documentation for the immigration department, but that was hardly the case. He stayed with a friend named John Steward; it was his first time in the United States.

After spending the summer back in England – when he saw Evelyn at Mad during August – he departed from Southampton, returning to Australia again via New York. Boom was still in Carthona, but had broken a finger, and for a while had to have his letters dictated as his finger was wrapped in plaster of Paris. He wrote to Coote to tell her the news that his servant George had recently married, but would carry on doing things for him until Hugh came out. Then, in November 1933, he wrote that Hugh had arrived, full of news of a trip with Coote to Ireland with his greyhounds.

Hugh stayed with his father for Christmas 1933.

Evelyn returned to Mad for a few days at the end of November. He wrote to Maimie, thanking her for her hospitality: 'God how sad not to see you and say thank you thank you for all your kind hospitality. It has been lovely staying with you. Thank you. Thank you.' His big news was that in anticipation of the annulment he had proposed to Baby: 'Just heard yesterday that my divorce comes on today so was elated and popped question to Dutch girl and got raspberry. So that is that, eh. Stiff upper lip and dropped cock.'

Mad proved a haven at this time of disappointment. He was back there in early December and again for Christmas. Then he returned home and told his parents that he planned to go to Fez in Morocco, where, as Arthur Waugh noted in his diary, 'he hopes to complete his new novel'. This would be *A Handful of Dust*.

> What I have done is *excellent*. I don't think it could be better. Very gruesome. Rather like Webster in modern idiom.
>
> (Evelyn Waugh, letter to Diana Cooper)

Diana Cooper saw him off on the boat bound for Tangier. Letters from Maimie and Coote arrived in no time: 'How very decent and surprising to get letters from you both so soon. It made me feel less than a thousand miles away.' He went on to describe Fez, which he found 'very decent' with little streams running through it and old houses with pretty walled gardens. In the tongue-in-cheek tone reserved for the sisters, he told of seeing 'little Arab girls of fifteen and sixteen for ten francs each and a cup of mint tea. So I bought one but I didn't enjoy her very much.' In the midst of this letter he mentioned that he was at work on the new book: 'I have begun the novel and it is excellent, first about sponger and then about some imaginary people who are happy to be married but not for long.'

'Sponger' was Murrough O'Brien, a major in the Irish Guards, who was one of the models for the character of John Beaver. But the claim that the people who are not married for long were 'imaginary' is disingenuous: Evelyn was drawing, in different ways, both on his own brief marriage and on the separation of the Earl and Countess Beauchamp. The novel was developing into a much more serious work than his earlier ones. In another letter he told Katharine Asquith that he was pegging away at it, but that it was 'very difficult to write because for the first time I am trying to deal with normal people instead of eccentrics. Comic English character parts too easy when one gets to be thirty.'

Meanwhile he told Diana Cooper that he had seen the English papers and that the latest news was Lady Sibell's row with her uncle, the Duke of Westminster. There was a 'huge photograph' of her on the front page with the headline 'DUKE SUES NIECE'. He clearly knew all about why they were at loggerheads, but was discreet and even made a joke: 'the consul's wife said "Let me see, Lady Sibell Lygon is the Duke of Westminster's *fourth* wife isn't she?"' He also joked: 'Has Maimie married the pauper prince?' This is a slightly mysterious allusion: either she had renewed her involvement with Prince George or she had begun her relationship with the exiled nephew of the last Tsar of Russia.

Sibell allegedly libelled her uncle in the *Oxford and Cambridge Magazine*, causing him to issue a writ. The matter was eventually settled with an apology. She had accused him of being unpatriotic and 'unwholly indifferent to his responsibilities to this country'. The story of course hit the headlines, with only those in the know guessing the underlying reason for her attack upon his extravagant lifestyle.

Controversy dogged Sibell, not least because of her on-off affair with Lord Beaverbrook, the great press baron. It was he who introduced her to a rising young Labour politician, Aneurin 'Nye' Bevan. He converted her to socialism and she celebrated her conversion in 1932 by drinking Black Velvets. Bevan fell in love with her and wanted to marry her. She famously said: 'Anyone who knows Aneurin for six months either becomes a Socialist or goes mad.'

Evelyn reported from Fez to his friends that he had become attached to a young prostitute called Fatima. She had a gold tooth and was covered in blue tattoos. Since they could not speak each other's language, there was 'not much to do in between rogering'. Maimie had given him a Lalique glass ring, which he didn't like. He told her: 'I gave Fatima that milk ring you gave me, now if you are angry I shant be able to send it back and be forgiven.' He asked her to send all the gossip, as he claimed not to see many newspapers and was eager to keep in touch with Mad World: 'Tell Bartleet the beer is no good here . . . best love to Mr Grainger and your dear sisters.' He did not tell Katharine Asquith, his more pious female correspondent, about Fatima. The friendship with Maimie was robust enough to take the confession – and, given what she had been through in relation to her father, nothing sexual could shock her.

He was pleased with the progress of the novel: 'My good taste book is two thirds done. I think I shall finish it in three weeks and then I shall come to England for a day or two and hope to see you and Poll and that ill-behaved Lady Sibell' (a reference to the Westminster libel case). He asked for Maimie's advice for his hunting scene, where the child is killed: 'I have written a hunting scene and I expect it will be full of mistakes so I will read it to you and you can correct it . . . Please keep writing to me.' Sibell always admired Evelyn's great loyalty to her family, especially to her sister Maimie, but they were also loyal to him; their letters to him whilst he was abroad meant a great deal. He told Diana Cooper: 'I get constant letters from the Lygons but no one else.'

When he returned to England at the end of February he sent Maimie a postcard from Chagford, where he was putting the finishing touches to the book. He mentioned the resolution of the libel case and jokingly told Maimie: 'I have got a pipe for you to smoke hashish in.' He also alluded once again to her aspirations to princessdom: 'I suppose by now the pauper prince will be on the high seas and you will be in the soup again.' That October, Prince George was created Duke of Kent and the following month he married Princess Marina of Greece.

In late March, Evelyn turned up at his parents' door with the Lygons' car. He had come to move his clothes to their home in Belgrave Square. Arthur chatted to him while he packed. The same month he went to Madresfield with the sisters and accompanied them to the Cheltenham Races. In Hugh's absence, Evelyn was their surrogate brother.

Hugh and Boom, meanwhile, were travelling from Australia to America. They arrived in New York, where they stayed at the Waldorf, in the company of Robert Harcourt Byron, the tall handsome valet-cum-secretary. The passenger list says that Lord Beauchamp's final destination was England – but this was not so. His exile seemed interminable and the strain was telling. His striking black hair had by now turned grey.

A Handful of Dust, the novel Evelyn was working on all this time, was published in September 1934. The title – taken from one of the avant-garde poems that Harold Acton had recited through his megaphone at Oxford, T. S. Eliot's *The Waste Land* – was a signal of the new seriousness of Waugh's theme: 'I will show you fear in a handful of dust.'

The novel's great themes are exile and barbarianism. The twist is that the true savages are not those in the Amazon jungle but rather the selfish monsters from the world of the Bright Young Things – Brenda Last and John Beaver. The most savage moment in the novel comes not in the depth of the jungle, but in the moment of Brenda's relief at hearing that it is her young son John Andrew who has been killed and not her lover John Beaver:

> 'What is it, Jock? Tell me quickly, I'm scared. It's nothing awful, is it?'
>
> 'I'm afraid it is. There's been a very serious accident.'
>
> 'John?'
>
> 'Yes.'
>
> 'Dead?'
>
> He nodded.
>
> She sat down on a hard little Empire chair against the walls, perfectly still with her hands folded in her lap, like a small well-brought-up child introduced into a room full of adults. She said, 'Tell me what happened. Why do you know about it first?'
>
> 'I've been down at Hetton since the week-end.'
>
> 'Hetton?'
>
> 'Don't you remember? John was going hunting to-day.'
>
> She frowned, not at once taking in what he was saying. 'John . . . John Andrew . . . I . . . oh, thank God . . .' Then she burst into tears.

John Andrew, the precocious child who is killed, was partly modelled by Diana Cooper's clever son, John Julius (who grew up to become the writer John Julius Norwich). The riding accident was perhaps inspired by a combination of the story about the death of the only son of 'Bendor'

Duke of Westminster and a hunting accident involving the child of a Lygon neighbour, which Evelyn had heard about at Mad.

The old-fashioned gentleman exiled from his country home is called Tony Last. He is the last of his kind. And the creation of his story owes a profound debt to Evelyn's knowledge of the last man to be hounded out of England: Earl Beauchamp. 'A whole Gothic world had come to grief . . . there was no armour glittering through the forest glade, no embroidered feet on the greensward; the green and dappled unicorn had fled.' Last's sense of betrayal and dispossession is Boom's.

Waugh's art of composite character portrayal reached a new sophistication in this book. At a superficial level – though Waugh denied the identification, as he always did – Tony and Brenda Last have elements of a well-known high-society couple, Lord and Lady Brownlow. 'I am so afraid that Periwinkle will think it is about him – it isn't but bits of it are like,' Evelyn had admitted to Maimie in a letter from Fez. Peregrine Francis Adelbert Cust, sixth Baron Brownlow (Eton, Sandhurst and the Grenadier Guards), sometimes called 'Perry' or 'Winkle', would be personal lord-in-waiting to Edward VIII at the time of the abdication crisis. He drove Mrs Simpson across France, pursued by the press, the week before the final announcement. But that was to come: at this time, he loved his ancestral home, Belton House, while his wife, Katherine, daughter of a brigadier, preferred to spend time in London. At another level, Brenda Last, with her marital infidelity, is shaped by She-Evelyn. But the profoundest and subtlest identification is that whereby Tony is fashioned out of a combination of Evelyn himself and Boom.

Hetton Abbey, Tony's ancestral home, is manifestly Madresfield Court. The architectural resemblance is much more obvious and thoroughgoing than that between Madresfield and Brideshead Castle. If we must attach to Madresfield the dubious phrase 'the real' – dubious because all Waugh's fictional people and places are subtle transformations, not direct portrayals, of 'reality' – then it was 'the real Hetton' more than 'the real Brideshead'. Like the real Mad, the fictional Hetton was 'entirely rebuilt in 1864 in the Gothic style'. Like Mad, it has a central clock tower and a moat. The medieval Great Hall and the dining room are described in language that could come out of a *Country Life* article about the architecture of Madresfield – the hammer beam roof festooned with red and gold flags; the lancet windows of armorial stained glass; the huge chandelier with twenty electric bulbs to light it by night, the minstrels' gallery. The comfortable smoking room just off the library, the shuttered drawing room, the dark inner courtyard, the cloistral passages, the chapel where daily prayers were once said: all were instantly recognisable to the Lygon girls when they read the novel. The collections of china and snuff boxes are the same; the treasures and the oil paintings, the rare books and manuscripts in the library. Evelyn even describes the fireplace in the Drawing Room of Mad, the dado rail and the plaster work. As at Mad, each bedroom has a medieval name, though these are changed so as not to make the identification too obvious. The champagne is decanted into large jugs in Hetton, just as Boom insisted on in Mad. Countless memories are woven into the texture of the narrative: autumn light filtering in through the stained-glass windows, green and gold, gules and azure on the emblazoned coats-of-arms; Brenda walking down the great staircase with the light falling on her; patches of coloured reflection, the mingling of dusk and rainbow. The description of Christmas reads like a diary account of festivities at Mad. All of this must have been very amusing for the Lygon sisters. Jokes about an ill-tempered Pekingese called Djinn were included for the special benefit of Maimie.

The novel is peppered with references to old houses being demolished to make flats, often for people like Brenda so that they can take a lover – the moral degeneracy of modern times. The desire to cover the drawing-room walls with chromium plating and to replace the priceless rugs with sheepskin carpets is a sign of the new barbarism.

When Tony, beginning to feel the heat, has a delirious vision of the Lost City in the jungle, it is Hetton that he sees: 'It was Gothic in character, all vanes and pinnacles, gargoyles, battlements, groining and tracery, pavilions and terraces, a transfigured Hetton, pennons and banners floating on the sweet breeze, everything luminous and translucent.' As he is sucked further and further into the darkness of the Amazon, he continues to see transmutations of his lost paradisal home. The writing is partly inspired by Evelyn's own memories of Mad, reactivated every time he wrote to the Lygon girls, on his own Amazonian adventure.

But the longer shadow is that of Lord Beauchamp: the man whose ancestors had remodelled his house in the style of English Gothic and who was now exiled in a hot climate and an alien culture thousands of miles from the gentle landscape of the Malvern Hills. In *The Stones of*

Venice, John Ruskin argued that Gothic was the true architecture because of the 'sacrifice' of the stonemasons in the work they put into the intricate decoration of every stone. Gothic was accordingly the model for a life of service to the greater good. Boom believed that he had lived just such a life of service to his God, his country and his family heritage. But he fell among savages, Bendor Duke of Westminster above all, and was himself sacrificed on the altar of sexual hypocrisy, then condemned to wander the earth. When Waugh created the figure of Tony Last, in exile from the petals of almond and apple blossom in the orchard of an ancestral home, in the depths of his imagination he was thinking of how Boom must have dreamed of the sights and the smells of the Madresfield that he had lost: 'Carpet and canopy, tapestry and velvet, portcullis and bastion, waterfowl on the moat and kingcups along its margin, peacocks trailing their finery across the lawns; high overhead in a sky of sapphire and swansdown silver bells chiming in a turret of alabaster.'

CHAPTER 16

Fiasco in the Arctic

A fiasco very narrowly rescued from disaster.

(Evelyn Waugh)

Hughie . . . was a sweet, sweet man. He was the gentlest of them all, very knowledgeable, very quiet, lovely companion . . . Evelyn was very unfit, but enormously brave, you see, he just never gave up.

(Sir Alexander 'Sandy' Glen)

Evelyn had in mind that his next project would be a biography of Pope Gregory the Great. In April 1934 he wrote to Maimie Lygon telling her that he had finished *A Handful of Dust*, which he called his Good Taste ('G.T.') book. He told her that he had hunted – 'a very good run and did not fall off' – and that he was going to stay with Gabriel Herbert on the way to London. This was his first visit to Pixton, the Herbert family home near Dulverton, Somerset, and probably where Laura first properly caught his eye. He told Maimie that all three 'tender Miss Herberts' were at home: 'there are so many dogs in this house and they all sit in chairs so that I have to stand all the time and that is tiring'.

During a June heatwave in London, he went down to Madresfield. Back in London, on 5 July, after a tea party given by Lord Berners, Evelyn wandered over to Halkyn House to see if any of the Lygon girls were home. Instead he found Hugh, alone in the library, drinking gin. Hugh told him that he was leaving for Spitsbergen in two days' time with Alexander Glen.

Glen was a Balliol undergraduate. In 1932 his life had changed as the result of a misapprehension. He thought that a friend had invited him to a debutante's party, only to be told that they were shortly to sail from King's Lynn. On remarking that the Norfolk coast was an odd place from which to set out for an evening's drinking and dancing, he was told that the *party* in question was actually a group going to explore the Arctic. But he went along anyway and fell in love with the Far North. He went back the next year, leading a sixteen-man Oxford University summer expedition, which carried out valuable topographical and geological surveys of West Spitsbergen. In the winter he spent some months with the Lapps of northern Sweden.

Now he proposed another trip, on a much smaller scale, which would be an exploratory mission for a full-scale Oxford University Arctic survey that he duly led in 1935–36.

Glen met Hugh at Madresfield, where he was staying after Sibell's Chepstow Races party. The young explorer asked him if he would like a jaunt and, he recalled, 'Hughie said he'd love a jaunt.' Many years later, Glen vividly recollected Hugh's sweetness and gentleness. Not only was he very quiet and altogether a 'lovely companion', he was also intelligent and bookish – not at all the image of him as remembered by others.

Late in life, Glen remembered that the third member of the party, before Evelyn got involved, was to be a man called Anthony Holland whose father had been one of the great West African explorers in the 1880s. He recalled taking Anthony up to Madresfield to meet Hugh. He said that they got on very well before dinner. Hugh's boxing trainer was there. The trouble began when Anthony got very drunk over dinner. There was a row that culminated in a fight between him and Hugh. Glen recalled that Holland knocked Hughie out when they were taking port and that there was a tremendous scene. He said that the girls, Maimie and Coote, were there. Holland was 'very stiff upper lip' and said that he'd better withdraw from the expedition.

According to Glen's recollection, Evelyn was staying at Mad at the time, and upon Holland's withdrawal Evelyn asked, 'Can I come along?' and he said: 'Of course you can come along, and this made it very jolly.' Evelyn's diary does not survive for June, when this would have been, so there is no confirmation that he was there at the time – Glen's recollection came from late in his life and it seems that he was conflating the evening at Mad with a meeting in London. The impression given by Evelyn's journal, which resumes after a long silence with the Berners tea party, was that his decision to join the party was made on a whim so as to escape the hot and tedious London summer: 'I said I would go to Spitzbergen too. Then I went back to dress. While I was in my bath Sandy Glen rang me up and came to see me. We had champagne while I dressed. He said it was all right my going to Spitzbergen with him. I gave him £25 for fares and he gave me a list of things I should need.'

This accords with the much less dramatic account of the origin of the trip that Glen recorded in his 1935 book *Young Men in the Arctic*: 'We were due to leave Newcastle on 7th July, and on the evening of the 5th I received a message from Lygon to say that Evelyn Waugh was very keen on joining us. Supplies had been ordered for two, but I had left a small safety margin which was nearly sufficient for a third person.'

The next day Evelyn met up with Hugh at Halkers where they drank gin. Then they went to Lillywhite's to buy equipment for the trip – skis and ice axes and balaclava helmets. Evelyn tried on windproof clothes and bought a sleeping bag and cover. Sandy was very pleased that Evelyn thought to lay in a crate of chocolate and a supply of morphine. Later on Evelyn rang 'The 43', an infamous club in Gerrard Street, Soho – 'half a speakeasy and half a brothel', according to Alec Waugh – and requested his favourite girl, Winnie (the name he gave to the daughter of the woman hired for the divorce assignation in *A Handful of Dust*). When they said that she had not arrived, he went to her flat. He noted drily in his diary that 'she put up a good show of being sorry for my departure'. In fact, when he departed Winnie was the only person who sent him a good-wishes farewell telegram. 'Nothing from Madresfield,' he told his diary.

The next morning he went to Mass 'to confess Winnie'. Then back to Halkers to drink gin. They drank Black Velvets in the heat of the afternoon on the train from King's Cross to Newcastle. Sandy struggled to keep up with the two seasoned drinkers. He had never drunk Black Velvet before and was soon feeling the effects.

On board the passenger ferry to the Far North they had more drink and met a Norwegian alcoholic who smashed light bulbs with his head. To kill time on the slow passage up the Norwegian coast, Hugh and Evelyn played piquet and had a beard-growing competition: 'Hughie's is golden and even. Mine appears to be black and patchy.' Evelyn cut his head and looked 'disreputable' in his bloodied bandage. Their appearance and their propensity to drink large quantities of alcohol meant that the English passengers 'ceased making friendly advances'.

Evelyn grew irritated by Glen, calling him 'the leader' in his diaries and telling jokes and stories that only Hugh would have known about, but Glen insisted on laughing and joining in. Glen was the experienced one and they had to follow his lead. Hugh and Glen were much fitter, physically, than Evelyn, who had allowed himself to get out of shape with his partying during the previous months.

On 14 July they set sail on the last leg of the journey, from Tromsø to Spitsbergen. Conditions were not good; there was a heavy swell and Hugh and Glen were sick. It was difficult to sleep with 'golden sunlight streaming into the cabin all night': Evelyn took a treble dose of sleeping draught and crashed out for thirteen hours. At about seven in the evening they came into sight of Spitsbergen, 'Black mountains with glaciers flowing down to the sea between them – occasionally a narrow silver strip between iron grey sky and iron grey sea, the glaciers brilliantly white.' At Advent Bay the view was desolate, cloudy and dark: 'the higher slopes below the clouds were marked like zebra with white streaks of snow'. Small copper-green icebergs floated near the banks. They rowed in a small whaling boat to get to their camp. Glen remembered that the rowing was fairly rough and that Evelyn struggled, but was terribly brave: 'He was frightfully out of condition but he'd never give up.'

Their base was called Bruce City. It consisted of four huts and a glacier. There were supplies there from Glen's earlier expedition. Evelyn and Hugh were annoyed when Glen gave a bottle of rum to the whaling crew. Terns swooped at their heads in a hostile manner, though Evelyn was fascinated to find that the supplies left from the previous year were in first-rate condition.

After a night's rest they rowed across a fjord to another, smaller bay. Evelyn described the scene in his essay 'The first time I went to the north':

> Seals bobbed up in the water all round us; there were innumerable small icebergs, some white and fluffy, others deep green and blue like

> weathered copper, some opaque, some clear as glass, in preposterous shapes, with fragile, haphazard wings and feathers of ice, pierced by holes. The whole bay was filled with their music, sometimes a shrill cricket-cry, sometimes a sharp, almost regular metallic ticking, sometimes the low hum of a hive of bees, sometimes a sharp splintering, sometimes a resonant boom, coming from the shore where another crag of ice broke away from the underhung glaciers. The fog cleared about midnight, the sun lay on the horizon and in the superb Arctic light, that is both dawn and sunset, the ice face shone clear and blue to the white snow above it and the water was dense indigo.

The trigger-happy Glen was startled by Evelyn's objection to his killing a seal on the grounds that all life was sacred. Glen was struck by this 'tenderness' in Evelyn and said that it made a great impression on him: 'he was very powerful' as a personality, he recalled. Glen's published account of the expedition contains a close-up photograph of a seal but not, alas, one of Evelyn and Hugh.

The first task was to move the stores. They planned to climb a glacier three miles away, across a mosquito-infested valley of mud and sharp stone. They had to carry everything on their backs: 'we made two journeys a day, taking between thirty and forty pounds in a load. It was beastly work.' Once they were on the snow they felt that the worst of their labours were over. They were wrong. On the second day there was heavy rain and the great thaw made trudging across the wet snow even harder, especially as they had now loaded the sledge and were without dogs. Hugh and Evelyn went in front, harnessed with the ropes to pull, while Sandy Glen, exercising the prerogative of the expedition leader, stood behind to steer and push. After two exhausting hours they had barely gone a hundred yards. Glen later remarked, 'Lygon and Waugh had never seen a glacier before, let alone taken part in a sledge journey, and they had pictured our travelling twenty miles or so a day over a crisp, smooth surface.' Far from the snow being crisp and smooth, it was wet and soft.

Hugh had a particular aversion to getting wet, but it was his fate to be constantly soaked through. Again, Evelyn struggled as he was not as physically fit as the others, but he never complained. They had to move the stores in two loads, and it took a week of ten-hour shifts carrying half the provisions on their backs and then returning for the sledge. In the exceptional thaw due to the warm temperatures their clothes and bedding became soaked, and it was impossible to dry them out. Their small primus stoves were used to boil oatmeal and pemmican (dried meat mixed with melted fat), which Evelyn found disgusting. He also found the skis very hard going in the soggy snow. Glen drew his attention to an excellent ski instruction manual in their supplies. It emphasised the necessity of not regarding skis as two boards glued to one's feet. 'Above all,' it said, 'be happy, whistle.' Evelyn had the utmost contempt for this, Glen reported: 'his skis were a painful necessity fixed rather inevitably to his feet, and he would not look upon them as anything but despicable athletic implements'. Hugh, by contrast, was 'amazingly good' on his skis. Evelyn had a similarly disdainful attitude to the porridge that was the basis of their diet, with the result that he lost even more weight than the others in the course of the expedition – Glen was amazed at how much work he got through, considering how little he ate.

There was fog all around and tempers frayed as Glen changed his mind about climbing the glacier. He decided to turn west in the hope of finding a trapper's hut and a boat used on his last expedition. Evelyn was extremely pessimistic about the prospect. They came to the mouth of the Mittag-Leffler glacier, from the base of which a small number of streams trickled into the sea. Dense fog surrounded them, so they set up camp and slept. When they awoke the fog had lifted and the landscape was beautiful, laced with Arctic flowers such as saxifrage and wild poppies. They breathed in 'the unique Arctic night, not a breath of wind, immaculate'. The next day was as blissful, as they moved among a mass of bird life: terns, duck and geese laying on nests so close together and in such a great mass that it was almost impossible not to stand on them.

They reached the trapper's hut and Evelyn was left to clean it while Hugh and Glen returned to the old camp for the stores and tent. Evelyn cleaned the hut, chopped wood, tended the stove and then fell asleep, but not for long. Soon after, Glen burst in 'in a state of some agitation'. The small streams had burst and turned into torrents in the few hours since they had crossed the river. Hugh had managed to wade across to their former camp, but Glen had not. Hugh, drenched to the skin, had stripped off his clothes, presenting Glen with the sight 'of an entirely naked man running along the side of a glacier six hundred miles from the North

Pole'. The problem now was that Hugh could not cross back again without the help of the other two.

Half an hour before they even reached the glacier, Evelyn could hear the roar of the water: 'the flow was terrific . . . running at a dizzy speed, full of boulders and blocks of ice whirling down in it'. The ice threatened to knock them off their feet. The danger of being swept away was extreme, so the two men tied themselves together with tarred twine and were able to pull each other through the freezing water.

When they saw Hugh, he was laden with supplies. They threw him the twine on a ski stick and managed to drag him across, but at the last minute, with Glen safely back on the glacier, Evelyn was knocked over by an ice boulder, pulling Hugh down with him. The powerful current swept them away together. 'I had time to form the clear impression,' Waugh remembered, 'that we were both done for.' But then the twine snapped, and 'I found myself rolling in shallow water and was able to crawl ashore.'

Hugh was stuck on a small iceberg upstream and there seemed to be no way of rescuing him. Evelyn and Glen shouted at him to throw away his backpack, but he wouldn't. Hugh finally got to his feet and waded across, still fully loaded. Evelyn had 'uncertain memories of how we got back to the hut'. He was badly shaken and it took Hugh a long time to thaw out: 'We seem to have rubbed one another with sand to get back our circulation. Our jaws were out of control, set tight with cold or chattering so that we could not speak.' Glen remembers making a massive fire with the large quantities of driftwood that lay about. They dried their clothes and themselves. They slept and then awoke to find themselves covered in cuts and bruises.

Evelyn was very angry about the incident. They only had flour and some sugar to eat and a decision had to be reached as to what to do next. They could attempt the river, they could wait for the trapper to return to the cabin, or they could climb up into the mountains, a longer route that would take them above the river and back to their original base, where there were supplies and their boat. Evelyn recalls that Glen wanted to wait for the flood to abate. Although Hugh's knee was badly injured, Evelyn suggested setting off across the mountains: 'I did not think it would be successful, but it seemed preferable to waiting.' Glen recalls that he favoured staying, thinking that the river would block itself again. Hugh, as always, was very detached and totally unconcerned in the nicest possible way. He did not complain about his knee, but they had to wait until he felt well enough to walk. Glen remembers Evelyn shrieking at him that the whole business was 'typical of your folly'. Glen was unperturbed and agreed to try the mountain route, a trek of seventy miles without proper supplies and only half a bowl of pemmican a day.

In the meantime, they had a further local difficulty. They had lost their hats in the disastrous river crossing. This not only exacerbated their coldness, but also created a problem with the terns. In *Young Men in the Arctic*, Glen explains their resourceful response:

> Many of them were nesting near the hut and they resented our presence. If one as much as ventured outside, a crowd of angry shrieking terns would dive in turn at one's head and only the thickest balaclava helmet gave adequate protection from their pecks. After much thought we hit upon our ration bowls as substitutes, but the loud ping, which announced that a tern had made a bull's eye, seemed to encourage every other bird in the neighbourhood to join in the attack. A few days later we made the great discovery that if we held a long stick above our heads, it, instead of the head, became their target.

Once Hugh was able to walk, they set off. They did the journey in three days. They slept two nights in the open in damp and windy weather. Going over the top of a col, they took shelter from an incoming storm under an overhanging rock. Evelyn, huddled close to Glen, made 'a splendid comment, saying "If I hadn't joined the Church of Rome four years ago I could never have survived your appalling incompetence"' – he stood bolt upright in the midst of the storm to make this pronouncement. 'Hughie, very typically, was making himself comfortable under the rock, taking no notice of this.'

They had been on their feet for over twenty-four hours when they at last saw their base camp, separated from them by a shallow stream. Hugh and Evelyn refused to take another step. Glen's hunger drove him on and when he got to the hut he lit a huge fire and made a meal. 'Then conscience struck': he made some scones, filled them with redcurrant jam and chucked them over the river. Waugh and Lygon fielded them very well, so Glen's conscience was salved. They finally came back to the hut and that was the end of the journey.

They slept for thirty-six hours, regained their strength and rowed back to the Norwegian coalmine from where they had begun.

For Evelyn, the experience was 'hell – a fiasco very narrowly rescued from disaster', as he put it in a letter to Tom Driberg. His essay on the adventure, published in a collection by various authors entitled *The First Time I –* , was duly subtitled 'Fiasco in the Arctic'. He said that he could have called it: 'The first time I ever despaired of my life'. Evelyn did, however, acknowledge that the Arctic had many advantages over the tropics. There was constant light in which to read, everything was clean, cuts healed quickly, food remained fresh for weeks at a time, there were no insects, no microbes and no poisons – none of that unending warfare against corruption, the sterilising and disinfecting, the iodine and the quinine, mosquito nets and snake boots that impeded one in the tropics.

The ever-sanguine Glen recalled the whole experience as a joyous one and had nothing but praise for Evelyn's courage and tenacity: 'Hughie was quite fit. Evelyn was very unfit, but enormously brave, you see, he just never gave up.' He looked back with pleasure on the evenings when they drank whisky and smoked cigars. The conversation was 'very far reaching and very good'. He was aware that, being a decade older than he was, Hugh and Evelyn knew more about life and art and people, though less about the Arctic, than he did. He found Evelyn an easy and pleasant companion: 'I found him sweet, absolutely.' He excused Evelyn's bad temper as mere insecurity – a tendency to panic. He admired Evelyn's response to the beauty of the landscape and the wildlife, though found it hard to understand a man who would exclaim 'I hate dogs.' Yes, Waugh had panicked over the torrent incident, but he had shown 'enormous bravery overcoming his own panic'.

Glen's account captures perfectly Hugh Lygon's insouciance and phlegmatic disposition. He comes across as a remarkable character: a tall, handsome, muscular young man with his golden beard and athlete's physique, but also calm (preternaturally so) and somehow finding his corner of the mountain to take shelter in. His gentleness was a foil to Evelyn's vivacity, vigour and irritability. He shone in his ability to joke and to talk intimately with Evelyn.

Glen saw that Hugh and Evelyn were 'very, very close'. There were non-stop jokes between them, which in time he began to share: 'Jokes were far more dangerous than anything else, because your tummy was so sore with laughter . . . it was hysterical.' The two friends were perfectly balanced. Evelyn was a worker, who drove himself too hard, while everything 'just bounced off' Hugh. The third man saw that in some ways Evelyn wanted to be Hugh. He also felt that Waugh was 'extremely kind' in not making him feel gauche and immature. And that he didn't leave him out, even though he and Hugh were such close friends.

Both Evelyn and Hugh had distant relationships with their own older brother, so they became brothers to each other. They talked a lot about Oxford and London life and mutual friends and of course Madresfield. And about politics and about Germany, but not, according to Glen, about religion. The intimacy created by their condition so far from home and in such a hostile environment led Evelyn to open up in a way that was rare for him. Glen listened in as Evelyn poured out his heart to Hugh: how he was conscious that Alec was always his father's favourite son and how different he was from Alec, not sharing his obsession with cricket and his womanising ways; how he longed to escape from Highgate and his father not because he disliked his father, but because he disliked his 'rather bourgeois dullness'; how he loved sophisticated frivolity, which he found cathartic; how he loved that Madresfield was run by the girls, and that Maimie and Coote were always so glad to see him.

Glen, who admired the Lygon girls himself, felt that Evelyn was especially close to Coote, though people always thought it was Maimie. He reckoned that Coote underestimated Evelyn's 'very great affection for her'. This was typical of her modesty. Glen recalled his own mental picture of Coote sitting in the window doing petit point – 'one of these vivid little pictures of life'. He regarded her as one of those people who was really unaware of whether she was rich or poor, with something of the gypsy in her (later she would work in Turkey, then live on a river boat on the Thames).

Sandy Glen's memories reveal Evelyn and Hugh at their best. They were not only brave and hard working, but also terrific company. He wrote in *Young Men in the Arctic* of how conversation ran often upon food, which was hardly surprising considering how hungry they always were. He remembered one particular conversational fantasia:

> Dordogne was eventually chosen for a later holiday by Lygon and Waugh. As good food and good wine can best be appreciated after

> exercise, they decided to take a valet-chauffeur. He would precede them and find the best villages to which they, in their turn, would walk from their previous evening's abode. Baths run, clean clothes laid out, and finally the most carefully chosen dinner and wines would await their arrival. Books, people and travel were the main subjects when we tired of food itself. We cut out lunch and ate twice a day, so it was in the morning and evening that we did most of our talking. The greatest joy in sledging comes when supper is over and conversation exhausted: then there are no limits to the flights to which thoughts may take one. The while one's pipe sends up its drowsy smoke, in intertwining streaks of blue and grey.

The Dordogne remained a fantasy. Evelyn and Hugh would never share such intimacy again.

They returned to Mad at the end of August, informing Coote and Maimie that they had had mountains in the Arctic named after them.

There is a remarkable passage in *Brideshead Revisited* after Cordelia's long description of Sebastian and his doomed future as an alcoholic. Charles lies awake, tossing and turning, thinking about his friend:

> And another image came to me, of an Arctic hut and a trapper alone with his furs and oil lamp and log fire; the remains of supper on the table, a few books, skis in the corner; everything dry and neat and warm inside, and outside the last blizzard of winter raging and the snow piling up against the door. Quite silently a great weight forming against the timber; the bolt straining in its socket; minute by minute in the darkness outside the white heap sealing the door, until quite soon when the wind dropped and the sun came out on the ice slopes and the thaw set in a block would move, slide, and tumble, high above, gather way, gather weight, till the whole hillside seemed to be falling, and the little lighted place would crash open and splinter and disappear, rolling with the avalanche into the ravine.

This extraordinary metaphor of destruction, building in a rolling sentence that is itself like an accumulating snowball, is a memory of the trip to the Arctic with Hugh. It is the literary legacy of the fiasco in the north.

CHAPTER 17

Ladies and Lapdogs

While Hugh and Evelyn were narrowly escaping disaster in the Arctic, Lord Beauchamp was once more wandering the globe. He returned from Australia to Lord Berners's flat in Rome. Maimie took her turn to go out and stay with him. Evelyn returned to Highgate again, using his parents' home as a base while he saw his friends and regaled them with his Arctic adventures. His father's diary grumbles that he came in late when everyone else had gone to bed, leaving lights on and doors open. Lupin had returned from yet another harebrained scheme to annoy and frustrate his parents. Arthur's diary certainly has the aura of Mr Pooter: 'Evelyn brought gin bitters, and I drank them for lunch . . . went up to K's, did 1/3 of the crossword and had a nap . . . Had a good dinner of egg-salad, duck and green peas and pears. Went early to bed, leaving K and Evelyn to argue and play cards.'

Evelyn wrote to Maimie: 'Well it must be decent at Rome but very full of traffic because all roads lead there. If you see the Pope please tell him to jolly well get a move on with my annulment.' Then another letter: 'Darling Blondy, So I too am staying with my Boom. At present it is all dignity and peace but I expect we shall soon have a quarrel and black each others eyes and tear our hair and flog each other with hunting crops like the lovely Lygon sisters.'

He told Maimie that he was going to spend a studious autumn writing the life of 'a dead beast' (i.e. Catholic priest) – the Jesuit martyr,

Edmund Campion. He also wrote that he had dined with the Yorkes and that 'Henry loved your Boom' – so Henry Yorke must have been another of the old Oxford set who went out to stay with the exiled earl. And, he continued, 'I wish you had seen me at the N. Pole. I had great sex appeal – thin as Bartleet.' He was very pleased with the reception of *A Handful of Dust*: 'the good taste book I wrote about sponger is being a success and wherever I go the people shout Long Live Bo and throw garlands of flowers in my path and I have a brass band to play to me in my bath'.

'Handfulers', as they called it, was published in September. In the library at Madresfield there is a first edition inscribed 'To Hughie, to whom it should have been dedicated'.

Diana Cooper told him that everyone was raving about the new book. She shared the general admiration, but she also chided him: 'You were so very hostile when you left for the Pole that you froze the voicing of my praise.' In his reply he tried to explain to her how he felt about friendship, but later he crossed out the paragraph:

> The trouble is that I find the pleasures of friendship need more leisure than you can possibly give to it at the present. Also that I am jealous and resentful and impatient though you are none of those things. It is of no interest to me to see you in a crowd or for odd snatches of ten minutes at a time. Perhaps in thirty years time when some of your adherents have died or fallen away.

This self-censored comment provides a good insight into his exacting view of the requirements of friendship. There are shades of that other goddess Diana (Guinness) whose friendship had been so important to him but whom he had lost because he was jealous and couldn't bear to be in second place. By contrast, his friendship with the Lygons endured, because they put him at number one or at the very least had the grace to give him the impression that they did. Later that month he took two of the sisters (Sibell and Coote) to a boxing match. And he wrote to Maimie to tell her that he had seen lots of mutual chums at Nancy Mitford's wedding to Peter Rodd.

He was at home for most of September and then went off to Chagford, asking the sisters to write to him. He planned to make a start on the

Campion biography and also wanted to finish two short stories, 'Mr Cruttwell's Little Outing' and 'On Guard'.

He wrote to 'Darling Poll' from Chagford: 'Did you know that in the glorious epoch 1900–1914 [does he mean 1914–18?] the word "poll" was used by our gallant boys . . . to mean a tart . . . so now I shall give up calling you Poll on account of its being disrespectful. Darling Dorothy.' He once again joked that he had found a prospective husband for her: 'I went to Longleat yesterday and thought it a bad taste house and there was a poor lonely old man called Lord Bath and he had his little dinner laid out on the table god it was sad why not marry him?' The letter also includes a smutty joke of the kind that he liked to reserve for letters to her: he had been reading a 'feelthy' book which 'says that in rogering the cock should never be withdrawn so much as a millimetre and this gives the maximum pleasure to the lady on account of pressing her bladder'. On a rather different note he told her that he had visited a chapel where there was a stained-glass window with a portrait of the local earl as a child and that this had reminded him of her family chapel – 'as it might be Elmley etc at Mad'. He begged her to send him a birthday card because he got 'none last year and it made me very sad'. He asked her to 'tell Hughie to hurry up and have catholic lessons' – despite Sandy Glen's protestation to the contrary, the question of faith may have been something they discussed at Spitsbergen. The letter ended with the news: 'I wrote a funny short story about a loony bin and a very dull one about a dog who bit a lady's nose. That dog was rather like Grainger only not as intellectual perhaps more like Wincey but god it was a bad story. Please give my best love to your sweet sister and your disgusting friends, Bo.'

Wincey, Baby Jungman's dog, was a Blenheim spaniel given to her by the Duke of Marlborough. Evelyn had never been fond of the dog and the feeling was mutual. Grainger had also been very hostile to Evelyn in the early days of Evelyn's friendship with Maimie. 'On Guard', the story in question, finally went to *Harper's Bazaar*. The heroine is a fusion of Baby Jungman and Maimie Lygon. This is a good example of Evelyn's art of composite character creation. His old Oxford friend Terence Greenidge considered that his characteristic literary device was to roll together two real life characters into one fictional one, 'very often adding some lurid vice'. This was certainly true of Anthony Blanche in *Brideshead*, whom Evelyn admitted was a composite of Harold Acton and Brian

Howard. His rake, Basil Seal, in *Black Mischief* and *Put Out More Flags*, was a combination of an Oxford charmer called Basil Murray and Nancy Mitford's husband, Peter Rodd. When one of Evelyn's friends asked him how he got away with using real life models for fictional characters, his reply was that you can draw any character as near to life as you want and no offence will be taken provided you say that he is attractive to women. In the case of 'On Guard', neither Maimie nor Baby took offence because the heroine of the story was supremely attractive to men.

It tells the tale of a suitor who leaves for Africa and buys his girl a dog that is tasked to keep away other suitors in his absence. The dog, called Hector after the suitor who purchases it, obliges by spoiling all romances for his owner, peeing on all-comers and barking at them. Grainger and Wincey both had this characteristic, but so as to offend neither of them Hector is made a poodle rather than a Pekingese or a spaniel. Evelyn's father always had black poodles.

The heroine, Milly Blade, like Baby and Maimie, is a beautiful blonde: 'she had a docile and affectionate disposition, and an expression of face which changed with lightning rapidity from amiability to laughter and from laughter to respectful interest'. As with Maimie in real life, her best feature is a beautiful button nose that 'more than any other, endeared her to sentimental Anglo-Saxon manhood'. Small and snub, it was 'a nose which made it impossible for its wearer to be haughty or imposing . . . it was a nose that pierced the thin surface crest of the English heart to its warm and pulpy core; a nose to take the thoughts of English manhood back to its schooldays, to the doughy-faced urchins on whom it had squandered its first affection, to memories of changing room and chapel and battered straw boaters'.

Men fall hopelessly in love with her and she, beautiful, careless and vague, usually returns their affection for a few months. Four is her normal track record. Mike Boswell (Evelyn) is a platonic friend who has enjoyed a wholly unromantic friendship with Milly since she first came out. 'He had seen her fair hair in all kinds of light, in and out of doors, crowned in hats of succeeding fashions, bound with ribbon, decorated with combs, jauntily stuck with flowers; he had seen her nose uplifted in all kinds of weather, had even, on occasions, playfully tweaked it with his finger and thumb, and had never for one moment felt remotely attracted to her.'

All of this changes when he is having tea with Milly, Hector growling quietly. Mike (a tall and personable man of marriageable age) makes the mistake of patting Milly on the knee. Hector attacks and bites him, causing Milly to rush for the iodine bottle: 'Now no Englishman, however phlegmatic, can have his hand dabbed with iodine without, momentarily at any rate, falling in love.' Seeing the nose in such close proximity as she dabs his hand, he becomes her 'besotted suitor'. Meanwhile, Hector continues to ruin her chances, defeating suitor after suitor with his bad behaviour. Milly is more in love with her dog than the erstwhile Hector in Africa. He performs doggy tricks to amuse and delight her, but also disrupts the tender moments by peeing or being noisily sick.

Finally a suitor manages to get the better of the dog, and in response to his usurpation Hector bites off Milly's nose, leaving her with a 'fine, aristocratic beak – worthy of the spinster she is about to become'. Like all spinsters, she is doomed to spend her life alone with an ageing lapdog. In his bitterness towards Baby, Evelyn half-hoped that would be her fate. He would never have wished or dreamed that Maimie might be the one to end her life as a lonely old drunk sitting silently with only a Pekingese for company.

At the end of December, Evelyn returned to Pixton, the Georgian house on a wooded hillside near Dulverton that belonged to the Herbert family. He was becoming more and more taken with Laura Herbert. Then on to Mells, the home of Diana Cooper's friend Katharine Asquith, from where he opened his heart on paper to Maimie, who had been so close to him throughout his disastrous courtship of Baby Jungman.

First Evelyn told her how he felt sad and guilty that his former lover, Hazel Lavery had died aged only fifty-four: 'I feel a shit.' He was having a Mass said for her, which would require him to drive six miles in the cold and dark. He then turned to Laura, the 'white mouse', whom he had barely noticed at Portofino:

> I have taken a *great* fancy to a young lady named Laura. What is she like? Well fair, very pretty, plays peggoty beautifully. We met on a house party in Somerset. She has rather a long thin nose and skin as thin as bromo as she is very thin and might be dying of consumption to look at her and she has her hair in a little bun at the back of her neck but it is not very tidy and she is only eighteen years old,

> virgin, Catholic, quiet and astute. So it is difficult. I have not made much progress except to pinch her twice in a charade and lean against her thigh in pretending to help her at peggoty.

Evelyn was falling in love with another large chaotic family. Pixton was solid and shabby genteel, rather than aristocratic and beautiful, homely and hospitable rather than grand and elegant. The dogs ruled as they ran about jumping out of windows and sitting proprietorially on chairs, leaving guests like Evelyn to stand. Laura's mother, Mary Herbert, was another of the fierce, formidable and (unintentionally) funny matriarchs that Evelyn loved. She disliked him at first but came to be devoted to him. Evelyn Gardner was a close cousin of Laura's on her father's side. One of Laura's relations was heard to remark: 'I thought we had heard the last of that young man.' The family and guests were noisy – drinking, smoking and talking, mainly about arrangements for horses and hunting, and of course Catholic matters.

There was a converted chapel outside the house. It had been a laundry room. Father Knox and Father D'Arcy were frequent visitors. A nanny lived upstairs, often to be found quietly playing patience. This kind of country house living was very different to the lifestyle at Mad. But it was comfortable and it was here that Evelyn became drawn to the eighteen-year-old Laura. She may have looked like his favoured type – blonde, fragile-looking, shy, in need of protection – but she was not afraid to stand up to him. Unlike the glamorous flapper girls that had previously attracted him, she was stable, with a very strong sense of self. She also had the all-important sense of humour, and shared Evelyn's love of nicknames.

At her young age she was taking on a lot with Evelyn, who was himself such a strong character, and had not lived by half in his thirty-one years. But, bolstered by her strong sense of family pride, she was more than up to the task. Though not as musical as the rest of her family, she liked amateur dramatics and after finishing school in Neuilly she enrolled at RADA.

Evelyn wrote to her in London: 'Darling Laura, I am sad and bored and need your company. If you have a spare evening between now and when you leave London, please come out with me. Any time will suit me as I have no engagements that I cannot gladly break. Ask your mother first and tell her I wanted you to ask.'

In February 1935 an event loaded with heavy symbolism occurred. Evelyn wrote to Maimie with plans for her birthday: 'for your birthday we will have a stately orgy' (orgy meant party in Mad parlance). He joked that Jessel (he of the foie gras episode) had arranged a party on the eve of his wedding to Lady Helen Vane-Tempest-Stewart so that they could reciprocate for his Christmas faux pas at Mad by stealing all his presents. He told her that he had seen Laura in London but that the meeting had not been a success because he had an appalling hangover and after eating three oysters was 'sick a good deal on the table so perhaps that romance is shattered'. At the very end of the letter he wrote: 'I set my booms house on fire last Monday.' It may have sounded casual but Evelyn was very upset about the incident.

His father's diary records the events of the night: 'woke at 4 am to a smell of burning. On opening the bookroom door found the room ablaze. Called K [his wife], and Evelyn called the firemen . . . many books were burned, the armchair, Rossetti chair, carpet, curtains all scorched . . . Evelyn went to bed again.' Not only the precious chair that had once belonged to Rossetti, but also many of the books were irreplaceable. An account by Evelyn, written a couple of years later, says remorsefully: 'My father is a literary critic and publisher. I think he can claim to have more books dedicated to him than any living man. They used to stand together on his shelves, among hundreds of inscribed copies from almost every English writer of eminence, until on one of my rather rare, recent visits to my home, I inadvertently set the house on fire, destroying the carefully garnered fruits of a lifetime of literary friendships.' Evelyn, a book-collector himself, knew what this meant to his father. This incident – beside his sense of humour – explains why when he was later in the Army he infamously asked for his wife to save his books before his children, since books can never be replaced, whereas children can.

Whilst writing about Campion, who spent much of his time travelling between the grand homes of the aristocracy, Evelyn did the same – albeit without the inconvenience Campion faced of having the Elizabethan secret service on his tail. At Newton Ferrers he shocked the aristocratic company by talking crudely about love, which upset Sir Robert Abdy. If he was in the habit of sucking up to aristocrats, the accusation that has dogged his reputation, then this was a curious way of doing so. In Mad

World, the private code for boring was 'Hugh D. Mackintosh', or rather 'Makingtosh', an allusion to an Australian businessman friend of Lord Beauchamp's whom the Lygon girls found unutterably tedious. Evelyn's letters to his favourite aristocrat, Lady Maimie Lygon, include several references to Makingtosh of the following kind: 'I missed that train so I have to wait wait wait wait god it is sad Hugh D. Makingtosh H.D.M Hugh D Hugh D I think I am about to die I missed the train What will Laura say? say? Hugh D. Mackingtosh Grainger is impuissant as the frogs . . . GRAINGER CAN'T FUCK.' This is not the customary language of sucking up.

His life at this time was all 'wait wait wait wait'. He wanted to propose to Laura but could do nothing until he heard from Rome.

Evelyn and Maimie both suffered from depression and insomnia. They shared tips on pills and draughts to combat their problems: 'This is better than what I meant to send. Dissolve both in boiling water (½ tumbler) and drink. Very delicious and you will have 8 hours. Can't bear to think of you unhappy.' In April 1935 he wrote to Maimie from Bridgwater to thank her for reciprocating by sending him the 'beautiful pills. I think I will take to my bed and sleep for a few weeks.'

Maimie was full of news that her eldest brother had met a Danish widow to whom he had taken a great fancy. Evelyn mentions the relationship between Elmley, who he mocks as 'the Viscount', and his lady, 'the melancholy Dane'. He had formed a clear impression of the latter on the basis of Maimie's account of her origin: 'I suppose she will be like Ophelia and walk about with garlands of wild flowers and drown herself.'

The melancholy Dane was Fru Else Dornonville de la Cour, daughter of an actor and widow of a property developer. Known as Mona, she was very beautiful. Elegant and well travelled, she spoke a number of languages. She had been brought up in Copenhagen by her mother, after her father had left when she was just a young child. He was a well-known character called Viggo Schiwe, who played the part of Jean, the footman who has sex with the aristocratic young woman of the house in the original production of August Strindberg's scandalous play *Miss Julie*. Else tended to keep quiet about her theatrical connections, preferring to emphasise that her grandfather had been an admiral in the Danish navy. She was eight years older than Elmley and had a nineteen-year-old daughter from her first marriage. She had been educated at a good school in Copenhagen, which she thought gave her an advantage over the Lygon sisters: 'I'm sure I got a better education than my sisters-in-law brought up by governesses.'

She first met Elmley getting off the train at Worcester railway station. She was actually on her way to Madresfield. She had been invited to the house in her capacity as a friend of Lady Carlisle, who knew the Lygons well. Elmley had been travelling on the same train and was mesmerised by the beautiful Danish widow with the beguiling accent. He introduced himself as Lord Elmley, though she had no idea that he was connected to the Lygon family. 'I was going to stay with people called Lygon,' she recalled years later, 'and I knew their father was Earl Beauchamp, but I didn't know of someone called Elmley.' Mona was disappointed when the young man left her. She thought that she would never see him again. On arriving at Mad, she was overwhelmed by the sheer scale of the house, with its bachelor wing, visiting maids' rooms and nursery wing. There she saw the dining table which seated several dozen, the well-stocked library, long gallery, the crystal balustrade, ebony furniture, the Bronzinos on the walls, the cases full of Sèvres china and ornate snuff boxes, the Buhl furniture from Versailles, the carpets and tapestries. Then at dinner that evening she was amazed to see the young man she had met on the train taking his place at the head of the table.

All four sisters were at Mad that weekend and they welcomed Mona warmly. But it was Elmley who particularly singled her out. She had just learned to play backgammon and so he sat her on the sofa and they played all weekend. They agreed to meet up in London and that was the start of their relationship. The Lygon sisters grew to dislike Mona and had very little sympathy with their brother for marrying her. They were sure that, given her age, he would never have children and the longed-for heir. Hugh was not likely to marry and have children, which left only Dickie who was estranged from Madresfield and living with his mother. Mona, for her part, disliked the sisters. She remembered that they were pretty and glamorous and spoilt, 'financed by their father in a big way'.

Evelyn had turned against Elmley. What had happened to the champagne-swilling man in the purple suit, carousing in the Hypocrites' Club and making irreverent films with Evelyn Waugh at his home in Underhill? He had grown pompous and stiff. He found it very hard to get along with people and was still very angry with his father. In later life, perhaps fittingly for a man who met his wife on a train, Elmley's greatest pleasure as a peer of the realm came from sitting on House of Lords committees to do with the railways.

Evelyn was hard at work on Campion, even refusing invitations to Maimie's cocktail parties as he pushed towards the end. He was still depressed about his relationship with Laura, but hoped that the biography of one of England's greatest Catholic martyrs would help to convince her and her family that, notwithstanding the divorce, he was a good Catholic writer who was worthy of her.

He then made plans for a return trip to Abyssinia and secured an assignment for the *Daily Mail*, expenses paid, as war correspondent reporting on Mussolini's invasion. Diana Cooper had put in a good word on his behalf with Lord Rothermere – as Julia Stitch does with Lord Copper of the *Daily Beast* on behalf of William Boot (though the wrong William Boot, with hilarious consequences) in the great comic novel that came out of the trip, *Scoop*. Diana was delighted to have inspired the character of Mrs Stitch.

Arthur Waugh's diary records two visits that Evelyn had from Oxford friends before he left for Abyssinia. The first was probably Joyce Gill, whom Evelyn had known since his college days (she had been renowned in Oxford for dressing as a boy). Despite being desperately in love with Laura, Evelyn asked Joyce to leave her husband and go with him to Abyssinia. She later told one of her daughters that choosing not to go had been one of the most painful decisions of her life. She was in love with Evelyn. A letter written to him after the birth of his first child shows the extent to which he could induce strong passion in others: 'I think of you all the time when I am making love, until the word and Evelyn are almost synonymous! . . . I have only to remember your eyes – your mouth and my heart aches as if it were a stone cut by a diamond.'

The other person he saw was Hugh Lygon, who arrived by car on 27 July and took him down to Madresfield for a couple of days. Once again, the house would represent the last of England as he set off for foreign parts.

En route to Abyssinia, Evelyn visited Rome to try and move along his annulment. He wrote to Maimie from the Grande Hotel de Russie, possibly the most luxurious establishment in the city (the *Daily Mail* expense account was being well used): 'Now I must go to Naples and then sail to Africa. I do not want to go. Not at all. I cry a great deal on account of not seeing LAURA.' From Addis Ababa he wrote love letters to Laura: 'The thing I think about most is your eyelashes making a noise like a bat on a pillow.' He told Laura how unpopular he was with the authorities in Abyssinia, that his name was mud at the legation 'because of a novel I wrote which they think was about them (it wasn't)'. His friend Patrick Balfour, who was representing the *Evening Standard*, told his mother: 'I rather dread his arrival as his name is mud here since *Black Mischief* and half the European population is out for his blood.' Sir Sidney Barton and his family at the British legation had been deeply offended by Evelyn's cruel caricature of them as the Courtenays in 'Blackers'. Sir Sidney's daughter Esmé, who was convinced that she was the model for the promiscuous Prudence, was so angry with him that when she bumped into him at one of the town's three nightclubs, the Perroquet, she threw a glass of champagne in his face.

Once again it was 'wait wait wait wait'. Evelyn kept himself going by writing ribald letters to his women friends back home and gathering material for his next comic novel. He hinted to Maimie that he would love another Christmas invitation to Mad. In fact he was in Jerusalem for Christmas, first at a Franciscan monastery and then moving to a hotel for Christmas Day. He paid a visit to Bethlehem: 'It was decent to have Christmas without the Hitlerite adjuncts of yule logs and reindeer and Santa Claus and conifers,' he wrote to Katharine Asquith, 'but I was appalled to discover that we have no altar at all in the Basilica at Bethlehem . . . I don't really want to return to Europe until I know one way or another about my annulment and can arrange things accordingly.'

CHAPTER 18

A Year of Departures

Evelyn Waugh arrived back in England from Abyssinia in January 1936. This was a very significant year for him and the Lygon family. His biography of Edmund Campion won the country's most distinguished literary award, the Hawthornden Prize, and in July his long wait for news from Rome was over. It was also a year heralded by the death of King George V on 20 January. His last words were reportedly 'bugger Bognor', a sentiment which Evelyn would have heartily echoed in view of the miserable time he had spent there working on his travel book.

Lord Beauchamp was still living his peripatetic existence, writing to Coote of excursions from Sydney to Tahiti and to Wellington in New Zealand. In February 1936 he was aboard the SS *New Holland*. Coote had written with news of Christmas and the Hunt Ball. Her father wrote that he had sent her a birthday telegram but that it had been misdelivered to Malvern, Australia. In this letter he mentioned the names of his two travelling companions: 'Byron and I go straight to some mountain hotel in Java while David inspects Bali and then we motor along to Batavia.' He was still the tourist even in his exile. 'Byron', identified by his surname, was the tall and handsome valet. 'David', always referred to by his first name, had taken the position of Beauchamp's secretary. They would stay together for the rest of his life.

On landing in Europe, Beauchamp stayed in Paris. His former secretary, the Liberal politician Robert Bernays, stayed with him and reported that 'he was still vainly hoping that with the change of monarchs he will be allowed to return' to England. This suggests that he was fully aware that it had been King George V as much as the Duke of Westminster who had been his nemesis. The new King, with his own unorthodox sexual arrangements and his closeness to Prince Georgie, might take a more relaxed view of the exile.

Evelyn was back at Madresfield in February. He then borrowed a remote place in Shropshire to bang out his 'serious war book', for which he had no appetite. It was published under the punning title *Waugh in Abyssinia*. He told a correspondent: 'If the book bores its readers half as much as it is boring for me to write it will create a record in low sales.' Much more importantly, during this time, spring 1936, he sent a quietly honest letter to Laura asking her to marry him: 'I can't advise you in my favour because it would be beastly for you, but think about how nice it would be for me.' He went on to give a typically accurate self-portrait: 'I am restless and moody and misanthropic and lazy and have no money except what I can earn and if I got ill you would starve . . . Also there is always a fair chance that there will be another bigger economic crash in which case if you had married a nobleman with a great house you might find yourself starving, while I am very clever and could probably earn a living of some sort somewhere.' He also told her that he had a small family: 'You would not find yourself involved in a large family and all their rows . . . All of these are very small advantages compared with the awfulness of my character.'

From Shropshire he also wrote Maimie some letters entirely in (cod) French, in honour of her being on the continent with her father. As well as giving the information that he had won 'un cadeau' for 'le livre de bon gout, *Edmund Campion*' and that 'M. Jackson a coupé un "arser" dans les cours de chevaux à Worcester', he asked about her father, expressing the hope that he found himself well 'avec tous ses aimants' ('with all his lovers'). Maimie travelled on from Paris to Venice where Boom had taken a palazzo for the summer.

The flame-haired mistress of the last Kaiser of Germany leased Lord Beauchamp the *piano nobile* of the Palazzo Morosini on the Grand Canal, a stone's throw from the Rialto. Inside, the palace was peaceful, with only the sound of water lapping against stone, but outside was a hive of activity as cargo boats unloaded fish and vegetables for the nearby markets.

Venice had long been known for its tolerant attitudes towards sex. And it was a city that had always attracted writers, painters and exiles. All about this city of domes and bell-towers lurk the shadows of famous men. Casanova was born in Venice; Wagner wrote the gloriously erotic second act of *Tristan* there; Robert Browning died in the house of the Doge; Byron's lover threw herself from the balcony of the Palazzo Mocenigo.

Foreigners had always rented Venetian palaces for the season. For Virginia Woolf, the watery city was 'the playground of all that was gay, mysterious and irresponsible'. In the early part of the twentieth century, Baron Corvo, the noted homosexual ex-priest and writer, set himself up in a palazzo on the Grand Canal, where he conducted numerous love affairs with the beautiful young gondoliers who moonlighted as rent-boys servicing rich English lords. Beauchamp knew Baron Corvo's work from *The Yellow Book*.

Corvo's novel, *The Desire and Pursuit of the Whole: A Venetian Romance*, published in 1934, was a thinly veiled homosexual romance involving an English man and a boy-girl child called Zilda. He also wrote *The Venice Letters*, detailing his uninhibited real life sexual adventures with teenage Venetian male prostitutes. In lurid detail, Corvo described his exploits with stevedores called Piero, Gildo, Carlo and Zildo and with the sixteen-year-old Amadeo Amadei, who looked as if he came out of a Renaissance painting – 'young, muscular, splendidly strong, big black eyes, rosy face, round black head, scented like an angel'.

Amadeo is in search of an English lord to supplement his paltry wage, as are scores of his friends, who have lost custom to the university boys from Padua. At a Venetian trattoria he shows the baron what he has to offer by stripping off his clothes: 'he was just one brilliant rosy series of muscles, smooth as satin . . . he crossed his ankles, ground his thighs together . . . and stiffened into the most inviting mass of fresh meat conceivable, laughing in my face as he made his offering of lively flesh. And the next instance he was up, his trousers buttoned, his shirt tucked in and his cloak folded around him.' When the baron tells him that he is not rich, Amadeo begs him to recommend him to other rich English nobles. He will do anything for his patron – full anal sex is on offer and a lurid description ensues. Amadeo tells Corvo that many of his friends model for foreign painters and offer sexual services as an added extra. Baron Corvo knows that he must act immediately. 'Amadeo is ripe, just in his prime . . . he'll be like this till Spring . . . then some great fat slow cow of a girl will just open herself wide, and lie quite still and drain him dry.' Then his bloom will be gone; 'he'll get hard and hairy' and he will be 'just the ordinary stevedore to be found by scores on the quay'.

There is no way of knowing whether Lord Beauchamp availed himself of the services of such stevedores and gondoliers. His secretary, David Smyth, and the aptly named valet, Byron, may have sufficed to fulfil his needs by this time in his life. But he would have enjoyed looking at the dancing, prancing stevedores unloading their cargo outside his palazzo, just as he loved looking at the young Australian men sunning themselves on Bondi Beach.

In *Brideshead*, just after describing Lord Marchmain as a Byronic voluptuary, Anthony Blanche alludes to the gondolier at the Marchmain palazzo: 'once I passed them and I caught the eye of the Fogliere gondolier, whom, of course, I knew, and, my dear, he gave me *such* a wink'. Waugh obviously knew all about the Venetian homosexual underworld.

From his palazzo, Lord Beauchamp heard the news that his eldest son had got married. There was no question of his attending. The couple were married on 16 June at St Clements Dane, a small Christopher Wren church on the Strand. The bride's dress was by Maggy Rouff, who designed gowns for silver screen legends such as Greta Garbo. Rouff was known for evening dresses that clung close to the body and were sewn with airy, slanting tiers of ruffles. For the wedding, Mona wore a gown of cream lace with a gold embroidered floral pattern and a fashionable cream cap trimmed with white flowers. She carried orchids.

The wedding was one of the most glittering society occasions of 1936. Guests included Beauchamp's old political master, Lloyd George. Evelyn was there; it was shortly before he received the Hawthornden Prize. The Countess Beauchamp attended the wedding and Hugh was his brother's best man. This was one of the few times after 1931 when the Lygons saw their mother.

The man conspicuous by his absence was, of course, Lord Beauchamp. He wrote to Coote to beg for news. Never had he felt his isolation more. David Smyth, who had become a trusted figure, almost a member of the family, had been invited to the wedding. He had now returned to Venice: 'David is safely back and has given news of the wedding . . . Did you give a dinner that night. Who came? Was Dickie asked? What besides miniatures (by whom?) did your mother give? I hear her memory is getting worse.'

The wedding reception was held at Halkyn House and then the couple went to Vienna and Budapest for their honeymoon. On a later occasion they went to see Boom. Mona vividly recalled the first time she met her father-in-law: 'I liked him very very much. A charming man. He had a flat in Paris and we stayed with him.' She remembered that he would send her a little present every morning on her tea tray. Her husband, she said, was 'not kind to his father. He never answered his letters.' According to her own account (which may of course be self-serving), it was only her intervention that brought them together. Mona knew that her father-in-law was not a happy man and knew that it was to do with his sexuality, though she had a somewhat simple-minded view of his homosexuality: 'I don't think he was very happy. He was really bisexual and if he'd had a very sexy wife he might not have been homosexual.' Mona was not particularly enamoured of the countess, whom she described as 'very very dull', though granting that she must have been very pretty when she was young. She acknowledged that the countess was very kind to her – 'nothing wrong there'. She never met the Duke of Westminster, but took the view that, 'He was pretty awful. It was jealousy. My father-in-law had so many high offices . . . and Westminster had nothing. He had money but no office.' She did meet Evelyn, whom she remembered as 'a great friend of my sisters-in-law'.

On 7 July, Evelyn finally got the news from Rome for which he had waited for so long. He received a telegram from the archbishop handling the case: 'Decision favourable. Godfrey.' He phoned Bruton Street, Laura's London residence, to tell her the news. She was at church so he hurried to find her. In the church porch he told her that they were finally free to marry. He wrote to Maimie to tell her the good news: 'Darling . . . You will be greatly surprised to hear that I have got engaged to be married to Miss L. Herbert . . . She is lazy with a long nose but otherwise jolly decent . . . don't tell Capt. Hance or he will take Miss H. away from me on account of his superior sex appeal.'

Evelyn's diary for 9 and 10 July shows him dining with Maimie and

Hubert Duggan and lunching the next day with Hugh and Maimie. He was very happy and full of news and plans about Laura and his wedding. He dined with Coote on 13 July; the next day he had drinks with Hubert and Maimie, who were probably still conducting their affair. He was happy, sleeping well, visiting friends and spending most of his time with Laura. He went to a cocktail party with Maimie on 21 July. A letter written to Laura expresses his deep happiness: 'I shall think about you for about 17 hours in the 24 and dream of you for the other five. Darling Laura. I love you. Thank you for loving me.'

While this was a happy time for Evelyn, for the Lygons it was the worst since the events of summer 1931. They experienced two tragedies, one after another. First came the unexpected death of the countess from a heart attack.

Evelyn had made plans to return to Abyssinia to finish the novel that was published as *Scoop*. On 28 July 1936, the day before he left England, he wrote in his diary: 'Had arranged to meet Hubert at Halkyn House but Lady Beauchamp had just dropped dead so my arrival, tipsy and with Brownlows, was not opportune.'

That night he met and got drunk with his old love Olivia Plunket Greene, now in her thirties and an alcoholic: 'she very drunk. Put her to bed.' He was saddened to see the state of her but relieved that the relationship hadn't worked out, now that he had Laura. The meeting signalled the close of a long chapter but also his determination never to desert his old friends.

Lady Beauchamp's death set off a chain of events that was, in Waugh's words, 'Shakespearian in its elaborate impossibility'. The death of the countess propelled Lord Beauchamp into action. The moment he heard the news, he contacted his lawyer, Richard Elwes, who happened to be on holiday in Venice, and told him that he was determined to return to England as soon as possible to attend his wife's funeral. Coote was in Venice with her father and they set off for England by train.

Elwes hurried back to London and saw Norman Birkett, who held a senior position in the office of the Attorney General. The Attorney General's office was sympathetic to Lord Beauchamp's plight and the proposition, put forward by Elwes, that the warrant for his arrest should be regarded as non-operative during his attendance at the funeral. However the ultimate decision lay with Sir John Simon, the Home Secretary, who was very upright. The Duke of Westminster wasted no time in speaking to Sir John and appealing against any provision that Beauchamp should be allowed to 'desecrate by his odious presence the interment of his beloved sister'. Sir John was in an awkward predicament but finally decided that the law must run its course.

Father and daughter arrived at Dover on a cross-Channel steamer. At the point of embarkation they saw a man frantically waving his arms. It was unclear whether he was waving them on or not. He was dressed in striped trousers and a short black lawyer's jacket. They realised that it was Richard Elwes.

Lord Beauchamp, after five years of exile, was about to set foot on English soil when at the last minute Elwes went aboard and urged him to stay on board or else risk arrest and public humiliation. With his sister still warm in her coffin, the Duke of Westminster was on the point of exacting his revenge for the lack of a public trial and the refusal of the Lygon children to testify against their father. Elwes told Lord Beauchamp the news: 'He said, No.' There was no choice but for him to return to his palazzo in Venice. His daughter remembered that, stoical and tough as ever, Boom did not make a fuss. They waited for the steamer to turn around and sailed back to France.

Coote returned with her father and did not attend her mother's funeral. Nor did Maimie, who was said to be ill.

Lady Beauchamp's funeral took place in Chester. The countess, said the newspapers, had been 'a great political hostess' noted for two things: her devotion to her mother and her 'staunch churchmanship'. There was, of course, no mention of the scandal and the separation – though a friend subsequently wrote to *The Times* quoting a poem that once had been written for her by Laurence Binyon, including the lines: 'What wrongs are borne, what deeds are done/ In thee', and adding the pointed comment that 'in her mature years these lines were equally applicable in the sense that she possessed a great simplicity of character. Experience of life had brought very great moral courage and devotion to duty.' Another correspondent recalled her hospitality at Madresfield in happier days:

> I can only see her now with her fair head thrown back and her hand outstretched in welcome . . . 'I have put you in the same room, as I know you loved it so' were her words to me once; and at dinner the

same night she whispered to me that there was to be ice pudding as she remembered my love for this, too . . . Thus one thinks of those fragrant memories which recall her as we knew her then. Her nursery, her garden, her stables with the pair of white Austrian horses, the long gallery where she wrote her letters, and the chapel with the white pigeons circling round it.

Hugh was distraught by his mother's death and also by the death five days later of his cousin, Lady Alington. A healthy girl with a fistful of swimming medals, she was struck down by acute appendicitis at the age of just thirty-three. Hugh was in a bad way. Coote recalled that he had been feeling unwell for some months. His failures had multiplied. His desperate attempts to get back on the wagon had come to nothing and, as Evelyn's friend Christopher Sykes put it, 'the violent physical exertions by which he thought he could restore his health failed utterly; he still refused to consult a reliable doctor'.

He had been injured falling from his horse and his face had been damaged by a stray pellet on a shooting trip. Photographs taken at the time show him looking much older than his years. He was no longer the gilded youth of photographs taken in the twenties and the lovely portrait of him executed by William Ranken. Hugh was persuaded to recuperate abroad, but his devotion to his dogs, Dan and Luke, made him reluctant to leave. The dogs were inconsolable, he said, if he left them for even an hour, so how would they cope being left for three weeks?

He decided on a motoring tour of Bavaria and left on 14 August. This was the month when the Olympic Games were held in Hitler's Berlin and the whole of Germany was in the grip of Nazi fever. Hugh travelled with an artist friend, Henry Winch, described by Coote as a 'dull dog'. On Sunday, the 16th, the day of the Olympic riding finals in Berlin, they spent many hot hours driving hatless in an open car. Hugh was afflicted with sunstroke. Or he might have been drinking. Near the end of the day, he got out of the car to ask passers-by for directions, fell on the kerb and in so doing fractured his skull. He was taken to Rothenburg ob der Tauber hospital.

Henry Winch sent a telegram to Coote in Venice. Her father chartered a plane and they rushed to Hugh's bedside. Lady Sibell also made her way there. Maimie was recovering from an appendix operation and couldn't travel. Despite the attention of the very best German doctors,

Hugh never regained consciousness. He died on 19 August in the early hours of the morning. He was thirty-one.

This time nothing was going to stop Boom from returning to England. He insisted on bringing the body of his son home to be buried. He simply didn't care if he were arrested. The *Daily Express* reported that he 'felt he had to bring the boy home . . . it had broken him up'. Lady Sibell claimed, late in life, that Lord Beaverbrook prevailed upon Sir John Simon to lift the warrant. She recalled that on her arrival at Ostend with her father and sister, she received a telegram saying: 'Safe for your father to land.' But she was probably exaggerating her own part in the affair. The truth was that Lord Beauchamp had once again instructed Richard Elwes, telling him that regardless of the risk of arrest he was returning to Madresfield for his son's funeral. Elwes put the case to Birkett and they renewed their case to the Home Secretary. This time Sir John felt moved to mercy. It was felt that Lord Beauchamp had suffered enough, and to the great indignation of the Duke of Westminster and his entourage, the warrant was suspended for the period of the funeral.

On 24 August the Honourable Hugh Lygon was buried at Madresfield. Lord Beauchamp had longed to return home, but never in such a circumstance as this. A Tiger Moth aircraft was kept on standby in case he had to make a hurried exit.

The church and churchyard were so packed with friends that the funeral was delayed: those who remembered Hugh's habit of always being late smiled at how he was late for his own funeral. Lord Beauchamp's emotions can only be imagined. It was the first time he had seen Dickie, his youngest son, in five years. He had a lot of people to face, including a smattering of aristocrats (the Dowager Lady Ampthill, the Countess of Coventry, Viscountess Deerhurst) and even his former lover, Ernest Thesiger. Hugh's pallbearers were his devoted friends: Wally Weston, Jack Hood, Walter Hanson, Robert Bartleet and Henry Winch. Captain Hance attended with Jackie and Reggie. Evelyn was still away in Abyssinia and did not hear the news until he returned home. Among the friends who did make it to the funeral were Patrick Balfour, John Sutro, Christopher Sykes and Hugh's old acting coach, Willie Armstrong.

Appreciations and obituaries were written for Hugh, with his friends remembering his gentleness, 'quiet charm' and his capacity for laughter. 'Only to hear his irresistible laugh was a tonic,' wrote Armstrong in

The Times. His alcoholism and homosexuality were tactfully ignored. His devotion to friends was emphasised, along with his kindness to his servants and employees, who considered him, it was said, their friend more than their master.

'He could not do enough for his friends and in their happiness he knew what it was to be happy.' The 'close friendship' with Evelyn Waugh was particularly remarked upon, with due mention of their intimacy at Oxford (Mr Waugh and Mr Acton being described as leaders of 'Aesthetic Oxford'). There was mention too of their adventure in Spitsbergen, where Hugh, despite injuries, had shown remarkable fortitude. His friends and family would long mourn him, Armstrong concluded, 'for it was quite impossible to know "Hughie" Lygon and not love that smile and that indefinable charm which were his very own'.

After the funeral, Lord Beauchamp returned to Venice. Coote remained convinced that her beloved Hughie's death had been brought on by the vicissitudes of his wasted life, his needless bankruptcy and his unhappiness in those last few weeks after the death of their mother:

> He may well have been poorly before he went off and no doubt was shaken by my mother dying so suddenly from a heart attack without any preliminary illness. Also I think he had a long term malaise from Lady Sibell and Elmley letting him go bankrupt for a very paltry sum a couple of years or so before; although he was reinstated and farming a living in a pretty house not far from Mad called Clevelode, all his plans for training and so on had come crashing about his ears, and I think this had a shattering effect on him.

At this terrible time Coote was a rock to her father and he could not have coped without her. She put aside her own despair to comfort and support him. She later described Hugh as a man of 'tremendous energy': 'he was such fun to be with, it came as a great blow to me when he died'. Boom wrote to her on 30 August from his palazzo on the Grand Canal: 'Darling Dorothy, I want to write a special line of thanks for all your loving sympathy these last dreadful days. You had more courage than I and I can never forget your help. How bad it has been I now begin to realise and have collapsed – not ill but just unhappy . . . your loving Daddy. What a lucky man your husband will be.'

For those who loved Hugh, it was the waste of a young life. He was a young man who had seemed to have everything – wealth, connections, a first-class education, let alone his formidable personal charm. It was the thwarted promise that was so upsetting for his family. For those who knew him best, the added tragedy was that Hugh had seemed to overcome his demons. His farming at Clevelode was going well: he had returned to the embrace of the Malvern Hills and the support of the loyal locals.

When Evelyn returned to England he was shocked and deeply upset to hear the news, especially as he had thought that Hugh was finally turning his life around. It was on 10 September that he arrived back from Abyssinia and learnt the news. He immediately wrote to Maimie:

> Darling Blondy,
>
> I have just got back and have learned for the first time the tragic news of Hughie's death. At least I have heard as much [as] my parents remember from the newspaper report. Do write and tell me what happened.
>
> It is the saddest news I ever heard. I shall miss him bitterly. It is so particularly tragic that he should have died just when he was setting up home and seemed happier than he had been for so many years. I know what a loss it will be to all of you and to Boom. Please accept my deepest sympathy. I am having Mass said for him at Farm Street . . . I long to see you again in October.
>
> My dearest love to you, Bo.

CHAPTER 19

Three Weddings and a Funeral

Laura was now foremost in Evelyn's thoughts. He had stopped at Assisi on the way to Abyssinia and from there he wrote her one of his most tender letters:

> Sometimes I think it would be lovely to lead the sort of life with you that I have led alone for the last ten years – no possessions, no home, sometimes extravagant and luxurious, sometimes lying low and working hard. At other times I picture a settled patriarchal life with a large household, rather ceremonious and rather frugal, and sometimes a minute house, and few friends, and little work and leisure and love. But what I do know is that I can't picture any sort of life without you . . . And I don't at all regret the haphazard, unhappy life I've led up till now because I don't think that without it I could love you so much. Goodnight my blessed child. I love you more than I can find words to tell you. E.

The 'large household, rather ceremonious and rather frugal' would have been like Mad as he imagined it must have been during the childhood of the Lygon sisters.

His journal records that he saw Maimie in October, 'fat, and sweet, and inconsequent'. What had happened to the beautiful, lithe girl he had known for the past five years? She gave him the details of Hugh's death, which he did not record in his diary. He spent time with her the following day. She was still grieving for Hugh. Later, she sent a photograph of him. He wrote back to thank her, saying he was house-hunting and that he was touched by the gesture, though he didn't like the picture much. He was always frank.

In December he wrote to ask her if Grainger the dog was upset about the abdication of the King. He was busy writing his happiest novel, *Scoop*, and wondered whether it would be possible to renew the old regime of working at Mad: 'Would you like me to visit you for a week and work in your beautiful schoolroom with the camphor wood chest or would that disgust you?' It somehow wouldn't be the same after all that had happened.

Some time in 1936, Evelyn wrote a beautiful letter to Maimie, who was depressed and unhappy. Her love affair with Hubert Duggan was over and she was lonely. It seems that she had asked him to visit and he hadn't:

> My Darling Blondy,
>
> I am afraid I was like Bloggs and Teresa and worse about coming down this weekend. I didn't know what would have been most helpful for you so ended as usual by doing nothing. And I don't know what I can say that would not be impertinent.
>
> But listen. I know from experience that being very unhappy is necessarily lonely and that friends can't help and that sympathy means very little – but please remember always that if there is ever anything I can do to help you have only to tell me, and I will chuck anything or do anything. The sort of dislocation you have had is a pain which can't be shared – but being unhappy is not *all* loss and I know you have the sort of nature that won't be spoilt.
>
> I only dare to say this because I was unhappy some years ago in rather the same way as you are now.
>
> All my love – don't answer. Bo.

Evelyn was planning his wedding. When asked what they wanted for a wedding present, he suggested a bed. He was very keen for his Lygon friends to meet Laura, but was conscious of her diffidence: 'It would be nice to bring Miss H to see you for a night or two at yr Highclere. She is a shy lady and would be scared if a lot of grown up people were there. Is there ever a time, either week end or mid week when we could find you alone?'

With regard to Laura, he showed his usual sharpness and unfailing honesty, writing to Alec: 'She is thin and silent, long nose, no literary ambitions, temperate but not very industrious. I think she will suit me ok and I am very keen on her.' But to Diana Cooper he wrote: 'I find new depths of beauty and sweetness in L. Herbert daily.' Nancy Mitford described her as an exquisite piece of Dresden china, so fragile that one felt she must snap in two.

The wedding day was set. Evelyn was looking forward to being settled after so many years in the wilderness. But he continued to write and think about the theme he identified in one of his later essays: 'Man, as an exile from Eden'.

In March 1937 he spent Holy Week at Ampleforth, visiting Castle Howard on the way. One time on retreat at Ampleforth he took Hubert Duggan with him, sober, and in a state of 'exalted gratitude' for his rescue from the horrors of alcohol. It all went well, as with Duggan's brother on the Adriatic cruise, until Hubert suddenly vanished and was discovered drunk in Scarborough.

In April, Evelyn wrote to Maimie to tell her that Captain Hance had said yes to his wedding invitation but that all his other chums were abroad. 'Do please all of you come without fail to the wedding and to the party the day before because I shall be very lonely among all Laura's high born and [illegible] aunts. Mr Herbert sent the invitations with ½d stamps so all my friends thought they were bills and tore them up. G how s [God how sad]. So Laura is very pretty and well and it will be decent to be married to her and she sends her love.' His best presents, he said, were silver from the Asquiths and a beautiful glass chandelier from the Coopers that arrived broken.

The ceremony took place at the Church of the Assumption in Warwick Street, London, on 17 April 1937. Captain Hance and his family did not make it to the wedding. Maimie and Coote were there, to Evelyn's delight. The bride was given away by her brother, Auberon (her father was dead). Henry Yorke was Evelyn's best man. The guest list, which duly appeared in *The Times*, reveals that Evelyn had drifted away from the Bright Young Things into a new, more respectable milieu. John Sutro attended in addition to Henry Yorke, but otherwise there was not much of a showing from the old Oxford set.

After arriving at their honeymoon destination of Portofino, where he had first seen 'the white mouse', he wrote in his diary: 'Lovely day, lovely house, lovely wife, great happiness.' He told Coote how moved he was that she had attended the wedding despite being ill at the time. 'So it is very decent to be married, very decent indeed,' he wrote, before adding: '*A bas milady Sibell and ses jockeys*' – down with Lady Sibell, who was the only one of the three sisters who had not gone to the wedding.

He asked 'Darling Poll' to come and stay after their return in June. Coote knew Laura's elder sister from hunting circles, but did not know Laura, who did not ride. Coote's recollection was that Mrs Herbert disapproved of Evelyn, the previously married man, and thought him most unsuitable for Laura: 'They were a very enclosed circle, and it is another aspect of Evelyn's courage that he took it on and won. It was a long, long fight.' Coote liked Laura immensely, remembering that she was very quiet in company, that she was very loyal and that, although she never contradicted Evelyn over small things and gave him his way over nearly everything, if she felt strongly about something, she would put her foot down and he would accept it.

In August the Waughs moved into their marital home, Piers Court, an elegant Georgian house that Evelyn found at Stinchcombe in the Cotswolds. Costing £4,000 – the money having been given by Laura's grandmother as a wedding present – it immediately became known as Stinkers. From there they paid a visit to Mad, where it would seem they had an unexpected encounter.

Lord Beauchamp heard that the warrant for his arrest had finally been revoked. On 19 July 1937, the *Normandie* docked at Southampton. This time the earl (accompanied by David Smyth) was able to step onto his native soil with no fear of there being a policeman waiting to welcome him. He was at last returning to his beloved home. The summer was spent at Mad. Though there is no mention of the fact in letters or reminiscences (and there are no Waugh diary entries for these months), it is probable that on his August visit Evelyn met Boom for a second time. If this is the case, it may be assumed that they would have reminisced about their previous encounter in the cramped surroundings of Lord

Berners's flat overlooking the Forum in Rome (Berners himself visited Boom at Mad in September).

For Boom, Mad was haunted by ghosts and painful memories. He could not settle. Accustomed to a wandering life, in October he returned to Venice with David. He wrote to Coote from the Grand Hotel: 'Energetically I have already been to the Accademia and now David is at High Mass at St Mark.' That David was a practising Catholic makes one wonder whether, late in life, Boom ever contemplated conversion – Lord Marchmain's road. Once again writing of Smyth as if he were a member of the family rather than a paid employee, he also observed that David had enjoyed riding on the autostrada, though they had a puncture and needed to purchase a new tyre.

In December he was back at Madresfield and writing to Coote about her debts: 'Is it gradual or did something big and bad happen suddenly?' He didn't want her to run into the kind of money trouble that had been so damaging to his lost Hugh. That same month, he and his daughters hosted a coming-of-age dinner-dance at Halkers for young Dickie. The surviving members of the family were together again – in company with David – and entertaining lavishly. Lord Beauchamp wore black, white and pink studs in his shirt front and spent the night at the Ritz to save his household staff any fuss and bother.

But he was in no position to re-enter London society. In January 1938 he and David were aboard the *Europa*, heading across the Atlantic. He wrote to Coote from Cuba: 'We are both much better since we got here.' They lunched out at Sloppy Joe's bar and drank mint juleps made with Spanish brandy. A month later, they were to be found half way across the Pacific. The *Stella Polaris* landed in the Fiji Islands and the earl, with David as his fellow guest, dined with the Governor of Suva.

Lord Beauchamp had now taken up knitting as well as embroidery. He wrote to Coote of his shipboard routine: 'Shave at 8. Embroider and orange juice with a visit from David till 10.30. Then deck. Cocktails at 12.45. Luncheon and coffee.' A month later another letter followed, this time from the Hotel Suisse in Kandy in the hills of Ceylon (Sri Lanka). Beauchamp had by this time received a letter from his daughter with the news that she had been travelling on the continent: 'I imagine you escaped before Hitler arrived,' he wrote. 'What a surprise it was!' ('it' being the Anschluss).

Another round-the-world voyage completed, Beauchamp returned to Mad. During the summer of 1938 a cinefilm was made of the family. The reel is in colour and shows the earl in the gardens of Madresfield. The film begins with a panning shot of the house, and then Lord Beauchamp's Packard drives through a clump of golden yews. Lord Beauchamp features in white trousers, smoking a cigarette. He is surrounded by his adoring girls, Sibell in a blue dress and holding a black chow. The handsome butler Bradford appears. Then the camera shows His Lordship sitting in the moat garden pouring tea. Other shots show people swimming in the outdoor pool and walking in the maze. Looking at the film, one would never imagine the tragedies that had befallen the family – nor that Lord Beauchamp had already been diagnosed with the cancer that would kill him just a few months later.

The family planned a trip to New York together. Beauchamp insisted on going, against the advice of his doctors. For the second time, he had agreed to host a reunion dinner for an association of Americans with the surname Lygon. Travelling with him were Coote, Maimie and Richard – though fully grown now, Dickie was shorter than his brothers at five feet eight inches with blond hair and green eyes. They checked into the Waldorf Astoria. Boom stayed on after the children set sail back to England. A few days later, he was taken ill. A telegram summoned Elmley and his wife, who took the first available ship and arrived a couple of days before he died. They then brought his body home.

The seventh Earl Beauchamp was buried at Madresfield on Friday 25 November 1938. Cars were laid on to meet the Paddington train when it arrived at Malvern Link. All the family attended. Evelyn was not present, but some of his Oxford friends were there to support the girls – Sutro, de Trafford and Duggan. Boom was laid to rest in a grave beside Hugh's. According to Sibell, he was buried in a cardinal's robe, a purple garment made of watered silk. If this is so, it suggests that he had, indeed, been having Romish thoughts. But he died in the High Anglican faith in which he had lived. There was a memorial service at St Paul's, Knightsbridge, on the same day, attended by an eclectic mix of Liberal Party grandees and Bright Young Things from the circle of the Lygon daughters, including Robert Byron, Patrick Balfour, Jessel's boy, Christopher Sykes and Henry Yorke.

Aware that his cancer would probably prove fatal, Lord Beauchamp had signed a will at Mad in the summer. Elmley and Maimie were named as executors. Each of the three unmarried girls – Sibell, Maimie and Coote – was given an income sufficient to yield £1,000 a year. The residue of the estate – and thus Madresfield itself – was bequeathed to Elmley. There was really no choice about this, unlikely as Mona was to produce an heir. Neither Lettice – who ever since her marriage had kept away from family affairs – nor Dickie, were mentioned in the will. David Smyth was tasked with going through 'all my letters and personal effects'. He also received a legacy: 'I GIVE and BEQUEATH all my Australian property of whatsoever nature to the said David Smyth for his own use and benefit absolutely.'

Evelyn, ensconced in his new home, Piers Court, heard the news when he read the morning newspaper. He wrote immediately to Maimie about the 'very sad news' and how he had feared the worst when reading press reports of Boom's illness. 'My thoughts have been with you during this anxious time,' he wrote; 'I know how much your father has meant to you, and how much you meant to him, and I send you all my love and sympathy. Will you please tell Coote and Sib and El and Dicky? . . . I am having a Mass said for your father. I am afraid he would not have approved in his life time, but I think you will.' His affection for Maimie was as strong as ever: 'Please remember that I still love you all just as much as in the old days when I saw you more often, and that it would always be a delight to see you here if you could face the discomfort.'

Evelyn finished *Scoop* at the start of 1938, and his first child, Maria Teresa, was born in March of that year. His last recorded visit to Madresfield took place towards the end of April, a couple of weeks before *Scoop* was published. Now Evelyn had a family and a substantial country house of his own, albeit on nothing like the scale of Mad. He had found a home but lost his freedom. He was happy and settled. His correspondence with Maimie and Coote would continue for the rest of his life, but he was no longer a true inhabitant of Mad World. His absence from Boom's funeral that November – whatever the reason – is symptomatic of the change.

He was, however, still a traveller. Straight after *Scoop* was published, to high acclaim for its comic brilliance, Evelyn was on a train bound for a Catholic convention in Hungary, the Eucharistic Congress. He was upset that the Nazis had prevented thousands of Catholic Austrians from attending: 'near neighbours abruptly and cruelly deprived of their primary human right of association in worship'. After this he went to Mexico with Laura to write about the political situation there. His account was published in a book called *Robbery Under Law*, which was more a political treatise than a travel book, and for that reason his least funny and least successful work.

The immediate consequence of Boom's death for the Lygon sisters was that they lost their family home. Elmley wasted no time in initiating the formalities to assume the title of the eighth Earl Beauchamp, take his seat in the House of Lords and move to Madresfield from the disused lighthouse where he had lived in his parliamentary constituency in Norfolk. Madresfield had a chatelaine again: middle-class Mona, now the Countess Beauchamp. It was Mad World no longer. By this time the sisters cordially loathed Elmley and Mona. Sibell only returned to Mad once during the reign of Mona, which lasted for fifty years.

The best hope for the sisters would be a sequence of good marriages, but there was little prospect of that. As his condolence letter suggests, Evelyn was concerned about them. Throughout his long friendship with Maimie, Sibell and Coote he made jokes about possible suitors, but not even his wild imagination could have predicted that they would make such disastrous matches. Apart from Lettice, who had married her country baronet before the scandal, none of the Lygons married into the aristocracy or even the gentry. Perhaps this more than anything shows the legacy of their father's disgrace.

Of the three sisters, Sibell was the first to marry. She had had many affairs with prominent men such as Lord Beaverbrook. And she had some repute as a journalist. Though most of the pieces that appeared under her name in the *Daily Express* were actually by Beaverbrook, her column in *Harper's Bazaar* was her own. She was very attractive, extremely tall, over six feet, and many were surprised that at the age of thirty-two she was still unmarried. It was said that like the big horses she rode, she was too headstrong to control. Ominously, she had a history of small confrontations with the wrong side of the law. On one occasion a policeman called at Madresfield, believing that she did not have a licence for her dogs. He was told that it was inconvenient for Lady Sibell to receive him. When he called again, he discovered that the new licence had been taken out just a few hours after his first call. The matter went to court and she was fined thirty shillings.

She found herself a handsome pilot eight years her junior, named Michael Rowley. His mother had married (and would later divorce) Bendor, Duke of Westminster, the architect of the Lygons' misery. She had owned a hairdressing salon on Bond Street, and briefly employed Sibell there.

The wedding was announced at the beginning of 1939. It would be a quiet affair, 'due to mourning'. The ceremony was then postponed three times. A date in early January at Caxton Hall was scratched when the groom's father claimed never to have heard of Lady Sibell. The second date at the Oratory was cancelled. A third plan for a wedding at Marlow was also aborted. The ceremony finally took place at the Brompton Oratory in February 1939, in the presence of close family and friends.

Two weeks later, apparently thinking it a great joke, Rowley told his new wife that he had been married to someone else the previous July. Something to do with a German girl while on holiday in Mexico – 'But he didn't think it was legal,' Sibell later recalled. Unfortunately, the first wife, living in Bavaria, found out. She told of the passionate letters that Michael had written to her professing his love: 'It is almost unbearable to be away from you'; 'I adore you and will never give you up for one day'; 'Nothing shall separate us.' Her name was Eleonore, and they had been secretly engaged, but initially had no intention of marrying. After a drunken lunch while on holiday in Mexico, they had spotted a sign outside an office saying 'Get Married Here'. When they went in they saw a young American couple in the process of marrying. The couple agreed to act as witnesses, and so they got married too. It was on his return to England that Rowley met and fell in love with Lady Sibell. The couple went over to Germany to see the first Mrs Rowley, and she appeared to accept the situation. Things came to a head later.

Meanwhile, things had not been going well for Maimie. Some time before the war, Evelyn had written to her from Chagford commiserating with her for having contracted a sexual disease: 'Decent to hear your voice on telephone. V. sorry about your ear and crabs. Odd we should both have crabs together. It is worse for me to have no bush than it is for you. But it will grow again I hope. Perhaps we should get wigs to wear.' 'I expect there will soon be a war,' he added, to pile general misery onto local difficulty.

All her love affairs had ended in tears. Her beauty would not last for ever. Maimie had no choice but to make the best match she could. She too married in 1939. The girl who had consorted with Prince George and been spoken of as a possible royal bride had to make do with a Romanov instead of a Windsor. She married an exiled Russian prince, called Vsevolode Ivanovitch. The nephew of the last Tsar and second in line to the dissolved imperial throne, he was three at the time of the Bolshevik revolution. His English governess smuggled him out of Russia and he went to Eton and Oxford. He partly survived by selling off such family silver as had been brought out of Russia, but he could not get by without working. At one time he set himself up in business selling lubricants in north London, where he became known as Mr Romanoff.

Maimie called him Vsev. Photographs show him as an earnest bespectacled man with black slicked-back hair. He does not look at all glamorous, unlike her other lovers such as Hubert Duggan and Prince George. Nevertheless, it gave a certain pleasure to place an announcement in *The Times* on 1 February 1939 to the effect that Lady Mary Lygon had become engaged to 'Prince Vsevolode of Russia, son of the late Prince John Constantinovitch and of Princess Hélène of Serbia'.

Evelyn wrote to Maimie to congratulate her on her engagement and she told him that she had a 'v. decent engagement ring' and joked that she wanted the title Princess Grainger but that Vsevolode said 'no, she is the Princess Pavlosk'. Maimie told Evelyn that she was receiving instruction in the Orthodox Church from a nice beast. As with Evelyn, love led her to religious conversion. She also told Bo that she was very popular with Vsev's family as 'Boom jiggered some Patriarchs some time ago so they think I'm wonderful.' She asked: 'Can we come and sponge one weekend?' In the same letter she also asked with concern about the appendix operation that Laura had just undergone. This led her to remember her own operation at the time of her mother's funeral: 'I wonder if her scar is bigger than mine which is one and a half inches. There is a lot of snobbery over that.' She told Evelyn that Coote had bought a house in Upton upon Severn, and that Grainger was ill. Apart from her concern for Grainger, she seemed happy and ebullient: 'V and I are going to be quite rich and you must come often to our luxurious Highclere – I am longing to see you.' The expectation of riches was either a joke or seriously over-optimistic. The reality was that Vsev lived from hand to mouth. He, not George, was the genuine 'pauper prince'.

His tsarist origin and her popularity in society were enough to get them some good wedding presents: a silver cigarette case with lighter from the Queen (in the photographic portrait taken for the wedding Vsev has a matching cigarette holder), a stack of jewellery from the groom's mother, Hepplewhite dining-room furniture from the Lygon siblings, a television radiogram set from some of Maimie's girlfriends, and a silver casserole dish from her former lover, Prince George (and Princess Marina). Maimie gave Vsev a set of solid silver dinner plates inscribed with his crown and initial – the only crown left to him. He gave her an ostrich-skin dressing-case and a couple of antique cigarette cases. They married on 31 May in the Chelsea Register Office, with a religious ceremony the following day in the Russian Orthodox Church on Buckingham Palace Road. Maimie, perhaps casting a wistful eye towards the Palace up the road, thus became the Princess Romanovsky-Pavlovsky.

Young Dickie gave her away because Elmley was 'ill'. Her dress was in oyster satin with flounces of old family Brussels lace. There was a good turnout of exiled Romanovs and society figures, along with some of the old set – Henry Yorke, Christopher Sykes and of course Evelyn and Laura. A *Tatler* photographer caught the moment during the Orthodox service when crowns were placed over the heads of bride and groom.

Evelyn disliked Maimie's husband, calling him the 'intolerable Russian'. He met him properly for the first time in July, when he drove to Malvern to meet Coote, Maimie and her new husband at the Hornyold Arms. He also lunched with Coote at her new house in Upton upon Severn: 'commodious, nondescript, very cheap house', he noted in his diary. It was very strange to be with the girls in Worcestershire, but excluded from Mad itself.

There was little sign of heavily built and thickly spectacled Coote getting married. Evelyn still joked with Maimie about possible suitors for her sister, but Coote herself was happy to remain single. The prospect of war overshadowed everything. Everyone's lives were about to change.

CHAPTER 20

Waugh's War

> What really hung over us then, like a great storm cloud, was the idea of Hitler.
>
> But like all parties, it had to come to an end.
>
> (Maimie Lygon)

In July 1939, Evelyn was busy at Piers Court. His journals are full of industry: he is hanging portraits, planting bulbs, digging paths and restoring panelling. He also began work on a new novel, whose heroine owed not a little to Diana Mitford. It is not a novel in any direct sense about the Lygon family – though in the manuscript there is an interesting excised episode in which a gentleman is blackmailed by his servants, a fate that had befallen Lord Beauchamp when he was blackmailed by the Madresfield cook, Mrs Harper, who threatened to expose his homosexuality. Evelyn had heard about this incident from Maimie. The novel also details a quasi-autobiographical father/son relationship that is distant and formal.

Both father and son despise the modern age and view life as a 'huge, grim and solitary jest'. A major theme is the erection of blocks of jerry-built flats adjacent to the family home, Hill Crest Court. The destruction of ancient houses was always a deep concern of Evelyn's. Barbarians were taking over the modern world. The arrival of Mona at Madresfield was perhaps a symptom of the changing times. This novel also introduced a new character type, Atwater, who would assume a prominent place in Evelyn's post-war novels. Vulgar and touchy but also a clown, he is the symbol of the new age of the common man – half-educated, blasé, an insensitive bore, he will be reincarnated as Hooper, Apthorpe and Trimmer. The type is everything that was diametrically opposed to Lord Beauchamp.

The book was unfinished, but eventually published as a fragment, called *Work Suspended,* in 1942. An exceptionally incisive account of it in the *Partisan Review* highlighted the key theme: 'For fifteen years, Waugh has sung the house, and with it the precious furnishings he finds suited to it . . . And in this love of house, of continuous domicile and individual roof, Waugh appears for the defence in one of the most important struggles in English poetry and letters of the past twenty years.' For this critic, Nigel Dennis, Waugh's preoccupation with country houses was bound up with his hostility to the poets and intellectuals of the New Left:

> These young mainly upper-class men, he argues, tried to purge themselves of their upper-class preferences, their acceptance of the old, rural order . . . The intellectual pledged his new fidelity to the city, to the waste land that must be recreated . . . Like these intellectuals, Waugh saw the ghosts in the old houses, the flies lovely in amber; unlike them, he totally rejected the plea to 'advance to rebuild'. The ghosts must be materialised; or, if that were impossible, they must be preserved as the best available wraiths.

But as Evelyn worked on the novel through the long hot summer of 1939, it was becoming increasingly clear that the threat to England and its old ways was not the New Left at home, but the far right in Germany.

As soon as war was declared, Evelyn abandoned the novel in order to sign up for soldiering. But his age (thirty-six) put him at a disadvantage. He felt bitter that he appeared to be of the generation who were too young to fight in the first war and too old for the second. A desk job on government business was a possibility, but that would kill him as a writer. His inclination was to join the Army as a private – the 'complete change of habit' would be the best possible stimulus to his imagination.

Just over two weeks after the declaration of war, Sibell unexpectedly arrived for lunch, in company with her new husband in his shiny RAF uniform. She was 'in a great state of nerves, full of laments about black-out and rationing'. Evelyn took her rather too literally and it was left to Laura to point out 'that she was apprehensive for Michael's safety'. Waugh, by contrast, had no immediate prospect of war action. After various knockbacks he came to the conclusion that someone at the War Office was blocking his chances. Worse, all of his friends seemed to have positions (apart from Harold Acton, who was turned down by everyone and, in a development that would have appalled the fictional Anthony Blanche, was reduced to teaching English to Polish airmen in Blackpool).

Stinchcombe was preparing itself for evacuees from the East End of London. The local schoolmistress told Evelyn that Piers Court was designated as a billet. During the war many country homes were requisitioned by the Ministry of Defence and used for army quarters, training camps, schools or hospitals. Waugh eventually let out Piers Court to a Dominican order of teaching nuns.

In *Brideshead* the Castle is requisitioned as army billets. The troops do their best to destroy the house's architectural features, though not the chapel with its enduring flame. In reality, many great stately homes suffered immense damage because of wartime requisitioning. Madresfield Court, unusually, remained intact. There was good reason for this. The eighth countess, Elmley's wife, was often asked why Madresfield had not been requisitioned. She would reply that this was because 'treasures from the tower' were coming. The treasures were the two princesses, Elizabeth and Margaret. Madresfield was the place designated for safety if the princesses were required to leave London, and thus the house was perfectly conserved during the war years. In preparation for the possible day of arrival, Elmley and Mona would place a book on the bedside table for the princesses, appropriate to their ages. As the war went on, they changed the book annually.

The requisitioning of large houses during the war was exploited to hilarious effect in Evelyn's next novel, *Put Out More Flags*. The incorrigible scam-master Basil Seal, acting as billeting officer for evacuated children, extorts money from the gentry for *not* sending the awful Connolly children to their stately homes. Waugh had no time for those members of the upper classes for whom the war effort did not extend to willingness to having their homes invaded by working-class children.

While the country mobilised, Evelyn pulled every string he could in order to join up. But there seemed to be no demand for middle-aged 'cannon fodder' – until his friend Brendan Bracken (Rex Mottram in *Brideshead*) exerted influence on Winston Churchill to support his application to join the Royal Marines.

Meanwhile, Maimie wrote to Evelyn from her home in Lennox Gardens: 'We are here indefinitely and later running a Russian unit of the Red Cross though from what I know of A. Russians and B. Red Cross even a 100 years war will have been long over by the time we are ready.' They had one ambulance and the outfit was known as 'Princess Pavlovsky's Unit'. Grainger, her beloved Pekingese, was at last dead. She joked that they hoped to form another ambulance unit as a memorial to him and take it to Peking via the Trans-Siberian Railway, 'but of course we've got to win Russia first'. She also gossiped that Captain Hance had a 'very special secret job and is to be sent overseas', but 'I can find nothing to be said in favour of this war . . . I am leading a life of doing nothing but knit operation stockings.'

Other friends were less involved in the war effort. The Coopers, to Evelyn's disgust, had decamped abroad. John Julius had been evacuated to Canada and Diana joined her husband on a lecture tour of America: 'My heart bleeds for you and Duff,' wrote Evelyn with heavy irony; 'I can think of no more painful time to be among Americans and to be obliged by your duties to pay attention to their ghastly opinions.'

The Waughs' first son, Auberon, was born on 17 November 1939. Six days later, Evelyn went to London for his interview for the Royal Marines. He returned for the boy's christening. 'Laura has had a son,' he wrote to Maimie; 'Will you be its Godmother? I know you won't be able to come for [the] christening on account there's a war, but I could have a proxy for you. It is to be called Auberon Alexander. It is quite big and handsome and Laura is very pleased with it. We should so love it if you would accept. Please do.' He was tremendously proud and excited. In the event, three of the godparents, Chris Hollis, Frank Pakenham and Maimie, were cut off by weather and failed to show for the christening. Only Katharine Asquith got through. Maimie was the only one of the four godparents who was not a Catholic. Evelyn wrote to her afterwards: 'It is very nice indeed to have you as Godmother of my son. He was christened this morning under the names Auberon Alexander. As soon as he can speak he shall have to say Romanovsky-Pavlovsky.'

He also told her his big news: 'I have been given belligerent rights by Mr Churchill in a private army he is starting for purposes of his own and go into training on Jan 1st. I shall be in London to buy uniform before then and will call and see you with great love.' He knew that he would get good copy out of the war and he duly did: the 1942 novel *Put Out More Flags* and the autobiographical trilogy *Men at Arms, Officers and Gentlemen, Unconditional Surrender* (republished collectively as *Sword of Honour*) are arguably the finest Second World War novels to have come out of England.

As Christmas approached, he thanked Maimie for sending a beautiful christening cup. He hadn't yet seen it, but Laura had drawn a picture. He wrote that he was sorry she had influenza and told her how much he was enjoying the barracks at Chatham in Kent where he was in preliminary training for the Royal Marines, joking that compared to Captain Hance's riding academy it was not 'very frightening'. Despite his talk of joining up as a private, he was commissioned as a second lieutenant and immediately took to the gentlemanly camaraderie of the officers' mess – not to mention the port. At first he loved everything about the Army, with the exception of the physical training. His love of the good life became a company joke: 'Mr Wuff, that's a rifle in your hand, not a cigar!' He liked the Royal Marine jargon, too: the men saying 'going ashore to see the madam' when they meant going home to see their wives.

The men were affectionate enough in calling him Uncle Wuff. They liked his subversive streak, especially when it was directed against his fellow officers. Once he enquired of a pompous visiting officer if it were true that in the Romanian army no one beneath the rank of major was permitted to wear lipstick. On another occasion he argued in favour of sending in sheep to set off enemy mines. His men were less enamoured of his being a stickler for etiquette and proper procedures and of his love for the past, as when he tried to convince the young men how much better the world was before the invention of electricity. He had cases of claret and burgundy sent up from home. These were known as 'Waugh's stores'. He wrote to Laura with news of his little triumphs and disasters:

'Did I tell you that I have won a complete victory over the Stilton cheese question and it is now properly served?'

A fellow officer, John St John, later said that *Put Out More Flags* and the three autobiographical novels gathered as *Sword of Honour* provided 'the truest as well as the funniest guide to what the war was really like'. As Peter Pastmaster says in *Put Out More Flags*: 'Most of war seems to consist of hanging about. Let's at least hang about with our own friends.'

When his unit was transferred to less elegant barracks at a disused holiday camp at Kingsdown in Kent. Evelyn moved out of the main, cold house into one of the huts and installed an oil stove and fur rug sent down from Pixton. It was like boarding school all over again. At Kingsdown he met the brigade commander, St Clair Morford, describing him in his diary as looking 'like something escaped from Sing-Sing and talks like a boy in the Fourth Form at school – teeth like a stoat, ears like a faun, eyes alight like a child playing pirates. "We then have to biff them, gentlemen." He scares half and fascinates half.' Evelyn immortalised him in the figure of Brigadier Ritchie-Hook in *Men at Arms*.

At the end of January, officers were given leave to live out with their wives. Evelyn sent for Laura and took rooms at the Swan Hotel in Deal. He used this interlude in *Put Out more Flags*:

> Alastair had a bath and changed into tweeds . . . Then he took a whisky and soda and watched Sonia cooking . . . after luncheon he lit a large cigar; it was snowing again, piling up around the steel-framed windows, shutting out the view of the golf course; there was a huge fire and at tea-time they toasted crumpets.
>
> 'There's all this evening, and all tomorrow,' said Sonia, 'Isn't it lovely?'
>
> During one of those week-ends Sonia conceived a child.

After further training at Bisley near Aldershot and an aborted plan for his company to go and defend the coast of the Republic of Ireland from a German invasion, he was sent to Cornwall, having achieved the rank of captain. 'Our task is the defence of Liskeard,' he informed Laura; 'None of us can quite make out why anyone should want to attack it.' After various other postings around Britain, in early September 1940 he found himself serving as battalion intelligence officer on an expedition, undertaken in conjunction with General de Gaulle's Free French, to capture the port of Dakar in French West Africa.

This was the first of a number of major military fiascos in which Captain Waugh participated. All of them were described with alarmingly little exaggeration in *Sword of Honour*. The assault on Dakar was a balls-up from start to finish, ending in an ignominious retreat. In spite of a message from Churchill urging the expedition to complete its mission, the decision was made to turn around. Two other ships in the expeditionary force were badly damaged. Evelyn wrote to Laura: 'Bloodshed has been avoided at the cost of honour.' He was so disgusted by the conduct of the Royal Marines that two days later he wrote to the War Office requesting a transfer. With his customary honesty, he told his wife that 'during the time when we expected to be sent into an operation which could only be disastrous, I realised how much you had changed me, because I could no longer look at death with indifference. I wanted to live and was pleased when we ran away.'

In Gibraltar, on the way back to England, he received the excellent news that Colonel Robert 'Bob' Laycock had got him into the independent company of Army commandos that he had been commissioned to raise. Back in London, he tried to find Laycock in order to confirm the transfer. This took some time (Bob was in fact in Scotland), so there was an opportunity to see old friends – though he was disgusted to find some of them, such as the Coopers, huddling in the Dorchester, sharing rooms and anxiously whispering that the hotel was not steel-framed. He had marched through an air raid in search of Laycock: this cowardice was not what he was expecting.

The next day he saw Maimie, and her new husband, and here found the sangfroid absent from the Coopers. Vsev was working as a wine merchant by day and an air-raid warden by night. As usual, Evelyn was irritated by him, though he liked the access to fine wines from Saccone & Speed. The Romanovsky-Pavlovskys had moved from their big house to a cottage behind the Brompton Oratory. 'She is living a life of serene detachment among acres of ruin,' Evelyn reported to his wife:

> Her minute house full of opulent furniture, a disorder of luxury – lapdogs, orchids, dishes of grapes, boxes of chocolates, about 50

> mechanical toys with which she and Vsevolode play in the evenings. She, very stout, and oddly dressed, exactly like eccentric royalty. She was giving a cocktail party at 12 in the morning 'because people are so dutch about jaggering me at night', full of cosmopolitans who kissed her hand. Pam Chichester was staying there with a broken rib having been blown out of two houses. When the party left we had a great luncheon of oysters and gruyere cheese, with two bottles of very old champagne. Then Vsevolode and I smoking cigars a yard long and Maimie smoking one of a good six inches, we went to a matinée. It is not at all London life as Hitler imagines it.

This was much more to his liking than the quivering aristos in the Dorchester. Despite his admiration for Maimie's redoubtable disregard for the bombs, he was quietly alarmed that her behaviour was not quite normal.

He also told Laura other bits of gossip. His brother Alec had three girls living with him (all admirals' daughters) and spent his days experimenting with a flame-thrower. Maimie's brother Elmley, by contrast, 'sits at Madresfield in the crypt of the chapel, in a bomb-proof waistcoat'. Coote, meanwhile, had joined the Women's Auxiliary Air Force and become an expert photographic interpreter.

The Commandos were raised to supply raiding parties on occupied France and were to be led by youthful officers. The normal rules did not apply to them and they were endlessly fascinating to Evelyn in those early halcyon days: 'We rise above all the troubles of normal administration. The troops are simply given large sums of money and told to arrange their own food and lodgings. There are no punishments because if anyone is a nuisance he is simply sent back to his own regiment.' Once again he was in an eccentric libertarian community, a Mad World like those of the Hypocrites at Oxford and Madresfield after the parents had left.

Laycock had recruited most of his men from the 'smarter' regiments, such as the Household Calvary, the Grenadiers and the Coldstream Guards. 'Nothing could be less like the Marines,' Evelyn recorded. He was drawn to the Commandos as mavericks who made their own rules. Privately, he called them 'Buck's toughs' – an allusion to a gentlemen's club that was a kind of London equivalent of the Bullingdon.

In a letter to Henry Yorke, Evelyn referred to 'Bob Laycock whom you may remember in the first post-Duggan Maimie period'. This refers to Maimie's affair with Duggan in the early thirties, just after her father's exile. Bob was a frequent visitor to Madresfield and was best man at the wedding of Lady Lettice Lygon and Richard Cotterell. He was nicknamed 'Chucker' for his tendency to 'chuck' social engagements at the last minute. Tall, self-possessed and effortlessly charming, Bob and his officers were the types that Evelyn revered. They were soldier-dandies, most of them fine sportsmen, and very spoilt. The Commandos are depicted brilliantly in *Sword of Honour*, especially in the figure of Ivor Clair, with his pet dog and his turban: 'All the officers have very long hair and lapdogs and cigars and they wear whatever uniform they like . . . Officers have no scruples about seeing to their own comfort or getting all the leave they can.' Ivor is drawn principally from Bob Laycock, but Evelyn performs his usual trick of colouring the portrait with strokes of other acquaintances – it was actually a fellow officer, Randolph Churchill, who had a lapdog (Pekingese, like Grainger), to whom he was devoted.

Evelyn initially saw them as Rupert Brooke's spiritual sons: 'There was something of the spirit which one reads in the letters and poetry of 1914.' He loved the house party atmosphere, though he felt on the outside and could not afford to join his fellow officers at their fine restaurants or the gaming tables. His job as liaison officer he described as really meaning 'being on the waiting list for a job'. But Laycock liked and admired Evelyn, and Randolph Churchill became a great, if tempestuous, friend.

He wrote to Laura, convincing her that he was not 'drinking up all your children's money'. She was in the late stages of pregnancy. The baby, named Mary, was born on 1 December and died soon afterwards. Evelyn came to Pixton to see her: 'Poor little girl, she was not wanted.' His father Arthur wrote: 'There seems to me something quite pathetic in this little star of life, which just flickered and went out. She wasn't wanted and she did not stay.' It was at this time that Evelyn wrote to Laura telling her he was thinking of starting a new book for his own pleasure and not for publication – 'a kind of modern Arcadia'. This would become *Brideshead*.

In the new year of 1941, Laycock's Commandos (two battalions, 500 men, known collectively as Layforce) sailed for Egypt. They went by the long route around the Cape, and reached Suez in March, too late to do anything about the German invasion of North Africa. Indeed, the company had been moved around so much that the unit was nicknamed 'Belayforce', and graffiti appeared on the ship, which Evelyn grimly enjoyed: 'Never in the history of human endeavour have so few been buggered about by so many.' 'It is funnier if you are as familiar as Randolph makes us with Winston's speeches,' he told Laura. He said that he had found a *Country Life* book of English country houses and almost wept.

In April, still with no sign of action, they were permitted a raid on Bardia (a Libyan coastal town). Intelligence had reported that there were 2,000 Germans stationed there, but when they got there the Germans had gone. The one German that was left patrolling the town escaped, one of their own officers was shot and a group of men lost their way and had to be left behind. It was a catalogue of ineptness and embarrassment. Evelyn met Colonel Colvin, the commanding officer, and later regretted failing to report his incompetence. Colvin was the 'Fido Hound' of *Officers and Gentlemen*.

In his 'Memorandum on LAYFORCE', Waugh remarked on the tension between the Army and the Navy: 'No 8 Commando was boisterous, xenophobic, extravagant, imaginative, witty, with a proportion of noblemen which the Navy found disconcerting; while the Navy was jejune, dull, poor, self-conscious, sensitive of fancied insults, with the underdog's aptitude to harbour grievances.' The Commandos both attracted and repelled him: he was gleeful when calling them 'Buck's toughs' and even 'scum' in his letters to Laura. He was never a mere apologist for aristocratic thugs (remember the beginning of *Decline and Fall*) and his relationship with his 'batman' (soldier-servant) Ralph Tanner was anything but condescending.

Tanner was interested in archaeology, and so Evelyn arranged an interview for him with the curator of the Cairo museum. The men lived together in extremely arduous circumstances, and in 1975 Tanner was interviewed by *Punch* magazine, resisting at every turn the imputation of Evelyn's snobbery:

> 'There was a rumour, wasn't there, that [Waugh] was so unpopular he had to be protected from the other soldiers?'

'Absolute rubbish. He fitted in very well. He was everything you'd expect an officer to be, if you were an ordinary soldier.'

'A bit of a tyrant, you mean?'

'Not at all.'

'He didn't exploit you the teeniest, weeniest little bit?'

'I'd say he behaved as a model employer to a servant.'

'Waugh was famous for being irascible when bored. How did you cope?'

'He wasn't irascible with me.'

[Tanner is finally forced to concede] '– Well, yes – maybe other people did say Waugh was "a bit fond of the Honourables".'

'Didn't Waugh ever get roaring drunk with them, or something like that?'

'No.'

'You never had to clean up his vomit, or rescue him from a cold bath in which he had fallen in full evening dress?'

'Never. In fact he was so considerate, I'd wait up for him with some hot water, just to return the courtesy.'

In April 1941, German troops invaded Greece and Yugoslavia, but Crete remained in British hands until May, when there began a twelve-day battle for the island. Allied troops far outnumbered the Germans, but after suffering heavy losses in the first few hours, the British, to their astonishment, were ordered to retreat. On the seventh day the Commandos reached the island as reinforcements, only to learn that the situation was both dire and shambolic.

Their orders were to oversee the evacuation and to be the last to go, 'to embark after other fighting forces but before stragglers'. Colvin, suffering from 'battle fatigue', had completely lost his head and Bob Laycock had to relieve him of his duties. After five dreadful days of battle, Laycock ordered his men to fight through the rabble and embark, leaving behind hundreds of Commandos, New Zealanders and Australians.

Evelyn's personal memorandum of this disastrous campaign is an important eyewitness account. But he also played a major part in creating the official record – and in falsifying it. As an intelligence officer and Bob Laycock's personal assistant, he took responsibility for the battalion diary.

Bob dictated to him an entry recording that the order was given for the Commandos to evacuate the island 'in view of the fact that all fighting forces were now in position for embarkation and that there was no enemy contact'. This was patently untrue. After the ignominious withdrawal, a rumour went round that there would be a special evacuation medal for the survivors inscribed '*EX CRETA*'.

To all intents and purposes it was a cover-up. Evelyn, in private, felt enormous shame and dishonour. The feelings never left him. In a letter to Coote Lygon written in 1962 he referred to 'Laycock's and my ignominious flight'. And to Laura he wrote of 'my tale of shame' and 'my bunk from Crete'. 1962, as he noted wryly, was the twenty-first anniversary of the Cretan disaster: 'I celebrated . . . without pomp.'

It was difficult for him to relinquish his hero-worship of Laycock, to recognise that the supposed model commander had committed an act of cowardice. When Evelyn came to write his war novels, his complex feelings about his tainted hero were clear. In *Officers and Gentlemen* (the second novel in the *Sword of Honour* trilogy), Guy Crouchback burns the 'Hookforce' diary that contains the account of Ivor's disgraceful flight. Evelyn based two characters in this novel on Laycock: Tommy Blackhouse and Ivor St Clair. In the fictionalised account of the battle for Crete, Tommy breaks his leg and stays aboard the ship. It is Old Etonian gentleman-soldier Ivor who abandons his men and saves his own skin. Guy's destruction of the Hookforce war diary marks his complicity in the guilt, as did Evelyn's real life falsification of the Laycock war record. Yet he continued to support Bob Laycock publicly and even dedicated the novel to him, with the words 'To Major General Sir Robert Laycock KCMG CG DSO, that every man in arms should wish to be'.

By putting many of the positive aspects into the character of Tommy, Evelyn hoped that the identification with Ivor would be obscured. When *Officers and Gentlemen* was published in 1955, he was horrified that his friend Ann Fleming sent him a telegram. 'Presume Ivor Claire based Laycock dedication ironical.' He responded angrily: 'If you suggest such a thing anywhere it will be the end of our beautiful friendship . . . For Christ's sake lay off the idea of Bob = Claire . . . Just shut up about Laycock, Fuck You, E. Waugh.' Ann replied calmly: 'Panic is foreign to your nature and you rarely use rough words. Why do you become hysterical if one attempts to identify your Officers and Gentlemen?' Evelyn's diary says it all: 'I replied that if she breathes a word of suspicion of this *cruel fact* [my italics] it will be the end of our friendship.'

This altercation over the novel wasn't the end of his friendship with Ann Fleming in the 1950s, but the debacle in Crete in 1941 was the beginning of the end of Evelyn Waugh's love affair with the Army. In particular, it marked the onset of his deep disillusion with the stylish, handsome and brave gentleman-soldier figure he had revered since his hero-worship of J. F. Roxburgh at Lancing. A sentence in *Officers and Gentlemen* was omitted when the novel was republished as part of the *Sword of Honour* trilogy: it refers to 31 May 1941, when he bunked from Crete, as 'the fatal day on which Guy Crouchback was to resign an immeasurable piece of his manhood'. This was exactly what Evelyn felt and it was only to the women he loved and trusted most, his wife Laura and his old friend Coote Lygon, that he confessed his true shame.

His return to England in June 1941 after the ignominy of Crete was followed by a frustrating two-year period of inactivity. Layforce was temporarily disbanded and Evelyn returned to duty with the Royal Marines, though he was not to serve overseas for nearly three years.

On the way back from Alexandria he had written the short novel *Put Out More Flags* ('POMF', he called it for short). He described it to his father as 'a minor work dashed off to occupy a tedious voyage'. He wrote to tell Randolph Churchill that he had dedicated it to him and that it was quite funny.

That autumn saw Evelyn in hot water over an essay written for American *Life* magazine, 'Commando Raid on Bardia'. Unknown to him, the article was syndicated to the London *Evening Standard*. Evelyn suddenly found himself being presented in a news story as 'A Bright Young Man Who is One of the Toughest of Our Commandos'. But the Commandos were supposed to be a secret outfit, and there was a question about whether he had secured the appropriate permissions clearance for publication. Evelyn claimed that he was given permission by Brendan Bracken, who later 'backed out of his responsibility and I got reprimanded'. After this, Evelyn was told by his agent to make sure that he cleared all permissions. The article damaged his standing with the Royal Marines and his military future was irrevocably jeopardised. He did not see combat until his Yugoslavian mission in 1944.

In these intervening years, he threw himself into his writing and his friends. His sixth novel, *Put Out More Flags*, was published in March 1942 and was an immediate success, selling 18,000 copies despite wartime paper restrictions. As usual, he hit the Zeitgeist: his chronicle of the 'Phoney War' or the Great Bore War, 'that strangely cosy interlude between peace and war, when there was leave every week-end and plenty to eat and drink and plenty to smoke', touched a vein of short-term nostalgia when British fortunes were at their low point. Small and perfectly formed, it is perhaps his most underrated novel.

Characters from his previous books reappear and are shown to be affected by the war. The first half is comic, centring on bureaucratic and official ineptness at the newly created War Office and Ministry of Information, while the second half shows a new seriousness in tone as it creates a sense of how the world of the Bright Young Things had vanished. This part of the book read like a valediction to both a lost age and his own youth. Characteristically, a great house under threat plays a major part in the story. Its name, Malfrey, is somewhat evocative of Mad, his own lost paradise, though architectural parallels are not established.

A new character makes his debut: Ambrose Silk, 'a cosmopolitan Jewish pansy', later to be transmogrified into Anthony Blanche. Silk is elegant, part Jewish, homosexual, flamboyant, melancholic, witty in speech, and has a German lover. He is a modernist with fashionable left-wing pretensions. He is,

> an old queen. A habit of dress, a tone of voice, an elegant, humorous deportment that had been admired and imitated, a swift, epicene felicity of wit, the art of dazzling and confusing those he despised – these had been his; and now they were the current exchange of comedians. There were only a few restaurants, now, which he frequented without fear of ridicule, and there he was surrounded, as though by distorting mirrors, with gross reflections and caricatures of himself.

He was, to anyone in the know, an instantly recognisable portrayal of Brian Howard. His old Oxford friend was furious when he read the book. 'Evelyn Waugh has made an absolutely vicious attack on me in his new novel *Put Out More Flags*. You come into it, too,' Howard complained to his German lover, Toni.

This reaction, though understandable, misses both the enormous affection with which Evelyn represented his witty monsters such as Basil Seal and Ambrose Silk, and the serious side to his depiction of his comic villains. At Oxford, both Howard and Peter Rodd (known as Prodd, married to Nancy Mitford and the primary original for Basil) had been arresting, precious talents, and very charming. Ten years on, everyone knew that they were pretty much failures who had simply not lived up to their stupendous promise, and, worse, that they only had themselves to blame for squandering their lives.

There is also affection in the portrayal of the 'ghastly' working-class evacuee children, the Connollys, and admiration for their street wisdom. But there is no mercy for cowards such as Parsnip and Pimpernell (thinly disguised portraits of Christopher Isherwood and W. H. Auden), who run away to America to escape the war.

In the second half of the novel, we see the altered mood in the transformation of a character called Alastair Trumpington, an Old Etonian and a member of the Bullingdon in Oxford. Before the war, he lives a futile life. But on the outbreak of war he abandons his useless life and finds a sense of purpose, joining up as a private soldier: 'He went into the ranks as a kind of penance,' says his wife. Alastair dies in battle. Likewise, the dandy aesthete Cedric, though initially ridiculous, dies a hero, fearlessly carrying his message through enemy fire. Even irresponsible Peter Pastmaster and Basil Seal do their duty as soldiers. Basil tells his mistress, Angela Lyne, 'that racket was all very well in the winter, when there wasn't any real war. It won't do now. There's only one serious occupation for a chap now, that's killing Germans. I have an idea I shall rather enjoy it.' Waugh's own transformation by the war and his reaction to the social elite among the Commandos help to shape the pattern of the book, but there is also a profound sense in which Trumpington is his embodiment of what he imagines Hugh Lygon would have become, had he lived.

Angela Lyne, Basil's lover, is closely based on Olivia Plunket Greene. She is drawn with great sympathy as she inexorably descends into alcoholism. In a beautifully realised vignette towards the end of the novel, she collapses in a drunken stupor in the cinema and is helped home to her maid, Grainger, by Lady Mary Meadowes, who is out on a date with

Peter Pastmaster. Lady Mary, the second of the three daughters of a lord who is 'among the survivors of the Whig oligarchy', is a character of slender beauty (she does not carry 'a pound of superfluous flesh'), exquisite manners, graceful speech, sharp wit and great kindness. She also has a pet dog with peculiar habits. She is evidently an affectionate portrayal of Maimie.

The choice of the name Grainger for Angela's maid is a private joke for Maimie's benefit, but – consciously or not – by giving the name of her dog to the alcoholic character's maid, Waugh reveals that he is beginning to fear for her own future. 'Only Grainger, her maid, knew what was the matter with Mrs Lyne, and she only knew the shell of it. Grainger knew the number of bottles, empty and full, in the little pantry; she saw Mrs Lyne's face when the blackout was taken down in the morning.'

Maimie was drinking far too much with her wine merchant husband. She was beginning to behave rather oddly, much to Evelyn's concern. On leave in London in April 1942 he saw a lot of her. They dined and drank together, mixing caviar and Black Velvets. Then they went off to Vsev's ARP post to drink port until the early hours. Later he saw Laura and felt that this was 'the happiest leave of the war'. The only blot on his happiness was the troublesome influence of Vsev on Maimie.

He confessed his fears to Coote who, with the WAAF, had begun, in her own words, 'a nomadic life of seventeen years'. Evelyn had been posted to Ayrshire, from where he wrote to Coote in the bantering style that characterises all his letters to her: 'Darling Coote, Can't you get posted to Ayrshire, which is full of Waafs . . . Could you not get into Combined Operations. Then we could write one another official letters full of deep double meanings.' Evelyn asked if they could meet in London to drink utility port together. But then he gave her news of her sister: 'Blondie, ever prone to bad company, seems to have fallen in with a very bad set of foreigners. I got her to dinner alone once and she was heavenly, like her old self. It seems she suffers from the delusion that she is a Queen. It is quite common (see Alice in Wonderland).' Evelyn unequivocally blamed Maimie's husband for her behaviour. Vsev was giving her delusions of grandeur and impossible hopes. Evelyn told Randolph Churchill that Maimie 'expects to be called to the throne of the All Russians any day and has become gloriously sedate'.

In April 1942, Laycock called him back to the Commandos: 'Chucker

Laycock has proved most unchucking,' he told Coote. But he remained mainly in London, with only menial tasks. He was drinking a lot and taking heavy sleeping drugs. He crashed two army cars. Charles Ryder in *Brideshead* says: 'Here at the age of thirty-nine I began to feel old.' That was Evelyn at this time.

In June, Laura gave birth to a daughter who was to become the favourite of all his children, Margaret. Two months later, at Combined Operations Headquarters, he disgraced himself by getting drunk. He had been to one of Maimie's early morning cocktail parties and after a day's hard drinking had dined with Laycock and his wife and the Randolph Churchills. He was so drunk that he could not even remember who else was there. 'I began to trace a decline in my position in Bob's esteem,' he noted in his diary. He had no fixed base and was living in hotel rooms until Maimie offered to take him in, so he moved into her home.

At the end of August she organised a fair and circus on Hampstead Heath in aid of Yugoslavia. He went with Coote and his godson, Jonathan Guinness, whose mother and stepfather, the Mosleys, were in prison. Maimie's circus was such a success that she sold the tickets twice over 'and indignant crowds were turned away'. Evelyn reported that 'she has no means of using the money she raises so lavishly'.

These were desultory months. 26 October: 'Went to see Maimie and, in a daze, walked around exhibition. Went to supper with her and sat up late talking. Stayed the night with her.' He wrote to Coote: 'It is not unfair to say I never draw a sober breath.' The same was becoming true of Maimie. They shared hangovers, oysters, long evenings of conversation over bottles, and then fell asleep together and felt much better. Vsevolode was made a major in the Serbian army: 'He is so excited about it he was sick at Lady Crewe's,' Evelyn told Coote.

'For two intimates, lovers or comrades, to spend a quiet evening with a magnum, drinking no aperitif before, nothing but a glass of cognac after – that is ideal': that was Maimie and Bo's life together in bombed-out London in the autumn of 1942, waiting for the fortunes of war to turn.

CHAPTER 21

The Door to Brideshead

Evelyn was still living with Maimie and her husband, in an uncomfortable single room in Montpelier Walk, SW7 (South Kensington). He would have preferred it without Vsevolode, who interrupted their late night drinking and gossip. He found the prince acutely silly and was irritated with their friends and dogs, so he decided to move out. He was doing a desk job, but waiting in hope that Laycock would ask for him to go to Africa.

In June his father died. On the very same day, the brigade left on 'Operation Husky' (the invasion of Sicily), without Evelyn. He was told that he would be sent for later. Evelyn was angry and bitter about this, but with Alec on active service in Syria it was up to Evelyn to go to his mother's aid and sort out his father's papers. Nothing survives in the way of grief-stricken letters or diary entries. His loathing of his father's sentimentality had meant that he was always reluctant to express his own romantic side, especially in print. With Arthur's death, it became possible for Evelyn to go forward with a more personal and sentimental novel than he had ever written before.

The promise to be called out to Italy in the first wave of reinforcements was overruled and he found himself removed altogether from the Commandos. Through the summer he remained on indefinite leave, waiting for a new posting. He spent time with friends, quarrelling with Diana Cooper but remaining close to Maimie. 'Dined with Maimie where, by good chance, Vsevolode became ill and left the dinner table and us to two hours gossip' goes a typical letter to Laura, down with her family at Pixton. She was pregnant again. Evelyn was once again the homeless wanderer awaiting his fate. The Army did not seem to need him and it seemed as though everyone else had something to do.

One evening in September he dined with Maimie and stayed the night. He got drunk and accused her husband of being a spy. Among the people they frequently talked about was Maimie's old lover, Evelyn's Oxford friend, Hubert Duggan. He was dying of tuberculosis. Evelyn wrote to Laura: 'The news of Hubert is very bad indeed. He is allowed to see no one . . . He never sleeps and drugs put him into a delirium but not to sleep. He is in the blackest melancholy and haunted by delusions. There is nothing that can be done for him medically. Supernatural aid needed.' Duggan had renounced his Catholicism for the sake of his longstanding mistress, Phyllis de Janzé. Now on his deathbed he had begun to talk of religion and returning to the Church, but felt that this would somehow be a betrayal of the memory of Phyllis, who had recently died.

Evelyn acted directly and decisively. There was nothing he wouldn't do to save the soul of one of his friends. He went to see a Father Dempsey (whom he described as a big, fat peasant). The priest gave him a medal to hide in Hubert's room and promised to call, saying, 'I have known most wonderful cases of Grace brought about in just that way.' But when Evelyn was told that Hubert would not survive the day he could not locate Dempsey. He found another priest, Father Devas. His interference annoyed Hubert's sister, who was watching over him, and his nurse, but he was committed to saving his friend from Hell. Father Devas gave Hubert absolution and his 'Thank you, father' was taken as assent. Evelyn then returned to White's Club and sat drinking with Randolph Churchill. When he returned to Hubert, the priest was still there, wanting to anoint him, much as his sister resisted. All of this is Evelyn's own account:

> Father Devas very quiet and simple and humble, trying to make sense of all the confusion, knowing just what he wanted . . . patiently explaining, 'Look, all I shall do is just to put oil on his forehead and say a prayer. Look the oil is in this little box. It is nothing to be frightened of.' And so by knowing what he wanted and sticking to that . . . he got what he wanted and Hubert crossed himself and

> later called me up and said, 'When I became a Catholic it was not from fear', so he knows what happened and accepted it. So we spent the day watching for a spark of gratitude for the love of God and saw the spark.

This was a crucial moment for Evelyn. He had witnessed the operation of Divine Grace. He used the whole of this incident at the climax of *Brideshead.* Critics complained that the conversion of Lord Marchmain was wholly unrealistic, but as far as Evelyn was concerned it was a piece of reportage. To his theological mentor, Ronnie Knox, he wrote after the publication of *Brideshead*: 'It was, of course, all about the deathbed. I was present at almost exactly that scene, with less extravagant décor, when a friend of mine whom we thought in his final coma and stubbornly impenitent . . . did exactly that, making the sign of the Cross.'

Twelve days later Evelyn returned to Pixton with the intention of starting his novel. Hubert's death had made a profound impression on him.

On 3 October he attended an unsuccessful dinner party with Maimie and her husband, writing in his diary 'The Russian's intolerable.' He also recorded a very rare row with Maimie over the Allies Club. The Russian alliance was becoming strained both privately and in the wider world of the war.

A Requiem Mass for Maimie's erstwhile lover, Hubert, was held at the Church of the Immaculate Conception on Farm Street, in Mayfair, on 3 November. Father Devas officiated. Evelyn went with Maimie. Vsev was conspicuous by his absence. Evelyn was furious at 'an untoward incident' that occurred at the end of the service when the trumpets of the Life Guards sounded off the Last Post and the Reveille. Evelyn noted that the congregation finally understood the point of the service and were moved to tears, but the emotional silence was broken by one of his friends being ticked off by 'an old warrior in plain clothes' for failing to stand to attention. The appropriate reply should have been, according to Evelyn, 'Sir, I have come to pray for my friend's soul. Kindly keep your parade ground truculence out of this sacred place.'

Before he could get started on his new novel, he had to attend a parachuting course at Tatton Park near Manchester. He loved the experience, describing his first jump as 'the keenest pleasure I remember'. But on his second jump he cracked his fibula, putting himself out of action again. He spent two weeks in the Hyde Park Hotel, being fussed over by friends.

At Christmas time, with Laura and the children still spending the war in the safety of Pixton, Maimie took Evelyn in. Much as he loved Christmas with her, he wrote in his diary: 'I find my dislike of Vsevolode so overwhelming that I cannot sit in the room with him . . . Maimie is lost to me.'

In January 1944, with no official duties, Evelyn formally requested leave in order to write a new novel. The leave was granted.

He stayed at Chagford, working with intense concentration, for the whole of February. Unusually for him, he revised as he went along. He was revealing more of himself than ever before, and he wanted to choose the right words.

Then a call came from the War Office to say that his leave had been cancelled and that he should take up a new post as ADC to an unknown general: 'so that ends my hopes of another two months' serious work. Back to military frivolities.'

Southern England was preparing for the second front and needed all available men. Evelyn travelled to London to meet his new commander, Major General Ivor Thomas. He was so rude to him that Thomas refused to take him. 'This is a great relief,' Evelyn wrote: 'the primary lack of sympathy seemed to come from my being slightly drunk in his mess on the first evening. I told him I could not change the habits of a lifetime for a whim of his' (the particular offence was that he had spilled a glass of wine over the general). When he was transferred to a new general, he persuaded him forthwith to give him six further weeks' leave to continue work on the novel. Back at Chagford he was annoyed to be turned out of the room in which he had grown accustomed to writing in order to make space for an adulterous affair between Lord Grantley and an actress. 'I am sick at heart and lonely,' he wrote, but in twelve days he had completed 28,000 words.

He sent a charming letter to his eldest child on her sixth birthday, telling her all about the present he had arranged for her – painting materials, colours and brushes of the kind 'which real artists use, and when a thing is the best of its kind, even if it is only a little thing like a paint brush, it should be treated like a Sacred Animal. Always remember it is not the size or price of things that is valuable but the quality.' Then he added, 'You have been a great happiness to your mother and me for five years. It is very sad that I see so little of you.'

He wrote to Coote on 23 March, telling her about his novel: 'I am writing a very beautiful book, to bring tears, about very rich, beautiful, high born people who live in palaces and have no troubles except what they make themselves and those are mainly the demons sex and drink which after all are easy to bear as troubles go nowadays.' It was a long and tender letter, honestly telling her all of his troubles and saying that when he was in London he barely drew a sober breath: 'I was beginning to lose my memory which for a man who lives entirely in the past, is to lose life itself.' He told her all his news, of his parachute accident, and how he had a lovely time when he broke his leg and all his friends visited him and cost him a fortune in drinks. Referring to himself as a dypsomaniac, he said: 'I drove a General mad, literally, and both he and I were expelled from that headquarters together.' He also told how Maimie's husband was being a 'great grief at all who love Blondie. It is impossible ever to see her alone and he has not now any wine left to sell one so there is no point to him at all.' He included lots of gossip about mutual friends, and at the end of his letter added: 'Don't go East. Come back to us.'

He also wrote mysteriously: 'What are the documents concealed at Mad?' Coote must have mentioned something in a letter to him that does not survive – perhaps something to do with the family scandal. Boom and Mad were much on his mind as he wrote.

He was recalled to London at the end of March. While they were still deciding what to do with him, he ensconced himself in the Hyde Park Hotel and corrected his typescript. 'My Magnum Opus is turning into a jeroboam. I have written 62,000 words.' He had come to a natural break in the story and was happy to spend a fortnight getting drunk in White's while he awaited orders. On 1 May, he gave dinner to two old Oxford friends, Harold Acton and John Sutro. He filled Maimie in with the details: 'a fine dinner – gulls eggs, consommé, partridge, haddock on toast, Perrier Jouet '28, nearly a bottle a head, liqueur brandy, Partaga cigars – an unusual feast for these times . . . I found their company delightful . . . Harold's descriptions of service life as seen by a bugger were a revelation. He combines his pleasures with keen patriotism' (Acton had finally been accepted by the RAF).

Two days later he returned to Chagford, struggling with 'a very difficult chapter of love-making on a liner . . . I feel very much the futility of describing sexual emotions without describing the sexual act; I should like to give as much detail as I have of the meals, to the two coitions – with his wife and Julia. It would be no more obscene than to leave them to the reader's imagination, which in this case cannot be as acute as mine.' He wrote to Laura with a warning: 'sexual repression is making mag. op. rather smutty'.

He made terrific headway through the month of May, during which Laura gave birth to his fifth child, Harriet Mary. At the end of the month he was assigned to No. 2 Special Air Service Regiment, though not given an active posting. On D-Day, Tuesday 6 June, he brought the book to its climax: 'This morning at breakfast the waiter told me the Second Front had opened. I sat down early to work and wrote a fine passage of Lord Marchmain's death agonies. Carolyn [Cobb] came to tell me the popular front was open. I sent for the priest to give Lord Marchmain the last sacraments. I worked through till 4 o'clock and finished the last chapter.' That same week, appropriately enough, the Americans liberated Rome.

'I think perhaps it is the first of my novels rather than the last,' he wrote. He again described it as his 'magnum opus' and said to his agent that it 'was very good', explaining to him that 'the whole thing is steeped in theology'. The epilogue and final tinkering were completed on 24 June, the Feast of Corpus Christi.

He was shaken by the advent of the new flying bombs (this was the time that he sent his books away from the Hyde Park Hotel back to the country and joked that his son should come to London – 'a child is easily replaced while a book destroyed is utterly lost'). He was discomposed that, as one low-flying bomb came over, 'for the first and I hope the last time in my life I was frightened'. He put this down to his being drunk and resolved to give up alcohol: 'It is a cutting of one of the few remaining strands that held me to human society.'

A message arrived with the news that Randolph Churchill had personally requested Evelyn to join him on a mission to Croatia. Evelyn claimed jokingly that the commission came 'in the belief that I should be able to heal the Great Schism between the Catholic and Orthodox Churches'. He was eager to accept, but worried that the posting wouldn't come off, as he had had so many setbacks in the last three years.

Yugoslavia had been invaded by Germany and Italy, but had a number of resistance groups. It was thought that the presence of Churchill's son would act as a visible symbol of Britain's solidarity. The main resistance group was General Tito's Partisans, now supported by the British, who had switched their allegiance from the Serbian Chetniks. Tito was presented to the British as a heroic figure who stood for religious tolerance. In fact, he was a shadowy figure with his own communist agenda.

Catholic newspapers in England had reported for some time the less palatable truth about Partisan activities, which included the murder of Slovenian priests and the desecration of churches. Evelyn had his own agenda for agreeing to Randolph's offer, and he did not see Tito in quite the same way as he appeared to Churchill's son. Evelyn initiated a fantasy that Tito was in fact a woman and a lesbian to boot. He called her 'she' or 'auntie', a joke that took advantage of Tito's elusiveness and the fact that he was so little known outside Yugoslavia that there were doubts that he really existed.

In July, Evelyn and Randolph were posted to the Italian port of Bari and then to an island off the Dalmatian coast called Vis. From there they headed to the small spa town of Topusko, the Partisans' headquarters. They flew in on 16 July but, just as they were about to land, the plane crashed. There were nineteen on board and ten were killed instantly. Before setting off on the flight, Evelyn had mentioned in a letter to his wife that he had abandoned a silver medal that she had given him because the silver chain had turned his neck green. He believed that whereas Baby Jungman's St Christopher had saved him in the Amazon, this time the lack of Laura's token had nearly cost him his life.

Badly burnt, he was sent to hospital in Bari. To his great good fortune, Coote Lygon was stationed near there with the WAAFs. For the last two years of the war, Coote had been posted abroad. Like many other women of her class, her life had been given new meaning and adventure by the opportunity to serve her country. Most of the time she was in Italy, in the small Apulian town of San Severo, below the mountains of the Gargano peninsula on the Adriatic. She remembered Evelyn and Randolph going in and out of Yugoslavia. Evelyn sent her a telegram to tell her of the plane crash and of his injuries. She immediately went to see him.

Coote was delighted to be of use to Evelyn, whose first concern was that she should contact Laura. His hands were so burned that he could not hold a pen and so she wrote to Laura for him.

Coote remembered the hospital visit for more than one reason. Late in life, she recalled Evelyn's burnt hands and the grumbling son of the Prime Minister, 'complaining of water on the knee . . . creating a fine fuss'. But she also remembered a significant moment in the course of her conversations with Evelyn. He told her about the new book he had just finished: 'It's all about a family whose father lives abroad, as it might be Boom – but it's not Boom – and a younger son: people will say he is like Hughie, but you'll see he's not really Hughie – and there's a house as it might be Mad, but it isn't really Mad.'

If Coote felt apprehensive, she didn't reveal it. She remembered that he 'talked on for some time in this vein, at pains to emphasise that, although he had chosen a situation which might be compared to ours at one time, he was going to treat it in a very different way – he had taken the bare bones, the skeleton, and intended covering it with muscles creating tensions, quite different from those which had influenced us'.

Evelyn was clearly anxious not to hurt Coote and the family that he loved. He told her that the Roman Catholic element was a key part of the novel and that the matrimonial problems of the fictional Flytes were very different from those that beset Lord and Lady Beauchamp. Nevertheless, it was bold of him to admit how close the parallels were. It shows the depths of Coote's devotion that she chose to accept Evelyn's excuse for using her family as copy. She loyally continued to claim that the resemblances between her own family and the fictional Marchmains were much exaggerated.

Evelyn was sent to Rome to convalesce before he and Randolph departed a second time for Yugoslavia. Coote went too to look after Evelyn, giving up her leave in order to nurse him, just as Maimie had taken him in after his parachuting accident. He stayed in a charming flat, 5 Via Gregoriana.

He was also treated for a carbuncle that had grown on his neck. It was a painful procedure: 'Suffering was intense and continuous.' Eventually they gave him antibiotics and it began to heal. He relished the fact that Coote was there to administer to him and soon he was enjoying Rome – 'a week of easy living, getting strong and eating better'. Their days were spent visiting churches and dining quietly in the evening. He was in pain and had lost most of his luggage in the crash, including his shoes, forcing him to walk in 'creepers' both made for the same foot. It must have been a difficult time for Coote, given the memories of Rome with Boom. She was short of money and Evelyn, always generous to his friends, insisted on loaning her 5,000 lire.

In September, Randolph and Evelyn returned to Topusko. Evelyn set about collecting information for an official report on church affairs. He was also awaiting the proofs of *Brideshead Revisited*.

Randolph proved to be an uncongenial comrade. Being together in close proximity was a great strain upon both men. 'He is not a good companion for a long period,' Evelyn wrote, 'but the conclusion is always the same – that no one else would have chosen me, nor would anyone else have accepted him.' The weather was dreadful, it rained night and day for a week, and he had run out of cigars. Nor did he have the comfort of hard drinking, since he despised the local spirit, Rakia. He thought that it had 'an all-pervading stench part sewage part stickfast paste'.

Coote, with typical understatement, observed that the two men had got on each other's nerves when they were together in hospital in Italy. In Yugoslavia, nerves frayed by lack of cigars and drink, Evelyn vented some of his most glorious invective upon his less intelligent companion. Randolph was a 'flabby bully who rejoices in blustering and shouting down anyone weaker than himself and starts squealing as soon as he meets anyone as strong. In words he can understand he can give it but he can't take it . . . He is a bore – with no intellectual invention or agility.' All he and Lord Birkenhead, who had joined them, could do were repeat witticisms spoken by their fathers. 'Of conversation as I love it – a fantasy growing in the telling, apt repartee, argument based on accepted postulates, spontaneous reminiscences and quotation – they know nothing.' At the end of his tether with Churchill's volubility, Evelyn laid a wager that he could not read the Bible in a fortnight. The wager backfired as Randolph had a wonderful time rediscovering the Bible. As Evelyn described it: 'He sits bouncing about on his chair, chortling and saying "I say, did you know that this came in the Bible 'bring down my grey hairs with sorrow to the grave?'" Or simply, "God, isn't God a shit."'

Evelyn wrote to Coote, complaining that he was short of reading materials, and she dutifully sent him packages of books. He thanked her for repaying the Roman loan and told her that Freddy Birkenhead's arrival was 'most opportune as I was beginning to have qualms about a winter tête-à-tête with Randolph'. He also told her how grateful Laura was for Coote's nursing of him while he recovered from the plane crash and that his wife had said, 'I always thought her the nicest of all your friends.' To which Evelyn added 'Hear hear'.

Evelyn told her that he was hoping to see her again in Bari, where he had applied for a transfer. Coote was much on his mind, not least because the novel, in which her younger self figured as Cordelia Flyte, was also consuming him. On 20 November the proofs finally turned up and Evelyn spent every minute that Randolph was out of the room correcting them. He later gave them to a Jesuit institution in Baltimore, who had awarded him an honorary doctorate. He described their extraordinary trajectory in war-torn Europe: 'This set of page proofs was sent in October 1944 from Henrietta Street to 10 Downing Street; from there it travelled to Italy in the Prime Minister's post bag, was flown from Brindisi and dropped by parachute on Gajen in Croatia, then an isolated area of "resistance"; was corrected at Topusko and taken by jeep, when the road was temporarily cleared of enemy, to Split; there by ship to Italy and so home, via Downing Street.' Having Winston Churchill as his father was one compensation for Randolph's awkward company.

The proof corrections made by Waugh in Yugoslavia between 20 and 26 November were, he told his agent, 'extensive and very important'. He changed such crucial passages as the one in which he described the trajectory of Charles's love from Sebastian to Julia to God; he introduced many alterations to the architectural history and layout of Brideshead Castle; he made Charles's wife Celia even less sexually desirable than she was in the manuscript; he inserted a key passage into Sebastian's letter and expanded upon the theme of Charles's aesthetic conversion to the baroque. There were numerous other minor changes, some of them bearing upon the Lygon connection: in the manuscript, Beryl Muspratt is a year or two younger than Bridey, but in proof she becomes a year or two older, heightening the resemblance to Elmley's wife, Mona the Dane. The question of explicit homosexual reference was a cause of some soul-searching. In the manuscript, when Bridey wonders whether Kurt's relationship with Sebastian is 'vicious', Charles replies that it can't be because, 'For one thing, I happen to know the man has syphilis.' In proof, this becomes a gentler 'I'm sure not. It's simply a case of two waifs coming together.'

Once he had inserted the final proof corrections (undertaken while Randolph Churchill was out at the cinema), Evelyn dispatched his magnum opus and asked for a new posting to Bari. He remained there a fortnight, meeting up once again with Coote. She loved Bari, describing it as 'Paris, London and New York rolled into one after San Severo'. He was still short of reading matter, so she lent him some Trollopes. She was so keen to spend time with him that she got herself to Bari whenever she could, even on some occasions hitchhiking in lorries. It was a long and tiring journey from San Severo, but his company was usually worth the effort. Not always though – once she came to see him looking 'very thin and almost pretty', arriving early, 'rather importunately, at 3.30'. 'I had a rather sticky time with her until 6,' Evelyn complained, 'failed to get a bath, took two Benzedrine tablets, found I had lost all appetite through fatigue and could eat little of the very fine feast we had arranged. For myself I found it a dull evening and wondered whether Coote found it worth the long hitch-hike.'

Evelyn was then posted to Dubrovnik. His role was to serve as intermediary between the Partisans and the Allies, but the Partisans, allied with the Soviet Union, were increasingly hostile to the British, and to Waugh especially. He responded by helping the townspeople (many of whom were desperate to escape the coming communist regime) with their requests for help and food: 'Looking back on the last few days I find that everything I have done, which is not much, has been benevolent – giving jobs to the needy, food to the hungry, arranging to get a Canadian moved towards Canada, helping a Dominican priest swap wine for flour. There are few in the Army can say this.' He was also collecting material on religious conditions for his report 'Church and State in Liberated Croatia'.

On Christmas Day 1944 he wrote to Coote, telling her that he had had a pleasant Christmas 'in unbroken solitude, which next to Laura's company and that of the few friends I can count on the toes of ones foot, is what I should have chosen'. He described his surroundings as tolerable and apologised for his behaviour at their last meeting. He also told her how Christmas made him think a lot about Madresfield:

> Mr H and the Capt and the handsome presents Blondie made us give them, and Jessel's boy's foie gras and the time we went to the top of the noble line after dinner and someone gave the late Maj Duggan a push and he could not stop running until he reached the gates of St James girls school and you and me and Hamish popping into Lord Beauchamps Home for Impotent Clergymen. Well well never again.

He sat for a bust in support of a local artist: 'it will be the next best thing to having myself stuffed'. And he arranged for fifty sets of proofs of *Brideshead* to be sent as Christmas presents to his friends. He waited anxiously to hear what they thought about his magnum opus. Laura was requested to keep all thank-you letters in a safe place and to copy out the most interesting sentences for him.

It was to his fellow novelist Nancy Mitford that he turned to discuss his book. She 'got the joke' about everything and saw the point of the central relationships: 'so true to life being in love with an entire family'. He begged her: 'Please tell me what everyone says behind my back.' He was anxious because the book was such a departure from all his previous novels, yet he felt in his heart that it was his most important book. Financially, it was to be in that it became his first bestseller in America. He was always grateful for that, but he later changed his mind about the book's merits, thinking it too sentimental and seeing it as a reaction to wartime deprivation.

Nancy also said: 'I'm so glad you are nice about Brian this time.' Along with all Waugh's friends, she had seen cruelty in his portrayal of Brian Howard as Ambrose Silk in *Put Out More Flags*. But, as Evelyn confirmed, Anthony Blanche was a composite of Brian and Harold Acton. Harold was very upset by the portrayal. The general consensus among those in the know was that it was a clever idea to combine the two Eton boys who had offered an inseparable embodiment of the Oxford Aesthete.

He asked Nancy to continue to 'keep your ear to the ground and report what they say. For the first time since 1928, I am eager about a book.' He was less pleased with Laura, who was too lazy to read it: 'What do you think of the book? . . . Can you not see how it disappoints me that the book which I regard as my first important one, and have dedicated to you, should have no comment except that Eddie is pleased with it.'

He had to be content with the approval of his literary friends, all of whom believed *Brideshead* to be a masterpiece. He was delighted with Nancy's next two 'splendid letters. What a bob's worth.' She had written to tell him that many of their friends thought it was '*subtle clever* Catholic propaganda'. But this was the bit that delighted him:

> Now about what people think:
>
> *Raymond* [Mortimer]: Great English classic.
>
> *Cyril* [Connolly]: Brilliant where the narrative is straightforward. Doesn't care for the 'purple passages' i.e. deathbed of Lord M. Thinks you go too much to White's. But found it impossible to put down (no wonder).
>
> *Osbert* [Lancaster]: Jealous, doesn't like talking about it. 'I'm devoted to Evelyn – are you?'
>
> *Maurice* [Bowra]: Showing off to Cyril about how you don't always hit the right word or some nonsense but obviously much impressed and thinks the Oxford part perfect.
>
> *SW7 (European royal quarter)* [i.e. Maimie]: Heaven, darling.
>
> *Diana Abdy*: Like me and Raymond, no fault to find.
>
> *Lady Chetwode*: Terribly dangerous propaganda. Brilliant.
>
> *General view*: It is the Lygon family. Too much Catholic stuff.

The response of the Lygon girls was what he most wanted and feared. Maimie's 'Heaven, darling' was encouraging, but it wasn't until the end of January that he heard from her in person. She did not reveal much: 'Darling Bo. Your book is very very interesting and is the talk of all the sages who think it is wonderful . . . Darling, thank you very very much for sending it.' Some weeks later Coote was a little more forthcoming: 'I read it once at a furious pace, and now more slowly, and like it very much, Sebastian gives me many pangs.'

CHAPTER 22

Brideshead Unlocked

Most novels are confessions in disguise; most 'Confessions' . . . are novels in disguise.

(Harold Acton)

I reserve the right to deal with the kind of people I know best.

(Evelyn Waugh)

On 25 April 1945 the politician and inveterate gossip 'Chips' Channon wrote in his diary: 'I am reading an advance copy of Evelyn Waugh's new novel "Brideshead Revisited". It is obvious that the mis-en-scène is Madresfield, and the hero Hugh Lygon. In fact, all the Beauchamp family figure in it.'

To Channon and everyone else in the know, it was clear that the exiled Lord Marchmain was a version of Boom and Lady Marchmain of the Countess Beauchamp, that Sebastian was Hugh, Bridey was Elmley, Julia Maimie and Cordelia Coote. And yet – or *because* the identification was so obvious – Waugh's epigraph to the book read: 'I am not I: thou art not he or she: they are not they.'* This is the paradox of *Brideshead.*

* Waugh revised the text of *Brideshead* on several occasions. Unless otherwise stated, all quotations are from the first mass-market edition of 1945.

In 1947, Evelyn wrote a memo to MGM in Hollywood regarding a proposed film adaptation of the novel. It clarifies the fundamental point for those 'Californian savages': 'the theme is theological'. The particular theological point on which the book turns is 'in no sense abstruse and is based on principles that have for nearly 2,000 years been understood by millions of simple people, and are still so understood'. In short, 'the novel deals with what is theologically termed "the operation of grace", that is to say, the unmerited and unilateral act of love by which God continually calls souls to himself'.

'Too much Catholic stuff' was the general view of his friends and has remained the view of many of his critics. The novel is about the hero Charles Ryder's conversion to Catholicism and the 'twitch upon the thread' that reels in Sebastian and Julia, lapsed Catholics who have rebelled against their mother and their religion, but who are in the end powerless to resist God's grace. As Evelyn's Hollywood memo made clear, 'the Roman Catholic Church has the unique power of keeping remote control on human souls which have once been part of her'. Though Charles and Julia must renounce one another, each is the catalyst for the other's spiritual redemption: 'The physical dissolution of the house of Brideshead has in fact been a spiritual regeneration.'

Many ordinary readers ignore the theological and spiritual element, so caught up are they by the glamour of the Flytes and the glorious locations – Oxford, Venice, Paris, Morocco, Mayfair and the stately home of Brideshead Castle – just as Charles is entranced by all the splendour that Brideshead and the Marchmain family represent. This distraction of surface is deliberate. But the clues are planted in the narrative all the way through from the prologue, when Hooper, visiting the Arts and Crafts R.C. chapel at Brideshead, the great house that has been requisitioned as army barracks, says to Ryder 'More in your line than mine', through to the all-important scene at Lord Marchmain's deathbed when atheist Charles prays for a miracle and witnesses 'God's grace'. The novel urges you to read it backwards.

Brideshead mattered so much to Evelyn because he put so much of himself into it: his distance from his father, his sentimental education at Oxford, his early love affairs, his initiation into the aristocratic world of the Lygons, his conversion to Roman Catholicism, his abortive love affair with the Army. Like his creator, Charles Ryder is born in October 1903 and wants to be a painter; like his creator, he hails from a minor public school and is an atheist. All the things that mattered most to Evelyn in the years up until the end of the Second World War went into the novel, even though many years later (now bitter and disillusioned) he grew rather ashamed of its excesses, its sentimentalism and richly ornate language. At the time he believed that it was his great work and that it would go on being read for many years to come.

'General View: It is the Lygons' was the other side of the coin. Despite his protestations to Coote in Bari that it isn't really Boom or Hughie, or Mad, and despite the prefatory author's disclaimer, the Lygons suffuse the book. The portrayal of their ancestral home with its Arts and Crafts chapel, their painful domestic situation, their startling beauty (like faces carved out of Aztec stone), the father as a disgraced Liberal politician who is now a social pariah exiled in Italy, the young people left to run wild in the great house, the pious mother, the alcoholic second son drifting from failure to failure, the lovely daughter who becomes a society beauty in an unhappy marriage, the cold and pompous heir to Brideshead unable to produce an heir himself, the plain and tender-hearted youngest daughter. The Lygons inspired all of these elements and more.

In his war trilogy, Evelyn satirises *Brideshead Revisited* by having one of his characters, Corporal Ludovic, spend his war writing an impossibly baroque novel that is described as 'a very gorgeous, almost gaudy, tale of romance and high drama . . . The plot was Shakespearian in its elaborate improbability. The dialogue could not have issued from human lips, the scenes of passion were capable of bringing a blush to readers of either sex and any age . . . [it was a book] which could turn from the drab alleys of the thirties into the odorous gardens of a recent past transformed and illuminated by disordered memory and imagination.' But the extra joke here, as he pokes fun at his own novel's perceived weaknesses, is that the elaborately improbable Shakespearean plot of *Brideshead* was a watered-down version of the real Lygon story. How much more improbable the plot would have been if Evelyn had retained the homosexual element instead of inventing the more socially acceptable figure of Lord Marchmain's exotic mistress, Cara.

Nancy Mitford, who loved the book, wondered how all the glamorous Flytes could fall in love with such a 'dim' character as Charles Ryder. Evelyn half agreed: 'Yes, I can see how you think Charles is dim, but then he's telling the story.' He was telling his own story and he knew that the Lygons had indeed fallen in love with him, as he had with them.

Charles has two love affairs, first with Oxford/Sebastian, and later with Brideshead/Julia. For many of his readers the first is much the more convincing. Evelyn sensed this himself, anxiously asking Nancy: 'The crucial question is: does Julia's love for [Charles] seem real or is he so dim that it falls flat; if the latter the book fails plainly.'

The problem is Julia, who, as Waugh's first biographer Christopher Sykes says, is 'dead as mutton'. Sykes believed that this was because Julia did not have a real life model; she was no more than a waxwork. The reality is a little more complicated: she did have a partial model in Maimie, but Evelyn's difficulty was that his platonic and playful relationship with her did not have the dramatic and emotional potency to match his translation of Boom and Hugh into Lord Marchmain and Sebastian.

Oxford Revisited

> Beware of the Anglo-Catholics – they're all sodomites with unpleasant accents.
>
> (Cousin Jasper's advice on going up to Oxford)

The Oxford part is especially haunting and beautifully written, to such an extent that Evelyn worried (to Nancy) that he had kept lapsing into verse. As befits the title of Book One, 'Et in Arcadia Ego', these chapters are suffused with a glow of sunlight on grey-golden stone, flowering chestnuts, young men on bicycles, light falling over the spires, grassy meadows, dappled streams, men in cricket whites, green spaces, punting and strawberries. Small wonder that many readers love the Oxford part of the novel best. Maurice Bowra, the quintessential don, thought the Oxford part 'perfect', while Harold Acton, Roger Fulford and Christopher Sykes loved the first third of the novel and thought that there was a falling off once Sebastian has left the story. Acton said that the Oxford part of the novel was 'the most successful evocation of the period I know'.

It is a testimony to how much Evelyn was loved by his friends that so few took offence when he used them as copy for his novels. Harold Acton loyally defended the novel's brilliance in public, but privately was hurt by Evelyn's depiction of him in the sinister Anthony Blanche. Evelyn had hoped to get round the problem by combining the characters of Brian Howard and Harold Acton, a neat device since the two men who revolutionised Oxford in the twenties were so close as to be indistinguishable in the eyes of their friends – or at least their enemies. Evelyn told his friends that Blanche was one-third Acton and two-thirds Howard. He recognised that people mistakenly assumed the character was pure Harold ('who is a much sweeter and saner man').

Acton hid his hurt feelings when he wrote to congratulate Evelyn: 'I slid my paper knife through ... [the pages] like an itching bridegroom, and was panting, trembling and exhausted by the time I had finished cutting them ... swept alternatively by pleasure and pain: pleasure at your ever-increasing virtuosity and mastery of our fast-evaporating language ... pain, at the acrid memories of so many old friends you have conjured.' Anthony Blanche himself could not have put it better.

Despite Evelyn's assurances to Harold that the bulk (and, by implication, especially the malicious aspects) of Blanche was Howard, there are many Acton hallmarks, most famously the recitation of Eliot's *The Waste Land* through a megaphone from the balcony of his rooms in Christ Church (the chosen passage being 'I Tiresias ...', a specific allusion to bisexuality). The attempt to break into Blanche's rooms to duck him in the Mercury fountain is based on the same incident with Harold. Most of Evelyn's friends made the identification when they received their copies of the book. Christopher Sykes claimed that Evelyn used the very same phrases that Acton used, and portrayed him 'as the ruling aesthete'.

Anthony Blanche even has Harold's distinctive gait, 'moving as though he had not fully accustomed himself to coat and trousers and was more at ease in heavy, embroidered robes'. Evelyn removed this description from later editions of the novel, as it was too much like Harold. After Brian's death he strengthened the identification with him by adding some extra Howardesque descriptions, no doubt to make amends to Harold. The stammer and the turns of speech, the repetition of 'my dear', are Brian, as are Blanche's half Jewish, half American origins, his elegance and his malevolence: 'waxing in wickedness like a Hogarthian page boy ... he dined with Proust and Gide and was on closer terms with Cocteau and Diaghilev . . . he had aroused three irreconcilable feuds in Capri; he had practised black art in Cefalu; he had been cured of drug-taking in California and of an Oedipus complex in Vienna.'

It was the smaller roles that were the harshest. Privately, Evelyn admitted to Christopher Sykes that Rex Mottram was an unkind caricature of the Minister of Information, Brendan Bracken, the man who gave him leave to write *Brideshead.* Maurice Bowra was secretly annoyed at his portrayal as the toadying don, Mr Samgrass, but he put on a different face in public, saying to his friends: 'I hope you spotted me. What a piece of artistry that is – the best thing in the whole book.' The role of Samgrass may have been partly inspired by the Lygons' habit of bringing tutors of various kinds down to Mad in order to keep an eye on Hugh.

Brideshead is, along with *The Ordeal of Gilbert Pinfold*, the most autobiographical of Waugh's novels. The plot manifestly mirrors Evelyn's own experiences as a young man, especially in the Oxford chapters: a lonely middle-class boy goes to Oxford and languishes in the company of dull but clever friends until he is befriended by a group of glamorous Old Etonians who introduce him to an enchanting world of cosmopolitan culture, heavy drinking, beautiful clothes, friendship, stimulating conversation and a childhood that he has missed out on. In terms of his sentimental education, it is not examinations and prizes that he takes with him or academic learning that Oxford bequeaths. Rather, 'that other, more ancient lore which I acquired that term will be with me in one shape or another to my last hour'.

And yet the Oxford section, so heavily autobiographical, owes a huge literary debt to Book Three, 'Dreaming Spires', of Compton Mackenzie's Edwardian novel, *Sinister Street* (mentioned by Waugh in both *Brideshead* and his autobiography as one of the Oxford novels that most influenced him). There are many parallels between Charles Ryder and Mackenzie's equally autobiographical hero, Michael Fane, a middle-class boy from a day school who loves art and is taken up by glamorous Etonians. His possessions and artwork are 'jejune' (the very word used of Charles's); he loves the grey and gold of the city, the 'golden fume of the October weather'. Fane thinks that Oxford should be approached with a stainless curiosity: 'Already he felt that she would only yield her secret in return for absolute surrender. This the grave city demanded.' These parallels point towards one aspect of the peculiar power of *Brideshead*: it is at once autobiographical and archetypal, both the portrait of an age and a book that speaks to the aspirations of youth in other ages.

'Sebastian gives me many pangs'

> 'Just the place to bury a crock of gold,' said Sebastian. 'I should like to bury something precious in every place where I've been happy and then, when I was old and ugly and miserable, I could come back and dig it up and remember.'
>
> (*Brideshead Revisited*)

In the Hollywood memo, Evelyn described his hero Charles Ryder as an 'intelligent, artistic and lonely young man'. Lord Sebastian Flyte, meanwhile, 'is the attractive, wayward and helpless younger son . . . the idol of the fashionable aesthetic set that was prominent in English university life in the 1920s'.

Sebastian is the most intriguing and lovable character in *Brideshead Revisited*, and perhaps this is why so many critics have tried to find his model. Though Evelyn went to great pains to reassure Coote that the younger son was not really Hugh, they both knew that their friends would make the connection. Coote insisted rightly that Waugh's characters were composites, 'transmuted by his imagination and his considerable powers of invention'. She thought that the interesting thing about the way that people were always intrigued to know who his characters 'really are' was that it showed he had succeeded in creating 'entirely credible people in plausible situations'.

And yet Coote's response, 'Sebastian gives me many pangs', is quietly unequivocal. Christopher Sykes said that in conversation Evelyn told him that he drew upon aspects of Hugh for Sebastian. Maimie told Waugh's second biographer, Martin Stannard, that Hugh might have suggested Sebastian Flyte as 'a younger son . . . under the shadow of not having an inheritance'. Her younger sister confirmed the parallel of the second son. Coote said that Sebastian was based on 'all the younger sons rolled into one – Hughie, Charlie Cavendish, John Fox Strangeways – characters who all lost out a little because the older sons had everything'. Unsurprisingly, all those mentioned had drink problems.

Evelyn's friends – Peter Quennell, Terence Greenidge, Somerset Maugham and many more – saw Hugh Lygon as the model for Sebastian Flyte. But he also drew upon his love affairs with Alastair Graham and Richard Pares. On occasions the name Alastair appears in the manuscript for Sebastian. The key to Evelyn's art was the combination of two characters. His deep feelings for Alastair are woven into the book. However, a closer look reveals that Hugh is much the more important of the two principal models for the incomparable Sebastian. In 1955 Evelyn responded to a letter about *Brideshead* from a Mr Gadd: 'I am glad you find "Sebastian" an interesting character. I don't think he had any egotism. He was a contemplative without the necessary grace of fortitude.' These words could have been applied to Hugh Lygon, but not to Alastair Graham, who was no contemplative and did have a good deal of egotism. More obviously, the character's aristocratic glamour and sweet nature are wholly Hugh Lygon's.

At Oxford he is 'the most conspicuous man of his year by reason of his beauty'. His lovely complexion is admired by Anthony Blanche. Whilst the other Etonian teenage boys have spots, Sebastian's skin remains clear – or at least very nearly so (Blanche spitefully calls him 'Narcissus with one pustule'). Nanny also notices that he always looks as if his face is washed even when it isn't. For Charles, he has a face 'alive and alight with gaiety'. With his outer beauty goes an inner purity.

Among Waugh's many revisions of the text of *Brideshead* is a change from 'he was magically beautiful, with that epicene quality', to 'he was entrancing with that epicene beauty which in extreme youth sings aloud for love and withers at the first cold wind'. There was something about this type of beauty that brought out Evelyn's protective instincts. In his Hollywood memo he confirmed that part of Charles's 'romantic affection' for Sebastian was 'the protective feeling of a strong towards a weak character'.

It is Anthony Blanche who fleshes out Sebastian, as he had known him since Eton. The words are almost certainly a memory of what Evelyn had heard Brian Howard say of Hugh Lygon, whom he adored: 'I was at school with him . . . everyone in Pop liked him, of course, and all the masters. I expect it was that they were all really jealous of him. He never seemed to get into trouble . . . he was the only boy in my house never to be beaten at all.' Sebastian's charm and kindness give him immunity from the bullying that usually comes from the jealousy of other boys. Like Hugh, 'he isn't very well endowed in the Top Storey', but, as Blanche admits, 'those that have charm don't really need brains'. Sebastian is equally impeccable in his manners and his taste in clothes (Charvet ties, dove-grey flannel, white crepe de Chine). His beauty and eccentricities of manner endear him to all social classes. Even the grumpy barber and Charles's manservant, Lunt, are captivated by him.

It is Sebastian who leads Charles into Arcadia, through the 'low door . . . to a secret and enclosed garden'. He is a symbol not only of Oxford and undergraduate love, but also of childhood. Famously, Sebastian is first seen with a teddy bear and he first encounters Charles when vomiting through an open window on the ground floor of the quad. He then writes his apology in child-like crayon all over Charles's best drawing paper. He takes him to meet his nanny; he loves his pillar-box-red pyjamas – and of course that teddy bear. Aloysius is in the best Waugh tradition of composite character creation: he is based on a combination of John Betjeman's bear, Archie, and the teddy that Terence Greenidge observed Hugh Lygon carrying round Oxford (whose name, alas, is lost). Sebastian, like Hughie in real life, is spoilt and irresponsible, yet one cannot help loving him. In all this, he is just like a child. Lord Marchmain's mistress Cara tells us that he is in love with his childhood.

Sebastian is also given Hugh Lygon's darker side: his alcoholism, his weakness, his inability to grow up, his ill luck in love. Evelyn's memo to Hollywood makes it clear that the drinking is an attempted escape. Evelyn stresses the importance of conveying 'the gradual stages of differentiation between the habits of a group of high-spirited youngsters, all of whom on occasions get drunk in a light-hearted way, and the morbid, despairing, solitary drinking which eventually makes Sebastian an incurable alcoholic'.

'His days in Arcadia were numbered.' Sebastian's fragility is treated with great sympathy. Waugh's portrayal of his dypsomania is masterly: 'He was more than ever emaciated; drink, which made others fat and red, seemed to wither Sebastian.' He is shown stealing money from friends, skilfully escaping his minders, the trembling hands lighting a cigarette. Every detail is observed from life: 'the drunken thickening in his voice', the pallor 'fresh and sullen as a disappointed child'. He is unkempt and there is a 'look of wariness in his eyes'. He drinks in a 'nervous, surreptitious way, totally unlike his old habit'. Lady Marchmain, powerless to help her son, remarks: 'One of the most terrible things about them [drunkards] is their deceit. Love of truth is the first thing that goes.'

Evelyn used his experience not only of Hugh's alcoholism, but also of Hubert Duggan's, Alastair Graham's and Olivia Plunket Greene's. Julia, like the Lygon sisters in the understanding they showed to Hugh, apportions no blame for her brother's drink problem: 'It's something chemical in him.' Charles rejects this as cant: 'I got drunk often, but through an excess of high spirits, in the love of the moment, and the wish to prolong and enhance it; Sebastian drank to escape.'

Details from Madresfield are woven into the narrative, such as the grog tray in the library and the cocktails handed round by the footmen. There is a clear anticipation of Sebastian in Evelyn's depiction of Hugh wandering around the library at Madresfield, rotten drunk, holding a candle in his hand. The description of Sebastian drunk at dinner shows the effects that alcoholics have on those around them: 'A blow, expected, repeated, falling on a bruise, with no smart or shock of surprise, only a dull and sickening pain and the doubt whether another like it could be borne – that was how it felt, sitting opposite Sebastian at dinner that night, seeing his clouded eye and groping movements, hearing his thickened voice breaking in, ineptly, after long brutish silences.'

Coote Lygon may have been saddened by the portrayal of her brother, but she also saw that the novel was a tribute to Hugh, not a condemnation. As Cordelia makes clear, Sebastian in his fragility is close to God. Evelyn uses the word 'holy' to describe Sebastian in his decline. When he is ill he is described as the most patient of patients. It is left to Cordelia to describe his end, dying of alcoholism in a monastery near Carthage. The beauty has faded; he is thin, almost bald with a straggling beard; he never eats and is robbed 'right and left' by the people who are supposed to be looking after him. But, as Cordelia says, 'He's still loved, you see, wherever he goes, whatever condition he's in. It's a thing about him he'll never lose.' Like Hugh in his last years before dying at the age of thirty-one, 'he still has his own sweet manner'. Cordelia describes Sebastian as being like others she has known: 'I believe that they are very near and dear to God.' She has predicted his life 'half in, half out, of the community', pottering around the monastery, disappearing for drinking bouts, then coming back dishevelled and more devout than ever. She describes him acting as a guide for English-speaking tourists, being completely charming. 'Then one morning, after one of his drinking bouts, he'll be picked up at the gates dying, and showing by a mere flicker of the eyelid that he is conscious when they give him the last sacraments. It's not such a bad way of getting through one's life.'

Charles responds by thinking back to the youth with the teddy bear under the flowering chestnuts. 'It's not what one would have foretold,' he says. To which Cordelia replies: 'One can have no idea what the suffering may be, to be maimed as he is – no dignity, no power of will. No one is ever holy without suffering.' The association of holiness with suffering, applied to a character named Sebastian, suggests that there is another dimension besides alcohol to the story.

'The attraction of man to man'

> It is in many ways a great inconvenience (though there are manifest compensations) to have 'unnatural' sexual appetites.
>
> (Evelyn Waugh, review of Compton Mackenzie's *Thin Ice*)

> 'My dear, I should like to stick you full of barbed arrows like a p-p-pin-cushion.'
>
> (Anthony Blanche to Sebastian Flyte in *Brideshead Revisited*)

Sebastian Flyte is named after Saint Sebastian. His name is symbolic. His family name Flyte represents him in flight from his religion and his family, but it is also suggestive of the image of the martyrdom of Saint Sebastian, in which he is depicted with a flight of arrows assailing his body.

In the Italian Renaissance, Saint Sebastian was possibly the most frequently painted figure after Mary and Jesus. He was valued by artists who saw in him a figure of Hellenic beauty, and a rare opportunity to paint a male nude at a time when female nudes predominated. His highly eroticised figure was painted by nearly all the major artists of the period, including Bellini, Tintoretto, Mantegna, Titian, Guido Reni (seven times), Giorgione, Perugino, Botticelli, Veronese (a series of magnificent wall frescoes in the church of San Sebastiano), Bazzi (known as Il Sodoma), and many others. His story lent itself to great art, combining beauty, suffering and ecstasy. He is the embodiment of what is sometimes cruelly called 'Catholic porn'.

Saint Sebastian was born to a wealthy family in the third century and was executed for refusing to renounce Christianity. He was tied to a tree and fired at with arrows, but miraculously survived and was later clubbed to death and thrown into a sewer.

A beautiful young man, virtually naked, bound to a tree and pierced with arrows, with a face either passive or displaying religious ecstasy: Saint Sebastian is now known as the patron saint of homosexuality (as well as of athletes). It was in the nineteenth century that the homosexual cult of him took hold. Several of the classic twentieth-century texts of gay literature partake of the cult: there is an explicit allusion in Thomas Mann's *Death in Venice*, Tennessee Williams wrote a poem called 'San Sebastiano de Sodoma', and the adolescent protagonist of Yukio Mishima's *Confessions of a Mask* (1948) first masturbates over a photograph of a painting of Saint Sebastian. Oscar Wilde used the alias 'Sebastian' in Paris. When he visited Keats's grave in Rome, he compared the dead poet to the martyred saint: 'As I stood beside the mean grave of this divine boy, I thought of him as a Priest of Beauty slain before his time; and the vision of Guido's Saint Sebastian came before my eyes as I saw him at Genoa, a lovely brown boy, with crisp, clustering hair and red lips, bound by his evil enemies to a tree and, though pierced by arrows, raising his eyes with divine, impassioned gaze towards the Eternal Beauty of the opening Heavens.'

Anthony Blanche's parting shot at the end of Sebastian's luncheon party – 'My dear, I should like to stick you full of barbed arrows like a p-p-pin-cushion' – could hardly make clearer the connection between Lord Sebastian and the martyr. When Evelyn was in Venice with Maimie in 1932 he wandered the churches of Venice to escape the heat and became acquainted with numerous paintings of the saint and the Church of Saint Sebastian with its superb wall frescoes by Veronese. And then there was his memory of that other Church of Saint Sebastian Outside the Walls, in Rome, with Giorgetti's highly eroticised horizontal statue and the arrows of Saint Sebastian, where he waited in vain for Alastair Graham in 1927.

Charles and Sebastian's 'romantic affection' is partly sexual. Their 'naughtiness is high in the catalogue of grave sins'. Charles has no regrets about his Oxford sexual experimentation: 'all the wickedness of that time was like the spirit they mix with the pure grape of the Douro, heady stuff full of dark ingredients; it at once enriched and retarded the whole process of adolescence as the spirit checks the fermentation of the wine, renders it undrinkable, so that it must lie in the dark, year in, year out, until it is brought up at last fit for the table'.

Charles's attitude is very close to Waugh's own. And Evelyn's, in turn, is very close to that of Terence Greenidge, the Oxford friend who introduced him to the homoerotic environment of the Hypocrites. In 1930, Evelyn gave a largely favourable review in the *Fortnightly* to Greenidge's *Degenerate Oxford?* – the question mark was an integral part of the title, since the aim of Terence's book was to refute suggestions that had been aired in the press that Oxford was a haven for upper-class indolence and sodomitical indulgence. The core of the book was a defence of the Oxford 'Aesthetes' and their 'romances'.

'Oxford romances often are not pursued to lengths which would engender conflicts with our criminal code,' Greenidge asserted. He admitted that 'Queer deeds may occasionally get done among those who come from over-emancipated Public Schools', but claimed that 'the majority of us favour that vague romanticism which may be likened to a warm, misty July morning'. He then went on to argue that Oxford Aesthetes were 'young men who are in a state of transition . . . We become normal when we go down.' His own case, he suggested, was typical: he was now happily married with a wife and child – though, in reality, Greenidge would spend the next few years writing novels called *Brass and Paint* and *The Magnificent*, which were regarded by the police as homosexual pornography. All copies were called in and very nearly all were destroyed.

Greenidge's favoured term for 'the attraction of man for man' was 'Romanticism' rather than 'Homosexuality'. He argued that it came to the essence of the sensibility of the Aesthetes, suffusing every aspect of their Oxford lives. He was thinking of something deeper than the way that male-male relationships were inevitable in an environment where females were kept sequestered in separate colleges, though that was part of the story. Citing the character of Michael Fane in Compton Mackenzie's *Sinister Street*, he linked 'Romanticism' to the peculiar beauty and antiquity of Oxford as a city:

> The whole town possesses a charm so emphatically not of our twentieth-century civilisation that one tends to think – maybe more than one should – about romance, and to believe firmly that the romance must be of an exotic kind. Conventional frivolling with conventional girls just would not do. Oxford is so different from Lyons' Corner House. I have heard hard-bitten and respected men of the world confess that when they revisited their 'alma mater' they found their minds becoming full of thoughts and aspirations to which they hoped they were now for ever strangers. A queer lotus dust seems to blow around an unreal city.

This is a brilliant diagnosis of what might be called 'the Brideshead Complex', written fifteen years before *Brideshead* by the man who ushered Evelyn Waugh to the door of the world that would become Brideshead. In anticipation of Evelyn, Terence Greenidge had unlocked the Oxford secret that Q in 'Alma Mater' said 'none can utter'.

Greenidge went on to weigh up the advantages and disadvantages of Oxford 'Romanticism'. He suggested that the primary advantage was that it made its practitioners 'specially sympathetic and nicely sensitive', with the result that they would go on to treat women as friends rather than sexual objects:

> A girl once said to me, shortly after I had left Oxford, 'There's a thing I like about you. Although you are not actually feminine in nature, there are womanly bits to your mind, and they make you rather specially sympathetic and nicely sensitive.' I mention this remark not because it might seem complimentary to myself, but because it struck me at the time as being an interesting criticism, and an epitome of one of the defences which the Oxford Romanticist puts up for himself.

This is wholly applicable to Evelyn: it was his Oxford Romanticism – his 'homosexual phase', as would now be said – that made possible his incomparable gift for friendship with women.

The greatest disadvantage of the condition, Terence Greenidge went on to contend, was that 'in several cases – though not in all, as some of my earlier stories will show – Romanticism seems to be attended by a feeling of guilty secrecy', which is unhealthy and dangerous. 'I do remember an occasion,' he recalled, 'when all of a sudden some of us came across quite trustworthy evidence of the romantic friendships of a prominent undergraduate politician, who had shown such diplomacy in this particular department of his life that previously not a whisper of scandal had been wafted to ears which would have been most anxious to receive it.'

Guilty secrecy was the special preserve of the homosexual politician whose career would be ruined by scandal. And no one in the Oxford of Greenidge and Waugh knew this better than the sons of Lord Beauchamp. Hugh Lygon would never have made a politician like his father and brother, but his status and connections were such that in public, and even within his family, he had no choice but to harbour his homosexuality as if it were a guilty secret.

Evelyn's one reservation in his review of *Degenerate Oxford?* concerned Greenidge's coy substitution of the word 'Romanticism' for 'homosexuality': 'I could do with more plain speaking about homo-sexuality. By his implied assumption that homo-sexual relations among undergraduates are merely romantic and sentimental he seems to avoid the most important questions at issue.' Writing his review in 1930, Evelyn hinted that 'queer deeds' were a great deal more common among the Aesthetes than Greenidge implied. By the time he came to write *Brideshead* in 1944, he was more guarded. The hints about naughtiness 'high in the catalogue of grave sins' are there, but the primary emphasis is upon 'romantic affection'.

Whereas Charles Ryder grows out of his 'Romanticism', Sebastian is as reluctant to renounce his homosexuality as he is to relinquish his teddy bear, his pillar-box-red pyjamas and his nanny. As with Alastair Graham and Hugh Lygon in real life, Sebastian is unable to settle down. He becomes part of a nomadic, expatriate community in which he is left free to have male lovers. Sebastian, we are told by Blanche, finds a sailor in Athens who speaks American, 'lay up with him until his ship sailed, and popped back to Constantinople. And that was that.'

His German lover, Kurt, has syphilis, and when the monk views the relationship as an innocent friendship, Charles's reply is cynical: 'Poor simple monk . . . poor booby.' Charles, out of loyalty to Sebastian, tells his brother Bridey that there is 'nothing vicious' in his relationship with

Kurt, but in private he thinks differently. Rex Mottram, when recommending a therapist who can help Sebastian with his alcoholism, adds 'he takes sex cases too'.

Sebastian's homosexuality, like Hugh Lygon's, causes him to feel self-hatred and guilt: 'I wouldn't love anyone with a character like mine . . . I'm ashamed of myself . . . I absolutely detest myself.' Charles sees the damage that has been done by Sebastian's overbearing religious mother: 'Without your religion Sebastian would have the chance to be a happy and healthy man.' For Hugh, the combination of a secretly homosexual father and an almost maniacally religious mother was toxic. For him in life, as for Sebastian in the novel, alcoholism was the consequence of his sense of guilt and his desire to escape himself. Lady Marchmain contends that Sebastian's flight mirrors his father's: 'Both of them unhappy, ashamed, and running away.'

For his portrayal of Lord Marchmain, Evelyn drew heavily upon Lord Beauchamp, with one significant difference. In deference to the Lygon family, he removed almost all traces of Boom's homosexuality. Instead, Lord Marchmain is given a mistress, Cara, with whom he escapes the stranglehold of the pious Lady Marchmain. Coote insisted that the matrimonial problems of Lord and Lady Marchmain could 'in no way be equated with those which beset my parents'. Nevertheless, there is a strong hint in Anthony Blanche's comment about the breakdown of the marriage, which resonates vividly with that of the Beauchamps:

> She has convinced the world that Lord Marchmain is a monster . . . You would think that the old reprobate had tortured her, stolen her patrimony, flung her out of doors, roasted, stuffed and eaten his children, and gone frolicking about wreathed in all the flowers of Sodom and Gomorrah.*

Given how openly Lady Sibell and her sisters talked about Lady Beauchamp's overzealous piety, and its alienating effects on the family, it is significant that Lord Marchmain's reason for sexual infidelity is his wife's oppressive religiosity. The Lygons certainly never blamed their

* This was altered by Waugh in proof. In the original manuscript Blanche speaks of Marchmain 'indulging in what my step-father calls "English habits"' – a clear allusion to the purported English predilection for homosexuality.

father or were ashamed of his homosexuality. Their view was that their mother was impossible to live with and they always blamed the family catastrophe on Bendor's jealousy and homophobia rather than ever pointing a finger at their father.

Evelyn shared the Lygons' liberal views towards homosexuality. Of Oscar Wilde, he wrote: 'He got himself in trouble, poor old thing, by the infringement of a very silly law, which was just as culpable and just as boring as an infringement of traffic or licensing regulations.' In their later years, Maimie and Evelyn exchanged views on homosexual literature. In 1955, when Maimie was mentally ill and recovering in a rest home, Evelyn told her he was reading Christopher Isherwood's *The World in the Evening*. Isherwood's novel was a frank story about a bisexual man whose marriage implodes: 'Your dear father would not have approved,' he wrote, somewhat mischievously.

A year later, Evelyn wrote a favourable review of Compton Mackenzie's novel *Thin Ice*, applauding it for taking as its theme a subject that he says had been unduly neglected in English literature, 'that of the homosexual male'. Evelyn bemoaned the fact that most homosexual writers falsified and transposed their material by heterosexualising their material (hardly surprising in view of the law of the land prior to the Wolfenden Report of 1957). Evelyn went on to argue that 'normality' – a word which he insisted on placing between inverted commas – is 'certainly an almost meaningless expression': 'The absolute norm is an abstract from which all men vary in greater or less degree . . . the vagaries of human lust are fully catalogued . . . we have become less xenophobic in condemning sexual eccentricity . . . it is [Compton Mackenzie's] intention to utter a temperate and sage call to order.'

He greatly admired the novel, which takes as its theme a brilliant, young and well-born politician named Henry Fortescue who is adored by women and is described as a 'future Prime Minister'. He is also homosexual. Afraid to ruin his career, Fortescue exercises self-control in regard of his sexual appetites, but his political career fails for other reasons. Beset by his political failures, he throws caution to the wind and becomes 'first indulgent and then reckless' in his 'lawless pleasures'. He embraces a seedy underworld of male prostitution: 'It is this aspect of lawlessness, with the concomitant of blackmail, which characterises the life of the homosexual.' Evelyn was aware that the cook at Madresfield had tried to blackmail Lord Beauchamp and saw at first hand his rootless life.

Evelyn admired a scene in *Thin Ice* in which the politician is arrested in a gay bar, but then released by a merciful policeman, especially as it was based on a real incident that was common gossip during the latter stages of the war. 'It is delightful to see this highly diverting anecdote, which was unlikely to find its way into the protagonist's reminiscences, so admirably preserved for posterity.' The anecdote in question involved Evelyn's old school friend, the politician and journalist Tom Driberg. He was arrested for fellating a Norwegian sailor in an air-raid shelter, but released on the way to the station when the policeman discovered that Driberg was the author of the 'William Hickey' column in the *Daily Express*, of which he happened to be a great admirer. But in reading *Thin Ice*, Evelyn could not have avoided thinking about how Lord Beauchamp's increasing sexual recklessness ruined his political career. The appealing thing about Mackenzie's novel was its reversal of the pattern: 'a man whose moral character is ruined by political failure'.

Evelyn may have joked about 'buggers' and 'pansies' in his letters, but he was irritated by an American play about homosexuals which showed them in a poor light: 'they all commit suicide' he complained to Nancy Mitford; 'The idea of a happy pansy is incomprehensible to them.' In his own way, Sebastian is entirely happy with the sponger Kurt: 'It's funny, I couldn't get on without him, you know,' he tells Charles in Morocco, 'it's rather a pleasant change when all your life you've had people looking after you, to have someone to look after yourself.'

In *Brideshead* Waugh paid tribute to his formative homosexual affairs, and acknowledged the happiness they had brought. Despite the 'grave sins' committed at Oxford, 'there was something of nursery freshness about us that fell little short of the joy of innocence'. In the face of cousin Jasper's 'grand remonstrance' (based on a similar confrontation with his brother Alec), Charles has no regrets: 'Looking back, now after twenty years, there is little I would have left undone or done otherwise. I could match my cousin Jasper's game-cock maturity with a sturdier fowl . . . I could tell him too, that to know and love one other human being is the root of all wisdom.' That lesson of the novel was what led Henry Yorke, who did not indulge in 'Romanticism' whilst at Oxford, to thank Evelyn for his personal copy of *Brideshead* with the wistful words 'I wish

I had been in love at Oxford when I was up. I see now what I have missed.'

'So true to life being in love with an entire family'

> There was that slight, inherited stain upon her brightness . . . that unfitted her for the highest honours.
>
> (*Brideshead Revisited*, regarding Julia Flyte)

Nancy Mitford's reaction in her letter to Evelyn in Yugoslavia came to the heart of the novel. The story is that of the Golders Green boy who wrote it, lonely within his own family, so susceptible to falling in love with entire families: first the Fleming family, then the brotherhood of the Hypocrites, then the Plunket Greenes, and at last the enchantingly glamorous Lygons.

The Lygon sisters could not have failed to pick up on numerous specific details. The particular quality of the family's beauty, with its underlying sadness, resonates throughout. Blanche describes Bridey as having a face that looked 'as though an Aztec sculptor had attempted a portrait of Sebastian'. This is a brilliant description of Elmley, who nearly always looked so much more solemn than Hugh. Charles agrees with Blanche, but also sees that Bridey's 'smile, when it rarely came, was as lovely as theirs' – though Evelyn had turned against Elmley, he still remembered their good times among the Hypocrites.

Lady Julia, like Maimie, has 'A face of flawless Florentine quattrocento beauty', but with an air of 'Renaissance tragedy'. Cordelia has 'the unmistakable family characteristics, but had them ill-arranged in a frank and chubby plainness'. As compensation, 'all the family charm is in her smile'. This is the plump but smiling Coote, to a tee.

Elmley's response to the novel, if he read it, is not recorded. His wife, Mona the Dane, is cruelly portrayed as the suburban Beryl Muspratt. The transformation of Elmley himself into Lord Brideshead ('Bridey') is not exactly flattering either. To those in the know, the identification becomes clear from the moment that Bridey is described as a Magdalen man. In Blanche's eyes, he is 'a learned bigot, a ceremonious barbarian, a snow-bound lama'. When Bridey marries a naval widow with children who is some years older than him, Julia remarks caustically: 'I'll tell you one thing, she's lied to Bridey about her age. She's a good forty-five. I don't see her providing an heir.' Beryl's background is clearly a parody of Mona's inflated claims of her own naval connections: 'I imagine she's been used to bossing things rather in naval circles, with flag-lieutenants trotting round and young officers on-the-make sucking up to her.'

Elmley, whom Evelyn increasingly despised, is depicted in the novel as a repressed, aimless waste of time, though with the redeeming feature that his voice has 'a gravity and restraint' that in anyone else would have sounded pompous, but in him sounds 'unassumed and unselfconscious'. 'Bridey was a mystery,' muses Charles Ryder, 'a creature from the underground; a hard-snouted, burrowing, hibernating animal who shunned the light. He had been completely without action in all his years of adult life . . . at Brideshead he performed all unavoidable local duties, bringing with him to platform and fete and committee room his own thin mist of clumsiness and aloofness.' He lacks all the charm and charisma of his younger brother, Sebastian, and is deficient in social graces: 'emanating little magnetic pools of social uneasiness, creating, rather, a pool of general embarrassment about himself in which he floated with log-like calm'.

Bridey and his wife visit Lord Marchmain when they go abroad on their honeymoon, paralleling Elmley and Mona's visit to Boom in Paris. Lord Marchmain dislikes Beryl: 'She had no doubt heard of me as a man of irregular life. I can only describe her manner to me as roguish. A naughty old man, that's what she thought I was. I suppose she had met naughty old admirals and knew how they should be humoured.' Other than the reference to Sodom and Gomorrah, this is as close as we get to any hint of Boom's homosexual proclivities in the portrayal of Lord Marchmain.

The Flyte girls feel ousted from Brideshead, as did the Lygons, who left Madresfield after their brother's marriage. The good-natured Coote was revealingly and uncharacteristically acerbic when in her letter to Evelyn of 1956 she compared Elmley and Mona to Jane Austen's Mr and Mrs John Dashwood, adding: 'I often think of sending them an annotated copy.' One can readily imagine the annotations to the sequence in which the John Dashwoods viciously disinherit the three lovely sisters and force them out of their beloved family home.

Coote was discreetly silent on the subject of her reaction to the youngest Flyte daughter, Cordelia. The character's name is that of the youngest and most beloved daughter of Shakespeare's King Lear, the one on whom he pins his hopes of being looked after in exile. Coote's loyal correspondence with Boom was truly Cordelia-like. She was at Madresfield that first time Maimie brought Evelyn to the house in October 1931. Years later, she remembered 'running out over the bridge in the starlight when she [Maimie] arrived and seeing this unknown and unexpected figure emerging from the car – it was Evelyn'. Charles Ryder's first sight of Cordelia is his memory of this moment: she is a lively and engaging child, but without 'the promise of Julia's full *quattrocento* loveliness'. Later, Charles is shocked by how life's circumstances have changed her: Cordelia, like Coote, goes abroad for the war, Coote to Italy, she to Spain.

> It was odd, I thought, how the same ingredients, differently dispensed, could produce Brideshead, Sebastian, Julia and her. She was unmistakably their sister, without any of Julia's or Sebastian's grace, without Brideshead's gravity. She seemed brisk and matter-of-fact . . . hard living had roughened her . . . she straddled a little as she sat by the fire and when she said 'It's wonderful to be home,' it sounded to my ears like the grunt of an animal returning to its basket.

This is a harsh description, but Charles comes to see her inner beauty. Cordelia bluntly asks him whether he is disappointed in how she has turned out: 'Did you think, "Poor Cordelia, such an engaging child, grown up a plain and pious spinster, full of good works"? Did you think "thwarted"?' Charles replied that he did, but now does not, so much: 'she too had a beauty of her own'.

Lady Julia owes something to Olivia Plunket Greene, who was in love with religion, but she also owes much to Baby Jungman and Maimie Lygon: her beauty, her glamour, her spidery body, her way of talking, her flapper slang. Above all, Julia has a 'magical sadness' that draws Charles to her. Like Maimie, she graces the fashionable columns of the newspapers, is supremely elegant, well-dressed, wearing cloche hats and carrying her Pekingese, driving her motor car. She has none of the pomposity of Bridey, and all the ease and unaffectedness of Sebastian. In his various revisions of the novel, Waugh changed Julia's hair colour from dark to Maimie's gold, and then back to dark. Children and dogs adore her, as they adored Maimie. And she does not make the marriage that is expected of her.

The most remarkable detail suggesting that Evelyn was thinking of Maimie when he created the character of Julia Flyte is based on a piece of very private knowledge. Julia is described as outshining all the girls of her age. She is an obvious candidate for an answer to the question that preoccupies all the ladies in high society: 'Whom would the young princes marry? . . . They could not hope for purer lineage or a more gracious presence than Julia's; but there was this faint shadow on her that unfitted her for the highest honours.' That shadow is 'the scandal of her father'. The sequence is clearly based on Evelyn's knowledge of the reason why the affair between Maimie and Prince George did not lead to marriage.*

Waugh's Hollywood memo said that when Charles first meets Julia 'she has the world at her feet'. Maimie had the world at her feet, but, as with Julia, her father's disgrace ensures that she is ostracised by society. Julia says: 'I've grown up with one family skeleton, you know – papa. Not to be talked of in front of the servants, not to be talked of in front of us when we were children.'

Waugh's memo emphasised that Charles Ryder's love for Sebastian is in part a foreshadowing of his love for Julia. When Julia asks Charles why he married the awful Celia, he says:

> 'Loneliness, missing Sebastian.'
> 'You loved him, didn't you?'
> 'Oh yes. He was the forerunner.'
> Julia understood.

Later he repeats that Sebastian was the forerunner: 'I had not forgotten Sebastian. He was with me daily in Julia; or rather it was the Julia I had known in him, in those distant Arcadian days.' The idea of the forerunner, of a love for the brother and the sister that is somehow the same, is a brilliant device on Waugh's part: it allows him to express the idea that

* Maimie herself was spared from reading this passage in precisely this form: in the version she was sent in 1944, 'the scandal of her father' is mentioned as a reason for her not making a royal match, but it is secondary to the 'much blacker taint' of Julia's Catholicism.

what he is really in love with is the family, not any one member of it, and at the same time it makes *Brideshead* into one of the great expressions of what might be called the bisexual imagination.

Nevertheless, few readers have felt as compelled by the character of Julia as by that of Sebastian, or indeed feel convinced by the passion between Charles and Julia. Whilst it is unfair to describe her as 'dead as mutton', as Christopher Sykes did, there is a strong sense that the passion between Charles and Sebastian is better executed. For example, Charles's lingering gaze on Sebastian is intensely erotic: 'We lit fat, Turkish cigarettes and lay on our backs, Sebastian's eyes on the leaves above him, mine on his profile . . . the fumes of the sweet, golden wine seemed to lift us a finger's breadth above the turf and hold us suspended.' Charles is mesmerised by his mouth, 'watching the smoke from his lips drift up into the branches'. But there is much less eroticism when the image is repeated later in the story: when Charles lights Julia a cigarette, he takes it from his mouth to hers, revealing a 'thin bat's squeak of sexuality, inaudible to any but me'.

Late in life, Maimie laughingly dismissed any identification of herself with Julia, on the grounds that she and Evelyn were friends, not lovers: 'Evelyn was the last person I'd have fallen in love with: ours was just a great friendship. I would confide all my love affairs to him and he would confide all his to me.' The irony is that the relationship between Charles and Julia would have been more successfully portrayed if it had been closer to that in real life between Evelyn and Maimie: a deep friendship, not a love affair. But Waugh's hand was forced. The structure of the novel required him to introduce a love affair between Charles and Julia for two reasons. First, it was the way of creating the potential for Charles actually to become a member of the family – he nearly inherits Brideshead. And secondly, for Julia to have been the friend and Sebastian the lover would have been too overtly homosexual. As Lord Beauchamp's extra-marital involvements are made heterosexual in Lord Marchmain, so the sexual attraction has to be transferred from Sebastian to Julia. But it is no more than a bat's squeak.

Lord Marchmain's Palace of Sin

> 'He daren't show his great purple face anywhere. He is the last, historic, authentic case of someone being hounded out of society.'
>
> (Anthony Blanche on Lord Marchmain, in the original manuscript of *Brideshead*)

To those in the know, such as Chips Channon, Lord Marchmain in his crumbling palazzo on the Grand Canal in Venice was unmistakably Beauchamp.

Charles is interested in the effect of Lord Marchmain's disgrace on the rest of the family:

> 'It must have upset you all when your father went away.'
>
> 'All but Cordelia. She was too young.* It upset *me* at the time. Mummy tried to explain it to the three eldest so that we wouldn't hate papa . . . I was his favourite. I should be staying with him now, if it wasn't for this foot. I'm the only one who goes. Why don't you come too? You'd like him.'

This passage is one of the novel's few concessions to Lady Marchmain. It raises the possibility that one of the Lygon children may have told Evelyn about that moving letter their mother wrote to them. What he certainly did know was that Hugh was the child who spent most time with his father in the years of exile. In *Brideshead*, Sebastian is the family member most loyal to his father, the one who goes out to Venice with papers for signature.

As with Hugh, Sebastian's devotion and loyalty to his errant father is unquestionable. He tells Charles that 'papa is a social leper', that he lives in a 'palace of sin', and that the family has been tainted by sexual scandal, but this only adds to his glamour and mystery. Waugh admired Hugh Lygon's beauty, his loyalty, his courage and his gift for friendship. He also admired his way of dealing with his father's disgrace. It was Hugh who talked his father out of committing suicide. It was Hugh who travelled the globe to be with his father. Evelyn also saw how his vulnerable friend

* Like Dickie Lygon.

drank to escape his mother, his fear of failure, and, given what had happened to his father, his own homosexuality. At Oxford, at Madresfield and in the isolation of the Arctic, he had witnessed at first hand Hugh's great attraction and great despair.

The depiction in *Brideshead* of Lord Marchmain, whom Charles first meets in his 'palace of sin' in Venice, is drawn from Waugh's own first meeting with Lord Beauchamp in Rome: 'I was full of curiosity to meet Lord Marchmain. When I did so I was first struck by his normality, which, as I saw more of him, I found to be studied. It was as though he were conscious of a Byronic aura, which he considered to be in bad taste and was at pains to suppress.' The notion of his studied 'normality' takes on additional resonance when one recalls the context in which Waugh used the word, with probing quotation marks, in his review of Compton Mackenzie's *Thin Ice*.

Lord Marchmain is described as having 'a noble face . . . slightly weary, slightly sardonic, slightly voluptuous. He seemed to be in the prime of life; it was odd to think that he was only a few years younger than my father.' Anthony Blanche is more cutting in his description, but again it is an accurate and, to those who knew him, slightly uncomfortable description of Boom: 'a little fleshy, perhaps, but *very* handsome, a magnifico, a voluptuary, Byronic, bored, infectiously slothful, not at all the sort of man you would expect to see easily put down'.

Both Marchmain and Beauchamp are men of high culture with a keen interest in porphyry. Marchmain is described as 'following the sun', just as Beauchamp followed the sun by wintering in Australia and then returning to Italy and France for the summer months. Lord Marchmain advises Charles to 'stick to the churches' in order to avoid the searing Venetian heat, as Evelyn had loved the cool of the churches in Venice and visited churches in Rome with Lord Beauchamp.

The 'murky background' of the Flytes resonates with that of the Lygons. In *Brideshead* Lord Marchmain's status as social pariah is masterfully executed. He stays away from dining at the Luna restaurant, as it is 'filling up with English now'. Charles and Sebastian are taken to Florian's for coffee, where Lord Marchmain is snubbed by a party of English people, who are making for a table close to them and move away when they see who it is, suddenly talking with their heads close together. They are a Catholic man and woman that Lord Marchmain used to know when he was in politics. Just before this, Lord Marchmain is talking about how undignified the English are 'when they attempt to express moral disapproval'. He plays tennis with the professional coach, not with friends (Beauchamp was a keen tennis player). Lord Marchmain is also a Liberal, on the left of his party: 'I am all the Socialists would have me be, and a great stumbling block to my own party. Well, my elder son will change all that.' The latter allusion is to Bridey's defection to the Tories: when the Liberal Party split over participation in Ramsay MacDonald's National Government, Elmley joined the breakaway National Liberal grouping which later merged with the Conservative Party. Like Lord Beauchamp, Lord Marchmain despises his pious estranged wife, blaming her for his ostracism. And the references to footmen are striking. The syphilitic Kurt is described as a 'footman' from a popular film. Given all these connections, Chips Channon's knowing diary entry is hardly surprising.

Chapel and Fountain

> What a place to live in!
>
> (Charles Ryder, on first seeing Brideshead Castle)

Lady Dorothy Lygon said that there was no resemblance between the landscape and architecture of the fictional Brideshead Castle and the real Madresfield Court, with the exception of the chapel. This is not so. Although Evelyn's most direct portrayal of the physical characteristics of the house was in *A Handful of Dust*, many elements of Brideshead are shaped by Madresfield.

The surrounding landscape, the tiny village with post office and pub, the river, the sense of 'a sequestered place, enclosed and embraced, in a single winding valley', the house nestling out of sight, 'couched among the lime trees like a hind in the bracken': each loving detail offers an exact description of Madresfield. The 'blue remembered hills', as A. E. Housman called the Malverns, provide protection for Madresfield, just as with Brideshead, 'round it, guarding and hiding it, stood the soft hills'. The estate's woods of beech and oak, its avenues of lime and poplars, its wide green parklands, are all borrowed from Madresfield. On the other hand, Brideshead is not a moated house like Hetton Abbey. Nor is it red brick, nor

Victorian Gothic. There is always an element of distortion and a fusion of different models in Waugh's fictional recreation of people and places.

Coote observed that Brideshead is 'an epitome of stone of the Palladian style [Evelyn] loved so much'. It is grey-gold, with a distinctive dome. This is the main feature derived from Castle Howard, with its famous central dome by Sir John Vanbrugh, a highly unusual feature for a private dwelling. From the dome stretch out the fountain, the lakes, the temple and the obelisk, all reminiscent of Castle Howard and giving some justification to the use of that location in both the television and movie adaptations of the novel.

Evelyn's Hollywood memo cites the vital importance of two architectural features: the chapel and the fountain. 'I suggest that before I leave Hollywood,' he wrote, 'I should be allowed to see preliminary sketches of these two features drawn under my supervision.' The fountain represents the worldly magnificence and grace of the family which captivates Charles and the chapel symbolises his redemption.

The fountain was not in fact based upon Castle Howard's Atlas Fountain, as is often supposed. It was, in Evelyn's own words, 'brought from Italy and I see it as a combination of three famous works of Bernini at Rome . . . the Trevi and Piazza fountains and the elephant bearing the obelisk in the Piazza Minerva, which the Romans fondly call "the little pig"'. The Brideshead fountain is 'an oval basin with an island of formal rocks at its centre; on the rocks grew, in stone, formal tropical vegetation and wild English fern in its natural fronds; through them ran a dozen streams that counterfeited springs, and round them sported fantastic tropical animals, camels and camelopards and an ebullient lion all vomiting water; on the rocks, to the height of the pediment, stood an Egyptian obelisk of red sandstone'. Waugh has in a sense brought back to Mad the fountains that he visited in Rome with Boom.

The circumstances of the commissioning of the Arts and Crafts chapel, Boom's wedding present from his wife, are reversed in the novel: it is Lord Marchmain's present to his religious wife. The Brideshead chapel, as Coote admitted, was based precisely on the Madresfield chapel, with its Arts and Crafts decoration and the huge life-size frescoes of the earl and his wife and their children frolicking as angels. Even the firebuckets are in the Beauchamp colours of maroon and cream.

Evelyn, in common with his hero, professed admiration for homes that passed down the generations in the same family. Mad had done this since the eleventh century. In *Brideshead* Charles says: 'More even than the work of great architects, I loved buildings that grew silently with the centuries, catching and keeping the best of each generation.'

But with the modern age – the Great War, the introduction of death duties, then another war – the buildings were decaying. The Flytes' London home is Marchmain House, which they call 'Marchers', just as Halkyn House is called 'Halkers' by the Lygon family. 'It's sad about Marchers, isn't it,' says Cordelia near the end of the novel; 'Do you know they're going to build a block of flats and that Rex wanted to take what he called a "penthouse" at the top?' In reality, Mona had tried to convert Halkers into flats, though she had been turned down by – the old nemesis – the Westminster estate, who owned the freehold. It was sold instead to the Syrian Arab Embassy. It's now the home of the Ghana High Commission.

Lord Marchmain leaves his crumbling palazzo on the Grand Canal to die at his home in England. Knowing that, in the normal course of things, Brideshead would be inherited by Lord Brideshead and Beryl, he plans to leave the great house instead to Julia and Charles. According to Lygon family tradition, Lord Beauchamp did not want his eldest son to inherit Madresfield. He wanted to leave it to Hugh.

Conversion

> It was, of course, all about the deathbed. I was present at almost exactly that scene.
>
> (Evelyn Waugh to Ronald Knox)

Many of Evelyn's friends and critics were appalled by the deathbed conversion of Lord Marchmain. But for Evelyn himself, this scene was the whole point of the book. To those who complained that it was unrealistic, Evelyn replied that it was a piece of reportage. He had been present at the very scene – a moment of profound spiritual significance for him. This is one of the masterstrokes of his art of composite creation: he imagines Boom on his deathbed undergoing a conversion experience like that of Maimie's old boyfriend, Hubert Duggan.

Charles Ryder's spiritual epiphany occurs in this scene. The operation of divine grace upon him comes at Lord Marchmain's death, when he prays for a sign and the dying man makes the sign of the cross. The epilogue sees him kneeling at the altar of the Brideshead chapel, praying 'an ancient, newly-learned form of words'.

For most of the novel, Charles appears to be a non-believer, though there are clues that this is a novel narrated by a convert. The Flytes' faith is an enigma to Charles, 'and not one which I felt particularly concerned to solve'. But Charles is also shown fighting God, mocking Catholicism as 'mumbo jumbo' and 'an awful lot of nonsense'. Sebastian replies: 'Is it nonsense? I wish it were. It sometimes sounds terribly sensible to me.'

Early in the novel there is a strong clue in the lines: 'I have come to accept claims which then, in 1923, I never troubled to examine, and to accept the supernatural as the real.' In the end, Charles submits to God's grace as quietly as Evelyn, who wrote in *The Ordeal of Gilbert Pinfold*: 'Conversion suggests an event more sudden and emotional than his calm acceptance of the propositions of his faith.'

When Charles says that Catholics seem just like other people, he is rebuked by Sebastian: 'My dear Charles, that's exactly what they're not . . . they've got an entirely different outlook on life; everything they think is important is different from other people.' Charles's prayer for a miracle at Lord Marchmain's dying scene is a prayer for Julia. But when the miracle occurs, it is his own soul that is saved. In Evelyn's memo to Hollywood he says that the importance of the relationship between Charles and Julia is for each 'to bring the other to the Church'. Julia must renounce Charles in part to atone for her sins. She explains that if she gives up the thing she most loves, then God won't despair of her. Julia's bargain is very similar to Helen's in Graham Greene's *The End of the Affair*. She makes a plea with God to save Bendrick's life and if God spares him she will renounce him. This sort of plea makes sense to a Catholic, but not to anyone else. Charles himself makes this perfectly clear: 'I do understand.'

The Anglican Nancy Mitford was confused about the theology and Julia's renunciation of Charles: 'Now I believe in God and I talk to him a very great deal and often tell him jokes . . . he also likes people to be happy and people who love each other to live together – so long as nobody's else's life is upset (and then he's not so sure).' Evelyn patiently explained: 'It must be nonsense to say people never give up sleeping together for "abstract" principles. Anyway why "abstract"? Is the crown of England or the love of God abstract? Of course with Julia Flyte the fact that the war was coming and she saw her life coming to an end anyhow, made a difference.' In the memo, he goes further: 'I regard it as essential that after having led a life of sin Julia should not be immediately rewarded with conventional happiness. She has a great debt to pay and we are left with her paying it.' In other words, there will be no Hollywood ending for Charles and Julia.

The important point, Evelyn stressed, was that Charles is reconciled to Julia's renunciation: 'He has realised that the way they were going was not ordained for them, and that the physical dissolution of the house of Brideshead has in fact been a spiritual regeneration.' This message of hope, 'that the human spirit, redeemed, can survive all disasters', is made clear in the epilogue. Whilst the fountain is covered in barbed wire and debris, the chapel is unchanged. Charles comes full circle when he returns to the house, sees Nanny and then visits the chapel and kneels to pray.

> The builders did not know the uses to which their work would descend; they made a new house with the stones of the old castle; year by year, generation after generation, they enriched and extended it; year by year the great harvest of timber in the park grew to ripeness; until, in sudden frost, came the age of Hooper; the place was desolate, and the work all brought to nothing; *Quomodo sedet sola citivas.* Vanity of all vanities, all is vanity.
>
> And yet, I thought . . . Something quite remote from anything the builders intended, has come out of their work . . . something none of us thought about at the time; a small red flame . . . the flame which the old knights saw from their tombs . . . It could not have been lit but for the builders and the tragedians, and there I found it this morning, burning anew among the old stones.

This is the moment when Mad World is transformed into the Kingdom of Heaven. The big house slips away and the original title of *Brideshead* reasserts itself: 'the household of the faith'.

Evelyn had helped to save Hubert Duggan's soul. It was one of the great moments of his life. He had tried and failed to convert Hugh Lygon.

After the war, he tried to save Maimie, once Hubert's lover, begging her to let him pimp for her with the Holy Ghost. This was serious business. There was simply nothing he would not do to save his friends.

Maimie wrote to him in 1959 to tell him that she had lost her faith. He responded by asking her whether he could introduce her to a real 'beast' (priest) and asks her to come and see him: 'loss of faith is the saddest thing that can happen to one'. His next letter says that he knows a priest who was a friend of Hugh's at Oxford:

> I believe that everyone once in his (or her) life has the moment when he is open to Divine Grace . . . sometimes, like Hubert, on his deathbed – when all resistance is down and Grace can come flooding in . . . I don't know, darling Blondy, whether that is your condition now, but if it is, it's not a thing to dilly-dally about . . . I think it is just your soul opening up to God. I'd awfully like to pimp for you in that affair.*

Maimie was being offered her own moment akin to Charles's at the end of the novel. Like Hugh before her, she rejected the offer.

Snobs and Catholics

Those critics who disliked *Brideshead* did so on two grounds, that it was Catholic propaganda and that the novel venerated the aristocracy. The American critic Edmund Wilson, who greatly admired Waugh, was mortified: 'Waugh's snobbery, hitherto held in check by his satirical point of view, has here emerged shameless and rampant.'

When Evelyn was accused of being snobbish and in love with the aristocracy he defended himself vigorously: 'Class consciousness, particularly in England, has been so much inflamed nowadays that to mention a nobleman is like mentioning a prostitute sixty years ago.' In his diary he noted: 'Most of the reviews have been laudatory except where they were embittered by class resentment.'

* Remarkably, but typically of the relationship with Maimie, immediately after this heartfelt passage of the letter Evelyn changed the subject to a recently published memoir by Diana Cooper in which 'She plainly accuses Alfred [Hubert Duggan's brother] and me of buggery.'

He was well aware of inverted snobbery and could not have cared less that he was writing about a now unfashionable subject, and that writing about the working classes was all the fashion. In fact, he revelled in his position, saying 'I reserve the right to deal with the kind of people I know best.' As his son, Auberon, later pointed out, Evelyn's supposed romantic attachment to the aristocratic idea was employed chiefly to annoy people.

Evelyn loved to provoke his critics. In an interview in 1962 he said: 'I don't know them (the working classes) and I'm not interested in them. No writer before the middle of the nineteenth century wrote about the working classes other than as grotesques or pastoral decorations. Then, when they were given the vote certain writers started to suck up to them.' When Nancy Mitford was asked why she wrote about aristocrats, she said that it was because she knew them best. To ask her to write about factory workers would be 'like asking Jane Austen to write about Siberian Peasants'. Evelyn defended his position in the *Spectator*: 'In place of the old, simple view of Christianity that differences of wealth and learning cannot affect the reality and ultimate importance of the individual, there has risen the new, complicated and stark crazy theory that only the poor are real and important and that the only live art is the art of the People.'

When he was accused of being a snob by the *Bell*, a paper widely read by Irish Catholics, he said: 'I think perhaps your reviewer is right in calling me a snob; that is to say I am happiest in the company of the European upper classes; but I do not think this preference is necessarily an offence against Charity, still less against the Faith . . . Besides Hooper there are two characters in *Brideshead Revisited* whom I represent as worldly – Rex Mottram, a millionaire, and Lady Celia Ryder, a lady of high birth. Why did my reverence for money and rank not sanctify those two?'

Ryder and his creator do not love lords indiscriminately. Viscount Mulcaster is a mindless oaf, without the aristocratic grace of Sebastian. In the manuscript version of the novel, Mulcaster is 'a peer like pig', he is fat, badly dressed, with 'an idiot gape'. The members of the Bullingdon are presented as illiterate upper-class thugs, 'disorderly footmen', repressed homosexual Neanderthals. The Flytes themselves are deeply flawed. Lady Marchmain is cold and pious; Sebastian is a drunken wastrel and Bridey a pompous fool. Lord Marchmain also has his dark side: 'I had always been aware of a frame of malevolence under his urbanity.'

Only Cordelia, like the sister in Shakespeare's *King Lear* after whom she is named, is purely good.

The irony of Waugh's career is that having written this book for himself, not caring whether it sold well or not, knowing and believing that his subject was out of time and kilter (and loving it for all of these things), it became an immediate bestseller in both Britain and America. A Labour government was elected in 1945, the year of its publication, ushering in the age of the common man, the age of Hooper (and it must be said that the portrayal of Hooper is not without warmth, say, in comparison with that of Bridey the heir to Brideshead). By a further irony, the very same forces that led to the egalitarian aspirations which swept Labour to power also fed the nostalgia that made *Brideshead* a bestseller. Evelyn yet again found himself in tune with the Zeitgeist. Although his higher-brow literary friends and his sterner critics objected to his subject matter, ordinary readers were fed up with war, rationing and deprivation, and they loved the escapism of *Brideshead*, suffused as it was 'with a kind of gluttony, for food and wine, for the splendours of the recent past, and for rhetorical and ornamental language'. The country had been through so much that people no longer wanted to read about poverty and ordinariness. Waugh thus confounded his critics.

What really stung Evelyn was the impugning of his faith as a Catholic. To Conor Cruise O'Brien, who attacked him in *The Tablet* for his 'almost mystical veneration for the upper classes', he was quick to respond: 'In England Catholicism is predominantly a religion of the poor. There is a handful of Catholic aristocratic families, but I knew none of them in 1930 when I was received into the Church. My friends were fashionable agnostics and the Faith I then accepted had none of the extraneous glamour which your reviewer imputes to it.'

Edmund Wilson, in a wilful misreading of *Brideshead*, declared that 'what has caused Mr Waugh's hero to plump to his knees is not, perhaps, the sign of the cross, but the prestige, in the person of Lord Marchmain, of one of the oldest families in England'.

Yet Lord Marchmain is a social pariah, ignored by the great and good, hounded out of society. He is more like the gospel's woman taken in adultery than the protagonist of a traditional English 'silver spoon' novel. 'We were knights then, barons since Agincourt, the larger honours came with the Georges. They came the last and they'll go the first; the barony goes on.'* One can hear the family pride of Lord Beauchamp in Lord Marchmain's deathbed speech, but, with the Lygons as with the Marchmains, the ultimate irony is that the barony does *not* go on. Bridey and Beryl are childless, as Lord Marchmain reminds the reader in the marvellous phrase 'why should that uncouth pair sit here childless while the place crumbles about their ears?' It is hard not to think of Elmley and Mona, even to wonder whether Maimie told Evelyn the family story that Boom's last words to his beloved David Smyth, as he lay on his deathbed in Manhattan, were: 'Must we dine with the Elmleys tonight?'

The fountain is abandoned and vandalised; it is the faith that endures. Though Lord Beauchamp had seven children, there was no one to take the title to his grandchildren's generation. Hugh and Elmley and three of the sisters died childless. Only Lettice and Richard had issue – and both Richard's children were girls. The Earldom of Beauchamp is now extinct.

* Wording in this quotation follows Waugh's revised text of 1960.

CODA

'Laughter and the Love of Friends'

That day is wasted on which we have not laughed.

(inscription composed by Lord Beauchamp and his sister for the sundial at Madresfield)

Oh dear friendship, what a gift of God it is. Speak no ill of it.

(Fr Bede Jarrett, quoted by Evelyn Waugh in his biography of Ronald Knox)

In literary calendars 1945 is marked as the year that Waugh ended.

(Brigid Brophy)

The war ended the world that Waugh loved and he would never be the same again. Nor would the Lygons. Evelyn wrote to Coote on 3 March 1945: 'Here are the Trollopes, with many thanks – I enjoyed *The Way We Live Now* very much. I am glad my book about the way we lived then arrived safely.' His book about the way they lived then – in their Mad World before the war – was of course *Brideshead Revisited*.

His emotional and intellectual development ended in 1945. The writing afterwards is retrospective, the author estranged from the modern age. He became prematurely aged and embittered. If England was bad after the war, worse was to come: the Second Vatican Council would take the Roman Catholic Church in a direction of which he did not approve. And worst of all, he became a caricature of himself.

The Lygon girls were of more sanguine temperament. None of them seemed to be worried about their decline in prosperity. In an interview in the 1980s Lady Dorothy said that she saw the old days 'as a part of one's life that's now over. I was lucky to live the life I did, though I didn't think of it as privilege at the time.'

Maimie

After the war, Maimie descended into a haze of alcoholism and depression. Her mental condition caused much despair to her loved ones. Evelyn and Coote wrote to each other regularly to discuss the problem. She was suffering from persecution mania and was in a delicate state. Her friends claimed that Vsev had spent all her money. The prince and princess had no children, were heavy drinkers and were devoted to their Pekingese dogs. They got into the habit of throwing pots of boiling hot tea at each other.

In February 1946, Maimie wrote to Evelyn from the Georgian apartment in Alexander Square SW3 to which she and Vsev had moved. She had been to a ball and danced with a Colonel de Jouray, who was frightened of ladies: 'I suppose if we had all been great pansy sheiks with our pockets and shoes full of sand it would have been alright.' Somewhat incongruously, she had discussed modern novels with him, but did not dare to say that she liked *Brideshead* 'as now it is so popular in the USA he would despise me for bad taste'. Waugh's novel had become a hugely successful Book Club selection in America. Maimie also joked that a Danish count who was in love with Coote had asked her hand in marriage and promised a lot of certificates saying that he was not infected with the clap, 'but of course she has said no'.

Some months later, Evelyn told Nancy Mitford that Maimie's 'nasty little dog has been kidnapped and held to ransom. She paid up.' He was writing a treatise on wine for her husband in exchange for champagne. Two months later he reported that she had been burgled, losing wine and a gold cigarette case. Maimie wrote again with news that a different colonel had asked for Coote's hand in marriage but that she had refused, unimpressed by his great wealth. She also wrote: 'I think I have 2 pansy servants – Decent.'

Evelyn responded: 'My male instinct told me that your news was connected with Poll's nuptials. I thought you would tell me she was at least engaged but no it is no again. I think it would have been injudicious to marry Col Britain on account of his low birth, ungainly manners, insanitary and immodest habits with the chamber-pot. I hope she did not flatter him with a moment's hesitation but snapped out her No before he had finished his declaration.' Meanwhile he was negotiating to buy a house in Somerset – perhaps Coote could live there 'and keep out the vigilantes until I have sold this little house'.

He sent a postcard in September asking if she would eat oysters with him and then go to the cinema: 'Please do or are you too busy with your literary career?' This is a reference to her editorship of *Diversion*, a book she was producing to raise money for the Yugoslav Relief Society. It included short stories by Henry Yorke, Peter Quennell, Eddie Sackville-West and many other mutual friends. Elizabeth Bowen's contribution, a beautiful little story about the declining Anglo-Irish aristocracy, would have given Maimie a peculiar pang: entitled 'The Good Earl', it told of a lord who died far from home and of his daughter witnessing the unloading of his coffin from an ocean liner and taking his body home to bury it. On a lighter note, there was a story by Lord Berners that rewrote Evelyn's short story about Maimie – the beautiful girl with the snub nose and the Pekingese that damages her mistress's marital prospects. It even included the detail, taken from the life of Grainger, of the dog becoming a member of the Lord's Day Observance Society. When the book came out, Evelyn attached a clipping about it to a letter:

> Blondie, What is this I read? A book of stories composed by you and Mrs Chapman. Why has this been kept a secret? Are they obscene? Am I to have a copy? Are you trying to take the bread out of my children's mouths? 'Diversion' indeed. Is this the time for diversions with a labour government and squatters and famine and Poll still unmarried?

Maimie duly sent a copy and Evelyn replied gracefully: 'Thank you very much indeed for sending me your beautiful "Diversion". I am ashamed now that I didn't contribute. If I had known that Tito was not to profit I would have done so eagerly. I am sure it will be a very great success.'

He subsequently sent her a new book of his own, a slight novella entitled *Scott-King's Modern Europe*. The protagonist, a dim schoolmaster at a conference in an imaginary continental country, gets into conversation with an Anglophile engineer who asks him if he knows the Duke of Westminster. 'No,' replies Scott-King. 'I saw him once at Biarritz,' his interlocutor says; 'A fine man. A man of great propriety.' 'Indeed?' says Scott-King, his quizzical tone that of the Waugh who knew what Westminster had done to Beauchamp. 'Indeed, London is his propriety,' comes the answer – the misprision not only a joke at the expense of the foreigner but also an allusion to the legendary scale of the duke's property portfolio. 'I hope you are not furious at my mentioning the Duke of Westminster in my book,' Evelyn wrote to Maimie. 'You know how we love to gossip about our social superiors.'

Most of their letters during these years are a mix of gossip, booze, jokes, 'filthiness' and book talk. Maimie asked Evelyn if he would put her up for membership of the London Library. He made her claim on the basis of the publication of *Diversion*: 'I said you were a scholar of international repute but they said there was no chance of priority. It should not take longer than 9 months at the rate members are dying this winter of exposure and malnutrition.' She was duly elected and he gave her some solemn advice on the rules of the Library:

> NEVER write 'balls' with an indelible pencil on the margins of the books provided. Do not solicit the female librarians to acts of unnatural vice. When very drunk it is permissible to fall into a light doze but not to sing. Fireworks are always welcome in the reading-room but they should be of a kind likely to divert the older members rather than to cause permanent damage to the structure.

Maimie had a beautiful voice. A tribute by a friend after her death noted that she was incapable of singing out of tune and that she would warble out Gilbert and Sullivan or Victorian ballads as 'unself-consciously as a bird', to the piano accompaniment of Bloggs Baldwin – but there is no record of her having tried it out in the reading room of the London Library.

'How I dread Christmas,' she wrote towards the end of 1946; 'Do come to London soon and cheer us up.' Those joyous Christmases at Mad were now a very distant memory. Her letters revealed increasing signs of having been written when drunk. An obsession with homosexuality runs through many of them: an Isherwood novel that she 'thought would be about a pederast'; repeated references to a story that eighty people had been arrested in Hampstead for sodomy. 'How much my mind has sunk,' she commented.

Every now and then she wrote with Madresfield gossip, such as the news that Miss Bryan, her old governess, was very ill and that the cook who blackmailed Boom was dead. She said that Dickie, her youngest brother, had phoned to say that he had sent a wreath and written a card from her (noblesse oblige, even to a blackmailer) and then Elmley rang to say he had done the same and so did Lady Sibell, 'all after I had rung the gardeners at Mad and done the same so I expect many people will think I am heart-broken'. The one thing she never lost was her sense of humour. Her letters to Evelyn are peppered with references to her father ('high time someone wrote a lovely life of Boom') and with nostalgia for the good old days ('just think 18 years ago we were all in Venice').

By 1952 Evelyn informed Nancy Mitford that 'poor Maimie is broke'. She and her husband were following 'the old, almost abeyant custom, of residing together without speaking. Difficult without servants.' The next year she moved to Hove on the Sussex coast, where she had a bad fall down the stairs, probably when drunk, and was left concussed and bruised. Evelyn thought that she was going a bit crazy. Her lawyers and bankers were refusing to allow her to cash cheques. She had begun to pawn her jewellery. This provided short-term relief: 'I have £350 in notes and no bills,' she wrote to Evelyn, 'so come up and let's make whoopee.' She told him that she was in deep disgrace with her brother Lord Beauchamp and her sister Lady Lettice, who had asked her and Vsev to live 'as jagger in turns with them to save money'. Maimie was desperate not to have to resort to this – 'So darling,' she asked, 'suggest a way I can earn my living.'

Her Christmas was dreadful: 'Not like the old days with the Capt. G. B. H.' At this point Vsev was still living with her, but he was shortly to leave for good. Maimie had been reading her old letters to Boom: 'My word! I was hypocritical. I expect they made good reading for Boom all the same . . . I never see a soul nowadays. However have got used to being lonely.' She had also been reading diaries from the early thirties (alas, now lost): 'Plenty of you – all to your credit. Well deserved!' But her brave front was not fooling her loved ones.

In 1954, Coote wrote to Evelyn: 'I long to see you; we are all very concerned about Little Blondie. Being married to Vsev is bound to make anyone nuts.' Coote told Evelyn that she had made an appointment to see Maimie's doctor but had deemed it wise not to tell her sister of her plans. Coote was pretty much resigned: 'I don't think it will do any good. Why didn't we kill him [Vsev] at Hove?'

Maimie's mental condition worsened until she was admitted into a rest home for the mentally ill in central London in June 1954. Naturally, she faced it head on and wrote to Evelyn: 'So here am I in the bin . . . I have been ill since before Whitsun.' She longed to return to her little flat in Hove, but was persuaded to stay at the home in Weymouth Street. Evelyn was distressed to hear the news and wrote to comfort her and sympathise that he too had lost his reason in February and March. He made jokes about her being mad with the coming eclipse of the sun, asking 'is it not very expensive in your bin?' Like the rest of her friends and family, he was worried about her financial position. He wished he could come to see her with 'grapes, and flowers, and filthy stories'.

A letter she wrote to him in August 1954 reveals her fragility: 'Darling, What are the saddest words in the English language – If Only, Never Again, Kept Waiting, Too Late, No Answer, Just Because. I think If Only is the Saddest.' By the end of the year, Evelyn was writing that 'Poor Maimie is sunk in madness.' There were rumours of suicide attempts and desperate drinking, though she made periodic attempts to give up for Lent or out of 'vanity and parsimony'.

Maimie was divorced in 1956. Vsev had gone off with his Hungarian mistress and would soon remarry. She abandoned Hove, wrote off her car and reverted to her maiden name. Several collections of her jewellery appeared as star items in the sale rooms at Christies. She explained to Evelyn that Vsev's old wine firm had sacked him and offered her a job: 'There is quite a future for me in the Booze business.' The willowy debutante was becoming an overweight middle-aged lady.

In December 1954, the year he found Maimie 'sunk into madness', Evelyn had visited the don, Richard Pares, who was dying of motor neurone disease. He wrote to Nancy Mitford: 'I went to Oxford and visited my first homosexual love, Richard Pares. At 50 he is quite paralysed except his mind and voice and awaiting deterioration and death . . . No Christian Faith to support him. A very harrowing visit.' He could not bear the idea of his friends dying without faith. So when Maimie wrote to him some years later to tell him that she had lost her faith, he acted quickly. She had said she was: 'Poor, Persecuted, cold, tired, hungry and I have lost my faith which I mind but what to do?' The letter was signed: 'Yours despairingly, Blondie'. Evelyn asked her to elaborate and she tried to explain:

> When I say I have lost my faith I do not mean *belief* exactly as who am I to dare say that something is untrue which has been known to be true for centuries by ones of far greater learning and intelligence than I could ever have had a glimmer of. Perhaps I meant courage and the insight which I had. Perhaps it is that things have been too easy for me. Anyway perhaps I could see your Beast one day . . . I do value your friendship.

Apart from trying to set up a meeting with a priest, he asked his friends to visit her and sent his daughter Meg, whom she adored, to see her. Meg loved looking through Maimie's scrapbooks of the 1930s and chatting. They often went to dinner at the Hyde Park Hotel. By this time Maimie had a new job working at Sloane Galleries Antiques on the King's Road. When this fell through, she took a position at Ede Car Hire, writing to Evelyn to recommend the company. It was a far cry from driving down to Mad in her father's sleek Packard. In 1963 Evelyn, in all seriousness, suggested that Maimie should take over the position of hostess at the Cavendish Hotel, following in the footsteps of Rosa Lewis, 'The Duchess of Jermyn Street'.

Maimie was, in Evelyn's words, 'very poor, and pretty'. He often sent her cheques for her birthday and Christmas. In the early days of their friendship he used to write her cheques for thousands of pounds with a message: 'Here is some money in case you are poor', knowing that she would never cash them – this of course was a joke, the rich daughter of Lord Beauchamp needing money from a poor, aspiring writer. But in these last years, he gave her money in earnest. He always asked with great tact whether she would mind accepting cash rather than a present for Christmas.

When Maimie was seventy-one she was interviewed for *Harpers & Queen* in relation to the Granada television adaptation of *Brideshead.* She was living in an unprepossessing basement flat in juggernaut-begrimed Redcliffe Gardens in Earls Court – still in surroundings that eccentrically combined style and disarray. A once rather grand gilt table was strewn with clutter, indeed every surface was covered with junk – pieces of string, old magazines, pipes – as though the contents of drawers had been tipped out. Maimie was elegantly dressed and 'remarkably pretty with hair the shape and colour of an overblown white rose' as she sat poised on a 'threadless urn-shaped sofa' with Mister, her Pekingese, gnawing an old bone at her feet. She had, observed the interviewer, Julie Kavanagh, the 'self-possession and nonchalant disregard of convention that seems natural in people of great beauty and privilege'. Although it was only four in the afternoon, Maimie offered her visitor vodka: 'It's so much nicer than tea, I always think.' Kavanagh saw the vestiges of the anarchic streak and enormous sense of fun that had so appealed to Waugh and sustained their long friendship. Maimie said that the motto that summed up her relationship with Evelyn was that inscription on the sundial at Madresfield: 'The day is wasted on which we have not laughed.'

Lady Mary Lygon died of cancer on 27 September 1982. Coote had nursed her throughout the illness. Her friendship with Evelyn Waugh endured for over thirty years, from his arrival at Mad to his death. Her Pekingese, Grainger, has his name perpetuated in *Black Mischief, Scoop, Incident in Azania, Put Out More Flags* and *Work Suspended.*

Elmley, Mona, Sibell, and Dickie

Elmley, the last Earl Beauchamp, lived out a dull life as a 'backwoodsman' in the House of Lords. The high point of his year was the Three Counties Agricultural Show. He died in 1979, leaving Mona as chatelaine of Madresfield. She lived on for another ten years, riding around the estate either on a tricycle or in a powder blue Rolls-Royce with a cocktail cabinet in the back.

In the early part of the Second World War, Lady Sibell's husband, Mike Rowley, served as a fighter pilot with 601 Squadron. But in the course of 1940 he developed a brain tumour and Sibell took him home to care for him. Meanwhile in Germany, the true Mrs Rowley found herself in the awkward position of being an enemy alien by virtue of her marriage to a man who was married to someone else. A letter to Rowley was smuggled out of Germany, but Sibell made sure her husband never saw it. She wrote to the address given by Eleonore – that of a friend in neutral Switzerland – with the news, entirely false, that Rowley had been killed in action.

Mrs Eleonore Rowley survived the war and in 1949 got a divorce on the grounds of her husband's adultery with Lady Sibell. This meant that a decade after their bigamous marriage she and Mike could remarry legally. But the wartime deception still rankled, so in 1951, short of money, Eleonore sued Sibell in London, claiming that the letter stating that Rowley was dead had caused her, as his lawful wife, deep shock and had affected her heart. The jury found in her favour and awarded her damages of £814. There was also a story that Eleonore had blackmailed Sibell for £2,000 before the court case.

The following year her husband really did die. Sibell moved to Gloucestershire, less than an hour's drive from Mad. She was subsequently cited in a divorce case brought by Mrs Anne Warman, of Salwarpe Court, Droitwich, against her husband, Francis Byrne Warman. Sibell also had romantic involvements with Lord Rosebery and Lady Mairi Bury.

She devoted the rest of her life to her one great passion: hunting. As Master of the Ledbury Hunt, she was for many years the only female Master of Foxhounds in the country. Whereas Coote always rode side-saddle, Sibell sailed astride over the big ditches and fences of the Gloucestershire and Herefordshire countryside. The secretary of the Ledbury Hunt, who worked closely with her, was Major Peter Phillips, whose son would become a renowned three-day eventer and the husband of Princess Anne. In 2005 Sibell was to be seen on the lawn of Madresfield, at a meeting of the Croome Hunt, the last before the imposition of the hunting ban. She died later that year, at the age of ninety-eight.

Youngest brother Dickie never spoke about his parents. He shunned the aristocracy, preferring the middle classes. He married a vicar's daughter. They had two daughters, one of whom, Lady Rosalind Morrison, moved into Madresfield after a protracted legal wrangle following Mona's death in 1989.

Coote

Lady Dorothy Lygon was on leave in Venice on VE Day, which was celebrated there with fireworks. At the end of the summer, she was shipped home from Naples. The following year she was demobilised. Hers had been a good war. Whereas Maimie's life had been shaped by her good looks, Coote got by on her toughness and intelligence. Her work as a flight officer and then a photographic interpreter in the WAAF was well respected and the war had given her the opportunity to travel throughout Europe.

When peace returned, she followed a variety of paths. She farmed in Gloucestershire, but that seemed constricting after the horizons opened during the war. She accordingly went to work as a governess in Istanbul for six months and then moved to Athens to serve as social secretary to the British ambassador. She lived for a while on the Greek island of Hydra before returning to England to work as an archivist at Christies. She was loved by young and old alike.

She remained friends with Evelyn until the end of his life. They shared book talk as well as smutty jokes and frivolity, and he encouraged her to write about her life. She sent him a story, based on her Istanbul experiences, about the misadventures of a governess called Miss Coote. 'I could try to write my autobiography as you suggest,' she said in a letter, 'but Elmley, Mona, Blondie and Lady Sibell would never speak to me again, let alone any other friends or relations, who might also fall by the wayside, and while I don't really care about E and M, I feel some consideration otherwise.' Nevertheless, she told him that she was trying to write about her 'nursery days with a vague idea of following it up with adolescence and the summer I spent with Boom in Venice when Hughie died, as 3 more or less self-contained essays cum documentaries. Do you think this is feasible?' He got her an advance of £300 from Chapman and Hall, but the book was never finished.

In one letter he noted that she did not appear to be greatly cast down by the death of her uncle, the Duke of Westminster, the architect of the family's misery. Even gentle Coote was delighted by the death of Boom's nemesis.

When she was a governess in Istanbul in 1956, she had looked after a little girl called Julia, daughter of a Mr Rochester. She very much liked her but thought she was hopelessly spoilt. The youngest child in the family wet her knickers at the sight of Coote, who rather fancied the young Greek servant and felt that the Rochester family were like something out of an Ibsen play ('problem children and even more problematic parents'). When Coote first left for Istanbul, Maimie wrote to Evelyn with a playful turn on the 'Mr Rochester' connection: 'Poll came before catching the Night Ferry. I am sure that didn't happen to Jane Eyre before leaving Lowood.'

After many years of travel, Coote settled down near Faringdon House in Oxfordshire, the home of Lord Berners, who had left the house to his long-term lover and companion, the notorious 'Mad Boy' Robert Heber Percy. Coote knew both men, as they were friends of her father's and had often visited Mad.

Robert Vernon Heber Percy was born in 1911, the youngest son of Algernon Heber Percy of Hodnet Hall in Shropshire. He was nicknamed 'the Mad Boy' on account of his outlandish behaviour. He was handsome, elegant, high-spirited and a notorious homosexual – although that did not stop him marrying a girl called Jennifer Fry in 1942. They had one daughter, with whom Jennifer left home two years later. A divorce followed in 1947.

Mad Boy had met Lord Berners in 1932, when he was twenty-one. They were lovers for eighteen years, inseparable save during the war and the brief period of Heber Percy's marriage. When Berners died in 1950, he left Faringdon to Robert.

Faringdon was Mad World all over again, what with its flock of doves dyed in pinks and blues, and pewter tankards full of champagne. Mad Boy crashed cars and smoked furiously, burning holes in his stylish and expensive suits. There was a dog cemetery with one of the tombstones inscribed 'Towser: A short life but a gay one.'

Coote was fond of Mad Boy, on account of their shared passion for horses and entertaining. They had in common many friends and a taste for outrageous stories. They had been to many of the same places – Venice, for instance, where Heber Percy had lived with Berners, and where Coote had visited Boom. Berners worked for a time at the consulate there and was once asked to respond to a report in an Australian newspaper saying that Venice used to be a luxurious place but now it was full of nothing but beggars. He said that the only possible explanation was a misprint – 'for beggers, read buggers'.

By 1984, Mad Boy's health was failing and Coote nursed him through a bad fall. Paddy Leigh Fermor, the great travel writer who had often crossed paths with both the Lygons and Evelyn (he was a major player in the battle for Crete), visited Coote at Faringdon and noticed that they were close. However, neither he nor any of their friends could hide their shock when Coote announced that she was marrying Mad Boy. They married the following year, both aged seventy-three.

But Mad Boy had a loyal and ferocious Austrian cook/housekeeper, Rosa Proll. Her food was legendary, notably her summer puddings and her Pudding Louise, a confection of hot *marrons glacés*, boiling raspberry jam, and ice cream on top. Rosa was devoted to Heber Percy and left the house in high dudgeon when Coote became mistress of Faringdon. The fact that Coote was an excellent cook added insult to injury.

Rosa has been blamed for the failure of the marriage, but her influence cannot have been the only reason. For all the shared love of the hunt, Mad Boy and Coote were not exactly a natural couple. After all the years that Maimie and Evelyn had joked about possible suitors for their beloved Coote, not even they would have guessed in their wildest dreams the bizarre finale to her romantic life.

What possessed her? Some said it was a marriage of convenience to avoid death duties, but those who knew her best simply said that she was flattered and wanted to be married. Yes, Robert was homosexual, but so was her own father. Boom's problem, she thought, was not his sexual orientation, but his choice of a wife who didn't understand homosexuality. She would be different. The decision was, however, a disaster. Coote spent her honeymoon alone after Heber Percy turned against her, outraged at the thought that he might actually be expected to sleep with her.

After the marriage failed she retreated to her nearby bungalow, where she was happier. It seems that they never divorced, for she signed herself Dorothy Heber Percy in her will. In 2000 she helped a small press to republish a book by Lord Berners called *The Girls of Radcliff Hall*, a mischievous, racy, fictional evocation of life at Faringdon, in which all the boys (including Heber Percy) become girls at a boarding school, with Berners as the headmistress.

Coote died in 2001, at the age of eighty-nine. She had been busy planning her ninetieth birthday party. Despite all the trials and tribulations of her life, she had an admirable stoicism and resilience. Whereas the bigamy of Sibell's husband and Maimie's marriage to a penniless philandering Russian prince caused enduring distress, Coote's union with a notorious homosexual was a brief aberration. She had the happiest life of all the Lygons, filled with laughter and the love of friends. Even in her seventies she would think nothing of driving from Oxfordshire to the south of France for a party.

There is a wonderful glimpse of her in August 1990, at the twenty-first birthday celebrations of Debo Mitford's grandson. Debo, of course, had made the best match of all the Mitford girls – to the Duke of Devonshire. The party took place at Chatsworth and, like a throwback to Elmley's twenty-first at Mad, it lasted for three days. The celebrations began with an evening garden party for over two thousand people. The third day was for charity. Sandwiched between, was the main event, the ball. The grandchildren insisted on the formal dress code, much to Debo's amazement (though a few wore skimpy dresses, 'the sort that JUST covers the telling bits of body and show vast thighs, as if anyone wants to see them'). Debo herself wore 'a big crown of a tiara and felt like Mrs Toad of Toad Hall'. The young people were ferried from London in buses, with dinner served en route. There was only one gatecrasher, a 'beautiful, goat-like, tall creature' called Jerry Hall, some sort of model. Coote was there. She spent much of the night talking to old friends such as Paddy Leigh Fermor, though she could not have helped thinking of the old days at Mad.

In 1997, the BBC made a documentary about the changing fortunes of the British aristocracy. They interviewed Coote and Sibell, who were still following the Ledbury Hunt (though by car, not on horseback). Lady Sibell is tall and elegant, Coote large with spectacles. They talk about Evelyn and remember that he came out to hunt a couple of times, though it wasn't a great success. They also talk about how they were 'relentless about disturbing' him when he was trying to work in the old nursery at Mad. Coote wonders how he ever managed to finish his books.

Then she reads aloud the description of the chapel at Brideshead as the camera pans around Boom's chapel at Mad. They show family scrapbooks, beautiful photos of the 'Beauchamp Belles'. And they talk of Boom's exile for being a homosexual, Coote saying wistfully but stoically that it was 'quite, quite, quite an upset'. In the chapel they comment how the flowers in the stained glass have faded a little and recall how they were required to hold artificial doves when they were being painted for their frescoes. They talk about the wild weekend parties and then about how the war ended the world they knew. For Coote, it was an enormous watershed in everyone's life, while Sibell just says 'Never the same again.'

Evelyn

Ann Fleming killed Evelyn Waugh. She broke his spirit by passing on a piece of gossip. In November 1961 he went abroad with his favourite daughter, Meg. She was his last great love. In Trinidad they had stayed with Lord Hailes, Governor-General of the West Indies. In a move of unprecedented and uncharacteristic spite, Ian Fleming's wife Ann let Evelyn know that the Haileses had found him a great bore. This was a shock from which he never fully recovered.

It came on the heels of a similar incident that Evelyn himself recounted to that other noted wit, Nancy Mitford. Evelyn had been accosted by a man in White's (his gentleman's club in Piccadilly) who told him that nobody wanted to speak to him because 'you sit there on your arse looking like a stuck pig'. Evelyn, always slightly on the edge of persecution mania, became convinced that he had become boring. Nancy was furious about the Fleming incident: 'what makes Ann *tell* you that some friend of an expatriate . . . finds you a bore? The very last thing anyone could reproach you with.' But he was still upset a month later and tried to explain to Nancy precisely what this meant to him. The fine distinction that he stressed was that he had lost the ability to recognise his own dullness:

> I must explain about boring the Haileses because it has been what young people call 'traumatic' . . . The crucial point is that I was confident they both enjoyed my visit . . . I talked loud and long and they laughed like anything. Now I find I bored them. Well of course everyone is a bore to someone. One recognises that. But it is a ghastly thing if one loses the consciousness of being a bore. You do see that it means that I can never go out again.

He was quite serious about this. Nancy tried to comfort him: 'Do try and get it into your head that whatever else you may be you are *not a bore*.' But, never one to forget a criticism, Evelyn brought it up again with Nancy two years later, referring to himself as 'the man who bored the Haileses out of Trinidad'. Then yet again, in 1965, four years after it happened, he wrote to Diana Cooper: 'I first realised I had become a bore when the Haileses remarked on it to Clarissa. I had thought I was particularly bright with the Haileses. Traumatic.'

Evelyn's wit was legendary – often cruel but always hilarious – and he had made his career on being funny. He could be nasty, snobbish, cutting, acerbic, as his letters attest. But he could never have been accused of being dull. Not only did he have a life-long fear of boredom itself, but, in common with many of his generation, he had a pathological fear of becoming that most dreaded of things – a bore. Two other events added to his unhappiness towards the end of his life. His favourite daughter married and the reforms of the Second Vatican Council 'knocked the guts out of him'.

Ann Fleming, despite this aberration, was a loyal friend and she would have been upset to know how deeply Evelyn was hurt by the Hailes incident. Her friendship with Evelyn 'was a relationship giving nothing but joy'. She sketched one of the best descriptions of Evelyn in later life. For her, he was a great comedian like Charlie Chaplin – the little man, the figure of fun. She thought that like all great clowns 'he affected a grave demeanour of manner, he seldom laughed aloud, and a smile was very rewarding'.

Despite his great love for his wife and children he was beset by mood swings and fits of melancholy. When he was rude to his friends, his wife Laura made him apologise. On two occasions his rudeness provoked Ann Fleming to physical violence. She understood that his ill temper was partially due to his long-term insomnia, but that his bad moods were much improved by misadventures. Rafting on the Rio Grande he was delighted when the raft sunk and they had to swim to shore: 'Evelyn doing a slow breast stroke, blue eyes blazing and mood much improved, for he liked things to go wrong.'

Evelyn's problem after the war was that his life went right, so his fiction went wrong. His comedy depended on the misadventures and the sense of being an outsider. Settling down as a country squire with a happy brood of children was no recipe for the creation of another *Decline and Fall* or *Handful of Dust*.

Testimonies from his friends all emphasise his funniness, his incomparable companionship, his loyalty, his courage, his schoolboy sense of humour, his fierce intelligence and his humility about his own genius. He was a flirt (like his father) and adored fair, beautiful aristocratic women. All of his friends recall his blue eyes with their intense, piercing gaze. But no one gives a more accurate portrayal of the middle-aged Waugh than Evelyn himself. His autobiographical novel *The Ordeal of Gilbert Pinfold*, published in 1957, recounts a nervous breakdown that he suffered aboard a ship. It was brought on by an overdose of sleeping draught. In a chapter entitled 'Portrait of the Artist in Middle-age' he observes that 'the part for which he had cast himself was a combination of eccentric don and testy colonel and he acted it strenuously, before his children . . . and his cronies in London, until it came to dominate his outward personality'. This is late Waugh in a nutshell: a man who cast himself in a role that was really rather boring, with the result that he became a parody of himself, all too easily misunderstood as a curmudgeon, a snob and a testy misanthropist.

Gilbert Pinfold's crisis was his own. He went mad, began hearing voices in his head. One of them kept telling him that he was a homosexual. He wasn't – he loved women too much for that – but there is no question that the creator of Sebastian Flyte and admirer of Lord Beauchamp had one of the great bisexual imaginations of the English literary tradition.

His health was ruined prematurely by heavy drinking, smoking and addiction to the sleeping drugs that had blighted his life. But despite the ever more crusty persona, his late letters to his children reveal a tender, loving side that was rarely seen in public. To Bron, his eldest, he repeated his mantra: 'Most of the interest and amusement in life comes from one's friends.'

He died on Easter Sunday, 10 April 1966, of a heart attack. His friend Father Caraman said the Mass in Latin. He was deeply mourned by his friends. 'Probably the greatest friend I ever had,' said Nancy Mitford in a television interview just after his death: 'what nobody ever remembers about Evelyn is that everything with him was jokes. Everything. That's what none of the people who wrote about him seem to have taken into account at all.' His son Bron echoed this in the *Spectator* that May:

> The main point about my father, which might be of interest . . . is not that he was interested in pedigree – it was the tiniest part of his interests. It is not that he was a conservative – politics bored him . . . it is simply that he was the funniest man of his generation. He scarcely opened his mouth but to say something extremely funny. His house and life revolved around jokes. It was his wit – coupled, of course, with supreme accuracy of expression, kindness, loyalty, bravery and intelligence – which endeared him to everybody who knew him or read his books.

Late in life Evelyn Waugh completed *A Little Learning*, his memoir of his early years, in which Oxford plays such a vital part. When he heard that 'Frisky' Baldwin had had to buy a copy, he wrote a letter of apology, which Frisky inserted in his private proof copy of *Brideshead Revisited*. Evelyn said that the only reason he had not sent a complimentary copy was that Frisky had not really featured in the early years. 'In the second volume,' he explained, 'you will be a prominent character and I shall send you proofs for your permission to disclose the pleasures of the early '30s.'

All he managed of the sequel was a couple of pages concerning the brief period in 1925 when he was living in London with his brother Alec. His provisional title for the volume was 'A Little Hope', no doubt an allusion to his religious conversion. But if Evelyn Waugh had lived to complete the second volume of his autobiography, the centrality of Madresfield and the Lygons to his whole vision of life would have become fully apparent. The theme of the volume, like that of *Brideshead*, would have been 'the household of the faith'. What might he have called the chapter on Mad that would have been at the centre of it? He could not have done better than borrow that of the first of the three parts of his biography of Ronald Knox, published a few years before: 'Laughter and the Love of Friends.'

SOURCES

> The following list is not intended as a display of industry nor as a guarantee of good faith. They are the books which, while I was working on this subject, I found chiefly interesting and relevant; which I can commend to any reader who wishes to amplify details that I have stated too briefly, too vaguely, or too allusively.
>
> (Evelyn Waugh, Appendix to *Edmund Campion*, 1935)

Waugh prefaced his life of Edmund Campion with the comment that: 'There is great need for a complete, scholar's work on the subject. This is not it. All I have done is select the incidents which struck a novelist as important, and relate them in a single narrative.' In the case of Waugh himself, there is no further need for a complete, scholar's work on the subject: we already have one in Martin Stannard's two large volumes, *Evelyn Waugh: The Early Years, 1903–1939* (1987) and *Evelyn Waugh: The Later Years, 1939–1966* (1992), supplemented by Selina Hastings, *Evelyn Waugh: A Biography* (1994) and Douglas Lane Patey's acute *The Life of Evelyn Waugh: A Critical Biography* (1998). The first biography, *Evelyn Waugh* (1975), by Christopher Sykes remains invaluable because it was based on personal acquaintance (with the Lygons as well as Waugh). The best account of Waugh's Oxford friendships is Humphrey Carpenter's 'group biography' *The Brideshead Generation* (1989), though perhaps the one weakness of this engaging book is its lack of attention to the Lygons.

My aim, by contrast to that of the 'comprehensive' biographer, has been to select, if I may adapt Waugh's phrase, 'the incidents which struck me as important' in the genesis and aftermath of *Brideshead Revisited*, and relate them in a single narrative that illustrates what I believe to be the key themes of Waugh's life. It therefore seems appropriately in the spirit of Waugh himself to offer, in place of detailed reference notes, a brief listing of the principal published and unpublished sources on which I have drawn while working on the subject, together with a chronological list of Evelyn Waugh's book-length works and the major editions of his letters, diaries and shorter pieces.

For further details of sources and references, and background information on the writing of the book, please visit the author's website, www.paulabyrne.co.uk

EVELYN WAUGH'S MAJOR WORKS OF FICTION

Decline and Fall: An Illustrated Novelette (1928)
Vile Bodies (1930)
Black Mischief (1932)
A Handful of Dust (1934)
Scoop: A Novel about Journalists (1938)
Put Out More Flags (1942)
Work Suspended (1942)
Brideshead Revisited: The Sacred and Profane Memories of Captain Charles Ryder (1945)
The Loved One: An Anglo-American Tragedy (1948)
Helena (1950)
Men at Arms (1952)
Officers and Gentlemen (1955)
Unconditional Surrender (1961)
} revised and reprinted as the trilogy: *Sword of Honour* (1965)
The Ordeal of Gilbert Pinfold: A Conversation Piece (1957)

OTHER WORKS BY EVELYN WAUGH

Rossetti, His Life and Works (1928; biography)
Labels, A Mediterranean Journal (1930; travel)
Remote People (1931; travel)
Ninety-Two Days (1934; travel)
Edmund Campion (1935; biography)
Mr Loveday's Little Outing and Other Sad Stories (1936; short stories)
Waugh in Abyssinia (1936; travel)
Robbery Under Law (1939; travel)
Scott-King's Modern Europe (1947; novella)
The Holy Places (1952; travel)
Love Among the Ruins (1953; short story)
The Life of the Right Reverend Ronald Knox (1959; biography)
A Tourist in Africa (1960; travel)

Basil Seal Rides Again (1963; short story)
A Little Learning (1964; autobiography)
The Diaries of Evelyn Waugh, edited by Michael Davie (1976)
The Letters of Evelyn Waugh, edited by Mark Amory (1980)
The Essays, Articles and Reviews of Evelyn Waugh, edited by Donat Gallagher (1983)
Mr Wu and Mrs Stitch: The Letters of Evelyn Waugh and Diana Cooper, edited by Artemis Cooper (1991)
The Letters of Nancy Mitford and Evelyn Waugh, edited by Charlotte Mosley (1996)
The Complete Short Stories of Evelyn Waugh, edited by Ann Pasternak Slater (1998)

UNPUBLISHED MANUSCRIPTS

Some of Waugh's letters to the Lygon sisters are included in Mark Amory's selected edition of the *Letters of Evelyn Waugh*, but others remain in manuscript. A collection of eighty of those to Maimie is in the library of Georgetown University in Washington DC, while those to Coote, together with a second batch to Maimie, are in private hands. The letters from Maimie to Evelyn are in his incoming correspondence, which is in the British Library.

The published edition of *The Diaries of Evelyn Waugh* has been censored in places. Where necessary, I have silently restored omissions by consulting the original, which is in the huge and indispensable Evelyn Waugh collection in the Harry Ransom Center, University of Texas at Austin.

Alexander Waugh, Evelyn's grandson, has most generously allowed me to consult a wealth of material in his private family archive, including original manuscripts, transcripts of interviews, newspaper and magazine articles, photographs and Arthur Waugh's diaries. He has also provided me with some key references to Madresfield in a recently acquired and extremely important collection of Evelyn's letters that has long been thought lost.

Charles Linck, who unearthed the film *The Scarlet Woman*, kindly sent me a copy of his invaluable unpublished PhD dissertation, 'The Development of Evelyn Waugh's Career: 1903–1939' (University of Kansas, 1962). His privately published correspondence with Terence Greenidge is also an exceptionally valuable, almost unknown source: *Evelyn Waugh in Letters by Terence Greenidge* (1994).

The letters from the Earl and Countess Beauchamp to Lady Dorothy Lygon are in the private family archive at Madresfield. Materials for the servant's-eye view of Madresfield are in the local history collection of the Malvern Public Library and the Worcestershire Record Office.

The hitherto unseen Beauchamp divorce petition is in the National Archives at Kew. There are several small collections of unpublished Beauchamp papers, including his letters to Lloyd George, which are in the Library of the House of

Lords. Correspondence and papers relating to his governorship of New South Wales (in the State Library of New South Wales, Mitchell Library, Sydney) and his surviving papers at Madresfield provide the raw material for a full-scale political biography of this remarkable man, but because of the scandal nobody has yet undertaken one: perhaps it will now be possible.

OTHER SOURCES

Among the many other works consulted, the following have been especially useful:

Acton, Harold, *Memoirs of an Aesthete* (1948)

Amory, Mark, *Lord Berners: The Last Eccentric* (1998)

Barrow, Andrew, *Gossip: A History of High Society from 1920 to 1970* (1978)

Beevor, Antony, *Crete: The Battle and the Resistance* (1991)

Blow, Sydney, *Through Stage Doors* (1958)

Byron, Robert, *Letters Home*, edited by Lucy Butler (1991)

Chapman, Hester W., and the Princess Romanovsky-Pavlovsky (eds), *Diversion: published for the benefit of the Yugoslav Relief Society* (1946)

Cooper, Diana, *Autobiography* (1965; originally in 3 vols, 1958–60)

Davenport-Hines, Richard, 'Lygon, William, seventh Earl Beauchamp (1872–1938)', in *Oxford Dictionary of National Biography* (2004)

Davis, Robert Murray, *Evelyn Waugh, Writer* (1981)

De la Cour, John, *Madresfield Court* (undated guidebook)

Dickinson, Peter (ed.), *Lord Berners: Composer, Writer, Painter* (2008)

Dutton, David, 'William Lygon, 7th Earl Beauchamp', *Journal of Liberal History*, Summer 1999

Field, Leslie, *Bendor: The Golden Duke of Westminster* (1983)

Fielding, Daphne, *The Duchess of Jermyn Street: The Life and Good Times of Rosa Lewis of the Cavendish Hotel*, with preface by Evelyn Waugh (1964)

Fothergill, John, *An Innkeeper's Diary* (1931)

Glen, Alexander, *Young Men in the Arctic* (1935)

Green, Martin, *Children of the Sun: A Narrative of Decadence in England after 1918* (1980)

Greenidge, Terence, *Degenerate Oxford?* (1930)

Hance, Captain J. E., *School for Horse and Rider* (1932)

Hollis, Christopher, *Oxford in the Twenties* (1976)

Isherwood, Christopher, *The World in the Evening* (1954)

Kavanagh, Julie, 'Lady Mary Lygon Revisits Brideshead', *Harpers & Queen*, October 1981

Knox, James, *A Biography of Robert Byron* (2003)

Lancaster, Marie-Jaqueline (ed.), *Brian Howard: Portrait of a Failure* (1968)

Lygon, Lady Dorothy, 'Madresfield and Brideshead', in *Evelyn Waugh and his World*, edited by David Pryce-Jones (1973)

'Madresfield Court, Worcestershire', *Country Life*, 30 March 1907
Mosley, Charlotte (ed.), *The Mitfords: Letters Between Six Sisters* (2007)
Mosley, Diana, *Loved Ones: Pen Portraits* (1985)
—— *The Pursuit of Laughter: Essays, Articles, Reviews and a Diary* (2008)
Mulvagh, Jane, *Madresfield* (2007)
Nicolson, Harold, *Diaries 1907–1964*, edited by Nigel Nicolson (2004)
Parker, Peter, *The Old Lie: The Great War and the Public School Ethos* (1987)
Powell, Anthony, *Memoirs* (vols 1–3, 1976–80)
Rolfe, Frederick, 'Baron Corvo', *The Desire and Pursuit of the Whole* (1934)
Stannard, Martin (ed.), *Evelyn Waugh: The Critical Heritage* (1984)
Strachey, Julia, *Julia: A Portrait of Julia Strachey by Herself and Frances Partridge* (1983)
Taylor, D. J., *Bright Young People* (2007)
Treglown, Jeremy, *Romancing: The Life and Work of Henry Green* (2000)
Waugh, Alec, *A Year to Remember: A Reminiscence of 1931* (1975)
—— *My Brother Evelyn and other Profiles* (1967)
Waugh, Alexander, *Fathers and Sons* (2004)
Waugh, Auberon, *Another Voice* (1986)
Weaver, Cora, *A Short Guide to Charles Darwin and Evelyn Waugh in Malvern* (1991)
Williams, Dorothy, *The Lygons of Madresfield Court* (2001)

INDEX

P.S.

Ideas, interviews & features . . .

About the author

About the book

Read on

The Waugh Generation

Sarah O'Reilly talks to Paula Byrne

You reveal that to write, Waugh often escaped to the Easton Court Hotel in Chagford, explaining in a letter to Maimie and Coote Lygon 'the trouble about poor Bo is that he's a lazy bugger and if he was in a house with you lovely girls he would just sit about and chatter and get d.d.[disgustingly drunk] and ride a horse and have a heavenly time but would he write his book? No . . .' What distractions do you try to escape from when writing, and where do you go to escape them?
Evelyn Waugh made it clear, when he married Laura Herbert, that he would always need to be alone for his writing, and that he would find it impossible to write if surrounded by noisy children. With three young children of my own, I have huge sympathy for this viewpoint and, in an ideal world, I would love to escape to a remote location and immerse myself in the writing of my biographies. Practically, this rarely happens: my children would never forgive me and I would miss them too much. Happily, noise has never been a distraction. Coming from a large Catholic family, I learnt very quickly to write and read amongst chaos. Still, I secretly harbour fantasies of escaping to somewhere like Burgh Island in Devon, where I would be completely cut off – it worked for Agatha Christie!

Your last work of biography told the story of the eighteenth-century actress, poet, novelist, feminist, celebrity and royal

mistress Mary 'Perdita' Robinson. In turning to Waugh you swap the eighteenth for the twentieth century. Did writing about a different age bring different challenges?
I spent many happy years writing about the eighteenth century, which is where I am most comfortable, but I have always been drawn to the Jazz Age. I just adore the literature, the fashion, the excess, the music, the cars and the flappers. The research for *Mad World* was enormously exciting. I am also fascinated by the two world wars: one cannot fully appreciate the Roaring Twenties without understanding what came before and after, and I was mindful in writing this book that the Waugh generation was also a war generation.

Mad World was a challenging book to write in terms of the research – the Crete fiasco, for example, was so crucial to Waugh's disillusionment with the Army, but tricky to navigate. I also found writing about Waugh's (to my mind delightfully) irreverent and outrageous humour a challenge in an era obsessed with political correctness. When I wrote about Mary Robinson, I wasn't worried about offending any of the family, as it was so far in the past. It was quite different with *Mad World*, where family and friends are still alive – this led to some ethical considerations that I had never had to think about before.

'I have always been drawn to the Jazz Age. I just adore the literature, the fashion, the excess, the music, the cars and the flappers.'

You reveal in your preface that you set out to write this book 'because I believed that ▸

The Waugh Generation

(continued)

◀ Evelyn Waugh had been persistently misrepresented as a snob and a curmudgeonly misanthropist. I did not recognise Waugh in the popular caricature of him. I wanted to get to the real Waugh . . .' Where did your conception of the 'real Waugh' come from, or rather, how did you happen upon this other, lesser-known Waugh, which in turn led you to write your account of his early writing life?

I had long been convinced that people had got Evelyn Waugh wrong. Why would a man who was so unpleasant be so beloved by such a wide circle of friends? I admired Waugh's published letters and diaries, and thought that many of Evelyn's letters to his children were some of the most poignant, loving and wise letters ever written from father to child (especially those to his beloved daughter Meg). I felt the same way when I finally read Waugh's unpublished letters to Mary and Dorothy Lygon: here was a man who was generous, loving, loyal – and always uproariously funny. I felt that many of the reviews of the letters and diaries had quoted phrases out of context to perpetuate the caricature of the snobbish misanthrope. I was determined to show another side to Waugh. His relationship with the Lygon family was my key to unlocking that other side.

To what extent do you think that your own approach to the Lygon family has been shaped by Waugh's fictionalised portrayal of them? Dissenting voices such as Mona's – who argued that the girls were pretty,

glamorous and spoilt, 'financed by their father in a big way' – are few and far between in *Mad World*.

I do think that, inevitably, my view of the Lygon sisters was shaped by Waugh's fictional portrayal of them. For example, I argue that Julia Flyte's beauty and glamour owed much to Mary Lygon – her furs, her cloche hats, her Pekingese, her habit of always calling people 'darling' and, also, of course, her great sadness caused by her father's disgrace. However, my view of the Lygons was also influenced by the voices I heard in their own letters and essays, and by what their friends and contemporaries thought of them. Many of their friends stressed the sisters' courage and spirit in the face of the tragedies that tore apart their family.

You make the point, midway through *Mad World*, that 'instead of having children themselves, the Lygon girls were serving as midwives to Evelyn's books'. The girls' chances of making good marriages were blighted by the scandal surrounding their father, but were there also downsides to being involved with a man who demanded so much from his friends?

Yes, I think that there *were* downsides to the friendship. Evelyn's dependence, in later years, on sleeping drugs and alcohol made him a sometimes difficult friend. He could be irritable and rude. He also found it hard to conceal his dislike of Maimie's husband: 'Maimie is lost to me,' he wailed after she married her 'pauper prince'. Like many ►

❛ Like many friendships that endure for years, theirs had ups and downs, but Evelyn never abandoned the sisters. ❜

The Waugh Generation
(continued)

◀ friendships that endure for years, theirs had ups and downs, but Evelyn never abandoned the sisters. He was the first to lend money to Maimie and to support her when her marriage and mental health collapsed. He helped Coote get published and encouraged her in her writing endeavours.

In his 1944 letter to Colonel Ferguson of the Household Cavalry Training Regiment, Waugh sought a leave of absence from duty to write *Brideshead Revisited*, arguing that 'it is a peculiarity of the literary profession that once an idea becomes fully formed in the author's mind, it cannot be left unexploited without deterioration. If, in fact, the book is not written now it will never be written.' Do you, as a writer, share Waugh's need to plunge immediately into a new book once the idea has been hatched?
Biographers are very different from novelists. They don't necessarily have to wait for the Muse to strike or write quickly before inspiration fades. Evelyn's novels were often written very quickly whereas biographical research inevitably slows down the creative process. Also I like to spend a lot of time thinking as well as 'footstepping' – that is walking in the shoes of the writer, visiting important places. One of my happiest moments researching this book was finding Lord Beauchamp's palazzo on the Grand Canal in Venice.

Graham Greene wrote of the 'splinter of ice in the heart of a writer', the element of the artistic personality which uses others'

suffering for the writer's own creative ends. To what extent can it be said to be inevitable that a writer's friendships will be exploited in their work? And what made Waugh's use of the Lygons different?
Writers are indeed ruthless people. It is well known that Evelyn used his friends for copy, sometimes sending a postcard to friends saying 'Your turn next'. I think that, on some level, the Lygons would have felt a tiny amount of betrayal, but were too loyal to say so.

You refer to Stephen McKenna's dedication to Hugh Lygon of his novel *An Affair of Honour*, 'to whom I am indebted for the seed of truth from which this fantasy has grown'. With reference to your own work, should the origins of the fantasy always be looked into? What is the use of knowing about an author's life if what brought him to prominence was his work? How can – and should – biography inform our reading, enjoyment and interpretation of Waugh's novels?
I would always prefer to know biographical details about writers and their works. The very best of literary biographies bring writers alive for a new generation and encourage us to go back to the works. I'm thinking here of Richard Holmes's wonderful biography of Coleridge and Hermione Lee's *Virginia Woolf*. There is no doubt that these literary biographies increased my understanding and enjoyment of the works. Nevertheless, I would always sound a note of caution when considering the relationship between fact ►

' I like to spend a lot of time thinking as well as 'footstepping' – that is walking in the shoes of the writer, visiting important places. '

The Waugh Generation
(continued)

◀ and fiction. A novel is above all a work of the imagination.

You say, in discussing Waugh's biographical study of Rossetti, that 'To a greater or lesser extent, all biographers project themselves into their chosen subjects.' What aspects of you are revealed in your portrait of Waugh and his Mad World?
I come from a large, chaotic Catholic family, so I think that I was drawn to Evelyn's world. Like him, I am attracted to the panache and glamour exemplified by the English upper classes, whilst retaining a healthy cynicism towards them. I share Evelyn Waugh's irreverent sense of humour and I admire his generation and their 'stiff upper lip' mentality. I can't bear the self-pity and the victim culture that characterise our own age.

Did having his own family and family life put an end to Waugh's habit of falling in love with other families?
I think so. From the time he met Laura Herbert his search was over.

You refer to the decline and fall of the 'heavily footnoted biographical doorstopper' and champion the emergence of the 'partial life' in biography. As a practitioner of the craft, where do you foresee the next innovation in biography coming from?
I'm unsure as to how the genre of biography will develop, but I am convinced that partial life biographies are the way of the future. Nevertheless, there will always be a place for the 'cradle to grave' biographies. I think that the two can happily co-exist. ■

A Writing Life

When do you write?
I always write best in the mornings. During the rest of the day, I read or revise the morning's work.

Where do you write?
Usually at my lovely Georgian desk in my study. Sometimes I write at the kitchen table, so that I can see my hens (Dannii, Cheryl and Holly) clucking about.

Why do you write?
I write because I love it. When it goes well, time flies and then I feel like I deserve a nice glass of wine in the evening.

Pen or computer?
I like to write notes in ink (fountain pen is best), but then it's typing all the way.

Silence or music?
Music – always classical, usually Mozart, Haydn and Beethoven.

How do you start a book?
I buy a pretty notebook, a new fountain pen and then I start to take notes and it grows from there.

And finish?
My husband and children wrestle the pen out of my hand and take my laptop away and then I know that it's time to finish. ►

LIFE *at a Glance*

BORN
Birkenhead, 1967

EDUCATED
Marian RC High School for Girls; University of Liverpool

CAREER TO DATE
Schoolteacher, university lecturer, Royal Literary Fellow, writer

FAMILY
Husband: writer and critic Jonathan Bate. Three fabulous children: Tom, Ellie and Harry Sebastian.

LIVES
In a small village in Warwickshire

A Writing Life
(continued)

Which writer has had the greatest influence on your work?
Jane Austen – because she makes me laugh and she makes me cry.

What are your guilty reading pleasures?
The Twilight series, Harry Potter and E. Nesbit. ■

Other Worlds

by Paula Byrne

THE LYGONS WERE not the first family that Evelyn Waugh fell in love with. At the beginning there were the Flemings, then the Plunket Greenes, and then the Lygons: 'So true to life being in love with an entire family,' wrote Nancy Mitford.

Why do people fall in love with other people's families? That was the question with which I began my journey into Waugh's world. In Evelyn's case, he was in flight from his own upbringing. He was never close to his father. To all intents and purposes he felt like an only child – his brother was six years older and they moved in different circles. Waugh was drawn to large, chaotic households, often where there was a strong female presence. He loved, for example, hearing Nancy Mitford's tales about her eccentric clan. She was one of six sisters – infamous as the 'Mitford Girls'. It was Evelyn who, encouraging her literary endeavours, advised her to write about her own 'mad' family. *The Pursuit of Love* (he also gave her the title) was Mitford's most successful novel: a hilarious and poignant recreation of her home life in the Cotswolds.

Like Nancy Mitford, I hail from a large family. She was one of six sisters, I am one of five. I understand Waugh's fascination with big families. Whenever I have had a boyfriend from a small family, they have been enamoured of my own noisy, rambunctious siblings. We are drawn to the opposite of what we know. I think that one of the reasons why *Brideshead* is so ►

Other Worlds
(continued)

◀ beloved by readers (if not critics) is because of the way Waugh captures other worlds and reveals their magical quality.

He loved *Alice in Wonderland* – a book that was key to his comic vision. In his first, hilarious novel, *Decline and Fall*, Waugh depicts a hapless hero who unwittingly finds himself in a crazy, anarchic and topsy-turvy universe, full of lunatics and criminals masquerading as respectable people. Paul Pennyfeather's very dullness and conventionality only serve to highlight the contrast between him and the outrageous characters that inhabit his society.

Though far different in tone and style, *Brideshead Revisited* also takes its hero through 'that low door in the wall' which leads to an enchanted world. The sheer beauty of Oxford, with its ancient buildings of grey and gold, its tranquil, lush gardens and dreaming spires, casts the first spell over our shy lonely hero. Then at Brideshead, another magical castle, the hero finds Arcadia – not only in the bricks and mortar of the stately home, but also in the love of another human being.

One of the reasons why we read books is to escape into other worlds. Biographers, too, must enter imaginatively into the world they are trying to recreate. One of the reasons why I became a biographer is that I wanted to write about the books and authors that I love. I didn't want to be an academic critic and I don't see myself as a novelist. But in biography I found a form where I could do what novelists do – bring alive fascinating characters and relate a compelling plot – whilst also exploring how great books came to be written. I am always intrigued by the way in which writers draw upon their own experience but transmute it into their art, making all sorts of subtle changes. As I show, nearly all the characters in *Brideshead* are composites of different friends and acquaintances.

The other thing about biography is that it amply fulfils the desire to enter into a whole world totally different from your own experience. As a working-class girl from impoverished Birkenhead, I have always loved being transported to the elegance of the eighteenth century and the glamour of the Jazz Age. One aspect of the research for a biography that I especially enjoy is the process of bringing alive the atmosphere of the age. I immerse myself in newspapers and magazines, prints and photographs, gossip columns and memoirs. For *Mad World*, I pored over *Harper's Bazaar*, *Vogue's Book of Etiquette* and the Lygon family scrapbooks at Madresfield.

I regard Evelyn Waugh as one of the funniest writers in the English language, and, along with Jane Austen, he is one of my two favourite authors. Waugh and Austen have much in common: they are supreme social satirists, incredibly witty, masters of dialogue and character. Waugh's motto, 'laughter and the love of friends', could very well have been Jane Austen's – and it is certainly mine. ■

‘Why do people fall in love with other people's families? That was the question with which I began my journey into Waugh's world.’

Have You Read?

Other books by Paula Byrne

Perdita: The Life of Mary Robinson

To Coleridge she was 'a woman of undoubted genius', to others she was simply 'the most interesting woman of her age'. Mary 'Perdita' Robinson was, in her time, the darling of the London stage, mistress to the most powerful men in England, a renowned feminist thinker, and a bestselling author more famous for her poetry than Wordsworth. In this enthralling biography, Paula Byrne captures her life in all its extraordinary, disgraceful, triumphant and romantic glory.

'Enthralling and perceptive. A fine biographer has conjured up a dazzling personality and brought her, laughing, back to life'

Sunday Times

Jane Austen and the Theatre

Jane Austen was passionate about the stage. She went to the theatre in London and Bath whenever she could, acted in private theatricals and wrote a number of her early works in play form. Living in a great age of English stage comedy, she drew inspiration from Sheridan as well as Shakespeare. In this fascinating book, Paula Byrne traces the dramatic impact of the theatre on her masterpieces *Sense and Sensibility*, *Pride and Prejudice*, *Emma* and *Mansfield Park*. ■

If You Loved This, You Might Like . . .

The Mitford Girls
by Mary S. Lovell
Born of 'minor provincial aristocracy', the Mitford sisters came to epitomise the Bright Young Thing generation lampooned by Evelyn Waugh. They were Nancy, the literary dry wit; Diana, the iconic beauty who fell for the charms of Oswald Mosley; Pam, a countrywoman who married one of Europe's leading scientists; Unity, a member of Hitler's inner circle before her attempted suicide on the eve of World War Two; Jessica, the family rebel, who declared herself a communist in the schoolroom; and Debo, a future Duchess of Devonshire. This glittering group biography charts the disparate paths chosen by the blue-eyed sisterhood whose lives spanned the twentieth century.

Among the Bohemians: Experiments in Living 1900–1939
by Virginia Nicholson
Subversive, eccentric and flamboyant, the artistic community in the first half of the twentieth century was engaged in a grand experiment. The bohemians ate garlic and didn't always wash; they painted and danced and didn't care what people thought. They sent their children to co-ed schools; they explored homosexuality and Free Love. They were often drunk, broke and hungry but they were rebels. In this fascinating book Virginia Nicholson examines the way the bohemians refashioned the way we live our lives.

If You Loved This . . . *(continued)*

Memoirs of an Aesthete
by Harold Acton
Harold Acton listed as his principal recreation 'hunting the philistines'. From the balcony of his Oxford rooms he famously declaimed passages from *The Waste Land* through a megaphone, an event later recorded by Evelyn Waugh in *Brideshead*. In this remarkable memoir, he gives a witty and vivid account of the first thirty-five years of his life, from boyhood among the international colony of dilettanti in Florence before the First World War, to maturity in Peking. Between the two, he describes his experiences at the heart of a brilliant generation of postwar Oxford scholars, and his adventures amongst the bohemians of Paris.

Mr Wu and Mrs Stitch: The Letters of Evelyn Waugh and Diana Cooper, 1932–66
The correspondence between Evelyn Waugh and the celebrated beauty Lady Diana Cooper spanned thirty years. Prolific and candid, their letters are rich in anecdote, wicked, mischievous, affectionate, astringent, funny and, above all, fascinating for the insight they give into two of the most remarkable figures of their times.

Consuelo and Alva Vanderbilt
by Amanda Mackenzie Stuart
Consuelo Vanderbilt was one of the greatest heiresses of the late nineteenth century: a fabulously wealthy New York socialite and a

glittering prize for suitors on both sides of the Atlantic. When she married, a crowd of over two thousand onlookers gathered, and newspapers frenziedly reported every detail of the event, right down to the bridal underwear. Even by the standards of the day the glamorous eighteen-year-old had made an outstanding match: she had ensnared the twenty-four-year-old Duke of Marlborough, the most eligible peer in Great Britain. Yet the bride's swollen face, barely hidden under the veil, presaged the unhappiness that lay in the couple's painful twelve-year future. It was not Consuelo, but her domineering mother who had forced the marriage through. This captivating biography tells of the lives of mother and daughter: the story of the fairy-tale wedding and its nightmarish aftermath, and an account of how both women went on to dedicate their lives to the dramatic fight for women's rights. ■

Find Out More

WATCH:

Evelyn Waugh's caustic observations on British society brought to life in *Bright Young Things*, an adaptation of *Vile Bodies*, directed by Stephen Fry; *A Handful of Dust*, directed by Charles Sturridge; and the original *Brideshead Revisited* television series, directed by Charles Sturridge and Michael Lindsay-Hogg.

LISTEN TO:

Evelyn Waugh, a British Library CD which draws on previously unpublished BBC broadcasts from a period of over twenty-five years. The recordings range from the earliest surviving example of Waugh's voice, dating from 1938, to a speech given at the Royal Society of Literature in 1963, just three years before his death.

SURF:

http://www.evelynwaughsociety.org/index.php

The Evelyn Waugh Society was founded in 2005 to promote interest in his life and works. This is the homepage of their website, with links to further sources of information.